THE BIRTH OF THE CATHOLIC TÜBINGEN SCHOOL

American Academy of Religion
Academy Series

Carl Raschke, Editor

Number 37

THE BIRTH OF THE CATHOLIC TÜBINGEN SCHOOL:
The Dogmatics of Johann Sebastian Drey

by

Wayne L. Fehr

Wayne L. Fehr

The Birth of the Catholic Tübingen School: The Dogmatics of Johann Sebastian Drey

Scholars Press

Distributed by
Scholars Press
101 Salem Street
P. O. Box 2268
Chico, CA 95927

THE BIRTH OF THE CATHOLIC TÜBINGEN SCHOOL:
The Dogmatics
of Johann Sebastian Drey

Wayne L. Fehr
Ph.D., 1978, Yale University
New Haven, Connecticut

Library of Congress Cataloging in Publication Data

Fehr, Wayne L.
    The birth of the Catholic Tübingen School.

    (American Academy of Religion Academy
series ; no. 37) (ISSN 0277-1071)
    Bibliography: p.
    1. Drey, Johann Sebastian von, 1777–1853.
2. Tübingen School (Catholic theology) I. Title.
II. Series: Dissertation series (American Academy
of Religion) ; no. 37.
BX4705.D756F43   230'.2'0924   81-14545
ISBN 0-89130-544-0   AACR2

Printed in the United States of America
1 2 3 4 5
Edwards Brothers, Inc.
Ann Arbor, Michigan 48106

ACKNOWLEDGMENTS

I wish to express my gratitude to the scholars who have helped me with their counsel and encouragement. Rev. Avery Dulles, S. J., first suggested to me a research project on Drey. Professor Hans Frei, who directed the doctoral dissertation at Yale, was an unfailingly patient and supportive critic during the years of research and writing. Professor Walter Kasper, by his courteous interest in my project, helped me to clarify what was involved. Professor Josef Rief shared with me his own detailed knowledge of Drey's MSS and encouraged me to carry through my intention of examining closely the dogmatics notes. Abraham Kustermann has stimulated me by his own infectious interest in Drey, and has enriched my knowledge with some helpful references. Rev. Thomas O'Meara, O. P. and Professor Francis Fiorenza have both encouraged me to complete the original study and to revise it for publication. Rev. Justin Kelly, S. J., has stood by me as friend and perceptive critic, especially during the work of revision. To all these members of the fellowship of theologians I express my sincere thanks. I am grateful also to the staff of the Wilhelmsstift in Tübingen, who received me with kind hospitality in the summer of 1974, and especially Herr Rainer Funk, then Director of the Wilhelmsstift Library, who was most helpful and accommodating in allowing me to make use of Drey's papers and MSS.

TABLE OF CONTENTS

CHAPTER I

INTRODUCTION

The name of Johann Sebastian Drey (1777-1853) is little known today, even in theological circles, outside the area where he once exerted such a powerful influence: the Catholic Theological Faculty of the University of Tübingen. If he is remembered elsewhere, it is generally for having been the teacher of the much more renowned Johann Adam Möhler.

At the Catholic Faculty in Tübingen, however, Drey is well remembered,[1] and the style of theology which he initiated is pursued in conscious continuity by Walter Kasper.[2] The publication in English of Kasper's Christology has, in recent years, drawn the attention of English-speaking theologians both to Kasper himself and to the Catholic Tübingen School.[3] At the same time, there is a growing interest in the history of Catholic theology during the crucial nineteenth

---

[1]Cf. Max Seckler, "Johann Sebastian Drey und die Theologie," Tübinger Theologische Quartalschrift 158 (1978):92-109. In the 150th anniversary issue of the Theologische Quartalschrift, the catalogue of Tübingen theologians begins with Drey: 150 (1970):24-27. This issue also contains a reproduction of the only extant portrait of Drey. Hereafter, all references to this journal will make use of the abbreviation ThQ.

[2]Cf. Walter Kasper, "Verständnis der Theologie damals und heute," pp. 9-32 in his book Glaube und Geschichte (Mainz: Matthias Grünewald, 1970). Cf. also his small book Die Methoden der Dogmatik (Munich: Kösel, 1967), ET: The Methods of Dogmatic Theology (New York: Paulist, 1969).

[3]Walter Kasper, Jesus der Christus (Mainz: Matthias Grünewald, 1974), ET: Jesus the Christ (New York: Paulist, 1976).

1

century.[4] Several scholarly projects in Europe have recently
provided an overview of the leading theologians and movements
of Catholic theology in nineteenth-century Germany.[5] Even a
cursory view of this material shows that there was a rich and
varied theological enterprise among Catholics during the last
century, which has not received anything like the close study
devoted to Protestant theology of the same period.

The project of "rediscovering" nineteenth-century Catholic theology is motivated by the urgent concern to find the
roots of the current renewal of Catholic thought. It is of
great value to learn that these roots of a truly modern Catholic theology go deeper than the neo-Scholastic revival of the
late nineteenth century. In particular, there is much to be
learned from the vital and creative work done in the early
decades of the last century by a small group of theologians at
the University of Tübingen.[6] The most famous of these, of
course, was Möhler, whose place in the history of Catholic
theology has long been acknowledged. Drey, Hirscher, Möhler,
Staudenmaier, and Kuhn[7] have been regarded collectively as "the

---

[4]Cf. Gerald A. McCool, Catholic Theology in the Nine-
teenth Century: The Quest for a Unitary Method (New York:
Seabury, 1977). Cf. also the earlier book of Mark Schoof, A
Survey of Catholic Theology, 1800-1970 (Paramus: Paulist
Newman, 1970).

[5]Georg Schwaiger and Heinrich Fries (ed.), Katholische
Theologen Deutschlands im 19. Jahrhundert, 3 Vols. (Munich:
Kösel, 1975). Also the series Wegbereiter heutiger Theologie,
edited by Heinrich Fries and Johann Finsterhölzl (Graz: Styria,
1969--), each volume of which provides a selection of texts
from a particular author, preceded by a sketch of his life and
thought. Also a series of 19th-century studies funded by the
Fritz Thyssen Foundation: Studien zur Theologie und
Geistesgeschichte des Neunzehnten Jahrhunderts (Göttingen:
Vandenhoeck & Ruprecht, 1971--), which includes studies of a
number of Catholic authors.

[6]In addition to Kasper's instructive article "Verständnis
der Theologie," cited above, cf. also Franz Schupp, "Die
Geschichtsauffassung am Beginn der Tübinger Schule und in der
gegenwärtigen Theologie," Zeitschrift für katholische Theologie
91 (1969):150-71.

[7]Johann Sebastian Drey (1777-1853), Professor of Apologetics and Dogmatics at Tübingen; Johann Baptist Hirscher (1788-
1865), Professor of Moral Theology at Tübingen and later at

Catholic Tübingen School."[8]

Drey is of particular interest insofar as he may fairly
be regarded as the initiator and seminal thinker of this tradition.[9] He was among the original members of the Catholic
Faculty at Tübingen, beginning there in 1817, when the small
Catholic Faculty in Ellwangen (where he had begun teaching in
1812) was transferred to Tübingen and incorporated into the
University there. He lectured in Tübingen for nearly thirty
years, exerting a deep and lasting influence on many students
(among whom were Möhler, Staudenmaier, and Kuhn).[10]

The use of the term "Catholic Tübingen School" to refer
to Drey and his colleagues could, however, be misleading. For
one thing, there was not a complete uniformity of thought, nor
did Drey's students follow closely in all respects the master's
teaching. As a matter of fact, the theologians of this tradition were strikingly original and independent.

Moreover, as Rudolf Reinhardt has documented, there was
tension and disagreement within the faculty in the middle and
later periods (beginning with the ascendancy of Möhler in the

Freiburg; Johann Adam Möhler (1796-1838), Professor of Church
History at Tübingen and later at Munich; Franz Anton Staudenmaier (1800-1856), Professor of Dogmatics at Giessen and later
at Freiburg; Johannes Evangelist Kuhn (1806-1887), Professor of
Dogmatics at Giessen and later Drey's successor at Tübingen.

[8]Cf. Heinrich Fries' summary in Lexikon für Theologie und
Kirche, 2nd ed., edited by Josef Höfer and Karl Rahner, 10:390-
91 (Freiburg: Herder, 1965). Also Josef Rupert Geiselmann, Die
Katholische Tübinger Schule: Ihre theologische Eigenart
(Freiburg: Herder, 1964). Peter Hünermann also gives a brief
sketch of the Tübingen School's theology in Der Durchbruch
geschichtlichen Denkens im 19. Jahrhundert (Freiburg, 1967),
pp. 21-48.

[9]Cf. Geiselmann, Die Katholische Tübinger Schule, p. 13,
Schupp, "Die Geschichtsauffassung," p. 151, and Seckler, "J. S.
Drey," pp. 92-94.

[10]It is because of Staudenmaier's relationship to Drey
and his other teachers in Tübingen that he is ordinarily
regarded as a member of the School, even though he never taught
at Tübingen. Another well-known churchman who studied under
both Drey and Möhler, and is sometimes grouped with the School,
was Karl Josef von Hefele, Professor of Church History at
Tübingen and later Bishop of Rottenburg.

late 1820's).[11] A more "ultramontane" mentality grew strong,
in opposition to the older "reform" mentality represented by
Drey, Gratz, and Hirscher. Hence, Reinhardt is severely critical of the label "Catholic Tübingen School," since it tends to
ignore the differences and conflicts within the faculty.[12]

It would clearly be an unjustified simplification to
group together all the Catholic theologians who worked at
Tübingen over a century or more (as Reinhardt thinks Geiselmann
and others in the twentieth century tended to do), as if they
were all recognizably of the same mentality and method. Even
if one restricts the term "School" to Drey's own lifetime, the
term may suggest more uniformity of thought than was actually
the case.

On the other hand, the early period of the faculty (1817-
1830) does seem strikingly unified in its mentality and
approach to theology and Church, as Reinhardt recognizes.[13] It
is perhaps significant that contributions to the Theologische
Quartalschrift, the organ of the Catholic Faculty begun in
1819, were not attributed by name to individual authors until
1832. A perusal of these early volumes of the ThQ conveys a
strong impression of the shared concerns and presuppositions of
the faculty at that time.[14]

---

[11]Rudolf Reinhardt, "Die katholisch-theologische Fakultät
Tübingen im ersten Jahrhundert ihres Bestehens: Faktoren und
Phasen der Entwicklung," pp. 1-42 in Tübinger Theologen und
ihre Theologie: Quellen und Forschungen zur Geschichte der
Katholisch-Theologischen Fakultät Tübingen, edited by Reinhardt
(Tübingen: J. C. B. Mohr [Paul Siebeck], 1977), esp. pp. 19-26.

[12]Ibid., pp. 18-19, 41-42.   [13]Ibid., pp. 20-21.

[14]A clear expression of the prevailing attitude may be
found in the brief "Ankündigung" in the first issue of the ThQ,
announcing the purpose of the new periodical: ThQ 1 (1819):3-7.
This is reprinted in Stefan Lösch, Die Anfänge der Tübinger
Theologischen Quartalschrift (Rottenburg: Bader'sche
Verlagsbuchhandlung, 1938), pp. 15-17. On this, cf. Seckler,
"J. S. Drey," p. 97. Whether or not the omission of authors'
names was a deliberate expression of their unanimity, it is
clear that the change in policy--demanded by Möhler after an
1831 article by Hirscher on celibacy had stirred up controversy
--was a sign of disunity. Cf. Reinhardt, op. cit., p. 22.

For the early period, therefore, the continued usage of the term "School" seems justified. What was common to the early Tübingers (and continued to be evident in the later writings of Staudenmaier and Kuhn) was a certain perspective on the method of theology. Fries characterizes this commonality as the "formal element."[15]

There is no doubt that this formal, methodological stance is the heritage of Drey. His earliest published article (1812) addressed the "revision" of theology, and his first book (1819) was a thorough treatment of the appropriate method for an adequate contemporary theology.[16] To this extent, Drey's formal viewpoint may legitimately be regarded as a significant factor in the "birth of the Catholic Tübingen School." Hence, the present study of Drey's thought may also be regarded as contributing to the appreciation of that School's distinctive way of theologizing.

This book is not, however, an effort to account for the emergence of the Catholic Tübingen School in terms of preceding movements and influences. Nor does it attempt to establish the extent of Drey's influence upon other members of the School. Either task would far exceed both the competence of the author and the limitations of space.

The work of tracing Drey's intellectual antecedents and showing the multitudinous influences of other thinkers has already been done with great thoroughness by earlier studies.[17] In this respect, the emergence of the Catholic Tübingen School (as exemplified in Drey's thought) has been explained as far as such new intellectual movements can ever be accounted for. The influence of Drey upon his colleagues and students has also been documented in various studies of particular authors, and

---

[15]Fries, Lexikon für Theologie und Kirche 10:390. Schupp's judgment is similar ("Die Geschichtsauffassung," p. 151). Cf. also Seckler, "J. S. Drey," pp. 102-103.

[16]For references, see below.

[17]For references, see below.

may receive further illumination in forthcoming works.[18]

The aim of this book is, therefore, quite limited. It is devoted simply to the exposition and analysis of Drey's own thought. Since it was originally written as a doctoral dissertation, it remains rather specialized and technical, and for this reason might seem to be of limited interest. On the other hand, it can be related to wider concerns.

To understand Drey's distinctive approach to theology is to enter into the still relevant heritage of the Catholic Tübingen School. As Kasper and Schupp argue, it was in Tübingen more than a century and a half ago that Catholic theology for the first time took seriously the modern understanding of history and allowed history to become a constitutive dimension of theological method. If this orientation of the Tübingen School had prevailed in the Catholic Church, the crisis of Modernism would undoubtedly have been experienced differently, if not averted. In fact, the promising confrontation of Catholic theology with history was broken off around the middle of the nineteenth century.

Consequently, the renewal of Catholic theology in recent years has been faced with the enormous task of working through the intellectual developments of a century or more during

---

[18]On Drey's colleague Hirscher, cf. Walter Fürst, Wahrheit im Interesse der Freiheit: Eine Untersuchung zur Theologie J. B. Hirschers (Mainz: Matthias Grünewald, 1979). On Möhler, of course, the literature is vast. Cf. especially the lengthy introductions to Geiselmann's critical editions of Möhler's Die Einheit in der Kirche (Köln & Olten: Jakob Hegner, 1956) and Symbolik (Köln & Olten: Jakob Hegner, 1958), as well as Geiselmann's book Die theologische Anthropologie Johann Adam Möhlers (Freiburg: Herder, 1955) and his article "Johann Adam Möhler und die Entwicklung seines Kirchenbegriffs," ThQ 112 (1931):1-91. On Staudenmaier, cf. Peter Hünermann, Trinitarische Anthropologie bei Franz Anton Staudenmaier (Freiburg/Munich: Verlag Karl Alber, 1962), and William E. McConville, "Franz Anton Staudenmaier: Historical Theology and Theological Encyclopedia," doctoral dissertation for Vanderbilt University, in progress. On Kuhn, cf. Franz Wolfinger, Der Glaube nach Johann Evangelist von Kuhn (Göttingen: Vandenhoeck & Ruprecht, 1972), and Stephen F. Mueller, "Method and System in the Speculative Theology of Johannes Evangelist Kuhn," doctoral dissertation for the University of Chicago, 1981.

which Catholic thought had been largely isolated from contemporary challenges and opportunities. The problem of history,
in particular, has become ever more urgent for theology.[19]
From this perspective, a close look at the beginnings of an
historically-oriented Catholic theology might be an important
stimulus for the ongoing renewal of present-day theology.

Closely related to these considerations is Drey's conscious preoccupation with method in theology, as well as his
conception of Apologetics as a foundational discipline (what we
would today call "fundamental theology"). He thus anticipated
in a formal way some of the most burning issues of present-day
Catholic theology.[20] Even in his material treatment of these
issues, he can seem surprisingly modern. He attempted to
locate the phenomenon of Christianity in the widest possible
historical context, drawing upon the then new disciplines of
philosophy of religion and history of religions. At the same
time, he was aware of the beginnings of a critical-historical
treatment of the origins of Christianity and of its sacred
writings, and considered this relevant to theology.

That a Catholic theologian should self-consciously take
these factors as partly determinative of his theological method
is strikingly "modern," and must stand out as quite significant

---

[19]Cf. Kasper, "Verständnis der Theologie," pp. 13-14.

[20]The present-day concern with method is, of course,
reflected in almost all current discussions of the state of
Catholic theology. Besides Bernard Lonergan's Method in Theology (New York: Herder & Herder, 1972), one need only recall
David Tracy's Blessed Rage For Order (New York: Seabury, 1975)
and his more recent The Analogical Imagination (New York:
Crossroad, 1981), both of which are painstakingly concerned
with a responsible method. What Tracy says on the first page
of the earlier book could have been affirmed wholeheartedly by
Drey: ". . . each theologian must attempt to articulate and
defend an explicit method of inquiry . . ." (Blessed Rage,
P. 3). Both Hans Küng and Edward Schillebeeckx are equally
concerned with the appropriate method for Catholic theology.
Cf. Leonard Swidler (ed.), Consensus in Theology: A Dialogue
with Hans Küng and Edward Schillebeeckx (Philadelphia: Westminster, 1980). The closely related need for a fundamental or
foundational theology to establish meaningful categories for
formulating the truth of Christianity is likewise well represented by Tracy's earlier book.

in the history of Catholic theology--coming as it did a good
fifty years or more before the Modernist crisis.

In general, Drey shows a remarkable openness to the
intellectual resources of his day and a readiness to bring
contemporary philosophical thought and cultural values into a
creative dialogue with the Christian tradition. This was
characteristic of the Catholic Tübingen School, as has often
been remarked.

This openness seems clearly related to the University
setting in which the Tübingers worked. This was so important
to Drey that he considered moving to Freiburg when there was a
danger that the Catholic Faculty of Tübingen might be removed
from the University and resituated in an all-Catholic environment.[21] In contrast to such a closed confessional setting, the
University context encouraged Catholic theologians to do their
work in relation to the wider academic community, including (at
least at Tübingen) the Protestant theologians.[22]

The consequences of such a setting for the Catholic
Tübingen style of theology are manifest. There is a breadth of
vision and intellectual culture in the pages of Drey which
clearly springs from a wide and open attention to the resources
of his contemporary academic world.[23] In this, too, he anticipated a style of Catholic theology which is today increasingly
recognized as indispensable for grasping the truth of
Christianity in a secularized and pluralistic world.[24]

_____

[21]Cf. Rudolf Reinhardt, "Neue Quellen zu Leben und Werk
von Johann Sebastian Drey," Tübinger Theologen und ihre
Theologie, p. 128 and 163.

[22]That the relationship between Catholic theologians and
their Protestant colleagues in Tübingen was not without tension
is shown by Möhler's sharp controversy with F. C. Baur. Cf.
Joseph Fitzer, Möhler and Baur in Controversy, 1832-1838
(Tallahassee: American Academy of Religion, 1974).

[23]This quality is even more strikingly evident in Drey's
students Staudenmaier and Kuhn, who devoted much effort to a
careful appreciation and critique of Hegel and other major
thinkers of their time.

[24]Cf. David Tracy, The Analogical Imagination, Part I:
"Publicness in Systematic Theology," esp. pp. 14-21 ("The
Public of the Academy: Theology as an Academic Discipline").

One final point in which Drey may seem relevant to our
present situation is his view of the theologian's relationship
to the Church. Since the reality of development was basic to
Drey's understanding of Christianity in history, he regarded
the Church as an ever-changing phenomenon, moving through all
the diverse ethnic and cultural settings of the history of
mankind. This was the theological basis for his concern with
Church reform and renewal. He thought that the theologian had
an important role in criticizing the existing state of the
Church and in recommending the appropriate changes.[25] Hence,
the tone of the ThQ from the very beginning was free, open, and
"sachlich" in commenting from a serious theological viewpoint
on current issues of Church life and discipline.[26]

Then as now, such an attitude led to tension with Church
authorities.[27] Even within the faculty, as already noted,
there was eventually a shift to a more "ultramontane" viewpoint

----

[25]In 1821 Drey expressed this view in a letter to Johann
Baptist Keller, Vicar of the Rottenburg Diocese, who had
written a pastoral letter to the editors of the ThQ, reprimand-
ing them for their liberal and critical stance (especially with
regard to priestly celibacy). Drey defended the activity of
himself and his colleagues as a responsible exercise of their
role as theologians. For the texts of both Keller's letter and
Drey's response, see Reinhardt, Tübinger Theologen, pp. 152-161.
Cf. also Seckler, "J. S. Drey," pp. 97-98.

[26]The particular features of the liberal reform program
of the ThQ are enumerated briefly by Reinhardt, op. cit.,
pp. 20-21. It was especially Hirscher who advocated changes
which then seemed radical but have mostly been realized in the
twentieth-century renewal brought about by Vatican II. Cf.
Erwin Keller, "Gedanken Johann Baptist Hirschers zur Reform der
Kirche," pp. 91-101 in Georg Schwaiger (ed.), Kirche und
Theologie im 19. Jahrhundert (Göttingen: Vandenhoeck & Ruprecht,
1975) and Josef Rief, "Kirche und Gesellschaft: Hirschers
kritische Analysen und Reformvorschläge der vierziger Jahre,"
ibid., pp. 103-123.

[27]Drey himself had been condemned in Rome in 1815 because
of his small study of the history of confession which recognized that auricular confession of sins did not originate with
Christ or the apostles. See bibliography. Cf. Reinhardt,
Tübinger Theologen, p. 16. This reputation for unorthodoxy may
well have kept him from becoming bishop of Rottenburg in the
1820's. Cf. M. Miller, "Prof. Dr. J. S. Drey als Württember-
gisher Bischofskandidat (1822-1827)," ThQ 114 (1933):363-405,
esp. 367.

which reflected the general swing away from the liberal reform
mentality in the larger Church. Especially in later years,
Tübingen theologians were sometimes in trouble with the hier-
archy. In fact, their more open and historical approach to
theology and Church was rendered largely ineffectual by the
repressive power of Church authority in the later decades of
the century.[28]

In the more liberal atmosphere created by Vatican II,
Catholic theology today has recovered its sense of responsi-
bility for the critique of Church beliefs and practices. Hence,
for this reason also, the earlier work of Drey and his
colleagues may be of interest.

Because of the sometimes striking pertinence of Drey's
thought, I shall point out its connections with present-day
theological concerns wherever it seems appropriate in the
chapters which follow. Nevertheless, this study is limited to
the exposition of Drey's thought, and does not attempt the
further step of a constructive argument based on Drey.

Method of Presentation

In view of the apparent relevance of Drey and the
Catholic Tübingen School to contemporary theology, one can only
regret that there is at present next to nothing available in
English which could make this material accessible to serious
students who lack German. Neither the primary texts of Drey
nor the several excellent secondary studies of his thought have
yet been translated.

For this reason, it seems that an English-language study
of Drey may be of real service. Moreover, in view of both the
limited accessibility of even his published works and my
extensive use of unpublished manuscripts, the following way of
proceeding seems justified.

It is not my intention to interpret Drey through the
filter of secondary literature. My procedure is, rather, to
let the "specificity" of Drey's thought emerge from his own

---

[28]Cf. Reinhardt, Tübinger Theologen, pp. 32-41. For the
effect of the later Modernist crisis on the Tübingen faculty,
cf. ibid., pp. 271-352.

texts, in terms of his own purposes and concerns (which he
articulates clearly). Consequently, I make extensive use of
the primary sources--both published works and manuscripts--in
order to provide the reader with enough material to test and
judge my interpretation. The emphasis on primary texts may be helpful to readers
who wish to form for themselves a first-hand impression of the
character and quality of his thought. Accordingly, in every
citation of Drey's texts the original German (or Latin) is made
available in a footnote for the sake of exactness, while a
fairly literal but readable English translation is given in the
body of the text. In this way, the reader is provided with a
significant amount of primary material in a framework of interpretation, so that closer study of a particular point is made
possible without interrupting the flow of the argument.

From this point of view, this book is a major effort in
transposition of thought from its originating context to
another, rather different context. Hence, whatever its merits
as an advancement of the scholarly understanding of Drey, it
may also serve as a helpful introduction to Drey's thought for
English-speaking readers.

Life and Works of Drey

Johann Sebastian Drey was born of very poor parents in
Killingen, near Ellwangen in Swabia, on October 16, 1777.[29]

---

[29]The sources for Drey's biography are very scanty. For
the basic facts, all later writers are dependent upon the
obituary by Karl Josef von Hefele, published in the ThQ 35
(1853):341-349. Although scarcely any of Drey's personal
letters are extant, recent research by Rudolf Reinhardt and
others has brought to light some further information about
Drey's career. For a thorough and exact account of the sources
and the state of research on Drey's life, see Abraham Peter
Kustermann, "Zum 200. Geburtstag Johann Sebastian von Dreys:
Biographische Hinweise und Quellen," pp. 49-116 in Tübinger
Theologen und ihre Theologie. Cf. also Kustermann's later
article, "Vereine der Spätaufklärung und Johann Sebastian Drey,"
Ellwanger Jahrbuch 28 (1979-80):23-81. Finally, for a brief
account of Drey's life, see Josef Rief, "Johann Sebastian von
Drey," pp. 9-38 in Katholische Theologen Deutschlands im 19.
Jahrhundert, edited by Heinrich Fries and Georg Schwaiger,
Vol. 2 (Munich: Kösel, 1975).

Through the interest and financial help of the local pastor
(Martin Ziegler, a former Jesuit), the young Sebastian[30] was
given the opportunity for an education at the Gymnasium in
Ellwangen. In 1797 he went to Augsburg to study theology for
two years. After two more years in the seminary of the
Augsburg diocese at Pfaffenhausen, he was ordained a Catholic
priest in Augsburg on May 30, 1801.

For the next five years, Drey was a curate in his home
parish in Röhlingen. It was during these years that he read
contemporary German philosophy: Kant, Fichte, Schelling. This
philosophical education had a lasting effect on the form of
his thought.

From 1806 to 1812, Drey was a teacher at the Catholic
Lyzeum in Rottweil. His subjects were the philosophy of
religion, mathematics, and physics. The work in philosophy of
religion was to be of major and lasting importance for his
treatment of theology.

In 1812 he was called to be Professor of Dogmatics,
History of Dogma, Apologetics, and "theologische Enzyklopädie"
at the newly erected "Friedrichsuniversität" in Ellwangen.
This so-called University consisted, in fact, of a tiny theological faculty and a handful of students. But it was intended
by King Friedrich of Württemberg to become a major seat of
higher learning for the Catholic population of his kingdom.[31]

In 1817, to Drey's great satisfaction,[32] the entire
Ellwangen operation was transferred to Tübingen and incorporated into the University there.[33] This action--carried through

---

[30]Kustermann points out that Drey himself used only this
first name for a long time, and cites his signature in a letter
from 1806 (Tübinger Theologen, p. 61).

[31]Because of the redistribution of territories resulting
from the Napoleonic wars, the King of Protestant Württemberg
now found himself for the first time with a sizable Catholic
population. He wanted to provide for the education of their
clergy.

[32]Cf. Rief, "Drey," pp. 14-15.

[33]Cf. Joseph Zeller, "Die Errichtung der kath.-theologis-
chen Fakultät in Tübingen im Jahre 1817," ThQ 108 (1927):77-158;
F. X. Funk, "Die katholische Landesuniversität in Ellwangen und

by the new King, Wilhelm, against the opposition of the
Catholic hierarchy--created a remarkable new environment for
Catholic theology.[34] Catholic and Protestant theologians were
now colleagues at the same University, continually confronted
by the challenge of one another's differing traditions and
styles of thought. Moreover, as already noted, theology was
thus brought into a creative dialogue with the whole range of
contemporary academic disciplines. In this setting, Drey found
a place for the full employment of his considerable intellectual gifts.

Drey's critical, open attitude towards theology and
Church found embodiment in the journal which he helped to found
in 1819: the Tübinger Theologische Quartalschrift. In the
first decade of this journal's publication, Drey was a major
contributor of solid articles and numerous book reviews. He
continued to sustain the journal in later years, and even in
his retirement contributed book reviews.

Drey had already indicated something of his view of the
contemporary state and problematic of theology in an article
published in 1812.[35] In the year 1819 he published his first
major work: Kurze Einleitung in das Studium der Theologie,
which set forth with clarity and force his vision of the proper
method and subject matter of theology.[36] At the same time, he

---

ihre Verlegung nach Tübingen," pp. 3-30 in Festgabe zum 25-jähr.
Regierungsjubiläum S. M. des Königs Karl von Württemberg,
dargebracht von der Univ. Tübingen (Tübingen: H. Laupp, 1889).

[34]The advantages of this new setting were recognized
explicitly by the Government in Stuttgart. Cf. Seckler, "J. S.
Drey," pp. 100-101.

[35]"Revision des gegenwärtigen Zustandes der Theologie,"
Archiv für die Pastoralkonferenzen in den Landkapiteln des
Bistums Konstanz, Erster Band (1812):3-26. This article was
reprinted in J. R. Geiselmann's Geist des Christentums und des
Katholizismus (Mainz: Matthias Grünewald, 1940), pp. 83-97, and
in Franz Schupp's libellus Revision von Kirche und Theologie
(Darmstadt: Wissenschaftliche Buchgesellschaft, 1971), pp. 1-24.

[36]Kurze Einleitung in das Studium der Theologie, mit
Rücksicht auf den wissenschaftlichen Standpunct und das
katholische System (Tübingen: H. Laupp, 1819). This text was
re-issued in a photographic reprint in 1966 (Frankfurt/Main:
Minerva, 1966). Another photographic reprint was published in

published a long article in the first volume of the ThQ which
contained some of his most characteristic ideas: "Vom Geist und
Wesen des Katholizismus."[37]
The major work of Drey's life was his three-volume
Apologetics, which he began to publish in 1838.[38] This is the
work for which Drey has been remembered by historians of
Catholic theology.[39] To this he undoubtedly devoted his best
creative energies, so that it remains as the most impressive
monument of his theological career.

In addition to the subjects of "Enzyklopädie" (Introduction to Theology) and Apologetics, Drey also lectured for many
years on Dogmatics. Because of his severe illness in 1837, he
asked to be relieved of this subject.[40] But prior to that, he
had been lecturing on Dogmatics regularly each year since the
beginning of his career in Ellwangen in 1812. He never
published his Dogmatics, but the notes from which he lectured
(often written in his own hand) are preserved in the library of

---

1971, with a table of contents and introduction by Franz
Schupp (Darmstadt: Wissenschaftliche Buchgesellschaft, 1971).
Hereafter, this work will be cited as KE.

[37]"Vom Geist und Wesen des Katholizismus," ThQ 1 (1819):
8-23, 193-210, 369-391, 559-574. This article was reprinted in
Geiselmann's Geist des Christentums, pp. 193-234. An English
translation of this is currently being prepared at the Catholic
University of America.

[38]Die Apologetik als wissenschaftliche Nachweisung der
Göttlichkeit des Christenthums in seiner Erscheinung (Mainz:
Fl. Kupferberg, Vol. 1, 1838; Vol. 2, 1843; Vol. 3, 1847). A
second edition of Vol. 1 was published in 1844, and of Vol. 2
in 1847. All references are to the first edition, as re-issued
in a photographic reprint (Frankfurt/Main: Minerva, 1967).
Hereafter, this work will be cited as Apol.

[39]Cf. Karl Werner, Geschichte der katholischen Theologie
seit dem Trienter Konzil bis zur Gegenwart (Munich, 1866),
photographic reprint (Hildesheim: Georg Olms, 1966), pp. 473-
480, 497-499. Cf. also Avery Dulles, A History of Apologetics
Philadelphia: Westminster, 1971), pp. 180-181.

[40]Cf. Kustermann, in Tübinger Theologen, pp. 86-89.
Drey's successor as Professor of Dogmatics, beginning in 1838,
was his former student Kuhn.

the Wilhelmsstift in Tübingen.[41]

Drey was retired--somewhat against his will, it seems--in 1846.[42] The blow was softened by the award of the "Commenturkreuz" of the Württemberg "Kronorden" in recognition of Drey's outstanding achievements. (In 1823 he had received the "Ritterkreuz" which raised him to the rank of nobility and entitled this son of a shepherd to use the honorific von before his name.)

In his retirement he continued to work at the Apologetik. A second edition of Vol. 1 had been published in 1844. In 1847 appeared a second edition of Vol. 2 and the first (and only) edition of Vol. 3. He also wrote a number of articles for Wetzer and Welte's Kirchenlexikon and some reviews for the ThQ. In his old age he seemed to recover a more vigorous health than he had enjoyed in his younger years.[43] His death on February 19, 1853, came therefore as a sudden and unexpected event, after a brief and seemingly minor illness.

Sources

Besides the Kurze Einleitung and the Apologetik, there are a number of articles and book reviews which appeared over the years in the ThQ.[44] Drey's manuscripts and papers are

---

[41]See Chapter VI for a description and characterization of these MSS. They are gathered in three bound volumes and entitled (by the Wilhelmsstift library) collectively "Praelectiones Dogmaticae." Hereafter, references to these MSS will be given as PD, followed by the volume (I, II, or III) and the page number.

[42]Cf. Karl Josef von Hefele's article "Drey," in the Kirchenlexikon of H. J. Wetzer and B. Welte, 2d edition (1884), columns 2068-2069; also Reinhardt in Tübinger Theologen, p. 28, and Rief, "Drey," p. 17.

[43]Drey had suffered from hypochondria most of his life, and had undergone several periods of incapacitating illness. According to Rief and Kustermann, he likewise had experienced at least two major crises of an emotional nature, the first in 1827 (related to his unsuccessful, long-drawn out candidacy for the bishopric of Rottenburg), the second around 1836-1837 (a time of weariness and discouragement, climaxing in a serious illness). Cf. Kustermann in Tübinger Theologen, pp. 86-89, and Rief, "Drey," pp. 15-17.

[44]See Bibliography for a partial listing of these. A complete listing of Drey's articles and book reviews in the ThQ

preserved in the library of the Wilhelmsstift in Tübingen.[45]
The most important and interesting of these--besides the
Dogmatics lecture notes--are the Journals[46] and the MS of
Drey's lectures on the history of dogma.[47] Portions of the
Journals have been published by Geiselmann, as well as the com-
plete text of the lectures on the history of dogma.[48]

Secondary Literature

Josef Rupert Geiselmann has been the most important
contributor to the renewal of studies on Drey and the Catholic
Tübingen School. An early article in the ThQ drew attention to
the Dogmatics MSS.[49] In 1940 he published a valuable collection of writings from early nineteenth-century German Catholic
theologians, which included several articles by Drey, as well as
previously unpublished material from his papers in Tübingen.[50]

------

is to be found in Wolfgang Ruf, Johann Sebastian von Dreys
System der Theologie als Begründung der Moraltheologie
(Göttingen: Vandenhoeck & Ruprecht, 1974), pp. 37-53. For a
critique and expansion of Ruf's catalogue, see Abraham
Kustermann's brief notice in ThQ 156 (1976):232-234. For
Drey's authorship of pieces which appeared without the author's
name, see Lösch, Die Anfänge der Tübinger Theologischen
Quartalschrift.

[45]Ruf also provides a complete listing of Drey's papers
and manuscripts, pp. 29-36.

[46]"Tagebücher über philosophische, theologische und
historische Gegenstände . . .," Vols. 2, 3, 4, and 5 (1812-
1817).

[47]"Geschichte des katholischen Dogmensystems. I. Band.
Geschichte der drei ersten Jahrhunderte oder erste Periode.
Mit Benutzung von Münschers Handbuch dargestellt von Dr. J. S.
Drey Pr. 1812-1813."

[48]Geiselmann's Geist des Christentums und des Katholizismus, pp. 99-192 and 235-331. This printed version must be used
with care, since it contains some errors and misreadings of the
original handwritten text.

[49]Josef Rupert Geiselmann, "Die Glaubenswissenschaft der
katholischen Tübinger Schule in ihrer Grundlegung durch Johann
Sebastian v. Drey," ThQ 111 (1930):49-117.

[50]Josef Rupert Geiselmann (ed.), Geist des Christentums
und des Katholizismus: Ausgewählte Schriften katholischer
Theologie im Zeitalter des deutschen Idealismus und der
Romantik, Vol. 5 in the series Deutsche Klassiker der

In 1942 he had ready for publication his major study of the
Catholic Tübingen School's notion of "tradition," which included
a lengthy section on Drey. The printed copies of this were,
however, destroyed in the war before distribution, so that the
book had to be issued for the first time in 1964 as a photographic reprint.[51] Also in 1964, Geiselmann published <u>Die</u>
<u>Katholische Tübinger Schule</u>, a rather diverse collection of
material on Möhler, Drey, and other figures of the School from
the perspective of various themes.[52] Unfortunately, some portions of this volume are word-for-word repetitions of what had
been published already in the earlier work. Geiselmann's work
on Möhler, as already noted, also contains numerous clarifying
references to Drey.[53]

Prior to Geiselmann's publications, Drey and the Catholic
Tübingen School had been viewed somewhat negatively by Catholic
theologians formed in the neo-Scholastic mentality.[54] Edmond
Vermeil's careful study saw the Tübingen theology as an anticipation of the "Modernism" which so traumatized the Catholic
world around the turn of the century.[55] A later study by

---

katholischen Theologie aus neuerer Zeit (Mainz: Matthias
Grünewald, 1940). This work has already been mentioned several
times because of its valuable contents for Drey research.
Probably because of the war, this book is scarcely to be found
in North America. Hereafter, this work will be cited as <u>GdChr</u>.

[51]Josef Rupert Geiselmann, <u>Lebendiger Glaube aus</u>
<u>geheiligter Überlieferung: Der Grundgedanke der Theologie J. A.</u>
<u>Möhlers und der katholischen Tübinger Schule</u> (Freiburg: Herder,
1964).

[52]Josef Rupert Geiselmann, <u>Die Katholische Tübinger</u>
<u>Schule: Ihre theologische Eigenart</u> (Freiburg: Herder, 1964).

[53]See above.

[54]E.g., Michael Glossner, "Die Tübinger katholisch-
theologische Schule, vom spekulativen Standpunkt kritisch
beleuchtet, I. Drey der Apologet," <u>Jahrbuch für Philosophie und</u>
<u>spekulative Theologie</u> 15 (1901):166-194.

[55]Edmond Vermeil, <u>Jean-Adam Möhler et l'école catholique</u>
<u>de Tubingue (1815-1840): Étude sur la théologie romantique en</u>
Wurtemberg et les origines germaniques du modernisme (Paris:
Librairie Armand Colin, 1913). This interpretation of the
Catholic Tübingers as forerunners of Modernism was sharply
rejected by Léonce de Grandmaison, "L'école catholique de

Hermann Joseph Brosch also criticized Drey and the others from
the neo-Scholastic viewpoint.[56]
For a long time, Geiselmann seemed to be the only scholar
who was trying to retrieve and interpret sympathetically the
heritage of Drey and the Catholic Tübingen School. Eventually
several doctoral dissertations on Drey were done in Germany.[57]
But the first studies on Drey of major importance since
Geiselmann were those of Josef Rief[58] and Franz Schupp.[59]
     Rief's book is concerned with the social elements in the
thought of both Drey and Hirscher. He takes a wide view of
Drey's thought, and provides many helpful connections and
reference points to German intellectual history. Moreover, he
is intimately familiar not only with Drey's published works but
also with the Dogmatics manuscripts. This enables him to cite

---

Tubingue et les origines du modernisme," Recherches de science
religieuse 9 (1919): 387-409.

[56]Hermann Josef Brosch, Das Übernaturliche in der
katholischen Tübinger Schule (Essen: Ludgerus Verlag, 1962).
This had been completed in 1935 as a doctoral dissertation for
the Gregorian University in Rome, but its publication was
delayed by circumstances in war-time Germany. When it was
finally published in 1962, it occasioned a sharp response from
Geiselmann (cf. his review of it in ThQ 143 [1963]:422-453), who
published his large book Die Katholische Tübinger Schule as a
vindication of the Tübingen theology against Brosch's criticism.

[57]Hermann Lohmann, "Die Philosophie der Offenbarung bei
J. S. von Drey" (Doctoral dissertation, University of Freiburg,
1953); Wolfgang Ruf, "Johann Sebastian von Dreys System der
Theologie als Begründung der Moraltheologie" (Doctoral disser-
tation, University of Freiburg, 1958), later published with the
same title (Göttingen: Vandenhoeck & Ruprecht, 1974); Fridolin
Laupheimer, "Die kultisch-liturgischen Anschauungen J. S. von
Dreys" (Doctoral dissertation, University of Tübingen, 1960);
Elmar Klinger, "Das Alte Testament als heilsgeschichtliche
Größe" (Doctoral dissertation, University of Innsbruck, 1967),
later published as Offenbarung im Horizont der Heilsgeschichte
(Zurich: Benziger, 1969).

[58]Josef Rief, Reich Gottes und Gesellschaft nach Johann
Sebastian Drey und Johann Baptist Hirscher (Paderborn: F.
Schöningh, 1965).

[59]Franz Schupp, Die Evidenz der Geschichte: Theologie als
Wissenschaft bei J. S. Drey (Innsbruck: University of
Innsbruck, 1970).

many relevant texts to illustrate and clarify his interpretations. Rief is probably the one scholar now living who knows Drey's texts best from first-hand study and immersion in them. Since the earlier, massive book he has also published the interesting essay on Drey, already referred to. Written for a more general audience, it provides no textual references.

Franz Schupp's book is a brilliant survey of Drey's project, done as a "Habilitationsarbeit" for the University of Innsbruck. Since Schupp is interested in the question of theology as "Wissenschaft," he looks at Drey as an interesting example of how that question was dealt with creatively at a time of radical intellectual change. Like Rief's earlier study, Schupp's book is very helpful for identifying points of contact between Drey's thought and various influences in his intellectual milieu. It also gives a concise overview of Drey's entire system of theology. It is, however, rather dense and difficult reading for anyone who is not already quite familiar with Drey's own texts. (The same observation applies to Rief's much longer book.) Schupp has also provided brief but perceptive introductions to his photographic reissues of the Kurze Einleitung and of three Drey articles.

Besides the major studies of Drey, there are several articles which help to clarify his thought in terms of Geistesgeschichte. Hünermann shows the importance of German Idealism, especially Schelling.[60] Menke interprets and criticizes Drey's understanding of "dogma" against the philosophical background of Kant, Schelling, and Jacobi.[61] Schilson provides a detailed and valuable treatment of Lessing's influence upon Drey and other members of the Tübingen School.[62] Finally, there are some references to Drey in recent books devoted to

---

[60]Peter Hünermann, "Der Reflex des deutschen Idealismus in der Theologie der katholischen Tübinger Schule." Philosophisches Jahrbuch 73 (1965-66):48-74, esp. 51-63.

[61]Karl-Heinz Menke, "Definition und spekulative Begründung des Begriffes 'Dogma' im Werke Johann Sebastian von Dreys," Theologie und Philosophie 52 (1977):23-56, 182-214.

[62]Arno Schilson, "Lessing und die katholische Tübinger Schule," ThQ 160 (1980):256-277.

other authors or larger subjects.[63]

As this book goes to press, there is one other study of
Drey not yet available, which should be of considerable
importance for the interpretation of his thought: Abraham
Kustermann's doctoral dissertation on Drey's Apologetics.[64]

There is scarcely anything on Drey in the English
language, apart from the brief entries in the Catholic Encyclopedia.[65] Avery Dulles has an accurate but very brief report on
Drey's Apologetics.[66] Mark Schoof has a few pages on Drey and
the Catholic Tübingen School in his survey of Catholic theology
since 1800.[67] And Gerald McCool has a fifteen-page section on
Drey which relies on Geiselmann for the content of Drey's
thought.[68]

Focus and Nature of This Study

As indicated in the title, the thrust of this study is
towards the examination of Drey's unpublished Dogmatics lectures. The intent is to make use of these manuscripts in a
more formal and systematic way than previous studies have done.
Rief and Schupp have drawn upon this material to clarify and
illustrate certain points in Drey's thought. Geiselmann and

---

[63]Walter Fürst, Wahrheit im Interesse der Freiheit: Eine
Untersuchung zur Theologie J. B. Hirschers (Mainz: Matthias
Grünewald, 1979), pp. 342-367. Heinz Brunner, Der organologische Kirchenbegriff in seiner Bedeutung für das
ekklesiologische Denken des 19. Jahrhunderts (Frankfurt/Main,
1979), pp. 87-93.

[64]Abraham Peter Kustermann, doctoral dissertation (in
progress) for the University of Tübingen. Title not available.

[65]Johann Baptist Sägmüller, "Drey," The Catholic Encyclopedia, Vol. 5 (New York: Robert Appleton Co., 1909), pp. 159-
160, appears to follow closely Hefele's article in the
Kirchenlexikon of Wetzer and Welte. M. Csaky, "Drey," New
Catholic Encyclopedia, Vol. 4 (New York: McGraw-Hill, 1967),
1060-1061, shows the influence of Geiselmann's studies.

[66]Dulles, A History of Apologetics, pp. 180-81.

[67]Schoof, A Survey of Catholic Theology, 1800-1970,
pp. 22-28.

[68]McCool, Catholic Theology in the Nineteenth Century,
pp. 67-81.

Ruf have also reported on the systematizing use of the <u>Reich Gottes</u> concept to organize the themes of the Dogmatics.[69] But no one has taken the Dogmatics material for its own sake, in order to document and interpret Drey's distinctive way of treating the traditional content of dogmatic theology.

Hence, despite the valuable studies of Drey's published works, there remains an uncertainty about the nature of his achievement in Dogmatics. It has generally been taken for granted that this achievement was very incomplete. But, in view of Drey's recognized influence upon Staudenmaier and Kuhn --both of whom published works in Dogmatics--it must be of some interest to know more about Drey's own way of doing Dogmatics.

Two considerations, however, make it inadvisable simply to begin with the manuscripts. For one thing, Drey did not publish this material, nor is it in a condition suitable for publication. It can only be appreciated within the context of his life-work and in the frame of reference provided by his published writings. Secondly, what is most interesting about this material (and, in fact, the key to understanding it) is Drey's distinctive methodological viewpoint. But it can hardly be assumed that this viewpoint is already well known. Moreover, as noted above, it is precisely this "formal" aspect of Drey's thought which constitutes his abiding legacy to the Catholic Tübingen School and which is, therefore, of greatest interest to contemporary readers.

Hence, the greater part of this book is necessarily and appropriately an extended essay of interpretation, whose pur-pose is to make clear Drey's distinctive approach to theology. Based mainly on his published works, this exposition attempts to set up the indispensable context for presenting and inter-preting the unpublished Dogmatics material. To some extent, this involves going over ground that is already familiar to Drey scholars. Since, however, Drey is so little known in the English-speaking world, this may not be altogether superfluous for the readers of these pages. On the other hand, to the

---

[69]Geiselmann, <u>Die Katholische Tübinger Schule</u>, pp. 192-209; Ruf, <u>J. S. von Dreys System der Theologie</u>, pp. 114-126.

extent that my treatment highlights certain features of Drey's
thought which have not been sufficiently noticed, it may also
provide a fresh view of the material.

Overview

Since "revelation" is the key concept and problem in
Drey's apologetic grounding of theology, Chapters II and III
present his theory of revelation from two particular perspectives. Chapter II examines revelation as a divine activity in
and upon the world of "nature." Chapter III considers the
intrinsic relationship of revelation to human subjectivity, and
in particular to "reason" (Vernunft). These two chapters,
based principally upon the Apologetik, provide a partial context
for understanding Drey's thought on the proper method for
theology. A further important context for Drey's theological
method is provided by the early Schelling's ideas on
"Wissenschaft." Hence, Chapter IV is devoted entirely to a
detailed exposition of certain elements in Schelling's early
writings (documented extensively from the primary texts).
Against this background, Chapter V is then able to present
Drey's proposal for the method of theology, drawn principally
from the Kurze Einleitung and the Dogmatics manuscripts.
Finally, Chapter VI exploits the formal perspective that has
been clarified in the earlier chapters, in order to present
the system in Drey's Dogmatics. This chapter is based almost
entirely on the unpublished Dogmatics manuscripts, with
parallel texts from the published works to illuminate characteristic ideas of Drey. The study concludes with a chapter of
review and critical assessment.

CHAPTER II

REVELATION AS DIVINE CREATIVE ACTIVITY

The context of Drey's theological life-work was the
Enlightenment's denial of revelation.[1] This denial struck at
the foundation and source of theology, as Drey understood it.

Deistic naturalism ruled out the very possibility of a
divine revelation, since the world was understood to be a self-
contained whole that was, indeed, originated by God but not
subject to any further interaction with Him. The claims of
Christianity seemed to postulate a miraculous intervention
"from outside" into this self-contained universe. But this
was rejected as unreasonable and incredible.

For Drey, therefore, the indispensable first task of
theology was to rehabilitate the concept of revelation by
constructing a philosophically consistent theory of revelation
and by examining the actual history of mankind to show the fact
of revelation in mankind's religious development. Only such a
thorough-going treatment of the theme of revelation, he thought,
could establish a meaningful context for the claims of
Christianity.[2]

This was the task of Apologetics, as Drey conceived that
discipline. It was to be a foundational discipline, whose
purpose was to vindicate the possibility of a theology oriented
to a divine revelation in history. Without such a basis,
Christian theology would be impossible.[3]

---

[1]Cf. Apol I, "Einleitung" § 20, esp. p. 57; ibid., #8,
p. 11.

[2]Cf. Apol I, "Einleitung" § 9, pp. 11-13.

[3]Cf. Apol I, "Einleitung" § 5, pp. 6-7.

The entire first volume of Drey's great work Apologetik
is devoted to a theory of revelation. My exposition of his
thought will focus on two important aspects of this theory: his
conception of the divine activity in revelation (the present
chapter) and his understanding of human receptivity in relation
to that revelation (the following chapter).

The first of these themes correlates with the challenge
of deistic naturalism, since it attempts to re-conceive the
God-world relationship in a way that makes divine revelatory
activity thinkable.[4] This chapter is devoted, therefore, to
Drey's view of the God-world relationship as grounded in the
mystery of creation. For it is in the concept of creation that
he seeks the key for interpreting the distinctive character of
the divine revelatory activity.

This creationist view of the world in relationship to God
turns out to be of crucial importance for Drey's method in
theology--specifically, for his orientation to the "divine
positivity" of Christianity.[5] Moreover, it is also fundamental
for interpreting the key concept of his dogmatics, Reich Gottes.
It will be argued later that the most profound meaning of this
term is to be sought in the mystical intuition of finite reality as pertaining radically to God in the "relation of origin."

The Naturalist View

It is helpful to begin with Drey's perception of the
mentality which he wished to overcome. He characterized the
basic principle of "naturalism" in this way:

> The principle is this: to think of God as in immediate
> activity towards the outside, in immediate contact with
> the world, only in the act of creation; after this act of
> creation, to cut off all connection and all intercourse
> between the two, to let the world at once run alone,
> develop itself alone, while allowing God only to be a
> spectator . . .[6]

---

[4] The key text for this aspect of Drey's theory of revelation is Apol I §§ 20-24, pp. 178-204.

[5] Cf. Apol I, "Einleitung" §§ 1-3, pp. 1-4.

[6] Apol I § 32, p. 262: "Das Princip ist, Gott nur im
Schöpfungsakt in unmittelbarer Wirksamkeit nach Außen, in
unmittelbarer Berührung mit der Welt zu denken, nach dem

This view is unacceptable to Drey because it removes God from the world, so to speak, and does not allow for any interaction between Creator and creatures. He sees this as the root error which naturalism has in common with rationalism. They both isolate created reality from God, recognizing only an extrinsic relationship of origination in the initial act of creation. Naturalism does this with regard to the "nature-side" of the universe, rationalism does it with regard to the "spirit-side" of the universe, i.e., man or human reason. But the basic viewpoint is the same.

If one so understands God's relationship to the world, Drey maintains, it is really impossible to defend the concept of revelation as a divine activity within and upon the world. The only possible divine activity with regard to the world is thought to be the originating act of creation. All events and developments must be included in this initial act through divine predestination.

The Supernaturalist View

The defenders of revelation, on the other hand, often tended to go to an opposite extreme, Drey thought. In order to safeguard the reality of a divine initiative in the world, they conceived that divine activity as suspending the course of nature and contravening the known laws of nature.

. . . they imagined the activity of God in revelation to be such that <u>all</u> activity and cooperation of natural forces in the divinely caused transformations of things would be excluded, so that these transformations would result without any help from nature; moreover, these transformations were supposed to come about according to quite other laws, indeed, contrary to the laws of nature. Otherwise, they believed, there would be nothing supernatural in them, or they could not be regarded as worked by God.[7]

Schöpfungsakt aber alle Verbindung und allen Verkehr zwischen beiden abzuschneiden, die Welt sofort allein laufen, allein sich entwickeln, Gott aber dabei nur das Zuschauen zu lassen . . ."

[7]Apol I § 24, pp. 200-201: ". . . sie stellten sich die Thätigkeit Gottes in der Offenbarung als eine solche vor, durch welche nicht nur alle Thätigkeit und Mitwirkung der natürlichen Kräfte zu den göttlich bewirkten Veränderungen in den Dingen ausgeschlossen würde, so daß diese ohne alles Zuthun der Natur erfolgten, dieselben Veränderungen sollten auch nach ganz anderen Gesetzen, ja sogar gegen die Gesetze der Natur erfolgen;

Overcoming the Opposition

Wishing to maintain, against deistic naturalism, the active presence of God to His world, without adopting this extreme supernaturalist conception, Drey sought an alternative way of conceiving the God-world relationship--one which would transcend the terms in which the naturalist/supernaturalist opposition was set. This alternative view was generated from a profound meditation on the mystery of the world's origin from the eternal creative activity of God.

A "Religious Subjectivity"

In order to appreciate Drey's approach to this most basic question of theology, it may be helpful to consider the matter of what we would today call "subjectivity." Drey himself clearly recognized the relevance of the theologian's own religious sensibility to the task of theology.[8] In this, he anticipated the present-day awareness that all seemingly objective affirmations about God arise out of a certain kind of subjectivity.[9]

From this contemporary perspective, one can notice a certain similarity between the naturalist and extreme supernaturalist views of God, as Drey encountered them. What they appear to have in common is a rather extrinsic way of regarding God in relation to the world. For the deist, of course, God is the great Artificer who sets the world machine in motion. But for the supernaturalist as well, God is the extrinsic Creator who intervenes "from outside."

---

anders glaubten sie, würde nichts Uebernatürliches in ihnen seyn, oder sie nicht als von Gott bewirkt betrachtet werden können."

[8] KE § 40, p. 24: "Wie des Menschen Religion, wie seine Stellung gegen Gott, so ist auch seine Theologie." KE § 102, p. 68: ". . . Muß im Theologen zum Behufe seiner besondern Wissenschaft . . . auf eine hervorstechende Weise angeregt und ausgebildet seyn--der Sinn für das Heilige, der religiöse Sinn." Apol I, "Einleitung" § 3, p. 4: ". . . der Theolog soll . . . nicht blos von Gott reden, sondern in Gott leben, zumal jenes ohne dieses nie recht gelingen wird."

[9] On the importance of subjectivity and "conversion" to the method of theology, cf. Bernard Lonergan, _Method in Theology_ (New York: Herder & Herder, 1972), esp. pp. 130-31 and p. 338.

Underlying this rational formulation is an experience of
the world characterized by a kind of subject-object dualism.
The self is a thinking subject, over against a world of objects.
The predominant mode of relating to this world is a kind of
control through rational understanding. Such a subjectivity
does not perceive the world, therefore, as mysterious or
"divine." If the idea of God is nevertheless maintained, it
can only refer to a reality which is quite extrinsic to the
world.

From this perspective it is significant that Drey
regarded the naturalist view of the world as insufficiently
"religious."[10] His own contrasting view is scarcely to be
appreciated without acknowledging its religious, even mystical
subjectivity.[11]

Underlying Drey's thought is a kind of mystical awareness
of the ineffable unity of finite and Infinite, so that the
world is regarded as thoroughly "penetrated" by God and
radically characterized by belonging utterly to Him in the
"relation of origin." This perception is well expressed in the
opening sentence of Drey's first book:

> All faith and all knowledge rests upon the obscurely
> felt or clearly recognized presupposition, that everything
> finite which exists has not only come forth from an eternal
> and absolute ground, but also is still--with this its
> temporal being and life--rooted in that primal ground and
> carried by it.[12]

---

[10]Cf. Apol I § 32, pp. 265-67.

[11]Cf. Bernhard Welte, "Zum Strukturwandel der katholischen
Theologie im 19. Jahrhundert," in Welte, Auf der Spur des
Ewigen (Freiburg: Herder, 1965), p. 387. Cf. Drey, "Revision
des gegenwärtigen Zustandes der Theologie," in Franz Schupp
(ed.), Revision von Kirche und Theologie (Darmstadt:
Wissenschaftliche Buchgesellschaft, 1971), p. 18. Also Drey's
article "Ueber das Verhältniß des Mysticismus zum Katholizismus,"
ThQ 6 (1824):219-48, reprinted in Schupp, Revision, pp. 23-54,
esp. pp. 28-30.

[12]KE § 1, p. 1: "Aller Glaube und alles Wissen ruht in der
dunkel gefühlten oder deutlich erkannten Voraussetzung, daß
alles Endliche, was da ist, aus einem ewigen und absoluten
Grunde nicht nur hervorgegangen [ist], sondern auch mit diesem
seinem zeitlichen Seyn und Leben noch in jenem Urgrunde wurzelt
und von ihm getragen wird."

Influence of German Idealism

Such a statement reflects not only Drey's personal religious temperament but also the mentality of early nineteenth-
century German Idealism.[13] In contrast to the dualism of
Enlightenment thought, this view of reality is strongly
monistic. There is a sense of the Infinite in the finite, an
awareness of the whole, a tendency to understand all particulars only in their relation to the whole. Moreover, in the
Schellingian version of this mentality, which especially
influenced Drey, the self is not subject over against object,
but rather a limited participation in the ultimate oneness of
all reality, the ultimate "identity" of subject and object.
For Schelling, as well as for Drey, the self cannot be thought
of apart from the great whole, nor can the world be thought of
apart from God.

It is precisely this subjectivity which Drey characterized as "religious" in contrast to the Enlightenment mentality,
and which commended Schelling to him as providing a philosophy
that was suitable for Christian theology:

> Without a doubt, that [system] must prove most useful to
> [Christian theology] which is religious in its very basis
> and which vindicates the same view in both history and the
> world, not cutting them off from God; [this system] inter-
> prets as a great error the belief in the self-sufficient
> reality of history and of the world; on the contrary, it
> concedes reality to them only insofar as they contain the
> revelation of God, which appears on two sides or in two
> essential basic forms.[14]

---

[13]Rief notes Schelling's influence on Drey's conception
of the Urgrund (Reich Gottes, pp. 221-24). Schupp points out
that Drey shared the early Schelling's view that knowledge of
the Absolute is possible only if the Absolute is immediately
present to human consciousness (Die Evidenz der Geschichte,
p. 107), and that the Absolute is the immediate starting-point
of all knowing (ibid., p. 109).

[14]KE § 96, p. 64: "Am trefflichsten muß ihr [der
christlichen Theologie] unstreitig dasjenige [System] zu
statten kommen, welches in seiner Grundlage schon religiös
dieselbe Anschauung auch in der Geschichte und in der Welt
geltend macht, diese beyde von Gott nicht abschneidet, vielmehr
den Glauben an die für sich bestehende Realität beyder für den
größten Irtum erklärt, und dagegen eine solche ihnen nur
zugesteht, in wie ferne sie die nach zwey Seiten oder in zwey
wesentlichen Grundformen sich gestaltende Offenbarung Gottes
enthalten."

It will become clear in later chapters that the system
referred to here is that of the early Schelling. This is
confirmed by the pencil notation "Schelling" found next to this
passage in the margin of Drey's own personal copy of the Kurze
Einleitung (preserved in the library of the Wilhelmsstift in
Tübingen).[15]

It is understandable that Drey, wishing to avoid the
deist isolation of the world from God, would look to Schelling
for a philosophical orientation.[16] For if it was characteristic of German Idealism in general to conceive God and the
world in the closest possible unity, Schelling in particular
saw the world as the self-manifestation of the Absolute. In
Schelling's early philosophy, the pure identity of the Ideal
and the Real (of Subject and Object) becomes differentiated
into the two parallel orders of nature and spirit. Hence, both
nature and history (the latter being the realm of finite
spirit) are aspects of the self-manifestation of the Absolute.[17]

There is, of course, a considerable difference between
such a view (which Windelband characterizes as "an aesthetic
pantheism")[18] and the traditional notion of a transcendent,
personal, free Creator who reveals Himself. In Schelling's
view, nature and history are only aspects of God. Moreover,

---

[15]Despite this acknowledgment, Drey did not actually
follow Schelling's system closely in its technical, formal
categories. What he took from Schelling was rather a perspective on the God-world relationship and on the nature of
"Wissenschaft." This will be examined closely in Chapters IV
and V. For Drey's views on the role of philosophy in theology,
see KE §§ 92-98, pp. 61-66; § 261, pp. 173-74; Apol I, "Vorrede,"
pp. XI-XII; and ThQ 17 (1835):194. Also see below, pp.

[16]Cf. Rief, op. cit., p. 106. Drey was by no means the
only Catholic theologian of this period who looked to Schelling.
Cf. Thomas F. O'Meara, Romantic Idealism and Roman Catholicism:
Schelling and the Theologians (Notre Dame: University of Notre
Dame Press, 1982).

[17]See Chapter IV for the detailed documentation of this
summary statement.

[18]W. Windelband, Die Geschichte der neueren Philosophie,
Vol. II: von Kant bis Hegel und Herbart (Leipzig: von
Breitkopf & Härtel, 1880), p. 275.

self-manifestation is a necessary movement of the divine nature,
rather than the sovereignly free act of a personal God. Hence,
Drey could not adopt Schelling's conceptuality without some
considerable modifications.[19]

What he clearly found congenial in Schelling was the
denial of the "self-sufficient reality of the world [i.e.,
nature] and history," and the insistence that both of these are
simply forms of divine self-manifestation. This view appears
to underlie Drey's very close identification of the two concepts "creation" and "revelation." Drey does not, however,
conceive God simply as the Absolute, nor does he give up the
notion of a free, personal Creator. Hence, there remains a
tension in Drey's thought between the Christian substance and
the German Idealist form.[20]

Although it would not be accurate to accuse Drey of
pantheism, it is basic to his theological vision to conceive
God as intrinsic to finite reality. It is this understanding
which seems most obviously bound up with the "religious" or
mystical form of his subjectivity. In view of the later
treatment of the concept Reich Gottes[21] it might be more fair
to characterize Drey's view as a kind of "panentheism."[22]

Creation and Revelation

Drey's concern is to avoid a false opposition between
creation and revelation (the error common to both naturalists
and supernaturalists). Revelation is not to be conceived as a
disruption or contravention of creation. The question then
becomes: how is the divine revelatory activity to be conceived
so that it is manifestly not in opposition to the divine
creative activity?

Schelling's intuition of the finite world as the self-
manifestation of the Absolute seems to be in the background of

---

[19]Ultimately, the avoidance of the unacceptable consequences of Schelling's thought is to be sought in Drey's
theology of the Trinity. See below, pp.

[20]See below, pp.

[21]See Chapter VI.

[22]Cf. Rief, op. cit., pp. 215-16, note 7.

Drey's treatment of revelation in the Apologetik, for he says
explicitly, ". . . the creative activity of God [is] precisely
the activity by which He reveals Himself outwardly . . ."[23] An
earlier formulation of the same thought is found in the Kurze
Einleitung:

> The revelation of God is the presentation of His
> essence in an other, which is not God and--to this extent--
> is outside Him. Outside of God is the universe, and only
> this; all revelation of God, therefore, can only take place
> in the universe, and the universe itself--nothing else--is
> this revelation. . . . [Revelation] itself, therefore--
> like religion--is from the beginning; it continues, and can
> never end.[24]

With creation itself thus seen as constituting the
"original revelation," it becomes possible to conceive
historical revelation as the continuation of the very same
self-manifesting creative activity of God.

Drey stresses that God's creative activity is not to be
restricted to a momentary originating event, but rather is to
be understood as an ongoing divine activity which continues to
bring new realities into being.

> . . . just as God did not become Creator merely for a
> moment, but is Creator at all times and remains Creator
> forever, so His creative activity continues, and makes
> itself truly manifest and recognizable in new productions
> . . .[25]

---

[23]Apol I § 20, p. 180: ". . . die schöpferische Thätigkeit
Gottes [ist] . . . eben . . . die Thätigkeit . . . wodurch er
sich nach außen offenbart . . ."

[24]KE § 16, p. 10: "Offenbarung Gottes ist Darstellung
seines Wesens in einem anderen, was nicht Gott ist, und
insofern außer Ihm. Außer Gott ist das Universum, und dieses
allein; alle Offenbarung Gottes also kann nur geschehen im
Universum, und dieses selbst ist jene, nichts anderes. . . .
Sie selbst also [die Offenbarung], wie die Religion, ist vom
Anfange her, sie dauert fort und kann nie enden."

[25]Apol I § 20, p. 180: ". . . wie Gott nicht für einen
Augenblick Schöpfer ward, sondern es zu jeder Zeit ist und
immer bleibt, so auch seine schöpferische Thätigkeit fortdauert,
und in neuen Hervorbringungen sich wahrhaft offenbar und
erkennbar macht . . ."

In this way, Drey conceives the world to be proceeding always immediately from the creative activity of God. The possibility of new creatures being produced is not felt as an intrusion into a pre-set world process.[26] Rather, the new creations (in particular, the events of "historical" revelation) are simply added to the already existing world order. The same eternally active Creator who brings forth the order of "nature" continues His creative activity by bringing into being the "miraculous"[27] events of historical revelation.

The divine revelatory activity which causes historical revelation is, in this view, regarded as essentially the same as the creative activity which produces the order of finite reality. Drey makes this explicit: "We maintain that revelation is, in its essence, identical with creation, and that the concept of revelation is identical with that of creation."[28]

This gives Drey the point of view which he needs in order to rise above the naturalist/supernaturalist opposition and thus to vindicate the concept of an historical revelation. This opposition, he thought, cannot be resolved, and its relative character cannot be shown ". . . unless the historical revelation is brought back to the original revelation, and it is shown that the former is only the continuation of the latter."[29]

-----

[26]Drey supposed that the bringing-into-being of the natural order itself was gradual (reflected in the six-day account of Genesis). Cf. Apol I § 21, pp. 183-84. Moreover, he regarded certain features of the natural world as evidence of ever-renewed divine creative activity, e.g., the fossil remains of now-extinct plants and animals, the appearance of meteors and comets, stellar nebulae. Cf. Apol I § 23, pp. 194-96.

[27]The word "miracle," while appropriate in Drey's view for characterizing the facts of historical revelation, was freighted with ambiguities and false implications, arising out of the naturalist/supernaturalist dispute. Drey's use of the term will become clear from what follows.

[28]Apol I § 20, p. 180: ". . . wir setzen die Offenbarung ihrem Wesen nach als identisch mit der Schöpfung, und den Begriff der ersten als identisch mit dem der andern."

[29]Ibid.: ". . . wenn die geschichtliche Offenbarung nicht auf die ursprüngliche zurückgeführt, und nachgewiesen wird, daß sie nur die Fortsetzung von dieser sey."

If both "nature" and historical revelation are conceived
as originating with equal immediacy from the creative activity
of the same eternally active God, then there can be no opposition between them. Moreover, both may be seen to have a double
character, of being both "supernatural" and "natural." God
manifests Himself in both nature and historical revelation.
The reality which manifests itself is supernatural. That in
which it is manifested (the product of the divine creative
activity) is natural.[30]

"Nature" in Relation to God

Drey elaborates the implications of his point of view
through a careful analysis of the concept "nature," as this was
used in the naturalist/supernaturalist controversy. In this
context, the term referred to the immanently intelligible
totality of the world process. Any intervention of God in this
self-enclosed whole was felt to be unthinkable. To attribute
any event directly to God's action was to consider it as
"supernatural," i.e., as a miracle. And this was unacceptable
to naturalists.

Drey challenges this concept of "nature" by raising the
question of the origin of the world. This question forces the
mind to deal with the mystery of creation. Once the question
"Whence?" has been raised with regard to the world as a whole,
Drey thinks that there are only two responses forthcoming from
those who believe in God at all. Either one considers nature
itself to be God, or else one attributes the origin of nature
to "the power of the Creator, the creative will of God."[31] In
the latter case, there are profound implications for one's view
of this nature that is created by God. In particular, the
concept "miracle" is seen to be applicable to the very origin
of created nature itself from the infinite, eternal God.

One feels here again something of the immense distance
between Drey's religious sensibility and that of the deists

---

[30]Cf. Apol I § 21, pp. 182-83, 185.

[31]Apol I § 21, p. 182: ". . . durch die Schöpferkraft,
durch den schaffenden Willen Gottes."

against whom he did his theologizing. The latter were able to
affirm that there was, indeed, a Maker of this great whole.
The act of creation was conceived as a momentary act of
producing the totality. God's relationship to the created
world was extrinsic--a relationship of causal origin. God
himself was "outside" the world, and the world itself could, in
a sense, be taken for granted as a given. It was enormously
complex and orderly, allowing us therefore to draw some
inferences as to the nature of the Being who fashioned it
originally. But there was nothing of the mysterious or
miraculous about it.

In contrast, Drey felt the mystery of a finite world
proceeding from the infinite God. "God creates, and He creates
a world; the eternal creates a temporal, the infinite a finite,
the perfect an imperfect; is this not a mystery, the mystery of
all mysteries?"[32]

Drey drives back "behind" the seemingly self-contained
and taken-for-granted "nature" of the deists to uncover the
fundamental mystery of nature's origin. He calls this mystery
the "world-miracle":

> Nature comes forth from the one who is prior to everything
> and above everything, who is prior to and above nature . . . ;
> nature has its ground in the supernatural; is this not a
> miracle, the true world-miracle?[33]

This odd expression "world-miracle" expresses Drey's
sense of the mystery of being created as the enduring basis of
the God-world relationship. "World" or "nature" may not be
regarded as a totally profane, self-contained given. On the
contrary, its reality springs from the creative will of the
eternal, infinite God. It is appropriate to use the word
"miracle" (Wunder) to characterize this mystery of the world's

---

[32]Ibid.: "Gott schafft, und schafft eine Welt, der Ewige
ein Zeitliches, der Unendliche ein Endliches, der Vollkommene
ein Unvollkommenes; ist das nicht ein Geheimniß, das Geheimniß
aller Geheimnisse?"

[33]Ibid.: "Aus dem, der vor Allem und über Allem, vor und
über der Natur ist, geht diese hervor . . .; die Natur hat
ihren Grund in dem Uebernatürlichen; ist das nicht ein Wunder,
das wahre Weltwunder?"

source, because there is certainly an element of wonder or
amazement in the intuition of this relationship. Moreover,
since the word "miracle" attributes the phenomenon in question
to the immediate activity of God, it is manifestly applicable
to creation.

"Natural" and "Supernatural"

In this way, Drey deepens and modifies the concept of
"nature" so as to overcome the absolute dichotomy of natural
and supernatural. It is not as if the world itself were a
self-contained, fully intelligible reality, into the midst of
which God were thought to intervene "from outside" through
arbitrary actions that disrupt this immanent intelligibility.
Rather, nature itself is grounded in the supernatural reality
of God the Creator. The totality of the world itself is--in
this sense--supernatural or miraculous.

Consequently, one may say that the totality of "nature"--
as well as each individual part of it--is both natural and
supernatural. As Drey puts it, everything has two "faces":
"the one, with which it looks at us, and this is its nature-
face; the other, with which it looks towards God . . . its
divine or supernatural face . . ."[34]

The manifest regularity and intelligibility of nature
(newly discovered in the rise of the natural sciences in the
seventeenth and eighteenth centuries) is the "natural face" of
the world. This world exists in its own right, and things act
according to laws. There is an "immanent causality in nature"[35]
which is the proper object of investigation and scientific
understanding.

At the same time, however, the totality of the world
takes its origin from God in the mysterious relationship of
being created. This is the "supernatural face" of nature,
which "looks towards God" and reflects the image of the Creator.

---

[34] Apol I § 21, p. 183: ". . . das eine, womit es uns
anblickt, und dieß ist sein Naturgesicht, das andere, womit es
gegen Gott schaut. . . . Dieses göttliche oder übernatürliche
Angesicht desselben . . ."

[35] Apol I § 32, p. 267: ". . . die immanente Kausalität in
der Natur."

While affirming the ontological priority of God (the
Supernatural), Drey affirms the relative autonomy of created
reality by speaking of the "sabbath of God." This is a _relative_
"sabbath" insofar as God constitutes in existence beings which
exist, perpetuate themselves, and operate in their own right as
truly distinct from Him. God "rests" only in the sense that He
lets nature truly be and operate in its own right. But He does
not cease to be Creator, nor does nature cease to be "supernatural" in the sense of manifesting the Creator by being
utterly dependent on Him as ground.

> . . . since it remains eternally true that [nature] can
> only do what it does through God, and without Him would not
> even exist, much less be able to do anything, so, the
> appearance of the natural can never remove the supernatural
> in nature, and it should not even repress the supernatural
> in our consideration of nature.[36]

Hence, "nature" as the product of God's originating
creative activity has a double character that remains. There
is, he says, a "synthesis" of natural and supernatural in the
created world which we call "nature." This synthesis can be
regarded as the product of God's original revelation or self-
manifestation. Nature points to God because it is His self-
manifestation. Drey's reason for so conceiving the order of
creation is indicated by his question:

> . . . is this synthesis [of natural and supernatural] the
> only one, or--what is fundamentally the same thing--is
> God's activity in creation his only revelatory activity?
> Or can we believe in or know another, continued revelatory
> activity in addition to this one?[37]

---

[36]Apol I § 21, p. 185: "Da . . . es in Ewigkeit wahr
bleibt, daß sie [die Natur], was sie kann, nur durch Gott kann,
ohne ihn gar nicht wäre, vielweniger etwas könnte, so kann der
Anschein des Natürlichen das Uebernatürliche in ihr nicht
aufheben, soll es auch in unserer Betrachtung nicht einmal
zurückdrängen . . ."

[37]Ibid.: ". . . ob diese Synthese beider die einzige sey,
oder was auf den Grund zurückgegangen, dasselbe ist: ob die
Thätigkeit Gottes in der Schöpfung auch seine einzige
Offenbarungsthätigkeit, oder ob wir außer dieser noch eine
andere, fortgesetzte glauben oder wissen können?"

He wishes, of course, to say that there is indeed another, continuing revelatory activity of God in the world--in the phenomena of historical revelation. But he can only maintain this if he can show the possibility of new creative activities of God in the already existing world of "nature." If God's revelation-activity is identical in essence with His creation-activity, then revelation must take place as a new, continuing creation. The problem is in specifying just how this further creative activity of God is related to the already existing product of the original creative activity, i.e., to "nature."

God's Continuing Creative
Activity in Relation to
the "Course of Nature"

Drey challenges, as we have seen, the naturalist conviction that there is a pre-set "course of nature" which is fixed and impervious to any further divine creative activity. Yet he wishes to argue that the new creative acts of God in historical revelation do not contradict or dissolve the already existing "nature," as extreme supernaturalists tended to think.

Drey is concerned to maintain the supernatural character of the events of historical revelation. He thinks it insufficient to call these events merely "extraordinary" in contrast to the "ordinary" pattern of the divinely created world process.[38] For the category "extraordinary" does not really attribute the phenomenon in question to a new creative initiative of God. Drey does not think that revelation is a valid concept unless one affirms this kind of divine initiative within the world.[39]

The crux, therefore, is the appearance of new religious developments in mankind. (For revelation, as we shall see in Chapter III, is intrinsically related to man's religious development.) How are such new spiritual phenomena to be explained? Naturalism attempts "to explain the origin of new

---

[38]This was one way in which contemporary theologians of the rationalist type, such as Planck and Schott, tried to account for the origin of new religious developments without affirming a new intervention of God. Cf. Apol I § 22, p. 189.

[39]Cf. Apol I § 32, pp. 267-68.

religious developments without a new activity of God for this
purpose, but solely from the continuing efficacy of the
original activity of creation, and from the forces placed in
creatures . . ."[40]

God's Creation of "New Beginnings"

The critical point at issue is whether God can and does
act directly and immediately within the world, to bring into
being new realities (religious developments) which are not
explainable merely in terms of the already existing pattern of
natural forces and historical factors.

Naturalists are willing to admit only an indirect,
mediated influence of God upon the course of the world. His
only immediate activity is in the initial act of creating the
whole. After that, He can only work through the already existing orderly pattern of the world process. To such a viewpoint,
Drey observes, "all those phenomena must be very unwelcome, in
which the thread of mediacy is suddenly cut off, and the
context of interaction among things is interrupted . . ."[41]

This kind of interruption of the pattern of immanent
causality is what enables us to recognize a phenomenon as the
work of divine, creative/revelatory activity. Something new
exists which is not fully explainable from the preceding
pattern of causal interaction.

> . . . we can no longer explain [a phenomenon] from [the
> already existing nature] if it is something absolutely new,
> if it is--according to its character--a creation, and
> exceeds the known forces of its apparent cause.[42]

---

[40]Apol I § 22, p. 190: ". . . den Ursprung neuer religiöser
Entwickelungen ohne eine neue Thätigkeit Gottes zum Behufe
derselben, einzig aus dem Fortwirken der ursprünglichen
Schöpfungsthätigkeit, und der in die Geschöpfe gelegten Kräfte
zu erklären . . ." Cf. Apol I § 32, pp. 267-68.

[41]Apol I § 23, p. 194: ". . . alle Erscheinungen [müssen]
sehr ungelegen kommen, in welchem [sic] der Faden der Mittel-
barkeit plötzlich abgeschnitten ist, der Zusammenhang der
Wechselwirkung in den Dingen unterbrochen ist . . ."

[42]Ibid., p. 198: ". . . wir können [eine Erscheinung]
aber aus [der bestehenden Natur] nicht mehr erklären, wenn sie
etwas schlechthin Neues, wenn sie nach ihrem Charakter eine
Schöpfung ist, und die bekannten Kräfte ihrer scheinbaren
Ursache übersteigt."

"New Beginnings" in Relation
to the "Course of Nature"

As we have already seen, Drey understands the divine
activity of revelation to be essentially a creative activity,
identical in its fundamental character with the act of creating
the order of nature. The agent is God. The product of His
revelatory activity is "something new, which did not previously
exist and which--compared with what does exist or did exist--
represents a breaking-off, a complete turning-about."[43]

In the order of physical phenomena, revelation-events
"enter our earthly world as aliens, just as much as the heavenly
bodies mentioned above enter the stellar world as aliens."[44]
He is referring to the kinds of inexplicable physical phenomena
ordinarily called miracles. He distinguishes these from the
new, inexplicable phenomena in the realm of the human spirit
which accompany and indeed constitute new religious developments in history. These are no less the product of divine
creative activity and--in this sense--could also be called
miracles. But he respects the prevalent usage and employs
rather the term "inspiration" to refer to these revelatory
events in the realm of the human spirit. His point is the
absolute newness of both classes of phenomena. This is the
quality which requires that we attribute them to the immediate
creative activity of God.

> Therefore, insofar as the new phenomena can neither be
> conceived nor derived from preceding ones, insofar as they
> were not posited or included in the preceding ones, the
> activity of revelation which calls them forth appears as a
> creative activity, completely equal to the original crea-
> tion in the production of that which had never existed.[45]

---

[43] Apol I § 24, p. 199: ". . . etwas Neues, vorher nicht
Dagewesenes . . . und mit dem Daseyenden oder Dagewesenen
verglichen, einen Abbruch, eine vollkommene Umkehrung desselben
darstellt."

[44] Ibid.: ". . . treten ebenso als Fremdlinge in unsre
irdische Welt ein, wie jene oben erwähnte Weltkörper in die
Gestirnenwelt." (Cf. above, p. 32, note 26.)

[45] Ibid.: "Insoweit also die neuen Erscheinungen aus den
frühern weder begriffen noch abgeleitet werden können, sie in
diesen nicht gesetzt und eingeschlossen waren, erscheint die
sie hervorrufende Thätigkeit der Offenbarung als eine

There is, however, an obvious difference between the original creation and the creative activity of historical revelation. The former brings things into being "from nothing," as the tradition says, i.e., without any previously existing substrate or material. The latter brings something into being with relation to and in connection with what already exists.[46] There is a subject for whom the revelation takes place. There is an object in connection with which it takes place. And there are "the preceding states of both, through whose inexplicable change or turning-about the revelatory activity makes itself perceptible precisely as divine."[47] Revelation, therefore, is distinct from creation by being a creative transformation (Umschaffung) of the already existing state of reality.[48]

This brings us, however, to the nub of the difficulty. Does such a transformation not disrupt and contradict the existing order of nature? The extreme supernaturalist defenders of revelation, of course, did not hesitate to affirm this. In this they shared the naturalist view of God's relationship to the course of nature. Drey, however, thinks that he can avoid this intellectually unacceptable concept of revelation by virtue of his own more carefully nuanced view of the God-world relationship.

The key to Drey's solution is the continuity of creation (the original revelation) and historical revelation. The same God who created the order of nature continues to re-create it through His revelatory activity. It is unreasonable to think of God as negating the product of His own creative activity. Hence, it is wrong to think of revelation as the negation of the "nature and law placed in things by the Creator Himself."[49]

---

schöpferische, durch Hervorbringung von noch nie Gewesenem völlig gleich der ursprünglichen Schöpfung."

[46]Cf. Apol I § 20, p. 179.

[47]Apol I § 24, p. 200: ". . . die früheren Zustände beider, durch deren unerklärbare Veränderung oder Umkehrung die Offenbarungsthätigkeit sich eben als eine göttliche bemerkbar macht."

[48]Ibid.

[49]Ibid.: ". . . was . . . von dem Schöpfer selbst als Natur und Gesetz in die Dinge gelegt ist."

Moreover, it is impossible for any revelation to be perceptible and available to man except in and through this world that God has created.[50] The already existing world, with all its regularity and intelligibility, is and must be the locus and the material for any revelatory activity. Hence, for this reason, too, it is unreasonable to suppose that revelation simply negates the laws of created nature or that it operates according to other, unknown laws.

Nevertheless, there is an element of newness about revelation, Drey thinks, which makes it recognizable as the product of divine creative initiative. It is not that something altogether contradictory to or incongruent with the already created order of nature suddenly appears. Rather, something comes into being whose origin is not fully explainable in terms of the preceding state of affairs, something which exceeds the power of its apparent causes.

Drey is thinking not only of "nature-miracles" such as the healings and multiplications of loaves in the gospel stories. Even more, he is thinking of the new spiritual realities, the new qualities of mind and heart, brought into being with Jesus and the rise of Christianity. If one thinks that all this is fully explainable as the result of natural forces and historical factors, Drey insists that the category of "revelation" is not applicable.

The Need for a "Second Revelation" in Continuity with the "Original Revelation"

Drey's insistence upon these "new beginnings" in historical revelation is to be understood against the background of his general conception of the human condition before God. As we shall see in the next chapter, a divine revelatory activity in history (a continuation of creation) is intrinsic to this human condition. But the particular form which it has taken in mankind's actual development corresponds to man's sinful refusal to recognize and respond to the primal revelation (the created world itself as divine self-manifestation).

----

[50]Cf. KE §§ 16-17, p. 10.

In this context, sin is regarded as man's culpable refusal to recognize the revelation-quality of creation itself (the "original" or "first" revelation).[51] It is this refusal which necessitates a further revelation in a form that discloses unmistakably the "supernatural" reality of the One who is Creator both of the order of nature and of the events which seem to transcend it.[52]

The true perception of the world views it "purely as revelation, purely as the work and property of God . . ."[53] But the world no longer appears this way to man who "has raised himself from this original perception to the other one which is constituted by self-consciousness and freedom."[54]

Drey seems here to link the rise of man's consciousness of self with the sinful denial of his relationship to God. Yet it does not seem that Drey considers sin to be essentially connected with the rise of consciousness and freedom, but only factually joined with it. To use his own favorite categories, sin is "accidental" (even though universal), not "necessary."[55]

At any rate, the possibility of sin is given with the rise of consciousness. And, once man "posits" himself as an absolute, self-sufficient ego, he is no longer able to perceive the world as God's revelation. Drey characterizes this state of mis-perception as "the madness of selfhood" (der Wahn der Selbstheit).[56] This sense of the absolute autonomy of the self and of the world (the root error of Enlightenment thought, as

---

[51]For the full treatment of Drey's doctrine on sin, see below, pp.

[52]Cf. KE §§ 16-22, pp. 10-12.

[53]KE § 18, p. 10: ". . . rein als Offenbarung, rein als Werk und Eigentum Gottes . . ."

[54]Ibid., pp. 10-11: ". . . sich von jener ursprünglichen Anschauung zu der andern, durch Selbstbewußtseyn und Freiheit gesetzten, erhoben hat."

[55]For a fuller discussion of this point, see below, pp.   . The place of sin in Drey's system is somewhat ambiguous, and reveals the inadequacy of the Idealist thought-frame.

[56]KE § 26, p. 14.

Drey saw it) leads to a completely "profane view of the
universe" rather than "the religious view" which could recognize the primal revelation.[57]

Hence, there is need for a different form of divine
revelatory activity, a new creation which manifestly transcends
the immanent causality of nature.[58]   "Only in this form can a
revelation force man to recognize God in it."[59]

Such a conception may well appear problematical to
present-day theology, insofar as it seems to introduce God as
the immediate cause of particular events and thus to confuse
the levels of first cause and second causes. At the same time,
it seems to allow insufficient room for faith insofar as it
supposes that these events force man to recognize the divine
causality in them.

These objections should be weighed against the background
of Drey's whole treatment of "natural" and "supernatural." In
the case of "nature" itself, as we have seen, Drey affirmed a
"synthesis" of natural and supernatural aspects. Likewise, in
the case of the particular events of historical revelation, the
new realities (creative transformations of existing reality)
are to be regarded as both natural and supernatural.

. They are perceptible precisely because they belong to
this world and are modifications of the existing state of
things. In this sense they are natural. At the same time,
they are supernatural in a double sense. First of all--like
the product of the original creative activity--they spring
directly and immediately from the creative will of God.
Secondly, they are manifestly of divine origin because they
exceed the power of their preceding apparent causes. This
occasions the recognition of the fundamental, underlying
relationship of created reality to Creator.

---

[57]KE § 21, p. 12: "Die profane Ansicht des Universums
beherrscht und schwächt die religiöse."

[58]Cf. KE § 22, p. 12.

[59]Ibid.: "Nur in dieser Gestalt kann eine Offenbarung den
Menschen zwingen, Gott in ihr anzuerkennen."

But this "relationship of origin" is, of course, precisely what the "miraculous" events have in common with the totality of "nature" itself. In both instances, to use the word "supernatural" of the realities in question is simply to recognize God (who is "above nature") as the source and abiding ground of that which is manifest to us as created reality.

Such a recognition, however, is undoubtedly bound up with the kind of subjectivity which Drey regards as truly religious and, indeed, mystical. If this consideration is given suffi- cient weight, Drey's stress on the "supernatural" character of historical revelation may not seem quite so remote from present-day thought.

For the logic of Drey's position could lead to the reasonable conclusion that a false subjectivity may mistake and ignore even the most striking manifestations of a divine initia- tive in history (just as it may disregard the primal revelation of the world itself). Faith, as we might put it today, is therefore intrinsic to the revelation-event.

Conclusion

This chapter has been concerned with Drey's effort to clarify and defend the concept of revelation against the challenge of deistic naturalism. In this context, revelation has been viewed somewhat abstractly as a divine activity in and upon the created world of "nature."

It should be kept in mind, however, that this highly philosophical argument was important to Drey in order to vindicate the plausibility of a divine initiative within history, awakening and guiding the religious development of all mankind.

What still needs to be considered, therefore, is how the divine revelatory activity is related to man. Against the challenge of rationalism, Drey needed to show the intrinsic correlation between this divine initiative and the rational nature of man. This will be the subject matter of the next chapter.

CHAPTER III

REVELATION AS THE EDUCATION

OF HUMAN REASON

This chapter continues the examination of Drey's theory of revelation, which is the key to his apologetic grounding of Christian theology. Whereas Chapter II dealt with revelation as a divine activity in and upon the created order, this chapter is concerned with how that divine activity is related to the human subject--to the human being in his/her quality of "Vernunft."

The rationalist view of man, as Drey understood it, did not allow for any ongoing influence of God upon the human reason which He had created.[1] Man was conceived as self-sufficient in the possession and use of reason. Religion was considered a function or aspect of man's autonomous, rational nature. From such a viewpoint, revelation--even if philosophically conceivable as a divine activity within the created world --must seem arbitrary, superfluous, and extrinsic to human reason.

In order to defend the concept of revelation against this rationalist view, Drey argues that the divine revelatory initiative is intrinsic to the very functioning and development of human reason. Just as God's creative activity is not to be regarded as merely extrinsic to the finite order, so also God's continuing creative activity of revelation is not to be regarded as merely extrinsic to human subjectivity.

----

[1]For Drey, this was simply the application of the basic principle of naturalism (see above, p. 24) to that portion of created reality called "human reason." Cf. Apol I § 32, p. 262.

Before presenting Drey's thought in its particulars, a
brief overview of the main themes may be helpful. The first
topic is "religion," as something "natural" to man. It begins
as an intrinsic awareness of God but at the same time needs an
ever-present divine influence, mediated through the world of
objects, in order to grow and develop. The outcome of this
account of religion is a "scientific concept" of revelation,
correlative to the essential nature of the human being.

The second topic is the "education" of human reason by
the never-failing divine influence. This developmental and
universal-historical view of the human condition regards the
divine revelatory activity as a transforming stimulation of
human subjectivity (beginning with feeling, passing over into
ideas and ethical action) which brings about a new social
reality in history. (Drey's theory of revelation, in this
respect, connects closely with his general theology of history
and his understanding of Church.)

The third topic is the intelligibility of revelation.
Although God's education of human reason is not limited to the
imparting of truths, Drey wishes to give full weight to the
intelligibility of the divinely guided development of mankind.
There are, he thinks, divine "ideas" being made real in history
which--when awakened in man's reason by the educative influence
of revelation--can be appropriated by the human mind as its own
ideas. To this extent, revelation has a rational quality, and
a kind of knowing (arising out of faith) is possible for the
theologian. Such a "wissenschaftliche Theologie" is, indeed,
demanded for an intellectually responsible contemporary treatment of Christianity.

This anticipatory overview of the present chapter shows
its function in the overall study of Drey's thought. On the
one hand, it completes the treatment of his theory of revelation. On the other hand, it also leads towards the more
detailed examination of his method for theology, which consists
in seeking the speculative intelligibility of a divinely
"posited" history.

Religion and Revelation

Drey's treatment of revelation in relation to human
reason is grounded explicitly in a philosophical account of the

phenomenon of religion. He took this approach to revelation
in conscious response to the challenges of naturalism and
rationalism.

Religion as "Natural" to Man

The defenders of revelation, for the most part, shared
the prevailing view that human reason is capable of elaborating
"a so-called natural religion prior to and independent of
revelation."[2] Rationalists insisted that this natural religion
is sufficient, and that the only possible content of any
hypothetical revelation would be the truths of this "religion
within the limits of reason alone." Hence, the revelation
would be superfluous, or--at most--a pedagogical help.[3] Supernaturalists, on the other hand, tried to show a relative
necessity for revelation because of the weakness of reason and
the inadequacies of natural religion.[4]

According to Drey, the fundamental error of both parties
was to think that human reason could originate a "natural
religion" apart from divine influence. (This error, he
thought, was bound up with the naturalist isolation of created
reality from God.) Consequently, revelation could only be
regarded as a kind of supplement to man's basic condition--
the need for which was denied by rationalists and affirmed by
supernaturalists. Such an additional intervention by God in a
world that was already complete (communicating truths allegedly

---

[2] Apol I, "Einleitung" § 20, p. 58: ". . . eine sogenannte
natürliche Religion vor der Offenbarung und unabhängig von ihr
. . ."

[3] E.g., Lessing was of the opinion that revelation gives
"dem Menschengeschlechte nichts, worauf die menschliche
Vernunft, sich selbst überlassen, nicht auch kommen würde:
sondern sie gab und gibt ihm die wichtigsten dieser Dinge nur
früher." (Werke, ed. H. G. Göpfert [Munich: C. Hanser, 1970-79],
8:491. "Erziehung des Menschengeschlechtes" § 4.) Drey
criticized this opinion as an unproven and unprovable hypothesis
(Apol I § 34, pp. 294-95). Drey's reference to Lessing here is
not an isolated instance. As Schilson has shown, Drey was
familiar with Lessing's works and significantly influenced by
his thought. Cf. Arno Schilson, "Lessing und die katholische
Tübinger Schule," ThQ 160 (1980):256-77, esp. p. 262, 266-70,
273-75.

[4] Apol I § 10, p. 134.

beyond the limits of human reason) seemed to be an unnecessary
and unintelligible intrusion into the domain of reason.

In order to challenge this taken-for-granted state of the
question, Drey had to present a somewhat different understanding of religion. On the one hand, of course, he fully shared
the contemporary view that religion was an essential feature of
man's nature.[5] On the other hand, he was unwilling to conceive
this "nature" as self-contained and only extrinsically related
to God.

On the contrary, as he put it very pointedly in an
earlier article, ". . . the essence of reason, the deeper nature
of man, is inconceivable without his relationship to God: in
fact . . . that very nature is precisely only this relationship
itself . . ."[6]

Drey's Account of Religion

Drey's account of religion[7] is governed by this underlying conviction that man's very being is constituted by the
relationship of radical, ontological dependence on God. This
corresponds to his general "mystical" view of the world itself
as "rooted in God."[8] This "relationship of origin" is the

---

[5]Cf. Apol I, "Einleitung" § 14, p. 27, where Drey says
that precisely because religion is "a necessary and natural
phenomenon in the human spirit," philosophy of religion is
important to theology. For "positive" Christian theology must
"connect" with the general theological principles derivable
from the religious condition of man. This connection is made
by the discipline of apologetics. This is an important methodological observation, which would be widely affirmed today.
Since Drey's day, of course, the phenomenology of religion has
also become available to theologians, adding a new dimension to
our appreciation of "the religious condition of man." But this
might well be fitted into Drey's formal framework.

[6]"Aphorismen über den Ursprung unserer Erkenntnisse von
Gott," ThQ 8 (1826):272. ". . . das Wesen der Vernunft, die
tiefere Natur des Menschen [ist] nicht begreiflich . . . ohne
sein Verhältniß zu Gott, ja . . . eben jene Natur [ist] gerade
dieses Verhältniß selbst . . ."

[7]See KE §§ 1-15, pp. 1-9, and Apol I §§ 1-6, pp. 79-119.
The earlier treatment is more formal and abstract, as Drey himself points out, while the later treatment begins more empirically from the "fact" of religion in history. Both treatments
locate religion initially as feeling.

[8]See above, pp.

objective basis of religion (which may thus be regarded as man's
subjective feeling and recognition of his objective relatedness
to God).[9]

Religion begins, therefore, as an inarticulate awareness
of the God-relationship in the very event of human self-
awareness. "Man becomes aware of God, as he becomes aware of
himself."[10] Like Schleiermacher, Drey locates this original
sense of God as a feeling arising in the Gemüt, "the deepest
ground of the soul."[11] At the same time, he differs somewhat
from Schleiermacher in maintaining that this feeling is based
on an objective reality: the actual rootedness of all things in
God.[12]

Moreover, religion is not limited to feeling, but rather
penetrates and qualifies all of man's spiritual powers--of
thinking, imagining, and willing. What begins as feeling
passes over into thoughts, images, myths, artistic creations,
and moral behavior.[13] Moreover, because of man's social nature,
it leads to the formation of a religious community with its
activity of cult.[14]

Hence, Drey offers as his own succinct definition of
religion the following formulation: religion is "man's being

---

[9]KE § 7, pp. 3-4.

[10]KE § 6, p. 3: ". . . der Mensch wird sich Gottes bewußt,
wie er sich seiner selbst bewußt wird."

[11]Apol I § 3, p. 88: "Der tiefste Grund der Seele . . ."
On religion as "feeling," cf. also especially "Vom Geist und
Wesen des Katholizismus," in GdChr, p. 213 and p. 216, and
"Ueber das Verhältniß des Mysticismus zum Katholicismus." ThQ 6
(1824):222-23, reprinted in Schupp, Revision von Kirche und
Theologie, pp. 28-29.

[12]Rief points out that, for this reason, there is a
rational quality to Drey's account of religious feeling which,
he thinks, is missing in Schleiermacher's view (Reich Gottes,
p. 81). On Schleiermacher's influence upon Drey, cf. Schupp,
Die Evidenz der Geschichte, p. 7 and p. 39, as well as Rief,
Reich Gottes, pp. 80ff.

[13]Cf. "Ueber das Verhältniß des Mysticismus zum
Katholicismus," ThQ 6 (1824):223-26, in Schupp, Revision von
Kirche und Theologie, pp. 29-32.

[14]Apol I § 3, pp. 88-95.

thoroughly determined [bestimmt] by the original consciousness
of God."[15] The determining factor is the primal awareness of
God, which gives a definite character to the religious man's
spiritual existence, profoundly affecting and specifying all
human faculties and activities.

This primal sense of the divine is intrinsic to human
nature as such, and is the condition of possibility for all the
further developments of religion. In this sense, religion is
"natural" to man. Yet, it is not to be regarded as "natural
religion" in the rationalist sense, because it is God Himself
(the Supernatural) who is the cause of the innate primal sense
of God in human consciousness.

Drey makes this clear by examining the rise of self-
awareness in man.[16] He maintains that there is an awareness of
God as Other in the very same moment of initial consciousness
in which man is aware of himself as a distinct subject, over
against the Other.[17] Man is aware of God as the Other on whom
his own existence depends, but from whom he is separate.
Following immediately upon this comes the longing for nearness
and union with God. In this way, the very rise of self-
consciousness in man involves the fundamental elements of
religious consciousness or "Frömmigkeit."

This is understandable, Drey argues, only if there was an
earlier "moment" in which God and man were intimately united.
This is the moment of man's creation when he is intimately
united with and, indeed, "penetrated by" God. When God "lets
man go" as a being distinct from Himself, man therefore retains
the sense of God. In the moment of creation, man was totally
penetrated by God's own will and consciousness. This is what
constitutes man, indeed, as a being with consciousness and will

---

[15]Apol I § 6, p. 118: ". . . das durchgängige Bestimmtseyn des Menschen durch das ursprüngliche Bewußtseyn von Gott."

[16]Apol I § 5, pp. 109-113. On this argument, cf. Rief,
op. cit., p. 219, as well as Peter Hünermann, "Der Reflex des
deutschen Idealismus in der Theologie der katholischen Tübinger
Schule," Philosophisches Jahrbuch 73 (1965-66):55-56.

[17]This awareness of God is, to be sure, obscure and
undifferentiated, as he points out later. See Apol I § 8,
pp. 128ff. and the discussion of it below.

or--in other words, as an "image of God." Hence, as soon as
man becomes aware of himself, he is simultaneously aware of God
insofar as he himself is the image of God. This accounts for
the presence and spontaneous origin of the notion of God in
man's very nature.

This also allows Drey to regard religion as natural to
man without accepting the rationalist concept of "natural
religion." For the very nature of man--including religion--is
seen in the intimate relationship to God constituted by
creation. God is not extrinsic to man's being.[18]

Religion and Revelation

The innate sense of God is, therefore, a kind of
"original" revelation without which religion would be impossible. But this interior awareness of God is by no means the
total meaning of the term "revelation," as Drey wishes to interpret it. For this initial, obscure sense of God in the Gemüt
must develop into fully articulated concepts, attitudes of mind,
moral decisions and actions. Drey maintains that this development of religion (in the individual and the race) is possible
only under the ever-present and continuing divine revelatory
influence, mediated through the objects of this world.[19] In
order to justify this position, Drey recognizes that he must
show the intrinsic correlation of such externally mediated
divine influence to the essential nature of human reason.[20]

The "Scientific Concept" of Revelation

This way of formulating the problem reflects Drey's awareness of the epoch-making significance of Kant's critical
philosophy for the Christian theologian.[21]

---

[18]Cf. Apol I § 5, p. 109.

[19]See below.

[20]Apol I, "Einleitung" § 21, p. 72: ". . . die innern
Verhältnisse der Vernunft zu der Offenbarung genauer zu
bestimmen . . ."

[21]Cf. Apol I, "Einleitung" § 21, p. 71: ". . . von dieser
Wendung beginnt für die Theologie das neunzehnte Jahrhundert."

As the first favorable effect of the critical philosophy upon Apologetics, we must consider the making-conscious of the need for a <u>theory</u> and <u>critique of revelation</u>. For such a long time, one had argued for and against revelation, without having a scientifically determined concept of it and of its relationship to the spiritual and ethical nature of man . . .[22]

What Drey means by "scientific" (<u>wissenschaftlich</u>) is to be made clear in Chapters IV and V. For the present it is enough to point out that "Wissenschaft" has to do with what is understood to be "necessary" rather than "accidental." That which is seen to be intrinsically related to man's essential nature is "necessary." This is contrasted with that which is perceived merely as a contingent fact of history, which just "happens" to be the case (the "accidental").[23]

The "fact" of revelation (amply attested, Drey thinks, in the actual history of mankind's religious development)[24] may nevertheless appear to be merely extrinsic and "accidental."[25] Hence, the task of the scientific theologian is "to determine more precisely the <u>inner</u> relationships of reason to revelation"[26] and thus "to specify the concept of revelation and its relation to religion <u>from within</u> and as something necessary."[27]

---

[22]<u>Apol</u> I, "Einleitung" § 21, p. 73: "Als die erste der Apologetik zuträgliche Wirkung der kritischen Philosophie muß das in das Bewußtseyn hervorgerufene Bedürfniß einer <u>Theorie</u> und <u>Kritik der Offenbarung</u> betrachtet werden; schon so lange hatte man gegen und für die Offenbarung gestritten, ohne von ihr und ihrem Verhältniß zur geistigen und sittlichen Natur des Menschen einen wissenschaftlich bestimmten Begriff zu besitzen . . ."

[23]This distinction, of course, was a common point of reference for German thought at least since Lessing.

[24]<u>Apol</u> I § 7, pp. 119-27.

[25]<u>Apol</u> I § 8, p. 128: ". . . die Erkenntnis der Offenbarung und ihres Verhältnisses zur Religion, die auf dem Wege historischer Betrachtung möglich ist, ist . . . bloß eine <u>äußerliche</u>, und die Offenbarung selbst wie ihr Begriff erscheint hier als etwas zufälliges . . ."

[26]<u>Apol</u> I, "Einleitung" § 21, p. 72: ". . . die <u>innern</u> Verhältnisse der Vernunft zu der Offenbarung genauer zu bestimmen . . ."

[27]<u>Apol</u> I § 8, p. 128: ". . . den Begriff der Offenbarung und ihr Verhältniß zu der Religion <u>von innen heraus</u> und als etwas nothwendiges zu bestimmen."

Drey attempts to establish such a concept of revelation through a kind of transcendental analysis of the conditions for the rise of religious consciousness in human beings. Since he is thinking, as already noted, in the general context of Schleiermacherian "Bewußtseinstheologie," he directs his attention to "consciousness" (Bewußtsein) as "the inner seat of religion and consequently the innermost point of man which revelation--conceived as God's activity--must touch . . ."[28]

Since religion arises in consciousness, a scientific understanding of revelation's intrinsic connection with religion (and thus, with human reason) must begin from this "innermost point of man." Hence, the logic of Drey's argument: He presupposes that "the development of religious consciousness is subject to the conditions and laws of the development of consciousness as such."[29] These conditions are therefore first established, before showing how they also apply to the case of religious consciousness.

Consciousness as Such

Man comes to self-consciousness, Drey maintains, only in encountering the Other. This rise of initial consciousness takes place in what he calls the "collision" (Anstoß) with particular objects of experience, which throws the human spirit back upon itself in its distinctiveness. This meeting of the Other makes man aware, for the first time, of the boundary between the self and what is not the self.[30] This gives rise simultaneously to the awareness of self and the obscure, global sense of the Other--i.e., of the world in general (and for religious consciousness, of God).

---

[28]Apol I § 8, p. 128: "Der innere Sitz der Religion . . . und folglich auch der innerste Punkt im Menschen, welchen die Offenbarung--als That Gottes gedacht--treffen muß, ist das Bewußtseyn . . ."

[29]Apol I § 8, p. 128: ". . . die Entwickelung des religiösen Bewußtseyns [unterliegt] den Bedingungen und Gesetzen der Entwickelung des Bewußtseyns überhaupt . . ."

[30]Apol I § 8, p. 128: ". . . der Geist in seiner Thätigkeit muß in sich selbst zurückgetrieben werden durch einen Anstoß, welchen er außer sich findet, durch eine Schranke, die, indem sie ihm sein Ich zu schauen giebt, für eben dieses Ich zum Nicht-Ich wird."

This 'not-I' is, for ordinary consciousness, the world, for
religious consciousness, God. Therefore, in the original
self-consciousness, the consciousness of God and of the
world is already included, since the former could never
arise without the two latter and their objects.[31]

The further development of consciousness, he argues, is
conditioned by the same kind of relationship to objects. It is
only in continuing encounters with particular objects that man
comes to know the world in its particularity (in contrast to
the obscure initial sense of world as such). Drey uses the
word "Anschauung" to refer to this process.[32] "All consciousness, therefore, develops with reference to an outward
perception--this is how we will, from now on, designate that
collision and reflex--and with reference to its objects . . ."[33]

Religious Consciousness

Having thus set up the general law for the development of
human consciousness as such, Drey applies this to the case of
religious consciousness. Religion, as we have seen, takes its
origin from the primal sense of God which is inseparable from
the first moment of human self-awareness. Although this sense
of the divine is innate in man as the "image of God," it can
only be awakened insofar as man becomes aware of himself. But
this can only happen in the encounter with objects, by which
self is defined over against the global ideas of both world and
God.

Just as the origin, so also the continuing development of
religious consciousness is subject to the same condition of
"outward perception" of objects.

----

[31]Apol I § 8, pp. 128-29: "Dieses Nicht-Ich ist für das
gewöhnliche Bewußtseyn die Welt, für das religiöse Gott. Darum
findet sich im ursprünglichen Selbstbewußtseyn schon das
Bewußtseyn Gottes und der Welt eingeschlossen, weil ohne die
beiden letztern und ihre Objekte das erste nie entstehen
könnte."

[32]On this need for "Anschauung" of an object as a mediation of the "idea" for human reason, cf. also "Aphorismen," ThQ
8 (1826):251, ". . . daß vermöge der endlichen Natur unseres
Geistes jede Idee, zumal die von Gott, als ein an sich Unend-
liches enthaltend, für uns nur dunkle Ahndung bleiben muß - so
lange bis in irgend einer Erscheinung die Idee - nicht die
volle, dieß ist unmöglich - sich geoffenbart hat."

[33]Apol I § 8, p. 129: "Alles Bewußtseyn entwickelt sich

. . . just as the consciousness of the world, which is
likewise primal, develops only insofar as the world becomes
perceptible in the diversity of its phenomena, in the
multiplicity and diversity of its parts, so also the primal
consciousness of God can only develop on the presupposition
of a similar outward perception.[34]

That is, the original, unspecified idea of God gradually
takes on a specific content through the experience and apprehension of external objects of the world. In order to clarify
this thought, Drey uses a metaphor from astronomy. A nebula
appears to the naked eye as an undifferentiated mass of light.
In order for the observer to perceive the particularities of
this phenomenon (the individual stars), the light must somehow
be refracted and focussed. Similarly, the undifferentiated
idea of God--sensed obscurely in even the first stirrings of
human consciousness--must be "refracted" through specific,
finite, worldly objects, if man is to grow and develop in his
religious consciousness.

This requirement springs from the universal law of the
development of human consciousness as such. There must be the
outward perception of objects if the primal awareness is to
develop into particularized knowledge. On the basis of this
analysis of consciousness in general and of religious consciousness in particular, he is then able to conclude:

> External phenomena and perceptions which reflect the divine
> in an objective way are, therefore, the <u>necessary condition</u>
> for the development of religious consciousness and of
> religion as such; this is so <u>in accordance with nature</u>,
> i.e., according to the nature of the human spirit . . .;
> this is true <u>universally</u>, i.e., in relation to all
> knowledge of God whatsoever.[35]

---

also an einer <u>äußern Anschauung</u>--so wollen wir fortan jenen
Anstoß und Reflex nennen--und an den Objekten derselben . . ."

[34]<u>Apol</u> I § 8, p. 130: ". . . wie das Bewußtseyn der Welt,
gleichfalls ein ursprüngliches, sich nur dadurch entwickelt,
daß uns diese in der Manchfaltigkeit ihrer Erscheinungen, in
der Vielheit und Zerlegung ihrer Theile zur Anschauung kommt,
so kann sich auch das ursprüngliche Bewußtseyn von Gott nur
entwickeln unter der Voraussetzung einer ähnlichen äußern
Anschauung."

[35]<u>Apol</u> I § 8, p. 131: "Aeußere, das Göttliche objektiv
zurückstrahlende, Erscheinungen und Anschauungen sind daher die
<u>nothwendige</u> <u>Bedingung</u> der Entwickelung des religiösen
Bewußtseyns und der Religion überhaupt; sie sind dies <u>naturgemäß</u>,

In this way, he has arrived at his "scientific concept" of revelation, derived from a transcendental analysis of the conditions of human knowledge. He has shown a necessity of revelation which springs from the very nature of man as spirit. Moreover, he has shown that this revelation must take the form of objective, external phenomena of this world.

He took this position in conscious disagreement with the then prevalent tendency to identify revelation solely with man's interior awareness of God (the innate idea of God).[36]

> It was . . . a great error . . . when theologians imagined
> . . . that the primal awareness of God, or the innate idea
> of God, or (as they also called it) the revelation of God
> in reason, could develop through mere reflection, i.e.
> through the mere bending back of thought upon itself . . .
> without the mediation of thought by corresponding objects,
> and with reference to them. This error arose from the lack
> of a deeper insight into the nature and laws of our
> consciousness, and has produced both naturalism and the
> prevalent rationalism.[37]

Drey's alternative view has important consequences for his theology, since it leads him to regard history as the outcome of an ongoing and never-ceasing divine influence upon human consciousness in and through the objects and events of this world. This concrete history is the object which the theologian must study and interpret, since it is the divinely created context for reason's functioning and development.[38]

---

d.h., nach der Natur des menschlichen Geistes . . . sie sind es allgemein, d.h., in Beziehung auf alle Erkenntniß Gottes überhaupt."

[36]Cf. Apol I § 9, p. 133.

[37]Apol I § 8, p. 131: "Es war . . . ein großer Irrthum . . . wenn Theologen sich einbildeten . . . das ursprüngliche Gottesbewußtseyn, oder die angeborne Idee von Gott, oder wie sie es auch nannten, die Offenbarung Gottes in der Vernunft, könne sich entwickeln durch die bloße Reflexion, d.h. durch bloße Umbeugung des Denkens in sich . . . ohne Vermittlung des Denkens durch entsprechende Gegenstände und an ihnen. Diesen Irrthum, der aus dem Mangel einer tiefern Einsicht in die Natur und Gesetze unseres Bewußtseyns hervorgegangen ist, und den Naturalismus und gangbaren Rationalismus erzeugt hat . . ."

[38]Cf. Hünermann, "Der Reflex," p. 58, where the romantic view of history as "Boden der Vernunft" is made clear.

Revelation, then, is to be conceived as intrinsically related to the needs of human reason, yet other than reason and always active in relation to it.

> . . . the necessity of revelation . . . can only be
> [demonstrated] if one shows that reason could not--either
> in the beginning or afterwards--develop without those
> external appearances which we call the revelations of God
> in the history of mankind. Only in this way does revel-
> ation appear no longer as something merely accidental,
> which is added onto reason as an afterthought, but rather
> as something which is posited simultaneously with reason
> and is always posited, and yet is different from reason.[39]

Revelation as the Education of Reason

The logic of Drey's position leads, therefore, from the more abstract, "transcendental" analysis of human reason's need for externally mediated revelation to a consideration of the actual historical condition of reason in relation to this ever-present divine influence. This provides the full response to the rationalist denial of revelation.

Drey is concerned to overcome the apparent opposition between reason and that which is allegedly "above" or "beyond" reason. Rationalism, as he understands it, makes reason absolute in its historical existence and hence cannot allow for any ongoing interaction between God and man:

> It allows God to be the source of truth for reason only in
> the act of creation; but after this, it stops up this
> source, and lets reason, from then on, draw only out of
> itself, so that it cuts off all operative connection of man
> with God . . . At the same time--in opposition to history
> and its own consciousness--it ignores or denies every
> aberration of reason, in order not to be forced to acknowl-
> edge the necessity of a repeated revelation and the need
> for a continuing influence of God.[40]

---

[39]ThQ 10 (1828): 686, ". . . die Nothwendigkeit der
Offenbarung . . . kann . . . nur [nachgewiesen werden] wenn man
zeigt, daß die Vernunft, weder am Anfange noch nachher, sich
entwickeln konnte ohne jene äußere Erscheinungen, die wir in
der Geschichte der Menschheit die Offenbarungen Gottes nennen.
Nur so erscheint die Offenbarung nicht mehr als etwas blos
zufälliges, hintennach zu der Vernunft hinzukommendes, sondern
als etwas mit ihr zugleich und immer gesetztes, und von ihr
doch verschiedenes."

[40]Apol I § 34, pp. 288-89: ". . . indem er Gott als die
Quelle der Wahrheit für die Vernunft nur im Schöpfungsakte
gelten läßt, nach demselben aber diese Quelle verstopft, und
fortan die Vernunft einzig aus sich selbst schöpfen läßt, so

As we have seen, the conviction central to Drey's alternative view is that God is not extrinsic to the definition of
the human. The deepest level of this truth is the ontological
relationship established in God's creation of the world and, in
particular, of man. From this perspective, the concept
"revelation" is rooted in the fundamental God-man relationship
itself. To be human at all is to be in a relationship of utter
dependence on God as the source of all being and of all truth.

When this ontological dependency is placed in a historical
and developmental perspective, it follows that human reason can
function and develop only in relation to the divine Reality.
This is the conception of the human condition which Drey
proposes in order to overcome the apparent opposition of reason
and revelation.

"The Education of the Human Race"

In order to conceptualize the correlation between reason
and revelation, Drey makes use of Lessing's idea of "the education of the human race."[41] He formulates his conception in a
close paraphrase of Lessing: "Revelation . . . is for the whole
of mankind what education is for the individual."[42]

Drey argues from the obvious fact that human reason is
essentially in need of education in order to develop and

---

daß er hiedurch alle wirksame Verbindung des Menschen mit Gott
abschneidet . . . Zugleich ignorirt oder läugnet er, gegen die
Geschichte und das eigene Bewußtseyn, jede Verirrung der
Vernunft, um nur nicht gezwungen zu seyn, die Nothwendigkeit
einer wiederholten Offenbarung, und das Bedürfniß eines
fortdauernden Einflusses Gottes anerkennen zu müssen."

[41]The fullest treatment is found in the article
"Aphorismen über den Ursprung unserer Erkenntnisse von Gott,"
ThQ 8 (1826):237-84. A similar argument is presented more
succinctly in Apol I § 11, pp. 140-51. In the earlier article,
Drey explicitly acknowledges his dependence on Lessing, and
characterizes this idea as "der würdigsten und wahrsten, die
man sich von der Offenbarung machen kann." ThQ 8 (1826):266-67.
Cf. Lessing, "Die Erziehung des Menschengeschlechts," in
Lessings Werke, ed. H. G. Göpfert (Munich: C. Hanser, 1970-79),
8:489-510. On Drey's familiarity with this text, cf. Schilson,
"Lessing und die katholische Tübinger Schule," p. 262. For a
detailed documentation of its influence on Drey, cf. ibid.,
pp. 266-70.

[42]ThQ 8 (1826):266. "Offenbarung . . . ist für die ganze
Menschheit, was für den Einzelnen die Erziehung ist." Cf.
Lessing, "Die Erziehung des Menschengeschlechts," § 1.

function at all. To put it another way, reason can be
awakened and brought to development only under the influence of
already developed reason (as we see in the case of children).
"Just as reason, wherever it exists, presupposes for its very
existence a higher reason, so this same reason presupposes for
its development a reason which brings about the development."[43]

In order to show the role of revelation in relation to
the human race, Drey applies this same principle to the case of
the very first human beings. Supposing that their condition
must have been analogous to that of children, he argues that
their "education" to rationality is conceivable only under the
awakening and stimulating influence of God (mediated externally
through the world), for no "higher reason" other than God
Himself was available. Hence, the origin not only of religion
but of culture itself is attributed to divine revelatory
influence upon undeveloped human reason.[44]

Drey maintains, furthermore, that the basic relationship
of reason to its Source--this basic dependency on divine
educative activity--is a permanent and abiding feature of human
existence. The effect of revelation is, therefore, to promote
ever further the development and functioning of human reason in
all respects.

> Revelation remains a need of mankind through all periods of
> its existence; even in heaven it does not end . . .
> Education has no other purpose than the development of
> reason in the theoretical and the practical sense, and the
> promotion of the right use of reason. Insofar, therefore,
> as God educates men through revelation, he has no other
> purpose than to perfect their reason and the use of it. It
> is by virtue of reason that man exists . . . Therefore,

---

[43]ThQ 8 (1826):249. "Wie die Vernunft, wo sie immer
existirt, schon ihrer Existenz nach eine höhere Vernunft
voraussetzt, so setzt dieselbe Vernunft in ihrer Entwicklung
eine entwickelnde Vernunft voraus."

[44]ThQ 8 (1826):249. "Folglich ist alle Cultur der
Menschheit, alle Erziehung, schon die erste ursprüngliche, zur
Vernünftigkeit nothwendige--das Werk Gottes gewesen . . ." On
this point Drey seems close to the views of French traditionalism (as also in his strong sense of the social-historical
mediation of revelation). Yet, his emphasis on the rationality
of revelation and his ideal of theology as "Wissenschaft"
clearly distance him from Bautain's fideistic version of
traditionalism.

revelation . . . cannot be directed to the suppression of
reason, but only to the perfecting of reason as the epitome
of the entire spiritual nature of man.[45]

Above all else, of course, the purpose of revelation is
to awaken, guide, and promote the development of religion. But
religion, in Drey's view, thoroughly qualifies and determines
those very faculties of man which--collectively--are regarded
as "reason" (Vernunft).[46] Hence, if revelation is to promote
religion in man, it must clearly be regarded as for reason.

> . . . just as the determinate character of revelation is
> for religion and religious life, so also it is for reason.
> Revelation cannot be contrary to reason, since it would
> then also have to be contrary to religion; it cannot be
> above reason, i.e. unreachable and unable to be received by
> reason, since it could then have no effect on the promo-
> tion of religion and religious life. Therefore, it can
> only be for reason, and indeed, in such a way that this
> revelation can be recognized as such by reason, can be
> understood with respect to its content, can be grasped with
> respect to its purpose, and can--with respect to its effect
> --be translated into conviction and life. Revelation,
> therefore, is not merely extrinsically for reason--as a
> testimony of God; it is--as a power and action of God--
> intrinsically and utterly for reason. Everything from God
> --through reason--and for it.[47]

---

[45]ThQ 8 (1826):268-69. "Die Offenbarung bleibt Bedürfniß
für die Menschheit durch alle Perioden ihrer Existenz, sie
endet selbst im Himmel nicht . . . Die Erziehung hat keinen
andern Zweck, als die Entwickelung der Vernunft in theoreti-
schem und praktischem Sinne, und die Beförderung des richtigen
Vernunftgebrauches. Indem also Gott die Menschen durch
Offenbarung erzieht, hat er selbst keinen andern Zweck bey
derselben, als ihre Vernunft und den Vernunftgebrauch zu
vervollkommnen. Durch die Vernunft besteht der Mensch . . .
Also kann die Offenbarung . . . nicht auf Unterdrückung,
sondern nur auf Vervollkommnung der Vernunft, als des Inbe-
griffs der ganzen geistigen Natur des Menschen ausgehen."

[46]Cf. Apol I § 34, p. 290.

[47]Apol I § 34, pp. 290-91: ". . . wie also die Bestimmung
der Offenbarung für die Religion und das religiöse Leben, so
auch für die Vernunft. Die Offenbarung kann nicht gegen die
Vernunft seyn, weil sie dann auch gegen die Religion seyn
müßte, sie kann auch nicht über die Vernunft, d.h. dieser
unerreichbar, unaufnehmbar seyn, weil sie dann zum Besten der
Religion und des religiösen Lebens nichts wirken könnte, sie
kann also nur für die Vernunft seyn, und zwar so für die
Vernunft, daß sie von dieser einmal als solche erkannt, ihrem
Inhalt nach verstanden, ihrem Zwecke nach begriffen, ihrer
Wirkung nach in die Gesinnung und das Leben umgesetzt werden
kann; die Offenbarung ist also nicht bloß als ein Zeugniß

   This text shows that Drey by no means had a one-sidedly
intellectualist understanding of revelation. Just as religion
embraces and determines the whole human being, so also revelation affects all of man's spiritual faculties. Moreover, its
general purpose is eminently practical: to awaken and promote
religious life in mankind.

   Hence, while Drey includes "instruction" (Belehrung)
among the specific purposes of revelation,[48] he considers
equally important the function of "awakening" (Erweckung).[49]
This refers to the enabling of man's freedom, under the immediate influence of the Spirit, to choose and actualize a way of
life that is in all respects religious.

   There is, furthermore, a third specific purpose of revelation which corresponds to the social and historical character
of human existence: the establishing of a "positive religious
community" (positive Religionsgemeinschaft).[50] This is the
consequence of God's revelatory influence (in the form of
"inspiration")[51] upon certain individuals whose function it is
to become initiators of a religious community in history.
(Christ is, of course, the supreme instance of this, although
the category "inspiration" is inapplicable to him because of
his divinity.)[52]

   Revelation is not, therefore, directed merely to many
separate individuals, but is rather to be conceived as the
influence of God upon the entire human race--fostering and
enabling the formation of a great social reality in history.
Individuals have different roles to play in this process. Some
are initiators of community, others are instruments of its
growth and spread.

Gottes äußerlich, sie ist als eine Gotteskraft und Gottesthat
innerlich, und durch und durch für die Vernunft. Alles von
Gott--durch die Vernunft--und für sie."

   [48]Cf. Apol I § 15, pp. 158-62.

   [49]Cf. Apol I § 16, pp. 162-65.

   [50]Cf. Apol I § 17, pp. 165-68.

   [51]Cf. Apol I § 28, pp. 223-36.

   [52]Ibid., p. 235.

Drey thus takes a universal-historical view of the human race which is grounded in the belief that there is a "great plan of education, which God is carrying out for our race in the whole of revelation."[53] "A firm and consistent plan of God runs through the whole of these special leadings and revelations, and develops itself more and more."[54] The entirety of these revelations is unified and ordered toward the culminating revelation in Jesus Christ, from which springs the ultimately intended "Religionsgemeinschaft" that is to include all nations.

It is this religious community springing from Christ which Drey regards as the ongoing embodiment in history of the decisive, originating revelation-event. This is his characteristic and influential idea of "living tradition" as the "Selbstüberlieferung der ursprünglichen Offenbarung."[55]

The metaphor of "the education of the human race" thus provides Drey with a helpful way of unifying several insights into the relationship of revelation to human reason. It is a developmental and social-historical view, which takes seriously the historical context of human reason. In this respect, Drey belongs to the thought-world of Romanticism, with its awareness of history, in contrast to the rather unhistorical deism of the Enlightenment period.[56]

At the same time, this metaphor allows him to <u>coordinate</u> revelation with reason, thus overcoming the apparent opposition felt by both rationalists and supernaturalists.[57] Although

---

[53]"Vom Geist und Wesen des Katholizismus," GdChr, p. 195: ". . . des großen Erziehungsplanes, welchen Gott im Ganzen der Offenbarungen an unserm Geschlecht ausführt . . ."

[54]KE § 27, p. 15: "Ein fester und consequenter Plan Gottes lauft aber durch das Ganze dieser besonderen Leitungen und Offenbarungen hin, und entwickelt sich immer mehr."

[55]Cf. Apol I §§ 49-56, pp. 380-410, esp. pp. 381-82 and pp. 398-404. Cf. also Apol III §§ 1-3, pp. 1-17. See below,

[56]It should, however, be noted that Drey was, precisely in this point, significantly influenced by Lessing—a reminder not to oversimplify the heritage of the Enlightenment period. Cf. Schilson, "Lessing und die katholische Tübinger Schule," p. 267.

[57]In this, too, there is a close parallel with Lessing. Cf. Schilson, op. cit., pp. 267-68.

revelation is God's activity (hence, ontologically prior to and so "above" reason), it is regarded as a constitutive, accompanying feature of the human condition, whose purposes can be realized only insofar as it affects reason and is appropriated by it.

Conceiving revelation as God's education of the human race also enables Drey to view it primarily as a divine activity which creates and guides a concrete history. In this respect, his stress on "divine positivity" is faithful to the biblical notion of a God who acts in history. As already pointed out, this orients theology primarily towards a concrete, continuing history (rather than to a body of timeless propositions about God).

The metaphor of "education" also quite obviously includes the factor of intelligibility. Human reason is being educated to discover and appreciate the divine "ideas" being realized in the history that is created by the divine revelatory influence upon the human race. This orients theology to the work of speculative reason, which must strive to appropriate these divine "ideas."

Drey's treatment of revelation as the education of reason thus provides a theological basis for the style of thinking most characteristic of the Catholic Tübingen School: a resolute orientation to the concrete history of mankind's religious development (in which Christianity is central), combined with the speculative drive to understand and interpret this history as a whole, in a way which commends the truth of Christianity to the human mind.

Before concluding this treatment of revelation, therefore, we need to examine more closely Drey's conception of the intelligibility of revelation and his ideal of moving to a rational "construction" of the divinely created history.

Faith and Knowledge

This final section has to do with the "content" of revelation and the capacity of the human mind to receive and appropriate this content. Hence, it involves the relation between

"faith" (Glauben) and "knowledge" (Wissen).[58] Drey maintains
that the orientation of human reason in faith towards the fact
of revelation enables an ever-greater understanding of the
intelligible content of revelation, so that true knowledge of
the revealed truth is attained. This is the work of "scientific
theology." This discussion of faith and knowledge, therefore,
begins the exposition of Drey's method for theology, which will
be treated fully in Chapter V.

"Mysteries" as Problems Set
For Reason by Revelation

It had traditionally been maintained that revelation
contains "mysteries" which cannot be understood but can only be
accepted in faith. To regard these mysteries as absolutely
unintelligible, Drey thinks, is to deny that revelation is
truly for reason.[59] Hence, he takes a more nuanced view.

On the one hand, he acknowledges that the fundamental
truths of revelation exceed the capacity of the human mind to
comprehend fully, since they all concern the ultimate reality
of God and our relationship to Him. But even the so-called
"truths of reason" in the area of religion (e.g., the very idea
of God or the idea of creation) are equally beyond the mind's
ability to comprehend fully.[60] Yet one must concede that there
is some intelligibility in these truths, which the mind can and
does appropriate, even if it can never grasp fully the reality
which they express. (Otherwise, one would have to say that
religion itself is beyond the power of human reason, which is
manifestly absurd.)[61] Similarly, he argues, the mind can come--
through a gradual process--to appreciate ever more fully the

---

[58]Apol I § 35, pp. 296-307. NB: The English words "faith"
and "knowledge" are nouns which do not convey the sense of
activity included in the German substantival use of verb forms.
(In this respect, the archaic form Glauben--rather than the
modern form Glaube--keeps a perfect parallel with Wissen.)
There seems to be no graceful way to render this verb-quality
in English, but the reader should keep in mind the range of
meaning expressed by the German words.

[59]Cf. Apol I § 33, p. 283; ibid. § 35, p. 298.

[60]Apol I § 33, pp. 283-85.

[61]Ibid., p. 285.

truths of revelation. These truths are, therefore, to be
regarded as only relative mysteries.[62]

In order to characterize the relationship of reason to
the mysteries which revelation presents to it, Drey once again
makes use of the metaphor of education.

The purpose of education in the ordinary sense is not to
funnel information into the minds of students, but rather to
stimulate their minds to achieve their own insights into the
material. The most effective means to this end is for the
teacher to present problems which are not readily solvable.
This stimulates students to do their own thinking and eventually to understand the object of study through personal
discovery.[63]

Applying this to revelation, Drey says that God stimulates human reason by presenting it with ideas which are new
and therefore not immediately graspable in terms of past
experience and knowledge.

> There are the problems of revelation, which are
> presented to reason by God, to this end: that reason--
> struck and overwhelmed by the height from which these
> communications come--might feel itself driven to descend
> into its own depths, to illuminate these with the torch
> of revelation, and by thus moving within itself and
> detecting all the divine ideas which lie within itself,
> to find the meaning of the dark word (a meaning not
> measurable by the empirical intellect), so that the
> problem is solved and a new light is spread over the
> whole range of religious knowledge.[64]

Drey understands "mystery," therefore, as a problem set by
God for reason to solve. "That which reason does not, at the

---

[62] Apol I § 35, p. 299.

[63] Apol I § 35, pp. 296-97.

[64] Apol I § 35, p. 297: "Es sind die Probleme der Offenbarung, der Vernunft von Gott vorgelegt zu dem Zwecke, daß diese
betroffen und überwältigt durch die Höhe, aus welcher ihr diese
Mittheilungen kommen, sich getrieben fühle, in ihre eigene
Tiefen hinabzusteigen, diese mit der Fackel der Offenbarung zu
beleuchten, und indem sie so sich in sich selbst bewegt, und
alle in ihr liegende göttliche Ideen erspähet, die Bedeutung
des dunkeln Wortes zu finden, die der Verstand nicht ermißt,
wodurch das Problem gelöset, und ein neues Licht über den
ganzen Kreis der religiösen Erkenntnisse verbreitet wird."

very beginning, grasp--and which, in accord with the purpose of
revelation, it is not supposed to grasp at once--this is, for
reason, the mystery."[65]

Such mysteries are truly "above reason" by virtue of
their origin--from God, not from human reason's own resources.
Moreover, reason is incapable of deducing them as necessary
conclusions from its already developed ideas. These truths are
not, however, absolutely and forever beyond human reason, since
it is God's purpose in revelation to stimulate reason to an
eventual understanding of these ideas in their intrinsic
relationship to the ideas of reason.[66]

Faith as the Initial Attitude
of Reason Towards Revelation

The ultimate goal, therefore, is knowledge of the content
of revelation. But there is a gradual process which leads to
this knowledge. The beginning must be in faith, which is "the
natural attitude of reason to the mystery (and to revelation)."[67]

Following the analogy of education, Drey points out that
all learning begins with faith in the teacher.[68] Because of
this basic trust, the learner accepts what the teacher presents
for his attention, even though he has not yet achieved any
insight into the matter. Similarly, since reason must accept
the mystery on the authority of God, what is basic to reason's
functioning here is an attitude of faith towards God. "Faith
in the mystery, therefore, rests upon faith in God and coin-
cides with it, is equally fundamental."[69]

_____

[65]Ibid., p. 298: "Das, was die Vernunft nicht gleich
Anfangs begreift, und dem Zwecke der Offenbarung gemäß nicht
sogleich begreifen soll, das ist für sie das Geheimniß."

[66]Apol I § 35, p. 298. Cf. also ibid., p. 300: "Der
Geist . . . wenn er auch das Geheimniß noch nicht durchdringt,
hat doch eine Ahnung von der Verwandschaft seines Inhalts mit
ihm selbst, und von dem Zusammenhange seiner eigenen Ideen mit
der Idee oder den Ideen, welche das Geheimniß einschließt."

[67]Apol I § 35, p. 299: "Die natürliche Stellung aber der
Vernunft zu dem Geheimniß (und der Offenbarung) ist der Glauben."

[68]Ibid.

[69]Apol I § 35, p. 300: "Der Glauben an das Geheimniß ruht
also auf dem Glauben an Gott und fällt mit diesem zusammen, ist
gleich ursprünglich mit demselben." NB: Faith is here viewed

In this view, reason is presented with divinely given truths which it is not yet able to grasp. Unless reason denies the <u>fact</u> of revelation (against its own sense for truth),[70] it must submit in obedience to the Revealer of these mysteries. In order to characterize this attitude of reason in the face of revelation, Drey once again quotes Lessing with approval: "A certain taking-captive of reason under the obedience of faith follows from the essential concept of a revelation."[71]

This obedient submission in faith is not, however, an abdication of reason. Rather, it directs reason's activity towards that which is accepted as true on the authority of God.[72] There is something to be understood here. By holding fast to this not-yet-understood truth and being persistently and seriously attentive to it, reason gradually comes to understand and to <u>know</u>. "From the faithful exercise of reason in the service of faith, knowledge grows."[73]

The Relation of Faith and Knowledge

Hence, in order to characterize the relation of these two functions of reason,[74] Drey says:

primarily in an intellectual context. But the "submission" involved is to be related to Drey's general view of man's "Bestimmung." Man is to be united with God by freely acknowledging the "relation of origin" and thus finding his place in the great <u>Reich Gottes</u>. This involves love as well as faith, and is most profoundly a matter of "humility," by which man yields to the divine Reality and is reconciled with it. Cf. KE § 29, p. 17, and see below,

[70]<u>Apol</u> I § 35, p. 301.

[71]<u>Apol</u> I § 35, p. 303: "'. . . eine gewiße Gefangennehmung der Vernunft unter dem Gehorsam des Glaubens beruhet auf dem wesentlichen Begriffe einer Offenbarung.'" Cf. <u>Lessings Werke</u>, ed. H. G. Göpfert (Munich: C. Hanser, 1970-79), 7:462. As early as 1815, Drey had copied this quote into his journal (<u>Tagebücher</u> II, p. 114).

[72]<u>Apol</u> I § 35, p. 302.

[73]Ibid., p. 303: "Aus der treuen Übung der Vernunft im Dienste des Glaubens erwächst das Wissen."

[74]<u>Apol</u> I § 35, p. 307: ". . . Glaube und Wissen . . . bestehen nebeneinander als zwei wesentliche Funktionen der Vernunft . . ."

> Faith is the father of knowledge. There must first be
> something posited, which is to be understood . . . As the
> mind embraces it with love, holds fast to it with respect
> and cultivates it with fidelity, the mind can succeed in
> penetrating its object and producing a science of religion.[75]

This raises the further question of whether or not this
knowledge eventually replaces faith. In his early work, the
Kurze Einleitung, Drey envisaged scientific theology precisely
as such a movement from faith to knowledge. In § 45, he says,
". . . in the place of an immediate certainty through intuition,
there comes a certainty which is mediated by reflection; in the
place of simple faith, there comes a knowledge."[76] In the
following number, he makes this even more explicit:

> . . . the concept which is at first drawn from historical
> tradition and also from revelation is brought back to an
> idea as something which is immediately certain by virtue of
> rational intuition . . . This procedure . . . is called
> theological (positive) rationalism. . . . [it] attempts a
> knowledge of the very thing which was believed; it hopes
> to transform faith into knowledge.[77]

Drey later came to change his opinion about this, as
evidenced by his marginal notations next to the passages just
cited, in his personal copy of the KE. In § 45, next to the
words "an die Stelle" ("in the place of") he wrote unrichtig,
and added the comment: "properly--knowledge is added to faith;
religion is based now on faith and knowledge at the same time;

---

[75]Apol I § 35, p. 306: "Der Glauben ist der Vater des
Wissens. Es muß zuerst etwas gesetzt seyn, was begriffen
werden soll . . . wie [der Geist] nun dieses mit Liebe umfaßt,
mit Hochachtung festhält, mit Treue pflegt, kann es ihm
gelingen, seinen Gegenstand zu durchdringen, und eine
Religionswissenschaft zu erzeugen . . ."

[76]KE § 45, p. 27: ". . . daß an die Stelle einer
unmittelbaren Gewißheit in der Anschauung eine durch Reflexion
vermittelte, an die Stelle des schlichten Glaubens ein Wissen
tritt."

[77]KE § 46, p. 28: ". . . der Begriff aus historischer
Überlieferung, und auch Offenbarung, zunächst geschöpft wird
auf eine Idee, als ein durch Vernunftanschauung unmittelbar
gewißes zurückgebracht . . . Dieß Verfahren . . . heißt
theologischer (positiver) Rationalismus . . . [er] versucht ein
Wissen des Geglaubten selbst, hofft den Glauben in ein Wissen
zu verwandeln."

the former does not cease."[78] And next to the words cited
above from § 46, he noted ut supra (referring to his marginal
comment on § 45), and added at the end: "But neither excludes
the other."[79]

In the Apologetik, moreover, he mentions explicitly in a
footnote that he is repudiating the earlier published opinion
that knowledge replaces faith.[80] In order to justify his later
view of the matter, he distinguishes between the historical
"fact" of revelation and its intelligible content.[81] Faith is
the orientation of human reason to the historical reality of
God's initiative embodied in events of this world in a recognizable way (the fact).[82] Knowledge is human reason's appropriation of the "necessity and inner truth of the ideas"[83]
contained in this revelation.

Drey thinks that it is possible for some few people to
rise to this kind of insight into the intrinsic intelligibility
of what God has revealed. For these--who are capable of
"Religionswissenschaft"--a proper knowledge of the content of
revelation is possible, whereas most people must always remain
with the attitude of faith towards the fact of revelation.

Even for the few, however, knowledge does not replace or
abolish faith.[84] Faith must remain the fundamental attitude of

---

[78]Marginal notation on p. 27 of Drey's Handexemplar of
the KE, preserved in the library of the Wilhelmsstift in
Tübingen: "eigentlich--zu dem Glauben tritt das Wissen hinzu;
die Relig. ruht nun auf Glauben und Wissen zugleich; jenes hört
nicht auf."

[79]Ibid., p. 28: "Aber keiner schließt den andern aus."

[80]Apol I § 35, p. 307, note.

[81]Apol I § 35, p. 307.

[82]In Drey's view, the originating "fact" of the Christ
revelation continues to be present in the world in the Church
as "living tradition." Hence, faith orients itself to this
fact, since there must be "Anschauung" of a present reality, in
order to believe in the authority of God revealing. Cf. "Vom
Geist und Wesen des Katholizismus," GdChr, pp. 205-7. Cf. also
Tagebücher V, pp. 181ff., in GdChr, pp. 187-88.

[83]Apol I § 35, p. 307: ". . . der Nothwendigkeit und
innern Wahrheit ihrer Ideen . . ."

[84]Apol I § 35, pp. 306-7.

reason insofar as it is man's orientation to the abiding fact
of revelation, in which the reality of God is mediated historically. The knowledge of revelation's content that is possible
for some will always be finite, since the mind's capacity is
limited. Hence, even this knowledge in no way makes superfluous the attitude of faith towards God manifest in history.
Faith will become unnecessary, Drey observes, not by the
transition to knowledge but only by the passing over into
"vision" (Schauen), "when science (Wissenschaft) will also
cease to do its work."[85]

The Transition from Faith to Knowledge

Despite this qualification, the thrust of Drey's thought
is clearly towards the greatest possible systematic understanding of the content of revelation. In conclusion, therefore, we
present his brief treatment in the Apologetik of the movement
of reason from (mere) faith to true knowledge.[86] This will
open up a perspective on the major themes to be treated in the
two following chapters.

The effort to understand revelation is not a purely
theoretical pursuit, since God's truth always has to do with
our ways of living and acting. To understand the truths of
revelation, one must not only think about them but also allow
them to affect and determine one's attitudes and behavior.
This way of being ruled by divine truth gives some uneducated
but deeply religious people profound insights into the relationships of God and man.

When human reason works on the divine truths, therefore,
in both a theoretical and practical way in the community of
believers over a long period of time, the outcome is described
as follows:

> [reason] . . . manages to view the content of revelation
> in its full extent, and to grasp it in its coherence; one
> doctrine throws light upon another, the mystery gradually
> emerges from its darkness, it comes into a closer

---

[85] Apol I § 35, p. 307: ". . . alsdann wird auch die
Wissenschaft aufhören ihr Werk zu treiben."

[86] Apol I § 35, pp. 304-6.

relationship with what was already clear; the whole thing arranges itself into a system, in which the necessity of each individual part is recognized partly from itself, and partly from its relationship to the whole . . .[87]

Two words in this text--"system" and "necessity"--are characteristic of Drey's thought. His ideal of knowing is specified by the intuition of intelligible necessity in what might seem to be merely fortuitous. This requires the appreciation of each particular in the context of the great whole. He continues:

So, the truth which was at first merely believed becomes a truth which is understood; the content of revelation, which reason accepted on the testimony and authority of God, now appears to reason as a nexus of doctrines which bear in themselves their truth and necessity; the mystery passes over into the idea, and the truths of revelation pass over into truths of reason.[88]

There is another characteristic term here: "idea." Drey uses this word in the general context of German Idealist philosophy, especially as this was formulated by the early Schelling. One knows the truths of revelation to the extent that they are perceived as divine "ideas" which can be brought into a unified, systematic correlation with those ideas which human reason itself has elaborated. This is possible because God is the one Source of all ideas. Hence, a theology of revealed truths can be elaborated as a true form of knowing ("Wissenschaft").

---

[87]_Apol_ I § 35, p. 305: ". . . so gelangt sie dazu, den Inhalt der Offenbarung in seinem Umfange zu überschauen, und in seinem Zusammenhange zu erfassen, eine Lehre wirft Licht auf die andere, das Geheimniß tritt nach und nach aus seiner Dunkelheit, es tritt in eine nähere Verbindung mit dem gleich anfänglichen Klaren, das Ganze reihet sich zu einem Systeme, in welchem die Nothwendigkeit des Einzelnen theils aus ihm selbst, theils aus dem Zusammenhange mit dem Ganzen erkannt wird."

[88]Ibid.: ". . . so wird die anfänglich bloß geglaubte Wahrheit zu einer verstandenen, der Inhalt der Offenbarung, den die Vernunft auf das Zeugniß und die Auktorität Gottes annahm, erscheint ihr nun als ein Nexus von Lehren, welche ihre Wahrheit und Nothwendigkeit in sich selbst tragen, das Geheimniß geht über in die Idee, und die Offenbarungswahrheiten in Vernunftwahrheiten."

> Reason now not only grasps the ideas of revelation from
> within; it also recognizes in them its own ideas, and
> thereby recognizes their common source and their harmony.
> Thereby is initiated not only a knowing of what is
> believed, but also a science of the entire doctrine of
> revelation, a theologia revelata.[89]

Conclusion

The word Wissenschaft points us into the subject matter
of the next two chapters.

So far, we have been occupied with Drey's defense of
revelation against the challenges of naturalism and rationalism.
This theory of revelation is foundational for Drey's view of
the method and system of theology. "The idea of revelation
runs through the entire system of theology, just as the fact of
revelation runs through the entire history of the development
of religion."[90]

The preceding section has begun to indicate the kind of
intelligibility which Drey expects to find in the divinely
given revelation. The peculiar character of this intelligibility is only to be appreciated by examining the ideal of
"scientific" knowledge which Drey took from his contemporary
philosophical culture, in particular from Schelling.

The first task, therefore, is to present those features
of Schelling's early thought which were important for Drey's
notion of Wissenschaft. This will be the subject matter of
Chapter IV.

Then we will be in a position to look closely at Drey's
proposal for the method of theology, giving special attention
to his ideal of "wissenschaftliche Theologie." It will also
be possible, against the background of Chapter IV, to assess
both the affinities and the tensions between Drey's thought and
Schelling's. All this will be treated in Chapter V.

---

[89]Ibid., p. 306: "Die Vernunft erfaßt nun nicht nur die
Ideen der Offenbarung von Innen heraus, sie erkennt auch in
ihnen ihre eigenen, und damit ihren gemeinschaftlichen Ursprung
und ihre Harmonie, womit nicht nur ein Wissen des Geglaubten,
sondern auch eine Wissenschaft der gesammten Offenbarungslehre,
eine theologia revelata eingeleitet ist."

[90]Apol I § 34, p. 289: "So zieht sich die Idee der Offenbarung durch das ganze System der Theologie, wie die Thatsache
der Offenbarung durch die ganze Geschichte der Entwickelung
der Religion . . ."

CHAPTER IV

"WISSENSCHAFT" AND THEOLOGY

IN THE EARLY SCHELLING

The text of Schelling which manifestly influenced Drey's theological method was the Lectures on the Method of Academic Study published in 1803.[1] Drey refers to this work approvingly, as containing (in the 8th and 9th lectures) "individual observations well worth pondering on a more scientific conception of Christianity and a more scientific treatment of theology."[2]

This chapter is directed, therefore, primarily to Schelling's Lectures, with the purpose of highlighting those ideas which were important for Drey. There is, of course, no question of presenting the entire system of Schelling's early thought. Nevertheless, it will be necessary to give some

---

[1] "Vorlesungen über die Methode des akademischen Studiums," Schellings Werke, ed. Manfred Schröter, 3:229-374. There is an English translation of this: F.W.J. Schelling on University Studies, translated by E. S. Morgan, edited with an Introduction by Norbert Guterman (Athens: Ohio University Press, 1966). But all quotations from this text (as from other texts of Schelling) will be given in my own translation. All references to Schelling are to the Schröter edition: Schellings Werke nach der Originalausgabe in neuer Anordnung, herausgegeben von Manfred Schröter (Munich: C. H. Beck & R. Oldenbourg, 1927; newly issued in 1958). References are to volume and page (e.g., 3:535) of the principal volumes (Hauptbände) or to the first of the supplementary volumes (Ergänzungsbände). In the latter case, the reference is given as Suppl. 1, followed by the page (e.g., Suppl. 1:418-19).

[2] KE § 84, p. 57: "Einzelne sehr zu beherzigende Bemerkungen über eine wissenschaftlichere Auffassung des Christentums und eine wissenschaftlichere Behandlung der Theologie finden sich in Schellings Vorlesungen über die Methode des akademischen Studiums. Tübingen, 1803. in der VIII. u. IX. Vorl."

indications of this system, since the text under examination
takes for granted the perspectives of the Naturphilosophie and
Identitätsphilosophie. Hence, other relevant texts of
Schelling will be cited in order to clarify or amplify ideas
found in the Lectures.

"Urwissen" as the Basis of "Wissenschaft"

We may begin by recalling that Schelling is concerned in
his early writings with the problem of knowledge, and in
particular with the kind of absolutely certain knowing which is
characteristic of "Wissenschaft." It is this kind of knowing
which is the object of higher academic studies.

Schelling is convinced that the problem of knowledge cannot be solved unless the dualism of subject and object is overcome. He is, in fact, concerned to overcome all dualisms:
subject-object, Geist-Natur, God-world, finite-infinite. He
wrote in 1802:

> Only that which overcomes all duality [Entzweiung] is
> abiding since only this is truly one and unchangeably the
> same. Only from this can a true Universe of knowing
> develop, a configuration which takes in everything. Only
> that which proceeds from the absolute unity of the infinite
> and the finite, is immediately in itself capable of sym-
> bolic representation.[3]

His requirement of a valid starting-point and principle
of knowing leads him to postulate the absolute identity of
subject and object as the ultimate reality.[4] It is this identity which is the ultimate truth of things, not the diversity
and opposition which we experience.

The primacy is given to rationality and knowledge, in the
sense that this ultimate reality--the "Absolute"--is conceived
as infinite knowing (absoluter Erkenntnisakt).[5] But this

---

[3] 3:535 ("Über das Verhältnis der Naturphilosophie zur
Philosophie überhaupt," 1802): "Was bleibt, ist nur, was alle
Entzweiung aufhebt, denn nur dieses ist wahrhaft Eine und
unwandelbar dasselbe. Einzig aus diesem kann sich ein wahres
Universum des Wissens, eine alles befassende Gestaltung
entwickeln. Nur was aus der absoluten Einheit des Unendlichen
und Endlichen hervorgeht, ist unmittelbar durch sich selbst der
symbolischen Darstellung fähig.

[4] Cf. 3:354; 1:708.   [5] 1:711.

knowing, unlike our ordinary knowing, is not that of a subject over against an object. Rather, the Absolute knows itself.[6] There is a perfect identity of thinking and being, of the "ideal" and the "real."[7]

The world of finite beings is the differentiation of this undifferentiated identity. It is the self-objectification (Subjekt-Objektivirung) and self-perception of the Absolute.[8] This takes the form of two different "series" of finite beings: the "real" (nature) and the "ideal" (spirit, mind, human reason, the realm of history).[9]

There is a pattern of intelligibility in both series, because both are the manifestation of the Absolute which is pure knowing (of itself), which is the "absolut-Ideal." Schelling refers to this ultimate identity of thought and being, therefore, not only as the Absolute but also as the "Urwissen."

He begins his Lectures on the Method of Academic Study with this concept of "primal knowing," because it is the only way of grounding the diverse forms of finite, human knowing. That is, the primal knowing is absolutely certain because there is identity of Knower and Known, of thought and being. Human knowing can have the character of absolutely certain knowledge only to the extent that it is a finite, partial specification of the primal knowing.

> . . . the one thing upon which our entire investigation depends . . . is the idea of a knowing which is in itself unconditioned, which is simply one and in which all knowing is one, the idea of that primal knowing (Urwissen) which divides itself into branches on various levels of the ideal world of appearances, and so spreads out into the one immeasurable tree of knowledge.[10]

---

[6] 3:303: "Die reine Absolutheit für sich ist nothwendig auch reine Identität, aber die absolute Form dieser Identität ist: sich selbst auf ewige Weise Subjekt und Objekt zu sein . . ."

[7] Suppl. 1:418-19 ("Fernere Darstellungen aus dem System der Philosophie," 1802). Cf. also 3:238.

[8] 3:346. Cf. 3:349.   [9] Suppl. 1:462-63. Cf. 3:311, 1:717.

[10] 3:237: ". . . dem Einen . . . wovon unsere ganze folgende Untersuchung abhängig seyn wird, . . . Es ist die Idee des an sich selbst unbedingten Wissens, welches schlechthin nur Eines ist und in dem auch alles Wissen nur Eines ist, desjenigen Urwissens, welches, nur auf verschiedenen Stufen der erscheinenden idealen Welt sich in Zweige zerspaltend, in den ganzen unermeßlichen Baum der Erkenntniß sich ausbreitet."

Any knowing, therefore, has an absolute character only in
relation to the primal knowing. The totality of our knowing is
a kind of copy or reflection of the primal knowing, and particular knowing has its validity only as an organic part of the
whole.

> Through this first knowing, all other knowing is in the
> Absolute and is itself absolute. For, although the primal
> knowing in its perfect absoluteness dwells originally only
> in the Absolute as the absolutely-Ideal, nevertheless it is
> present in us as the essence of all things and as the
> eternal concept of ourselves, and our knowing in its total-
> ity has the character of an image of that eternal knowing.
> . . . To be sure, only knowing in its totality can be the
> perfect reflection of that exemplary knowing, but all indi-
> vidual knowing and every particular Wissenschaft is
> included in this whole as an organic part; hence, all know-
> ing which is not related directly or indirectly to the
> primal knowing (even if it be through many intermediate
> stages) is without reality or significance.[11]

In this way, Schelling's notion of "Wissenschaft" rests
upon the presupposition of a primal "Wissen" which is the pure
identity of subject and object. The human mind can only
attain to absolutely certain knowledge by participating in that
absolute knowing.[12] This is possible because human reason is
the finite differentiation and manifestation of the Absolute in
the ideal order (the order of mind), just as nature is the
manifestation of the Absolute in the real order.

> Knowing, in its totality, is one absolute appearance of
> the one Universe; being or nature is the other. . . . Man,
> and rational being in general, is placed as a supplement to
> the phenomenon of the world: from him, from his activity,

----

[11]3:238-39: "Durch dieses erste Wissen ist alles andere
Wissen im Absoluten und selbst absolut. Denn obwohl das
Urwissen in der vollkommenen Absolutheit ursprünglich nur in
jenem, als dem absolut-Idealen, wohnt, ist es doch uns selbst
als das Wesen aller Dinge und der ewige Begriff von uns selbst
eingebildet, und unser Wissen in seiner Totalität ist bestimmt,
ein Abbild jenes ewigen Wissens zu seyn. . . . Allerdings kann
nur das Wissen in seiner Allheit der vollkommene Reflex jenes
vorbildlichen Wissens seyn, aber alles einzelne Wissen und jede
besondere Wissenschaft ist in diesem Ganzen als organischer
Theil begriffen; und alles Wissen daher, das nicht mittelbar
oder unmittelbar, und sey es durch so viele Mitglieder hindurch,
sich auf das Urwissen bezieht, ist ohne Realität und
Bedeutung."

[12]3:240.

is to develop that which is lacking to the totality of the
revelation of God, since nature receives the entire divine
essence only in the order of the "real"; rational being is
to express the image of the same divine nature as it is in
itself, that is, in the order of the "ideal."[13]

This way of grounding the absolute character of human
knowing depends, of course, on Schelling's postulate of the
ultimate identity of thought and being, of the "ideal" and the
"real."[14] He recognizes this dependence, and insists that this
postulate or presupposition--though it cannot strictly be
proved even by philosophy--is essential to the practice of true
"Wissenschaft."[15]

"Intellektuelle Anschauung" as the Entry to "Wissenschaft"

It therefore becomes crucial to understand how the practitioner of Wissenschaft comes to the discovery of this ultimate unity of the ideal and the real. For without it he lacks
"the entry to all Wissenschaftlichkeit."[16]

The discovery of this unity takes place in what Schelling
calls "intellektuelle Anschauung." Perhaps the best way of
approaching what this term means is to recall Schelling's
characteristic concern to overcome all dualism. The dominant
insight in his thought is the ultimate unity of what we ordinarily experience as divided: subject-object, thought-being,
ideal-real, Infinite-finite, God-world.

---

[13]3:240: "Das Wissen, in seiner Allheit, ist aber die
eine, gleich absolute Erscheinung des Einen Universum, von dem
das Seyn oder die Natur die andere ist. . . . Der Mensch, das
Vernunftwesen überhaupt, ist hingestellt, eine Ergänzung der
Welterscheinung zu seyn: aus ihm, aus seiner Thätigkeit soll
sich entwickeln, was zur Totalität der Offenbarung Gottes fehlt,
da die Natur zwar das ganze göttliche Wesen, aber nur im Realen,
empfängt; das Vernunftwesen soll das Bild derselben göttlichen
Natur, wie sie an sich selbst ist, demnach im Idealen
ausdrücken." Cf. also 3:303-4.

[14]3:237: ". . . die höhere Voraussetzung . . . , daß das
wahre Ideale allein und ohne weitere Vermittlung auch das wahre
Reale und außer jenem kein anderes sey." Cf. also 1:708ff.

[15]3:237.

[16]3:237: ". . . da sie der Eingang zu aller Wissenschaftlichkeit ist . . ."

The privileged place where this unity can be discovered
is the finite self's awareness of itself as "I."[17] This is
thought, but at the same time being--since the "I" only exists
insofar as it thinks.[18] This is "intellectual intuition," and
is really a free, active event by which the self "produces"
itself as a conscious "I".[19]

What seems essential in this key experience is the elimin-
ation of all subject-object duality.[20] The self is emptied, so
to speak, of sensible objects of its attention. What it is
aware of is precisely itself, not as the subject which knows
objects, but simply as the self which is.[21]

This intellectual intuition of the self as identity of
thought and being is the opening to the intuition of the
Absolute. It provides the indispensable insight into the ultimate identity of thought and being which characterizes reality
as such. It is, however, essential to rise from the self-
knowing of the finite "I" to the sense of the Absolute as pure
Identity of subject and object. Schelling criticized Fichte
for failing to do this, and recommended as the corrective to
Fichte's subjectivism:

> . . . it is necessary to rise to the absolute Subject-
> Object, to the absolute knowing-act itself, and by abstract-
> ing completely from the subjectivity of the intellectual
> intuition, to recognize the Absolute in and for itself.[22]

What is, in this way, recognized is the ultimate unity of
thought and being, which Schelling calls the Absolute. This
perspective governs his use of the word "God," and specifies
the sense in which his system may be considered "religious."

---

[17]1:290 ("Abhandlungen zur Erläuterung des Idealismus der
Wissenschaftslehre," 1796-97): ". . . in mir ist die absolute
Einheit des Subjekts und des Objekts, des Erkennens und des
Seyns."

[18]2:366ff. This and the immediately following references
are to "System des transcendentalen Idealismus" (1800).

[19]2:369.   [20]2:366.   [21]2:367.

[22]Suppl. 1:412 ("Fernere Darstellungen aus dem System der
Philosophie," 1802): ". . . so ist nothwendig, sich zum absoluten Subjekt-Objekt, zum absoluten Erkenntniβakt selbst zu
erheben, indem von der Subjektivität der intellektuellen
Anschauung gänzlich abstrahirt wird, das Absolute an und für
sich zu erkennen." Cf. ibid., 407 and 423.

Since it is the Absolute which is ultimately real, finite
beings must be understood as the manifestation of this pure
Identity, by differentiation into the two series of "the real"
(nature) and "the ideal" (mind). Only this perspective makes
absolute knowing possible, as a sharing in the primal knowing
which the Absolute is.

It is noteworthy that Schelling links the principle or
starting-point of philosophy (as absolute Wissen) with religion.[23] This does not mean that intellectual intuition of the
Absolute is a kind of mystical knowledge of God as a transcendent reality. Rather, the crucial intuition which is the entry
into "Wissenschaftlichkeit" is the perception of all finite
reality as the manifestation of the Infinite, as the differentiation of the ultimate, absolute identity of subject and object.

Schelling's way of grounding absolute knowing is thus, in
a certain sense, religious. That is, he has a kind of monistic
sense of the world as the very reality of God unfolded, so to
speak. Fuhrmans characterizes this sensibility very effectively:

> Here is the center of the Schellingian experience of
> the world between 1801 and 1806. All being is mirror of
> the Absolute--this is the formula which determines every-
> thing. In the more precise formulation of this basic fact,
> however, Schelling actually relinquished all transcendence
> of the Absolute. God is not the "above" over the world
> which is his reflection; rather, he is ultimately the
> center of the world, he is the womb out of which everything
> is continually born, he is the Being which mirrors itself
> in ever new images, he is the eternal Knowing which regards
> itself in ever new objects. This is the proper perspective,
> around which everything circles.[24]

---

[23]3:536 ("Über das Verhältniß der Naturphilosophie zur
Philosophie überhaupt," 1802): ". . . weil wir eine Philosophie,
die nicht in ihrem Prinzip schon Religion ist, auch nicht für
Philosophie anerkennen, verwerfen wir eine Erkenntniß des
Absoluten, die aus der Philosophie nur als Resultat hervorgeht,
die Gott nicht an sich, sondern in einer empirischen Beziehung
denkt . . ."

[24]Horst Fuhrmans, Schellings Philosophie der Weltalter
(Düsseldorf: L. Schwann, 1954), p. 35: "Hier ist die Mitte des
Schellingschens Welterlebens zwischen 1801 und 1806. Alles
Sein ist Spiegel des Absoluten--das ist die Formel, die alles
bestimmt. In der näheren Fassung dieses Grundfaktums hat
Schelling aber faktisch jede Transzendenz des Absoluten aufge-
geben. Gott ist nicht das Oben über der Welt, die sein
Abglanz ist, sondern er ist letzthin die Mitte der Welt, ist
der Schoß, aus dem alles immer wieder geboren wird, ist das
Sein, das sich in immer neuen Bildern spiegelt, ist das ewige

Schelling's <u>Naturphilosophie</u> is inspired by this sense of the world as the very presence and reality of God.

> The goal of the highest <u>Wissenschaft</u> can only be this: to present the reality--in the strictest sense, the reality --the presence, the living being of a God in the totality of things and in the particulars . . . . . Nature is not merely the product of an inconceivable creation, but is rather this creation itself; not merely the appearance or revelation of the eternal, but rather it is simultaneously this very eternal itself.[25]

This view of nature overcomes all dualism of world and God, of finite and Infinite. Correspondingly, Schelling understands our finite rationality as the very rationality of the Absolute manifesting itself.[26] The unity of subject and object demanded in absolutely certain knowing is insured to the extent that the finite "I"--through intellectual intuition--shares in the absolute knowing (the <u>Urwissen</u>).

It seems that this term "intellektuelle Anschauung" has at least two distinguishable but related senses. Basic and primary is the sense already explained: the intuition of the ultimate identity of Subject and Object (i.e., of the Absolute), as this is revealed in the paradigm case of the finite self's awareness of itself as simultaneously subject and object. But there is a second sense of the term: the intuition by which one is able to grasp the universal in the particular. It is only by this kind of intuition that "absolute" knowing is possible.

> Intellectual intuition--not merely transitory but abiding as an unchangeable organ--is the condition of the scientific spirit in general and in all branches of knowing. For it is the capacity to see the universal in the

---

Erkennen, das sich in immer neuen Objekten anschaut. Das ist die eigentliche Sicht, um die alles kreist" (my translation).

[25] 1:444; 446 ("Über das Verhältniß des Realen und Idealen in der Natur," 1806): "Der Zweck der erhabensten Wissenschaft kann nur dieser seyn: die Wirklichkeit, im strengsten Sinne die Wirklichkeit, die Gegenwart, das lebendige Da-seyn eines Gottes im Ganzen der Dinge und im Einzelnen darzuthun . . . . . . Die Natur ist nicht bloß Produkt einer unbegreiflichen Schöpfung, sondern diese Schöpfung selbst; nicht nur die Erscheinung oder Offenbarung des Ewigen, vielmehr zugleich eben dieses Ewige selbst."

[26] Cf. Suppl. 1:442.

particular, the infinite in the finite, to see both
united in a living unity.[27]

This ideal of absolute knowing is, in several places,
compared to the kind of knowing characteristic of geometry and
mathematics.[28] Distinguishing between thought on the one hand
(the "ideal" or infinite, which finds expression in the concept)
and limited, particular being on the other hand (the "real" or
finite, expressed as an object), he says:

> Geometry . . . and mathematics in general are complete-
> ly beyond this opposition. Here thought is always adequate
> to being, the concept is always adequate to the object, and
> vice versa; and the question cannot even arise, whether
> that which is correct and certain in thought is also cor-
> rect and certain in being or in the object, or how that
> which is expressed in being becomes a necessity of thought
> . . .[29]

What the geometrician understands to be necessarily true
in thought corresponds perfectly to the finite, particular
object in which that intelligibility is exemplified. The
discovery of this perfect correspondence--or rather unity--of
thought and being, of concept and object, is the key to absolute knowing. Schelling considers this to be possible not only
in geometry but also in philosophy.

In order to know finite objects in this absolute way
(recognizing in them the infinite, ideal content of thought),
one must have risen to the intuition of the ultimate identity

---

[27]Suppl. 1:414 ("Fernere Darstellungen aus dem System der
Philosophie," 1802): "Die intellektuelle Anschauung nicht nur
vorübergehend, sondern bleibend, als unveränderliches Organ,
ist die Bedingung des wissenschaftlichen Geistes überhaupt und
in allen Theilen des Wissens. Denn sie ist das Vermögen überhaupt, das Allgemeine im Besonderen, das Unendliche im
Endlichen, beide zur lebendigen Einheit vereinigt zu sehen."

[28]3:274-78; 3:550-60. Suppl. 1:397ff. and 414ff.

[29]Suppl. 1:415: "Die Geometrie . . . und die Mathematik
überhaupt sind gänzlich von diesem Gegensatz hinweg. Hier ist
das Denken dem Seyn, der Begriff dem Objekt jederzeit adäquat,
und umgekehrt, und nie kann auch nur die Frage entstehen, ob
das, was im Denken richtig und gewiß sey, es auch im Seyn oder
im Objekt sey, oder wie das, was im Seyn ausgedrückt ist, zu
einer Nothwendigkeit des Denkens werde . . ." Cf. ibid.,
pp. 397-98.

of thought and being, viz., the Absolute. This takes place in
"intellektuelle Anschauung" in sense (1). A finite human mind
which has risen to this intuition of the Absolute is able to
recognize its own thought as a sharing in the "primal knowing"
or absolute act of knowing which the Absolute is. Hence, it is
able to recognize the absolute character of its ideas, their
"eternal necessity."

Moreover, since the identity of thought and being has
been recognized, there can be no problem of bridging an imagined
gap between the mind's ideas and the particular, finite objects
of its knowledge. Reality is ideal, thought is being. But it
is the thought of the Absolute which is real.[30] The thought of
the finite mind is identical with the real only insofar as it
is a share in and manifestation of the Absolute, the Urwissen.
It is because of this relationship of finite mind to the
Absolute that Schelling can speak in the following way about
the "I", about "Vernunft" and knowing:

> The "I think," "I am" is, since Descartes, the fundamental
> error in all knowing. Thought is not my thought, and being
> is not my being, for everything is only God's or the All's.
>   The one kind of knowing in which not the Subject but
> the unqualified Universal (the One) knows, and in which
> therefore also only the unqualified Universal is the known,
> is reason (Vernunft).
>   Reason is not a capacity, not an instrument, and does
> not allow itself to be used; there is no Reason at all
> which we might have, but only a Reason which has us.[31]

This is an extreme expression of Schelling's "monistic"
sensibility, comparable to the text cited earlier about "nature"

----

[30]Suppl. 1:422. Cf. 1:715.

[31]4:82-83 ("Aphorismen zur Einleitung in die Naturphilosophie," 1806): "Das Ich denke, Ich bin, ist, seit Cartesius,
der Grundirrthum in aller Erkenntniß; das Denken ist nicht mein
Denken, und das Seyn nicht mein Seyn, denn alles ist nur Gottes
oder des Alls.
    "Die Eine Art des Erkennens, in welcher nicht das Subjekt,
sondern das schlechthin Allgemeine (also das Eine) weiß, und in
welchem eben daher auch nur das schlechthin Allgemeine das
Gewußte ist, ist die Vernunft.
    "Die Vernunft ist kein Vermögen, kein Werkzeug, und läßt
sich nicht brauchen: überhaupt gibt es nicht eine Vernunft,
die wir hätten, sondern nur eine Vernunft, die uns hat." Cf.
also 3:246 and 3:560.

as the very reality of God.[32] But here the unique oneness of
God (or the "All") is affirmed with regard to mind or reason.
What Schelling means by "Vernunft" is here seen to be the
Urwissen, the absolute knowing which is identical with the
being of the Absolute.

Hence, what he envisages as absolute knowing for a human
mind (required for Wissenschaft) is really the Absolute insofar
as its knowing is present and manifested in this finite mind.[33]

This helps to see the link between the two senses of
"intellektuelle Anschauung" which were distinguished above.
Sense (2) is the discovery of the universal in the particular,
the perception of the perfect unity of thought and being. The
particular, finite object is seen as a realization of the
infinite, eternally valid idea.[34] Thought or knowing (the
ideal) is primary. The particular finite being is an objectification of the primal, absolute knowing (Erkennen).

When this kind of knowing occurs, Schelling says that it
is "Vernunft" which knows. As Kasper paraphrases the texts
just cited: "It is not 'I' who know, but the All knows in me.
. . . It is not the empirical subject, but the unqualified
Universal which knows."[35]

Hence, the indispensable way to rise to this kind of
knowing is to rise to the intuition of the Absolute as the
perfect identity of thought and being--"intellektuelle
Anschauung" in sense (1). Only in this way can one recognize

---

[32]Schelling states his view in paradoxical but unmistakable language, just prior to the text quoted above: "Es gibt
wahrhaft und an sich überall kein Subjekt und kein Ich, eben
deshalb auch kein Objekt und kein Nichtich, sondern nur Eines,
Gott oder das All, und außerdem nichts. Ist also überall ein
Wissen und ein Gewußtwerden, so ist das, was in jenem und was
in diesem ist, doch nur das Eine als Eines, nämlich Gott"
(4:82). Cf. also 1:444-45.

[33]He considers human reason to be "das unmittelbarste
Abbild der ewigen Einheit" (Suppl. 1:442).

[34]Much more will be said about this below, under the
topic "Construktion."

[35]Walter Kasper, Das Absolute in der Geschichte (Mainz:
Matthias Grünewald, 1965), p. 53: "Nicht ich weiß, sondern das
All weiß in mir . . . . . . nicht das empirische Subjekt
weiß, sondern das schlechthin Allgemeine weiß."

one's own thought as the Absolute's eternally valid ideas which
alone are ultimately real.

> The demand upon which every Wissenschaft bases its
> reality, is this: that what is known by it absolutely--the
> Idea--be also itself the Real. In the "construction" of
> geometry this is attained immediately, since it is granted
> to geometry to express its archetypes in external intuition.
> In the "construction" of philosophy, it is absolute unquali-
> fied intellectual intuition in which absolute knowing (das
> absolute Erkennen) is recognized as at the same time the
> Real kat' exochen, as the Absolute itself, and therefore
> also the Modi of this knowing are recognized as the unique-
> ly true and real things.[36]

The "Ideas" as the Form
of Absolute Knowing

This last phrase, "the Modi of this (absolute) knowing,"
refers to the "Ideas,"[37] a notion which is prominent in
Schelling's Lectures on Academic Study. This needs some close
attention.

We have already seen that the controlling perspective for
Schelling's ideal of Wissenschaft is the intuition of the
Absolute as the pure identity of Subject and Object. On the
one hand, there is in this identity no object of knowing which
is distinct from the knower. On the other hand, there seems to
be a primacy attributed to "ideality" or knowing, so that the
Absolute is called "Urwissen" or the absolute act of knowing,
or the "absolut-Ideal."[38]

It therefore becomes important for Schelling to account
for the actual knowing of itself which he considers characteristic of the Absolute. If there were only pure, wholly

---

[36]Suppl. 1:422 ("Fernere Darstellungen aus dem System der
Philosophie," 1802): "Die Forderung, auf die jede Wissenschaft
ihre Realität gründet, ist: daß, was von ihr absolut erkannt
ist, die Idee, auch das Reale selbst sey; in der geometrischen
Construktion ergibt sich dieß unmittelbar, da es ihr vergönnt
ist, in der äußeren Anschauung gleichwohl die Urbilder auszu-
drücken; in der philosophischen ist es die ohne alle Beziehung
schlechthin absolute intellektuelle Anschauung, in welcher das
absolute Erkennen zugleich als das Reale kat' exochen, das
Absolute selbst, und also auch die Modi dieses Erkennens als
die einzig wahren und realen Dinge erkannt werden." Cf. ibid.,
p. 399.

[37]Cf. 3:341: "Die Ideen . . . [sind] an sich Formen des
absoluten Erkennens . . ."

[38]Cf. 1:711-12.

undifferentiated identity, one could hardly call the Absolute
"knowing."

It is a matter, therefore, of the "Selbstanschauung des
Absoluten,"[39] or of "Subjekt-Objektivirung."[40] There is a
differentiation of the undifferentiated identity. Schelling
utilizes the doctrine of the Ideas as a kind of bridge between
the absolutely Universal (undifferentiated Absolute) and the
particulars of its differentiation.

Windelband notes that Schelling's Identitätsphilosophie
was thus modified by the influence of Plato:

> . . . This factor [i.e., the Platonic influence] consisted
> in the concept of intellectual intuition as the Absolute's
> intuition of itself. If this self-intuition was to extend
> also to the fully "developed" Absolute, which had gone
> through its differentiations to the totality of the uni-
> verse, then the Absolute in this latter sense had also to
> perceive all these its differentiations in itself. These
> differentiations are, therefore, present in a double way:
> first, as objective phenomena, i.e. as real developmental
> forms of the Absolute; and second, as the forms of the
> Absolute's self-intuition. It is in this second sense that
> Schelling calls them Ideas, and the more he follows this
> thought, the more he is accustomed to call the Absolute,
> which perceives itself in them, God. The Godhead perceives
> itself in those Ideas, and realizes these Ideas in the
> objective phenomena of nature and history.[41]

Schelling makes this perspective explicit in the 11th of
the Lectures ("Über die Naturwissenschaft im Allgemeinen"),
where he wishes to lead his hearers to an appreciation of the

---

[39]3:349.   [40]1:712.

[41]W. Windelband, Die Geschichte der neueren Philosophie.
II. Band (Leipzig: von Breitkopf u. Härtel, 1880), p. 276: ". . .
Dies Moment bestand in dem Begriffe der intellektuellen
Anschauung als einer Selbstanschauung des Absoluten. Soll sich
dieselbe auch auf das voll entwickelte und durch die Differ-
enzirungen zur Totalität des Universums hindurch gegangene
Absolute erstrecken, so muß das letztere auch alle seine
Differenzirungen in sich anschauen. Diese Differenzirungen
also sind darnach doppelt vorhanden, einmal als objektive
Erscheinungen, d.h. als reale Entwicklungsformen des Absoluten
und zweitens als die Formen der Selbstanschauung des Absoluten.
In diesem zweiten Sinne nun nennt sie Schelling Ideen, und je
mehr er diesen Gedanken verfolgt, um so mehr gewöhnt er sich,
das in ihnen sich selbst anschauende Absolute Gott zu nennen.
Die Gottheit schaut sich selbst in jenen Ideen an und realisirt
diese Ideen in den objektiven Erscheinungen der Natur und der
Geschichte." (My translation.)

higher intelligibility of nature.

> . . . the origin and significance of [the Ideas] . . . lies
> in the eternal law of Absoluteness: to be Object for itself.
> By force of this law, God's "producing" is an imaging of
> the entire Universality and Essence into particular forms,
> by which these, as particular, are nevertheless at the same
> time universals, and are that which the philosophers have
> called Monads or Ideas.[42]

In this way Schelling seeks both to maintain the primal
identity of Knower and Known, and at the same time to account
for the diversity and differentiation in the Knower's self-
knowing. This differentiation in knowing is the first "objectification" of the absolute Subject,[43] whereas the appearance
of these Ideas in the order of finite being may be considered
a further objectification.[44] Since the Ideas, though of particulars, are nevertheless merely modifications of the single,
unique act of knowing ("Modi des absoluten Erkennens"), the
unity of God is not denied by the doctrine of Ideas.

> It is shown at greater length in philosophy that the
> Ideas are the only mediators by which particular things
> can be in God, and that there are, according to this law,
> as many Universals as there are particular things; and yet,
> because of the equality of the [divine] essence, there is
> in all of them only one Universal.[45]

---

[42] 3:339: ". . . müssen wir auf den Ursprung und die
Bedeutung von diesen [den Ideen] selbst zurückgehen. Jener
liegt in dem ewigen Gesetze der Absolutheit, sich selbst Objekt
zu seyn; denn kraft desselben ist das Produciren Gottes eine
Einbildung der ganzen Allgemeinheit und Wesenheit in besondere
Formen, wodurch diese, als besondere, doch zugleich Universa
und das sind, was die Philosophen Monaden oder Ideen genannt
haben." Cf. 1:712-13.

[43] Cf. 3:339-40: ". . . die Ideen in Gott . . . sind . . .
die ersten Organismen der göttlichen Selbstanschauung . . ."
And 3:340: ". . . das Absolute in dem ewigen Erkenntnißakt
[wird] sich selbst in den Ideen objektiv . . ."

[44] Cf. 3:346: ". . . die absolute Idealität . . . wäre
ewig unverkennbar, verhüllt in sich selbst, wenn sie nicht sich
als Subjektivität in die Objektivität verwandelte, von welcher
Verwandlung die erscheinende und endliche Natur das Symbol ist."

[45] 3:339: "Es wird in der Philosophie ausführlicher
gezeigt, daß die Ideen die einzigen Mittler sind, wodurch die
besonderen Dinge in Gott seyn können, und daß nach diesem
Gesetz so viel Universa als besondere Dinge sind, und doch,
wegen der Gleichheit des Wesens, in allen nur Ein Universum."
Cf. 1:714-15.

This text indicates the paradox involved in Schelling's
notion of the Absolute. If reality is ultimately the sheer
identity of Knowing and Being, how can there be any particularity or differentiation at all? This is, of course, not felt as
a merely theoretical question about the divine essence. The
difficulty is perceived, rather, in terms of Schelling's ideal
of "absolutes Wissen." His ruling perspective is, indeed, the
sense of the Absolute, discovered in intellectual intuition.
It is this which he sometimes refers to as "the All," "the One,"
"the Universal." On the other hand, it is the particular
objects of experience which he wishes to know from this absolute perspective. How can a particular be known "absolutely"?
This is really the problem which he is addressing with his
notion of the Ideas.

> . . . the Ideas . . . [are] the sole possibility of grasp-
> ing the absolute profusion [Fülle] in the absolute unity,
> of grasping the particular in the Absolute, but precisely
> thereby, of grasping also the Absolute in the particular
> . . .46

In order to appreciate the role of the Ideas in absolute
knowing, it is essential to understand how the Ideas are present in the Absolute. Schelling seems to view the matter somewhat in the following way: Each Idea is _of_ some particular
reality, e.g., "plant" or "animal." But this particularity is
only potential, insofar as the Idea is not actually separate
from the simple Absolute, but is only a "Modus" or "form" of
that primal Knowing. Moreover, _each_ Idea is a possible
"imaging" (Einbildung) of the _entire_ Absolute, so that each
Idea is the possibility of the whole _as_, e.g., "plant" or
"animal." Here are two texts which express this more fully:

> . . . in the Absolute there is no Form [i.e., the Ideal]
> separated from its Being [Wesen, i.e., the Real], and
> everything is in each other, as one Being, one mass, and
> from this One come forth all Ideas as divine growths,

46Suppl. 1:457 ("Fernere Darstellungen aus dem System der
Philosophie," 1802): ". . . die Ideen . . . [sind] die einzige
Möglichkeit, in der absoluten Einheit die absolute Fülle, das
Besondere im Absoluten, aber eben damit auch das Absolute im
Besonderen zu begreifen . . ."

since each Idea is formed ["imaged": <u>gebildet</u>] from the
entire Being of the Absolute.[47]

. . . the various unities [the Ideas] have, as various, no
reality in themselves; rather, they are only ideal forms
and images in which--in the absolute Knowing--the Whole is
expressed; insofar as they are in the absolute Knowing,
they are themselves the entire world and have nothing outside themselves with which they could be compared or to
which they could be opposed. The entire Universe is in the
Absolute as plant, as animal, as human being; but, since
the Whole is in each one, it is there not as plant, as
animal, as human being, or as a <u>particular</u> unity, but rather
as <u>absolute</u> unity. It is only in appearance--where it
ceases to be the <u>Whole</u>, where the Form wills to be something in itself an̄d departs from its identity with Being--
it is only here that each [Idea] becomes a particular, and
a determinate unity.[48]

It seems, therefore, that the particularity which is only
potentially in the Absolute (as Ideas) becomes actual in the
order of appearances. A particular object is a manifestation
and partial realization of an Idea. Whereas the Idea is identical with the Absolute (the "Universal" as such), the determinate object is particular (while at the same time, of course,
ultimately rooted in the Absolute by being a manifestation of
the Idea).

To know a particular object "absolutely," therefore, is
to discover the Idea of which it is an imperfect manifestation.
But--in the light of the above texts--it is clear that such a

---

[47]Suppl. 1:461: ". . . im Absoluten ist keine Form
getrennt von ihrem Wesen, und alles ist ineinander, als Ein
Wesen, Eine Masse, und aus diesem Einen gehen alle Ideen als
göttliche Gewächse hervor, denn jede ist aus dem ganzen Wesen
des Absoluten gebildet."

[48]Suppl. 1:446: ". . . die verschiedenen Einheiten haben
als verschieden keine Wesenheit an sich, sondern sind nur
ideelle Formen und Bilder, unter welchen im absoluten Erkennen
das Ganze ausgeprägt wird, und insofern sie in diesem sind,
sind sie die ganze Welt selbst, und haben nichts außer sich,
mit dem sie verglichen oder dem sie entgegengesetzt werden
könnten. --Das ganze Universum ist im Absoluten als Pflanze,
als Thier, als Mensch, aber weil in jedem das Ganze ist, so ist
es nicht als Pflanze, nicht als Thier, nicht als Mensch, oder
als die besondere Einheit, sondern als absolute Einheit darin;
erst in der Erscheinung, wo es aufhört das <u>Ganze</u> zu seyn, die
Form etwas für sich seyn will und aus der In̄differenz mit dem
Wesen tritt, wird jedes das Besondere und die bestimmte Einheit."

discovery is not at all the same as merely forming a general
concept which is applicable to a concrete case. Rather, it is
the discovery--with respect to a particular thing--that it is
only a partial manifestation of a _divine_ thought (so to speak).
But this divine thought, this Idea in the Absolute, can only be
discovered in the intuition of the Absolute itself, in "intellektueller Anschauung."

"Construktion" as the Proper Method of Absolute Knowing

The intellectual operation just characterized is called
by Schelling "Construktion." He considers it to be the true
and proper method of philosophy, since it is the only possible
way of knowing particulars "absolutely."

> Presentation in intellectual intuition is philosophi-
> cal construction; but just as the universal unity which
> lies at the basis of all things can only be found in intel-
> lectual intuition [Vernunftanschauung], so also it is only
> there that may be found the particular unities, in each of
> which the same absoluteness of the Urwissen is received;
> they are, to that extent, Ideas. Philosophy is, therefore,
> the science of Ideas or the eternal archetypes of things.[49]

What the mind discovers in "construction" is the Idea, a
"particular unity" in which "the . . . absoluteness of the
Urwissen is received." What is thus intuited is that paradoxical unity of particularity and universality which Schelling
locates in the absolute Knowing itself. "The Idea is always
and necessarily absolute, since in it universal and particular
are necessarily equated."[50] "Every Idea is a particular which,
as such, is absolute . . ."[51]

---

[49]3:277: "Darstellung in intellektueller Anschauung ist
philosophische Construktion; aber wie die allgemeine Einheit,
die allen zu Grunde liegt, so können auch die besondern, in
deren jeder die gleiche Absoluheit des Urwissens aufgenommen
wird, nur in der Vernunftanschauung enthalten seyn, und sind
insofern Ideen. Die Philosophie ist also die Wissenschaft der
Ideen oder der ewigen Urbilder der Dinge."

[50]Suppl. 1:457: "Die Idee also ist immer und nothwendig
absolut, da in ihr Allgemeines und Besonderes nothwendig
gleichgesetzt sind . . ."

[51]1:714: ("Darstellung der allgemeinen Idee der Philosophie, etc.," 1797 & 1803): "Jede Idee ist ein Besonderes, das
als solches absolut ist . . ."

It is from this perspective that he can refer to "construction" as "the presentation of the universal and the particular in unity . . ." and "the absolute and _real_ equating of the universal and the particular."[52] And he can refer to the Idea as "the pure synthesis of the Universal and the particular."[53]

This attempt to account for the absolute character of scientific knowing must not obscure the reference to a particular, determinate object. For it is only with respect to it that the Idea is intuited. After all, the Idea in its particularity only becomes actual insofar as it departs from the primal identity and is manifested in appearance.

Hence, it is the particular object which is known "as absolute" or "in the Absolute." But its very particularity is, in a sense, "destroyed" or sublated (_aufgehoben_)[54] insofar as this particularity is intuited _as Idea_, i.e., as a particular, possible form of the absolute Knowing. Its particularity is thus viewed in relationship to the Absolute, in which all "forms" are simply "Modi des absoluten Erkennens."

The particular object is thus presented to the human mind not as an isolated and arbitrary fact, but as a manifestation of the divine Mind. Even though no one object can be an adequate realization of its _Urbild_ or Idea,[55] the human mind can discover--with respect to that object--the Idea as identical with the Absolute itself. This particular "form" can be grasped as an expression or imaging forth of the unqualified Universality which the Absolute is: "in every individual construction, this absolute Unity is expressed in the particular as the Universal, total and undivided."[56]

---

[52] 3:274: "Die Darstellung des Allgemeinen und Besondern in der Einheit, heißt überhaupt Construction . . ." 3:551-52 ("Über die Construktion in der Philosophie," 1803): ". . . die Construktion, als solche, ist in der Mathematik und Philosophie immer absolute und _reale_ Gleichsetzung des Allgemeinen und Besonderen."

[53] 3:560: ". . . die Idee oder die reine Synthesis des Allgemeinen und Besonderen . . ."

[54] Suppl. 1:445; 460; 461.   [55] 3:349.

[56] 3:559 ("Über die Construktion in der Philosophie," 1803): ". . . daß jene absolute Einheit in jeder einzelnen Construction als das Allgemeine _ganz_ und ungetheilt im Besonderen ausgedrückt sey."

In this entire discussion, of course, Schelling is strain-
ing language beyond its limits in the effort to express his
sense of the really ineffable Oneness of reality. The whole
ideal of "absolute knowing" is the effort to grasp all particular, seemingly diverse things as, in reality, rooted in the One.
To claim to know particulars "absolutely" is unintelligible
apart from the "intellectual intuition" of this ultimate Unity.
It is this perspective on reality which he articulates in texts
like the following:

> . . . Everything particular as such is form, but the source
> and origin of all forms is the necessary, eternal, and
> absolute Form. [He means the Absolute as Urwissen or
> reiner Erkenntniβakt.] The act of "Subjekt-Objektivirung"
> extends through all things and propagates itself in the
> particular forms. These particular forms, since they are
> all only various ways in which the universal and absolute
> Form appears, are themselves absolute in it.[57]

We are left, therefore, with Schelling's monistic view of
reality as the indispensable basis for his ideal of "absolutes
Wissen." This is why "intellectual intuition" of the Absolute
is the only possible entry into "Wissenschaft" as he conceives
it. For no true "Wissenschaft" is possible, as long as one
remains satisfied with "merely finite knowing";[58] that is, as
long as one takes finite things merely in themselves and in
relation to one another, without discovering their relationship
to the Absolute.

The "Higher Viewpoint" of Absolute Knowing

This perspective is expressed most clearly in a passage
of the Lectures on Academic Study where he contrasts two different ways of knowing "nature":

---

[57]3:347: "Alles Besondere als solches ist Form, von allen
Formen aber ist die nothwendige, ewige und absolute Form der
Quell und Ursprung. Der Akt der Subjekt-Objektivirung geht
durch alle Dinge hindurch, und pflanzt sich in den besonderen
Formen fort, die, da sie alle nur verschiedene Erscheinungs-
weisen der allgemeinen und unbedingten, in dieser selbst
unbedingt sind."

[58]3:278: "Eine negative Bestimmung ihres [i.e., der intellektuellen Anschauung] Besitzes ist die klare und innige
Einsicht der Nichtigkeit aller bloβ endlichen Erkenntniβ."

The one, which considers nature as the instrument of the Ideas or, generally, as the real side of the Absolute and hence as itself absolute; the other, which considers nature in itself, as separated from the ideal, and in its relativity. We can call the former, in general, the philosophical and the latter the empirical [way of knowing nature].[59]

The point of this distinction can be grasped only from the above mentioned perspective of intellectual intuition. What is inadequate about the empirical way of knowing is precisely its failure to rise to this perspective. It is a "purely-finite view"[60] of things which seeks intelligibility merely in terms of the causal interrelationships of finite things. This kind of understanding is called "Erklärung,"[61] and is correlated with the faculty of "Verstand."[62] As an account of nature, Schelling finds it quite inadequate, since it discovers only a mechanistic sequence of causal interactions of finite things.

The philosophical way of knowing nature, on the other hand, considers finite things as the objectification of the Absolute in the order of the "real," as the appearances of the eternal Ideas. Since this way of viewing nature is called here "Construktion" (in contrast to "Erklärung"),[63] the earlier examination of "Construktion" is relevant again in this context. The faculty which is able thus to view nature as a mirroring of the Absolute is called "Vernunft" (perhaps "intuitive intelligence") in contrast to "Verstand."

What makes it possible for the mind to take the empirical purely-finite view of nature is the fact that finite beings do have a reality of their own, which may be attended to without noticing their quality of "symbolizing" the Absolute's eternal Ideas.

---

[59]3:340-41: "Die eine, welche die Natur als das Werkzeug der Ideen, oder allgemein als die reale Seite des Absoluten und demnach selbst absolut, die andere, welche sie für sich als getrennt vom Idealen und in ihrer Relativität betrachtet. Wir können die erste allgemein die philosophische, die andere die empirische nennen . . ."

[60]3:342: ". . . rein-endliche Auffassung . . ."

[61]3:342.   [62]Suppl. 1:393-95.   [63]3:342.

. . . Nature is, in general, the sphere of the "being-in
-themselves" of things; by reason of the imaging of the
Infinite into their finitude, they have--as symbols of the
Ideas--at the same time a life which is independent of
their significance.[64]

The philosophical way of considering nature looks precisely for the "significance" (Bedeutung) of finite things by
discovering the Ideas which are thus imperfectly manifested.
It is only this level of comprehension which Schelling would
dignify with the term "knowing" (Wissen or Erkenntnis) in the
proper sense. For only this kind of knowing grasps the finite
particular as "necessary," by rooting it in the Absolute, which
is the unique identity of thought and being.[65]

Empirical knowing, on the other hand, remains on the
level of the finite as merely particular, as seemingly arbitrary and accidental. This kind of knowing, it seems, might be
called "Kenntnis."[66] It is not irrelevant; indeed, it is indispensable for any higher knowing. But it is only preliminary to
rigorous "scientific" knowing, whose goal is to discover the
necessity of the seemingly accidental by means of "construction"
in intellectual intuition.[67]

All this has been said with regard to "nature," in order
to clarify Schelling's ideal of "absolutes Wissen" against the

---

[64]3:311: "Die Natur ist allgemein die Sphäre des in-sich-
selbst-Seyns der Dinge, in der diese, kraft der Einbildung des
Unendlichen in ihr Endliches, als Symbolen der Ideen zugleich
ein von ihrer Bedeutung unabhängiges Leben haben." Cf. 1:717.

[65]Cf. 3:347.

[66]3:266: ". . . so kann man die Art von Wissen, die vor
dem akademischen Studium erworben wird, nicht wohl anders denn
als Kenntnisse bezeichnen. . . . Die höheren Wissenschaften
lassen sich nicht in der Qualität von Kenntnissen besitzen oder
erlangen."

[67]"Kenntnis" has to do with experience. But the goal of
Wissenschaft is to "raise to the dignity of an a priori" those
propositions which at first are merely experiential, by coming
to realize their necessity. Cf. 2:278 ("Einleitung zu dem
Entwurf eines Systems der Naturphilosophie," 1799): ". . . wir
wissen ursprünglich überhaupt nichts als durch Erfahrung, . . .
und insofern besteht unser ganzes Wissen aus Erfahrungssätzen.
Zu Sätzen a priori werden diese Sätze nur dadurch, daß man sich
ihrer als nothwendiger bewußt wird . . . . . jeder Satz, der
für mich bloß historisch ist, [ist] ein Erfahrungssatz, derselbe aber, sobald ich unmittelbar oder mittelbar die Einsicht

background of his monistic sense of the Absolute. "Nature" is thus seen to be the one "side" of the Absolute's self-manifestation, although this "imaging-forth" is almost more of a self-concealment, insofar as the pure "ideality" ("Urwissen" or "reiner Erkenntnisakt") is merely symbolized in that which is other than itself, viz., in being or the real.[68] And Schelling did attempt, in great detail, to work out a philoso-phy of nature which would show the quality of the universe as the symbolization of the Absolute. Our interest, however, is not in this, but rather in the other "side" of the Absolute's self-manifestation: "history," the realm of explicit ration-ality and mind.

Schelling's View of History

It is in history, Schelling thinks, that the Absolute is manifested in its proper nature, so to speak, as Mind or "ideality." "In the ideal world it [the Absolute] puts its veil aside, as it were, and appears as that which it is, as Ideal, as act of knowing . . ."[69]

"History" as thus contrasted with "nature" seems to be regarded primarily as the development of human rational con-sciousness, of thought and knowing (the realm of the "ideal"). As we noted earlier, human "reason" (Vernunft) is considered to be a share in the "Urwissen," so that the eternal Ideas of the Absolute become explicit in finite consciousness. It is in this sense that the "ideality" of the Absolute becomes manifest in history--but, of course, only as separate from the order of the "real" (i.e., "nature"), whereas ultimately (in the Absolute), the ideal and the real are identical.

---

in seine innere Nothwendigkeit erlange [wird] ein Satz a priori . . ." See below, pp. 162-63.

[68]Cf. 1:717: ". . . in der erscheinenden Natur wird nur die besondere Form als besondere erkannt, das Absolute verhüllt sich hier in ein andres, als es selbst in seiner Absolutheit ist, in ein Endliches, ein Seyn . . ."

[69]1:717: "In der ideellen Welt legt es die Hülle gleich-sam ab, es erscheint als das, was es ist, als Ideales, als Erkenntnißakt . . ." Cf. 3:311: "In der idealen Welt, also vornehmlich der Geschichte, legt das Göttliche die Hülle ab, sie ist das laut gewordene Mysterium des göttlichen Reiches."

Schelling, however, also speaks often of history in a
somewhat different sense, in which it seems parallel to nature.
This parallel becomes evident in the Lectures, in a passage
where he is speaking of history as Wissenschaft.[70] Schelling
distinguishes two viewpoints from which the events of the past
may be regarded. And this distinction is strikingly similar to
the distinction examined above between the "philosophical" and
"empirical" ways of regarding nature.[71] There is an empirical
way of treating history, also, which orders the facts according
to some limited interest of the historian (e.g., military
operations). This may be called the "pragmatic" way of doing
history. It has a limited validity and intelligibility which
seems parallel to the empirical explanation (Erklärung) of the
phenomena of nature. It is interesting that the same contrast
between Verstand and Vernunft is again drawn here:

> The pragmatic purpose of history, of itself, excludes
> universality, and also necessarily requires a restricted
> object. The purpose of instruction demands a correct and
> empirically grounded connection of events, through which
> the Verstand, to be sure, is enlightened, but the Vernunft
> --without something further--remains unsatisfied.[72]

What the Vernunft seeks in its quest for the intelligibility of history is precisely what it seeks in its knowledge
of nature: to discover the relationship of these finite particulars to the Absolute. For history--in the sense of this
complex, seemingly fortuitous sequence of events--is actually
just as much a manifestation of the Absolute, of its eternal
Ideas--as nature is. "History, too, comes out of an eternal
Unity and has its root in the Absolute just as much as does
nature or any other object of knowledge."[73]

---

[70] 3:328-33.   [71] Cf. 3:340-41.

[72] 3:331: "Der pragmatische Zweck der Geschichte schließt
von selbst die Universalität aus und fordert nothwendig auch
einen beschränkten Gegenstand. Der Zweck der Belehrung
verlangt eine richtige und empirisch begründete Verknüpfung der
Begebenheiten, durch welche der Verstand zwar aufgeklärt wird,
die Vernunft aber ohne andere Zuthat unbefriedigt bleibt . . ."

[73] 3:313: "Auch die Geschichte kommt aus einer ewigen
Einheit und hat ihre Wurzel ebenso im Absoluten wie die Natur
oder irgend ein anderer Gegenstand des Wissens."

History is thus considered as an object of knowledge. As such, it has this in common with nature: both are finite, particular realities which can be regarded in themselves, without reference to the Absolute. But this kind of knowing is "merely finite," and does not satisfy the Vernunft. Absolute knowing of either nature or history is achieved, as we have seen, only when these finite objects are grasped in their quality of being manifestation of the Absolute, i.e., of its eternal Ideas.

There is, however, a problem in so regarding history--a problem which is not felt in the "construction" of nature. The material of history appears to be the complex interaction of countless free human agents, which results in various groupings, relationships, and events. If history is thus created by the free choices of human beings, how can it be regarded as the inevitable self-manifestation of the Absolute? How can human freedom be reconciled with divine necessity?

Schelling thinks that there is a higher viewpoint on history--in contrast to the merely empirical--which can discover the identity of necessity and freedom. This viewpoint is both philosophical and religious. It is philosophical, because, like the higher viewpoint on nature, it is possible only in intellectual intuition of the Absolute. It is religious insofar as it views history as the work of divine "providence," i.e., "the wisdom which, in the plan of the world, unites the freedom of human beings with the universal necessity."[74]

Schelling's notion of history is best characterized by this strong sense of an eternally necessary pattern being wrought out, in and through the play of human freedom. What grounds this paradoxical unity of necessity and freedom in Schelling's view of history is his monistic intuition of the ultimate oneness of all things.[75]

The necessity of history is rooted in the Absolute. But it is not a "blind" necessity (as it often appears to us, under

---

[74]3:332: ". . . Vorsehung . . . die Weisheit . . . , welche in dem Plane der Welt die Freiheit der Menschen mit der allgemeinen Nothwendigkeit . . . vereinigt."

[75]Cf. Suppl. 1:463; 3:328.

the form of "fate"),[76] because the Absolute is a pure knowing
or "ideality" which is, at the same time, identical with Being
or "reality." Hence there is an intelligibility about all
reality[77] which can be recognized. Schelling praises Christianity precisely because it affirms this intelligibility with
regard to history, under the doctrine of "providence."[78]

The higher viewpoint on the events of history must not,
however, become explicit in the academic discipline of history
itself, Schelling insists. (For such an explicit treatment of
the Ideas belongs either to philosophy or theology.)[79] Rather,
history is to be written as "art," so that the real events are
presented objectively in such a way that the higher necessity
becomes evident. What is thus portrayed is a necessity that is
manifest but not understood; in other words, "fate" or "destiny"
(Schicksal).[80] Schelling compares this art of the historian to
that of the dramatist who writes a tragedy. The events portrayed have a reality and empirical character in themselves;
but at the same time, they are perceived as the working-out of
a purpose not envisaged by the human agents, which has the
character of inevitability.

> History reaches its fulfillment for the Vernunft only
> when the empirical causes, while satisfying the Verstand,
> are utilized as instruments and means for the appearance of
> a higher necessity. In such a presentation, history cannot
> but have the effect of the very greatest and most marvelous
> drama, which can only be composed in an infinite Mind.[81]

---

[76]Cf. 2:601.

[77]This is the conviction shared by all forms of German
Idealism. Mind is the ultimate reality, so that everything
which presents itself to the human mind already has the quality
of rationality or intelligibility. Schelling says, for example,
that "Vernunft" is the "Urstoff" of reality (Suppl. 1:442).

[78]More will be said about Schelling's view of Christianity shortly.

[79]There is an ambiguity involved here, which will be
pointed out below.

[80]3:333.

[81]3:332: "Erst dann erhält die Geschichte ihre Vollendung
für die Vernunft, wenn die empirischen Ursachen, indem sie den
Verstand befriedigen, als Werkzeuge und Mittel der Erscheinung
einer höheren Nothwendigkeit gebraucht werden. In solcher

Theology as "Wissenschaft"

It is this higher view of history which is the key to
Schelling's notion of theology as Wissenschaft. Since this
latter notion is an aspect of his thought which manifestly
influenced Drey, it deserves some close attention.

In the 7th of the Lectures, Schelling locates and characterizes theology within the organic whole of the Wissenschaften.
It must be recalled that all human knowing is a share in the
"primal knowing" (Urwissen) which the Absolute is. Philosophy
is the highest kind of knowing, since it is the "immediate
presentation and science of the Urwissen itself, but it is this
only ideally, not really."[82] The point of the latter distinction seems to be this: philosophy does share in the ideal
content of the Absolute's eternal Knowing; it is the "Wissenschaft der Ideen." But, whereas in the Absolute there is perfect identity of ideal and real--of thought and being--this is
not so for the finite human mind. Hence, the order of the
"real," i.e., the actual, concrete manifestations of the Ideas,
cannot be known by the human mind in one comprehensive act of
knowledge.

> If an intelligence--in one act of knowing--could grasp
> "really" the absolute Whole as a system complete in all its
> parts, it would by this very act cease to be finite; it
> would grasp everything actually as One, but for that very
> reason would grasp nothing as determinate.[83]

This distinction between "ideal" and "real" knowing is
the basis for the opposition which Schelling draws between

_____

Darstellung kann die Geschichte die Wirkung des größten und
erstaunenswürdigsten Drama nicht verfehlen, das nur in einem
unendlichen Geiste gedichtet seyn kann." Cf. 3:331: "Dennoch
ist selbst unter den Heiligsten nichts, das heiliger wäre als
die Geschichte, dieser große Spiegel des Weltgeistes, dieses
ewige Gedicht des göttlichen Verstandes."

[82]3:302: "Die Philosophie ist unmittelbare Darstellung
und Wissenschaft des Urwissens selbst, aber sie ist es nur
ideal, nicht real."

[83]3:302: "Könnte die Intelligenz, in Einem Akt des
Wissens, das absolute Ganze, als ein in allen Theilen vollen-
detes System real begreifen, so hörte sie eben damit auf endlich zu seyn, sie begriffe Alles wirklich als Eines, aber sie
begriffe eben deßwegen Nichts als Bestimmtes."

philosophy, on the one hand, as the "absolute Wissenschaft,"
whose object is the Ideas, and, on the other hand, all those
other branches of knowing which have, as object, some determinate portion of "the real." These disciplines are called "reale
Wissenschaften." Only the totality of them--taken together--
may be considered the "'real' presentation of the Urwissen,"
in contrast to philosophy as the "ideal" presentation of that
same primal Knowing. But no one finite human mind, as already
noted, can take this in; only the entire human race can achieve
this "real" knowing. And even the ability to conceive the
totality of the "real" Wissenschaften in this way depends on
intellectual intuition.

> The "real" presentation of the Urwissen is all other
> knowing [i.e., other than philosophy], which is distin-
> guished from the former by the element of the concrete, but
> in this knowing it is differentiation and separation which
> rule; it can never become really one in the individual, but
> only in the species, and this also only for an intellectual
> intuition which views the infinite progression as present.[84]

The "real" Wissenschaften, Schelling thinks, are to be
grouped according to the archetypal polarity of the Absolute
itself, which has repeatedly been characterized as the simple
identity of ideal and real. This provides him with the following basic structure for the organism of the Wissenschaften.

> The first [Wissenschaft], which presents objectively
> the absolute identity-point, will be the immediate Wissen-
> schaft of the absolute and divine Being, hence, theology.
> Of the two others, the one which takes the real side of
> philosophy for itself and represents it exteriorly, will be
> the Wissenschaft of nature . . .
> The one which objectifies the ideal side of philosophy
> separately for itself, will be, in general, the Wissen-
> schaft of history . . .[85]

---

[84]3:302: "Die reale Darstellung des Urwissens ist alles
andere Wissen, von jenem durch das Element des Concreten
geschieden, aber in diesem herrscht auch die Absonderung und
Trennung, und es kann nie in dem Individuum real eins werden,
sondern allein in der Gattung, und auch in dieser nur für eine
intellektuelle Anschauung, die den unendlichen Fortschritt als
Gegenwart erblickt."

[85]3:305: "Die erste, welche den absoluten Indifferenzpunkt objektiv darstellt, wird die unmittelbare Wissenschaft
des absoluten und göttlichen Wesens, demnach die Theologie,
seyn.
    "Von den beiden andern wird diejenige, welche die reele

These are the three basic Wissenschaften of the "real."
What they have in common is precisely their orientation toward
the "real" in contrast to philosophy which remains totally in
the order of the Ideas. But there is a correlation between
them and philosophy, which depends on that ultimate oneness of
"ideal" and "real" which the Absolute is. Just as "nature" and
"history" are the two sides of the Absolute's self-
objectification, so also the "real" Wissenschaften (which
Schelling also calls "positive") are partial objectifications
of that ideality which is the domain of philosophy. "It is
philosophy itself, which becomes objective in the three positive Wissenschaften, but it does not become objective in its
totality in any one of them."[86]

This correlation is important for the method of the
"real" Wissenschaften. For, although their material (Stoff)
is some portion of concrete, determinate reality (the "real"),
their properly wissenschaftlich way of grasping the intelligibility of this material must be philosophical. (Cf. the
earlier discussion of "Construktion.")

The "real" must be discovered empirically.[87] It is, in a
sense, given. (Perhaps this is why Schelling can also call the
"real" Wissenschaften "positive.") It is in this sense that
Schelling speaks of the "historical" as the distinctive element
in the "real" Wissenschaften. This usage seems to reflect the
historian's function of research, of finding out the given
facts of the past.

    . . . The real side of Wissenschaft can always only be
    historical . . .

Seite der Philosophie für sich nimmt und diese äußerlich
repräsentirt, die Wissenschaft der Natur . . .
    "Die, welche die ideele Seite der Philosophie in sich
getrennt objektivirt, wird allgemein die Wissenschaft der
Geschichte . . ."

[86]3:306: "Es ist die Philosophie selbst, welche in den
drei positiven Wissenschaften objektiv wird, aber sie wird
durch keine einzelne in ihrer Totalität objektiv."

[87]Cf. 2:278.

> The real Wissenschaften in general can only be distin-
> guished from the absolute or ideal [Wissenschaft] [i.e.,
> Philosophy] through the historical element . . .[88]

The goal of any "real" Wissenschaft, however, is to grasp
the intelligibility of the "real" through the higher kind of
knowing, to rise from a merely empirical view to an absolute
knowing which alone deserves the name of "Wissenschaft." Hence,
Schelling can characterize the "real" Wissenschaften in general
as "syntheses of the historical and the philosophical" ways of
knowing.[89]

As already noted, Schelling locates theology as the highest of these "real" Wissenschaften. But there is an inconsistency in the way he characterizes it and attempts to distinguish it from the other two basic "real" Wissenschaften:
"Naturwissenschaft" and "Geschichte." This inconsistency was
pointed out by Schleiermacher in his 1804 review of the
Lectures.[90] The latter's critical observations are helpful in
reaching a fuller understanding of how Schelling actually conceived the task and method of theology.

The difficulty arises from the characterization of theology as the Wissenschaft "which presents objectively the
absolute identity-point," as "the immediate Wissenschaft of the
absolute and divine being."[91] It is not at all obvious how

---

[88]3:351: ". . . die reale Seite der Wissenschaft [kann]
immer nur historisch seyn . . ." 3:308: "Die realen Wissenschaften überhaupt können von der absoluten als der idealen
allein durch das historische Element geschieden oder besondere
seyn." Cf. 3:334: "Wenn die realen Wissenschaften überhaupt
nur durch das historische Element von der Philosophie
geschieden sind . . ."

[89]3:329: ". . . die realen Wissenschaften [sind] Synthe-
sen des Philosophischen und Historischen . . ."

[90]Schleiermacher's review of Schelling's "Vorlesungen
über die Methode des akademischen Studiums" appeared in the
Jenaische Allgemeine Literaturzeitung for 21 April, 1804 (1804,
Bd I, No. 96-97), pp. 137-51. It was reprinted in Aus
Schleiermachers Leben in Briefen, edited by Ludwig Jonas and
Wilhelm Dilthey, 4 (Berlin: Georg Reimer, 1863), 579-93.
Especially relevant to our present discussion are pp. 583ff.

[91]3:305: ". . . welche den absoluten Indifferenzpunkt
objektiv darstellt . . ." ". . . die unmittelbare Wissenschaft
des absoluten und göttlichen Wesens . . ."

this Absolute can be taken as the immediate object of a
Wissenschaft which is to direct its attention to the "real,"
and which, must, therefore, deal with the "historical." As
Schleiermacher asks,

> How is it with this real and purely historical element
> in theology? . . . Can this happen at all? Can the
> identity-point become the object of a "real" Wissen-
> schaft?[92]

Referring to Schelling's general characterization of the
"real" Wissenschaften as the branches of knowledge where
"differentiation and separation rule,"[93] Schleiermacher asks
how "these can rule in the Wissenschaft of the absolute, divine
being."[94]

The obvious conclusion to be drawn from this is that
theology--as a "real" Wissenschaft--cannot actually take as its
immediate object the undifferentiated Absolute. Rather, it
necessarily must fall into the two parallel ways of knowing the
divine in its differentiated manifestations: "an intuition of
God in history as in the ideal, and in nature as in the real."[95]

Looked at in this way, however, theology does not seem
really distinguishable from the "higher view of history" and
the "higher view of nature." And, since it is precisely the
"higher viewpoint" which enables both Naturwissenschaft and
Geschichte to be truly Wissenschaften of the "real," theology
seems to "dissolve into the other two real Wissenschaften."[96]

Summing up his criticism, Schleiermacher observes:

---

[92]Briefe (Jonas & Dilthey) 4:583, 584: ". . . wie steht
es denn selbst um dieses reale und rein historische in der
Theologie? . . . Kann es überhaupt statt finden? Kann wol
überall der Indifferenzpunkt der Gegenstand einer realen
Wissenschaft werden?"

[93]3:302.

[94]Briefe 4:584: ". . . kann diese herrschen in der
Wissenschaft des absoluten, göttlichen Wesens?"

[95]Ibid.: ". . . eine Anschauung Gottes . . . in der
Geschichte als dem Idealen, . . . in der Natur als dem Realen."

[96]Ibid.: ". . . in die beiden andern realen Wissenschaften
zerfliesst . . ."

Thus one sees manifestly, that theology cannot be a "real" Wissenschaft in the same sense as the other two; it cannot be a knowing of the same type as they, which differs only by its object; nor can it be related to them as the objectification of the identity-point is related to the objectification of the differentiated sides. Rather, it has its object in common with them, but shows itself to be a completely different treatment of it.[97]

Schleiermacher thus draws out the logical implication of locating theology among the "real" Wissenschaften. What is "real" is comprised by the two parallel orders of "nature" and "history." This must, therefore, be the actual object of theology, so that the latter cannot be distinguished from Naturwissenschaft and Geschichte by reason of a distinct object. If there is a difference, it must be a matter of formal viewpoint and method of knowing this object.

There is evidence in the Lectures that Schleiermacher's perception of Schelling's implicit logic was strikingly accurate. This evidence is found in the 8th and 9th lectures, which treat explicitly of theology, and in the 10th lecture, which treats of history.

We have already quoted from the latter section in order to explain Schelling's "higher viewpoint" on history. It seems significant that this higher viewpoint is there identified as that of philosophy and religion, but is not allowed to become explicit in the academic discipline of history itself. Hence, history is not--strictly speaking--a Wissenschaft (since it does not treat explicitly of the Ideas), but is rather a kind of art which may be considered to be "on the same level as Wissenschaft"[98] insofar as it lets the Ideas be displayed in the real events which it recounts.

If the discipline of history, therefore, is not the "real" Wissenschaft whose object is past events, one might ask what is.

_____

[97]Ibid.: "So sieht man offenbar, daß die Theologie nicht in dem Sinne, wie die andern beiden eine reale Wissenschaft sein kann, ein ihnen gleichartiges, nur durch seinen Gegenstand verschiedenes Wissen, auch nicht sich zu ihnen verhalten, wie die Objectivirung des Indifferenzpunktes zur Objectivirung der differentiirten Seiten; sondern vielmehr hat sie den Gegenstand mit ihnen gemein, zeigt sich aber als eine ganz verschiedene Behandlung derselben [sic]."

[98]3:332.

And the answer is quite clear and explicit: it is theology,
which makes the "higher viewpoint" explicit by attempting a
philosophical "construction" of universal history. This is the
notion of theology which is sketched out in the 8th and 9th
lectures.

This seems to be a kind of confirmation of Schleiermacher's critique, in this sense: Schelling appears to acknowledge that the object of theology is actually the same as that
of history--namely, the totality of events. Schleiermacher's
suggestion that theology be distinguished from history by
virtue of its formal viewpoint is not, however, Schelling's way
of making the distinction. Rather, the formal viewpoint of
both is actually the same (the "higher viewpoint"). The only
difference is in the way of presenting the material. History
is to do this artistically, in a manner analogous to tragic
drama. Theology is to do it philosophically, by "constructing"
history explicitly in terms of the eternally necessary Ideas.

The following text expresses this view of theology as
philosophical construction, as well as recognizing, in passing,
that "nature" also is part of theology's object:

> The historical construction of Christianity--because of
> the universality of Christianity's Idea--cannot be con-
> ceived without the religious construction of all of history.
> . . .
> Such a construction, by its very nature, is possible
> only for the higher way of knowing, which rises above the
> empirical linkage of things. It is, therefore, not possi-
> ble without philosophy, which is the true organ of theology
> as Wissenschaft--in which the highest Ideas about the
> divine being, about nature as the instrument of God and
> history as the revelation of God, become objective.[99]

This view of theology fits the description of a "real"
Wissenschaft. That is, the material to be known is the real:

---

[99] 3:321: "Die historische Construktion des Christenthums
kann wegen dieser Universalität seiner Idee nicht ohne die
religiöse Construktion der ganzen Geschichte gedacht werden. . . .
"Eine solche Construktion ist schon an sich selbst nur
der höhern Erkenntniβart möglich, welche sich über die
empirische Verkettung der Dinge erhebt; sie ist also nicht ohne
Philosophie, welche das wahre Organ der Theologie als Wissenschaft ist, worin die höchsten Ideen von dem göttlichen Wesen,
der Natur als dem Werkzeug und der Geschichte als der Offenbarung Gottes objektiv werden."

the events of history. But the way of knowing this material
transcends the empirical viewpoint. It is the higher way of
knowing, the way of Vernunft and philosophical "construction,"
in the sense explained earlier. Hence, the general characterization of the "real" Wissenschaften fits theology par excellence:
". . . it [theology] is altogether the highest synthesis of
philosophical and historical knowing . . ."[100]

Schelling thus actually situates theology firmly in the
domain of history.[101] But it is essential to appreciate his
special viewpoint on history. It is only from this "higher
viewpoint," explained earlier, that theology is to regard history. In contrast, a merely empirical treatment of history--in
particular, of Christianity and its doctrines--is hopelessly
inadequate to the task of theology.

Schelling's View of Christianity and the Task of Theology

Schelling begins the 9th Lecture ("Ueber das Studium der
Theologie") by drawing precisely this contrast. The wretched
state of theology in his day, he thinks, is due to the failure
of all parties to rise to the higher viewpoint of history.
Whether orthodox or unorthodox, they all persist in treating
Christianity from a merely empirical point of view.

If I find it difficult to speak of the study of theology, it is because I must regard as lost and forgotten the
very way of knowing and the entire standpoint from which
its truths are to be grasped. All the doctrines of this
Wissenschaft have been understood empirically and, as such,

---

[100]3:308: ". . . so ist sie überhaupt die höchste Synthese des philosophischen und historischen Wissens . . ."

[101]The logic uncovered by Schleiermacher's criticism
seems to demand that nature, as well as history, be an object
of theology. Schelling does not speak of nature in quite this
way, but his notion of Naturwissenschaft actually ambitions a
discovery of the divine in the "real." (Cf. 1:444, 446 and
pp. 79-80 above.) And this seems altogether parallel to the
task of interpreting history as the manifestation of the divine.
Nevertheless, Schelling attributes to theology explicitly only
the "construction" of history. Hence, we devote our attention
only to this. If one seeks a reason for this apparent inconsistency, perhaps it is to be found in history's quality of
"ideality," which unveils the proper nature of the divine in a
way which nature does not. (Cf. 1:717 and 3:311.)

have been both asserted and denied. But on this ground
they are altogether out of place and lose completely all
sense and meaning.[102]

What Schelling considers important about Christianity is
its "Idea." This central intuition was expressed only
inchoately and imperfectly in the biblical books and, indeed,
through most of Christianity's subsequent development.[103] This
is why the immense philological and historical research of
German scholars into "Urchristentum" is largely irrelevant to
theology.[104] It is the Idea which is important, and which is
eternally valid whether or not it is found in the beginnings of
Christianity.

It seems that this central Idea is expressed in the
Christian notion of the "reconciliation" of the world with God
by God's becoming man.[105] But this doctrine must not be understood in an empirical sense, as something that "happened" at
one point in time.[106] Rather, it is a matter of perceiving
the eternal oneness of finite and Infinite, of world and God.
This oneness may be expressed by saying that the Infinite (what
Schelling usually calls the Absolute) has appeared in and as
the finite. This is the "esoteric" meaning of the "exoteric"
doctrine of the Incarnation. And there is also an esoteric
sense to the doctrine of the Trinity--so that the "Son" may be
understood as the whole finite universe.[107]

The word "reconciliation" (Versöhnung) is appropriate for
Christianity's central intuition, because what Christianity
brings into the world is a new way of perceiving the divine and
the finite in relationship. There seems to be an irreconcilable gap or separation between the two. But this seeming
alienation is overcome by the new way of perceiving the eternal
oneness.

---

[102]3:318: "Wenn ich es schwer finde von dem Studium der
Theologie zu reden, so ist es, weil ich die Erkenntnißart und
den ganzen Standpunkt, aus welchem ihre Wahrheiten gefaßt seyn
wollen, als verloren und vergessen achten muß. Die sämmtlichen
Lehren dieser Wissenschaft sind empirisch verstanden und als
solche sowohl behauptet als bestritten worden. Auf diesem
Boden aber sind sie überall nicht einheimisch und verlieren
durchaus allen Sinn und Bedeutung.

[103]3:322.   [104]Ibid.   [105]3:316.   [106]3:320.   [107]3:316.

The new viewpoint of Christianity is seen more distinctly
in contrast to the pagan religion of antiquity. The latter
experienced the divine in nature; its gods were really part of
this natural world, finite beings which were absolutized.[108]
By contrast, Christianity transcends nature to intuit the
Infinite (the Absolute) as the ultimate and, indeed, primary
reality.[109] It regards the finite world as the manifestation
of this Infinite--primarily as history. History, rather than
nature, becomes the primary locus of the divine. No one event
reveals God fully, but rather the totality of events is the
self-manifestation of the Infinite.[110]

The human predicament seems characterized by the various
possible ways of perceiving the finite-Infinite relationship,[111]
since human beings are that portion of the finite which has
self-awareness and a sense of freedom. As long as human beings
live in an unconscious oneness with the All, they experience
themselves as part of nature. But as soon as there is a conscious separation from the All, in self-possession and freedom,
man experiences "fate" (Schicksal) as the higher necessity
which seems to rule his life. This is an experience of alienation and separation (Entzweiung). This is overcome, then, by
Christianity's new "higher viewpoint" on the finite-Infinite
relationship--so that man experiences "reconciliation"
(Versöhnung) of world and God, of his human freedom and the
divine necessity. The reconciliation is expressed in the
doctrine of "providence" (replacing "fate") as the interpretation of history. The world is now seen as a history of free
human agents which is, at the same time, patterned by a higher
intelligibility, a divine necessity.

> Christianity, therefore, introduces into history the
> period of "providence," just as the dominant view of the
> universe for Christianity is the view of it as history and
> as a world of providence.
> This is the great historical direction of Christianity;
> this is the reason why the Wissenschaft of religion is, in
> Christianity, inseparable from history--indeed it must be
> completely one with history. But this synthesis with
> history, without which theology itself cannot be conceived,

---

[108]3:310.   [109]Ibid.   [110]2:603.   [111]3:312.

demands in turn as its condition the higher Christian view
of history.[112]

This "higher Christian view of history" is thus seen to
be the consequence of the new intuition of the God-world relationship. But Schelling's use of Christian concepts such as
"providence" and "revelation" does not mean that he accepts the
traditional biblical view of God "acting in history." He
explicitly disavows the concept of revelation "as an action of
God in time,"[113] because this view expects the divine to be
discoverable in particular events on the empirical level of
intelligibility. Rather, the divine is to be perceived only
from the higher viewpoint of the Absolute, not in particular
events and persons but in the totality of history.[114] As for
"providence," this must not be imagined after the model of a
Poet who, independent of his creation, writes the parts for all
his characters before the performance. Rather, the mysterious
unity of necessity and freedom in the spectacle of history is
understandable only if the characters are actually freely
creating their roles as they go, and yet it is the one eternal
Poet (the Absolute as Urwissen) which is acting and expressing
himself in each one.[115]

In this view, history may be regarded as the revelation
of God, in a certain sense, but not in the traditional understanding of a transcendent God intervening by specific actions
within history. Only the totality of events would be the

---

[112]3:312-13: "Das Christenthum also leitet in der
Geschichte jene Periode der Vorsehung ein, wie die in ihm
herrschende Anschauung des Universum die Anschauung desselben
als Geschichte und als einer Welt der Vorsehung ist.
Dieß ist die große historische Richtung des Christenthums:
dieß der Grund, warum die Wissenschaft der Religion in ihm von
der Geschichte unzertrennlich ist, ja mit ihr völlig eins seyn
muß. Jene Synthese mit der Geschichte, ohne welche Theologie
selbst nicht gedacht werden kann, fordert aber hinwiederum zu
ihrer Bedingung die höhere christliche Ansicht der Geschichte."

[113]3:318: ". . . eine Handlung Gottes in der Zeit . . ."

[114]2:603.

[115]This view of history is expressed in the "System des
transzendentalen Idealismus" (1800), 2:587-604, esp. pp. 601-3.

adequate revelation of the divine. Only then--when history is
"complete"--would God "be" objectively, so to speak. But then
the finite world of human freedom would no longer "be."[116]

It should be noted that--even though this way of regarding history may seem quite exalted and even mystical--Schelling
at the same time did have some specific content in mind for the
expected "shape" of history. He sees the goal of history as
the slow formation of a kind of world-state, what he calls, in
the section we are referring to, "eine universelle rechtliche
Verfassung" and "eine weltbürgerliche Verfassung . . ."[117] And
it seems that this view of history's development might be
equated with the phrase "moralisches Reich," which he uses
elsewhere to characterize Christianity's view of the universe.[118]

In other words, the intelligible pattern which the higher
viewpoint of "providence" sees being worked out in the seemingly
free interaction of human beings is this formation of a universal world order of law. If it were ever complete, it would be
the full expression of the divine "ideality" in the order of
history.

To return now to Schelling's conception of theology as
Wissenschaft, it is clear that theology's task is to interpret
universal history from this higher viewpoint. The history of
Christianity is, of course, part of this universal history.
But "exoteric" Christianity, with its empirical understanding
of its events of origin and its doctrines, must be transcended.
Theology's business is to view the (not-yet-complete) totality
of history from the viewpoint of Christianity's master Idea:
the "reconciliation" of finite and Infinite. All doctrines are
to be interpreted speculatively, rather than empirically, so as
to show their "esoteric" meaning. Christ himself who is, "as
an individual, fully comprehensible," must be grasped "as
symbolic person and in his higher significance."[119]

It would perhaps not be accurate to call this view of
Christianity "ahistorical," since Schelling does direct his

---

[116]2:603.   [117]2:591-92.   [118]3:309

[119]3:319: ". . . Christus, als der Einzelne, ist eine
völlig begreifliche Person, und es war eine absolute Nothwendigkeit, ihn als symbolische Person und in höherer Bedeutung zu
fassen."

attention to historical phenomena. Yet, what is clearly decisive for him is a kind of timeless intuition of the eternal
relationship of finite and Infinite. This is the controlling
perspective from which the data of history are to be viewed.
And this intuition--although, of course, it has been achieved
gradually, and even was introduced in imperfect form by historical Christianity--is really independent of particular persons
and events.

Schelling characterizes this intuition of the Infinite in
its finite manifestations as "mysticism." It has existed here
and there, apart from Christianity, but has been brought decisively into the world only in Christianity--so that "mysticism"
(in Schelling's sense) may be considered the distinguishing
feature of this religion:

> All the symbols of Christianity show the quality of
> representing in images the identity of God with the world;
> the direction which is proper to Christianity is the intui-
> tion of God in the finite; this springs from its innermost
> nature and is only possible in it, for the fact that this
> direction was also found individually before and outside of
> Christianity merely proves its universality and necessity
> . . .
> We can give the general name of "Mysticism" to this
> sense for the intuition of the Infinite in the finite . . .[120]

Although this sense is at the heart of Christianity,[121]
the full realization of the new perception of reality could
only develop gradually. The unity and reconciliation of finite
and Infinite was, in the beginning of Christianity, an object
of faith. This faith is to be understood as "the inner certi-
tude which anticipates for itself the Infinite . . ."[122]

---

[120] 3:537-38: "Alle Symbole des Christenthums zeigen die
Bestimmung, die Identität Gottes mit der Welt in Bildern
vorzustellen, die dem Christenthum eigenthümliche Richtung ist
die der Anschauung Gottes im Endlichen, sie entspringt aus dem
Innersten seines Wesens und ist nur in ihm möglich, denn daß
diese Richtung einzeln auch vor und außer dem Christenthum war,
beweist nur seine Allgemeinheit und Nothwendigkeit . . .
"Wir können diesen auf das Anschauen des Unendlichen im
Endlichen gerichteten Sinn allgemein Mysticismus nennen."

[121] 3:537: "Der Keim des Christenthums war das Gefühl
einer Entzweiung der Welt mit Gott, seine Richtung war die
Versöhnung mit Gott . . ."

[122] 3:537: "Glauben ist die innere Gewißheit, die sich die
Unendlichkeit vorausnimmt . . ."

This "faith," however, was destined to move towards a
kind of knowing which he calls "Schauen." The transition was
anticipated by the mystics of all ages, who were often condemned by the official Church precisely "because they changed
faith into 'seeing,' and wanted to pluck prematurely the not-
yet-ripe fruit of time."[123]

Schelling thinks that the time for this transition is now
ripe. Negatively, this is evident in the decay of the "exoteric" forms of Christianity. Positively, the new philosophy
has at last ". . . reached--with the truly speculative view-
point--also, once again, the viewpoint of religion . . ."[124]

Schelling's Notion of Religion

It is noteworthy that Schelling thus identifies the truly
speculative viewpoint of philosophy with that of religion. We
have had occasion to point out earlier in what peculiar sense
the starting point (and abidingly normative viewpoint) of
Schelling's early philosophy is "religious,"[125] and we can now
appropriately conclude our discussion of his thought by considering a bit more closely his notion of religion. For it is
the religious character of his "system" which Drey found so
congenial to theology.[126]

It seems that the essential feature of the new philosophy
which links it so closely to religion is its discovery of the
ultimate oneness of Infinite and finite, of God and world.
This perception is intellectual, a matter of "Schauen" or
"Anschauung"; hence, it rises above the opposition of faith vs.
unbelief. "Mankind has lived long enough in an unworthy and
unsatisfied way--whether in faith or unbelief; it is philosophy
which . . . must, at last, bring mankind into 'seeing'
(Schauen)."[127]

---

[123]3:538: ". . . weil sie den Glauben in ein Schauen
verwandelten und die noch nicht reife Frucht der Zeit zum
voraus brechen wollten."

[124]3:327: ". . . die Philosophie . . . hat mit dem wahrhaft speculativen Standpunkt auch den der Religion wieder
errungen . . ."

[125]Cf. above, pp. 79-80.   [126]Cf. KE § 96, p. 64.

[127]1:722: "Die Philosophie hat . . . die Menschheit, die
lange genug, es sey im Glauben oder im Unglauben, unwürdig und
unbefriedigt gelebt hat, endlich ins Schauen einzuführen."

What philosophy now offers to mankind as a commonly
shared perspective on reality is "the intuition of the absolute
identity in the most complete objective totality . . ."[128]
Schelling envisages this new, shared viewpoint as "the new
religion . . . which is a return to the first mystery of
Christianity and a perfecting of it . . ."[129] He uses traditional religious language to speak of it as "the absolute
gospel" and "the true gospel of the reconciliation of the world
with God."[130]

What he expects is a discovery of the divine in both
nature and history. This intellectual discovery will be the
overcoming of the dualism and "Entzweiung" which has characterized Western thought for centuries. "The first reconciliation
and resolution of the ancient discord must be celebrated in
philosophy . . ."[131]

Schelling expects this new religion to replace the empirical, "exoteric" version of Christianity by uncovering and
explicating the speculative, "esoteric" meaning of its doctrines. He thinks this is the logical fulfillment of the
historical development of Christianity, the appropriate unfolding of its "germ" (Keim).[132]

This new religion may be regarded as the synthesis of the
valid perceptions of both pagan religion and Christianity.
Schelling had attempted to bring out the distinctiveness of the
latter by contrasting it with the former. But the new religion
which is being introduced by philosophy is able to recognize

---

[128]1:723: ". . . die Anschauung der absoluten Identität
in der vollkommensten objektiven Totalität . . ."

[129]3:540: "Die neue Religion . . . welche Zurückführung
auf das erste Mysterium des Christenthums und Vollendung
derselben ist . . ."

[130]3:327; 3:540.

[131]3:540: ". . . die erste Versöhnung und Auflösung des
uralten Zwistes muß in der Philosophie gefeiert werden . . ."

[132]Cf. 3:537.

the Godhead in nature as well as in history. In fact, in his
early enthusiasm for "Naturphilosophie," Schelling considered
this to be the prior locus for the intuition of the Absolute.
"The new religion . . . will be recognized in the rebirth of
nature as symbol of the eternal Oneness . . ."[133]

This sense of nature as symbol of God, to be sure, was
not lacking in Christianity, as he notes: ". . . The highest
religiosity, which expressed itself in Christian mysticism,
regarded the mystery of nature and the mystery of the Incarnation of God as one and the same."[134]

Still, the characteristic form of Christianity's perception of the finite-Infinite relationship was in history, as
already explained. This is the other "side" of the Absolute's
self-objectification, as Schelling's philosophy sees things.
And history appears to be the actual material for theology's
discovery of the Absolute in the finite, as Schelling envisages
the "real" Wissenschaft of theology.

Nevertheless, the full self-manifestation of the Absolute
surely includes nature, as well as history. Hence, theology--
in its effort to know the divine--might logically be expected
to "construct" nature as well as history, even though Schelling
does not speak of this. In any case, the "new religion" is to
intuit the Godhead in nature as well as in history.

Since Schelling links religion so closely to the highest
speculative viewpoint of philosophy, it is not surprising that
his notion of theology is so strongly philosophical. The task
which he assigns to theology is to carry out a properly
religious interpretation of finite reality--in particular, of
history.[135] But this religious interpretation is simultaneously

---

[133]3:540: "Die neue Religion . . . wird in der Wiedergeburt der Natur zum Symbol der ewigen Einheit erkannt . . ."
Cf. 1:723.

[134]3:312: ". . . Die höchste Religiosität, die sich in
dem christlichen Mysticismus ausdrückte, hielt das Geheimniß
der Natur und das der Menschwerdung Gottes für eins und
dasselbe."

[135]Cf. 3:529-30, where he calls the Enlightenment view of
reality "irreligious" precisely because it separates the world
from God and the finite self from the Absolute. His own view
is religious in contrast, since it sees both "nature" and human
intelligence as inseparable from the Absolute, which manifests
itself in these differentiated forms.

philosophical, because it is possible only from the perspective
of the intellectual intuition of the Absolute.

We have already noted the difficulty Schelling has in
adequately distinguishing theology from a philosophy of history.
This is significant, because it follows from his rejection of
the traditional notion of revelation. Theology must not be
directed toward specific persons and events which would be
taken on the empirical level as an authoritative self-
communication of God. Rather, it is the totality of history
which is--taken together--the revelation of the Godhead. This
is why theology can only be a properly absolute knowing of this
totality. But such a knowing is philosophical; or, more precisely, it is a synthesis of historical and philosophical
knowing.

If Schelling wishes to call this kind of knowing "theology," this usage, nevertheless, cannot conceal its essentially
philosophical character. It is theological only insofar as it
is a "religious" interpretation of the finite. But "religion,"
in this period of Schelling's thought, is essentially a matter
of intellectual intuition of the ultimate Oneness of reality.[136]

It is perhaps superfluous to point out how much of
"religion" is missing from Schelling's perspective. One could
characterize his sensibility as a kind of aesthetic monism.
What seems demanded of man in his relationship to the Absolute
is to rise to the higher viewpoint (introduced by Christianity)
which perceives history as the mysterious identity of human
freedom and divine necessity. Although Schelling does speak,
in one text, of "die freiwillige Unterwerfung"[137] of the human
consciousness with respect to the Absolute, this does not seem
to be a matter of obedience or personal submission. It is,
rather, an intellectual event, the acknowledgement, so to speak,

---

[136]There is an instructive parallel with Schleiermacher's
view of religion in the Reden, 1st ed., pp. 50-55 (2d ed.,
pp. 46-52). Religion--though distinct from metaphysical specu-
lation--is the intuition and sense of the "Universe," without
which speculation lacks a touchstone for the truth of its
thinking about the Infinite, "Vom Anschauen muß alles ausgehen
. . ." (1st ed., p. 54).

[137]3:312.

of the ultimate Truth. To this extent, the human mind partici-
pates in the <u>Urwissen</u>, in the ultimate Rationality which is the
"Urstoff" of reality.[138]

There is no room in such "religion" for concepts like
salvation, grace, forgiveness, no point to prayer or desire for
personal union with God. Nor, of course, is there any notion
at all of man being addressed by a Word which demands a personal response of obedience.

We will have to return to Schelling's view of religion
when we try to assess the differences between him and Drey and
to point out the tensions in Drey's use of Schelling's conceptuality.

---

[138]Suppl. 1:442.

CHAPTER V

DREY'S METHOD FOR THEOLOGY

Introduction

The preceding chapter was meant to illuminate the ideal
of "Wissenschaft," as formulated in the early writings of
Schelling. The extent to which this influenced Drey will
become apparent in the present chapter. But we need a somewhat
wider perspective if we are to appreciate properly Drey's distinctive way of doing theology. Hence, we begin this treatment
of his method by recalling briefly the general intellectual
context of his life-work, as this was presented in the earlier
chapters. Following this introduction, the chapter is divided
into three principal parts. Since Drey's method is a synthesis
of the historical and the speculative, the first section deals
with the priority of the historical, while the second treats of
theology as "Wissenschaft." The third section returns to
Schelling, in order to assess the affinities and tensions in
Drey's appropriation of his thought.

As we have seen, the naturalist rejection of revelation
was the most radical challenge to Christian theology at the end
of the eighteenth century. This denial of an authoritative
divine initiative in the history of the human race was closely
related to rationalism, which took human reason as the unique
source and measure of truth. The underlying error of this
dominant intellectual attitude, Drey thought, was to isolate
both nature and reason from God.

Drey's Alternative to the Deist View

Drey's theological enterprise can be seen as an explicit,
systematic effort to work out an alternative to the deist

conception of the God-world relationship. The fundamental
intuition of an unceasing divine presence and activity within
the world was always basic to his thinking.[1] This eventually
found expression in his theory of revelation, which was the
mature product of a life-time of reflection. As we have seen,
this involved an account of the God-world relationship in terms
of God's unceasing creative activity, so that the human condition is understood to be constituted by the ever-present divine
influence, creating and revealing. The world as a whole
(including man) is thus conceived as utterly subject to God's
creative will, in an eternal relationship to the Creator. This
is a view of God and world in a unity, called by Drey the Reich
Gottes.[2]

His reason for insisting on this alternative vision of
reality is to make thinkable and credible precisely what deistic naturalism denied: God's eternal and unceasing influence
upon human beings in the realities and events of this world,
that is, in history. For it is history to which Drey's attention as a theologian is primarily directed. He seeks to interpret mankind's religious development as the outcome of God's
revelatory influence upon the spirit of man. This "education
of the human race" is to be regarded as a unified, consistent,
divinely guided process which reaches its culmination and
center in Christianity.

Divine Positivity

What is, therefore, of decisive importance for Drey's
approach to theology is the "divine positivity" of Christianity.
He uses the word "positive" to mean, first of all, what is

---

[1]Geiselmann calls this his "anti-deist" attitude, and
notes the influence of this on Drey's great student, Möhler
(Lebendiger Glaube aus geheiligter Überlieferung, p. 148).

[2]The initial account of this in KE §§ 1-11, pp. 1-7,
shows strong traces of both Schleiermacher's theory of religion
and the Idealist conception of the finite-Infinite relationship,
whereas the account in Apologetik, Vol. 1, is dominated by the
concept of creation. But there is a continuity in thought, and
a consistency in conceiving the harmonious unity of all created
things in relation to God as center.

historically given[3] (in contrast to what is universally knowable to human reason reflecting on the essential nature of man
and the world). In this sense, Christianity--like other world
religions--is "positive" (in contrast to the so-called "natural
religion" of reason). But Drey wishes to affirm more than this.
As he uses the word "positive," it comes to be a catchword for
the authoritative, divine character of Christianity. It is not
merely historically given, as a matter of fact. It is divinely
given as the work of God's creative activity, as revelation.[4]

Moreover, this divinely given Christianity is not limited,
in Drey's view, to certain events of origin, but includes the
entire subsequent development of the Church which is still continuing.[5] This is an historical perspective which is, at the
same time, profoundly theological. It involves a "higher viewpoint" on history,[6] and the conviction that all events and
developments are guided by the hidden, yet ever-active God.[7]
It is in this form that Drey's anti-deist attitude is present
from the beginning,[8] long before the carefully worked-out

_____

[3]Apol I, "Einleitung" § 3, p. 3: "Als eine positive und
historische Religion ist das Christenthum zunächst nur historisch erkennbar. Ehe es von Gott gegeben und in die
Weltgeschichte eingeführt war, wußte Niemand, auch kein
Philosoph von demselben . . ."

[4]Ibid.: ". . . von Gott gegeben . . ." Cf. KE § 34,
pp. 20-21: ". . . sie [die Ideen des Christentums] sind in
einem noch strengern Sinne positiv, indem der Ursprung dieser
Ideen als Folge einer besondern Veranstaltung, als Folge eines
unmittelbaren Eingreifens Gottes in den religiösen
Entwickelungsgang dargestellt . . . ist."

[5]Cf. "Vom Geist und Wesen des Katholizismus," ThQ 1
(1819), in GdChr, pp. 193-234.

[6]Cf. "Revision des gegenwärtigen Zustandes der Theologie"
in Schupp, Revision von Kirche und Theologie, p. 21: ". . . die
Geschichte als das Werk einer ewigen Nothwendigkeit, die der
religiöse Mensch Vorsehung nennt . . ."

[7]Cf. "Ideen zur Geschichte des katholischen Dogmensystems," GdChr, p. 248: ". . . alle Geschichte [entwickelt sich]
an den Menschen und zunächst durch ihre Thätigkeit . . . die
frei und daher zufällig gedacht werden muß. Dies ist die
Hülle, hinter der sich der handelnde Gott versteckt."

[8]Cf. "Ideen zur Geschichte des katholischen Dogmensys-
tems," GdChr, pp. 244-46, 248. Cf. also KE § 175, p. 118, and
"Revision des gegenwärtigen Zustandes der Theologie," in
Schupp, Revision von Kirche, p. 15.

account of the God-world relationship in Vol. 1 of the
Apologetik.

Drey's method for systematic theology follows from this
basic conviction of the "divine positivity of Christianity."
Because Christianity is historically "given," the theologian
must direct his attention primarily to history. Moreover,
because Christianity is divinely "given," there is an authoritative character to this history. Hence, the theologian does
not begin by speculating, but rather receives from God's
authoritative revelatory initiative what he is to understand.

The Intelligibility of
the Divinely Given

At the same time, precisely because this historical
reality is "given" by God, there is something to be understood.
There is intelligibility in the historically given insofar as
it is the work of divine Mind. Theology, therefore, must ultimately be directed to this intelligibility of a divinely given
history.

Putting the matter this way certainly shows the influence
of German Idealism on Drey's theological method, but one should
not overestimate this influence. It is tempting to regard Drey
mainly as an example of how Idealism found its echo in Catholic
theology of this period. The influence of Schelling, of course,
is manifest--nowhere more than in Drey's ideal of "Theologie
als Wissenschaft." In his speculative bent, Drey undoubtedly
appropriates the language and conceptuality of his contemporary
philosophical culture. Nevertheless, it would be a facile
simplification of Drey's rich and complex thought to categorize
him simply as an Idealist theologian. He is strongly oriented
to the concrete history of religion, and especially to the
Christian tradition. Moreover, he has an explicitly theological reason for taking history as primary for his method in
theology: the anti-deist conception of God as revelatory Agent
in the entire process of mankind's religious development.

An accurate and balanced exposition of Drey's methodology
must, therefore, show how he evaluated historical theology, as
well as how he envisioned a "wissenschaftliche Construktion" of
the historically given. The bulk of this chapter, therefore,
will be devoted to these two large topics.

The Priority of the Historical

History as Primary for
Christian Theology

There are two senses in which history is primary for
Christian theology. The most basic consideration is the
"divine positivity" of revelation. The object of theology's
intellectual endeavor is historically given by divine initiative, as a great "fact." Hence, the primary mode of coming to
know what God has revealed must be the empirical-historical.
Drey lays down as the first principle for the method of
theology:

> . . . the entirety of Christianity--according to its
> history and its doctrine--as something positive and given
> can be known initially only in an empirical-historical way;
> and the historical knowledge (Kenntniß) of it must abso-
> lutely precede the scientific knowledge (Erkenntniß) of it;
> the former is the material basis of the latter.[9]

There is, however, also another sense in which Christian
theology has to do with history. What God reveals, in the
positively given "fact" of Christianity, is precisely His
purposes for the development of all mankind. Indeed, His
revelation itself must be viewed as a great historical process
which began long before Christianity, so that the latter is
recognized to be in an intrinsic relationship to the entire
preceding religious development of both Israel and the
"nations."[10]

Taught by the historically given revelation, therefore,
theology is to attempt a religious interpretation of universal
history in terms of the master idea of God's revelation, the
sum total of all His purposes: "Reich Gottes."[11] It is in this

---

[9] KE § 64, p. 40: ". . . das gesammte Christentum--nach
Geschichte und Lehre--als etwas Positives und Gegebenes kann
zunächst nur empirisch-historisch erkannt werden, und die historische Kenntniß von ihm muß der wissenschaftlichen Erkenntniß
schlechterdings vorangehen, jene ist die materielle Grundlage
von dieser."

[10] Cf. KE § 61, p. 39. This is the perspective from which
Drey surveys the great world religions in Vol. 2 of the
Apologetik.

[11] KE § 61, p. 38: "Die christliche Theologie . . . umfaßt
also nicht bloß den geschichtlichen Zeitraum, der in der
Profangeschichte mit dem Namen des Christentums bezeichnet ist,

sense, also, that theology has to do with history. Because God
is active in the history of mankind, shaping and guiding its
development towards the realization of His Kingdom, the theologian who is instructed by revelation must interpret this historical reality.

Thus, Christian theology is thoroughly oriented towards
history: (1) as the locus of its divinely given object (revelation, which makes God's purposes known), and (2) as the
divinely wrought realization of these purposes.

This view of theology and history is founded on Drey's
conception of the God-world relationship. Because God is conceived as the ever-active creative Agent in all of history, it
is possible both to consider the specific "history of revelation" as His work and to expect that this special history will
provide the key to the interpretation of universal history.

> . . . the history of revelation . . . is organized and
> guided by the same eternal Spirit as is ordinary history;
> indeed, it is the archetype and the explanation as well as
> the transfiguration of this ordinary history . . .[12]

One can sense, here, something of the scope of Drey's
universalist perspective. His stress on history does not
spring merely from a concept of theology as the ordering and
systematizing of the beliefs of a particular religion (in this
case, Christianity). Rather, he envisions revelation as a
divine initiative which includes and guides universal history.
Hence, Christianity itself must be understood in this widest
possible context--in relation to all cultures and religions.

At the same time, Drey expects that the more limited
history of Christianity will be an explicit manifestation of
God's universal purposes for the human race. Hence, the theologian is to direct his attention primarily to the historically
given phenomenon of Christianity.

---

sondern die ganze Weltgeschichte vom Anfange an, und diese
Geschichte deutet sie für die Wissenschaft der Religion unter
Leitung der darüber in der Lehre Christi und der Apostel ausge-
sprochenen Ansichten."

[12]Apologetik I § 29, p. 244: ". . . der Geschichte der
Offenbarung . . . , welche von demselben ewigen Geiste wie die
gemeine organisirt und geleitet, ja das Urbild, und die
Erklärung wie die Verklärung von dieser ist."

The "Objective Phenomenon" of Church as Ongoing Development of the Divinely Given Fact

What Drey means by Christianity is not limited to a set of beliefs, nor is it limited to certain events of origin, nor to the writings which witness to those events. Rather, he conceives Christianity as a social, historical reality--as Church, which persists and grows through the centuries in continuity with its beginning. He regards development as natural and inevitable, since the divinely given "fact" must spread to all places and cultures. The original revelation thus perpetuates itself as Church.[13]

Drey affirmed this as a "Catholic" understanding of Christianity, in opposition to the classicizing, historical search for "Urchristentum" as the only pure form of Christianity. He was aware of change, but regarded it as development in unbroken continuity with the divinely caused beginning.

This view of Church is based on Drey's concept of revelation. Far from being limited to certain past events, God's creative, revelatory activity extends throughout the course of human history--shaping and guiding it. The Church, in continuity with its origin, is the gradual making-real of God's master idea: "the kingdom of God."[14] Since all of history is guided by divine providence, a fortiori the Church is guided in its development by the Holy Spirit.

Drey's valuation of history for the method of theology is clearly governed by this general perspective on revelation. Since he regards the entire development of the Church's existence as ruled and guided by the divine Spirit, he is able to attribute a divine authority to the specific development of the Church's system of dogmas.

The Development of Dogma as the Making-Explicit of God's "Ideas"

He gave precise expression to his basic methodological option in his lectures on "the history of the Catholic system

---

[13]Cf. "Vom Geist und Wesen des Katholizismus," ThQ 1 (1819), GdChr, pp. 195-234.

[14]Cf. KE § 71, p. 45.

of dogmas" (1812-13).[15] There, he observes that a truly systematic treatment of the history of dogma is possible only if there
is really a system in these dogmas (as the Catholic Church
affirms). But there is a further question: is this system to
be regarded as merely the work of human reason through the
centuries, or as the work of divine reason? Drey opts for the
latter alternative. While acknowledging fully the complicated
and ambiguous character of the human agency in the development
of dogma, Drey affirms the higher agency of the divine Spirit,
who brings about--through all this--a true system of divine
truths. He thinks that God's own ideas or decrees for the
education of the human race are gradually made explicit and
knowable in the church's system of dogmas.

> . . . I have become convinced that God has an eternal plan
> of education which runs through the entire history of the
> human race . . . and that in Christianity, insofar as it is
> speculative and contains dogmatic doctrines, this plan of
> education is revealed in a speculative way, for reason,
> and the entirety of dogmatic Christianity is nothing other
> than the eternal ideas of God on the education of the
> human race.[16]

He thinks that God thus makes known to man's mind those
divine ideas which He is making real in the history of mankind
and, especially, in the history of the Church. This distinction between the "ideal" and the "real" is familiar from

---

[15]Manuscript No. Gf 1081 in the library of the Wilhelmsstift in Tübingen, entitled "Geschichte des katholischen
Dogmensystems. I. Band. Geschichte der drei ersten Jahrhunderte
oder erste Periode. Mit Benutzung von Münschers Handbuch
dargestellt von Dr. J. S. Drey Pr. 1812-1813." This MS is
printed in its entirety under the title "Ideen zur Geschichte
des katholischen Dogmensystems" in GdChr, pp. 235-331. References are to this source. These lectures were given in
Ellwangen, where Drey taught for five years, before the Catholic theological faculty there was transferred to Tübingen in
1817.

[16]GdChr, pp. 244-45: ". . . einmal habe ich mir die Über-
zeugung zu eigen gemacht, daß sich durch die ganze Geschichte
des Menschengeschlechtes ein ewiger Erziehungsplan Gottes
hinzieht, . . . daß im Christentum, inwiefern es spekulativ ist
und dogmatische Lehren enthält, dieser Erziehungsplan auf
spekulative Weise und für die Vernunft geoffenbart ist, und das
ganze dogmatische Christentum aber nichts anderes als die
ewigen Ideen Gottes über die Erziehung des Menschengeschlechtes
ist."

Schelling's thought.[17]

> Christianity in general--and thereby also the dogmatics
> of Christianity as its innermost spirit--is revelation of
> the eternal decrees of God concerning our race; this
> revelation is such that it not only presents to us these
> decrees as they are in the intellect of God, but also as
> they reached fulfillment in time and with respect to our
> race. . . . . . . The history of the Christian system of
> dogmas is nothing other than the history of the development
> of those decrees for men's knowing capacity; parallel to
> this development of the ideas, there is an equivalent
> development in the real history of Christianity . . .[18]

What Drey articulates in these texts is really his reason
for taking history seriously, as the basis of theology. Since
it is the divine Spirit who rules and guides all history--and
especially the history of Christianity--the theologian must
look to history to find out the divine ideas or decrees for the
human race. Moreover, since these ideas become gradually more
explicit and are organized into a system through the development of the Church's dogmas, the theologian must attend not
only to the beginning of Christianity (Scripture) but also to
its entire subsequent development (Church history).

The First Task of Theology:
Attention to the Divinely
Guided History of Christianity

It is from this theological vision that Drey lays out the
separate tasks of theology. He groups "Bibelstudium" and
"historische Theologie" together, under the general heading of

---

[17]It is noteworthy, however, that Drey tends to speak
more of God's "decrees" (Ratschlüsse) than of "ideas." We will
have occasion to comment on this later.

[18]GdChr, pp. 250-51: "Das Christentum überhaupt und somit
die Dogmatik des Christentums als der innerste Geist desselben,
ist Offenbarung der ewigen Ratschlüsse Gottes über unser
Geschlecht, eine solche Offenbarung, welche uns nicht nur diese
Ratschlüsse Gottes, wie sie in dem Verstande Gottes sind,
sondern auch wie sie in der Zeit und an unserem Geschlechte in
Erfüllung gingen, darstellt. . . . Die Geschichte des christlichen Dogmensystems [ist] nichts anderes als die Geschichte
der Entwickelung jener Ratschlüsse für das Erkenntnisvermögen
der Menschen, welcher Entwickelung der Ideen auch eine gleiche
in der wirklichen christlichen Geschichte parallel laüft . . ."

"Historische Propädeutik."[19] The distinction between the two
is founded on the distinction between Christianity's "point of
origin and original form" and its "further continuance and
development."[20] But what both disciplines have in common is
their historical method and their object: viz., the one,
unbroken history of Christianity, as it unfolds and grows from
its origin. Drey notes, in this regard:

> One sees that, in spite of this division for the sake
> of historical reflection, the primitive history and the
> further development of Christianity are, after all, one
> history, just as Christianity is only one, even for common
> sense. For the knowledge of Christianity, therefore, its
> further development is just as important and necessary an
> object as its primitive history. --This is the Catholic
> view of historical theology.[21]

Drey's theological principle of the divine guidance of
Christianity's development does not make him indifferent to the
empirical shape of Christianity's actual history. On the contrary, it provides the motive for the most exacting possible
critical study of this complicated history.[22]

---

[19] KE §§ 107-220, pp. 73-149.

[20] KE § 174, p. 117: "In wie fern in der geschichtlichen
Betrachtung des Christentums der Zeitpunct seiner Entstehung
und ursprünglichen Gestalt sich unterscheiden läßt von dem
Zeitraum seiner weitern Fortdauer und Entwickelung, in so fern
unterscheidet sich auch das Bibelstudium von dem, was man
sonst historische Theologie genannt hat."

[21] KE § 174, pp. 117-18: "Man sieht, daß ungeachtet
dieser Trennung zum Behufe der historischen Reflexion die
Urgeschichte und der weitere Verlauf des Christentums doch nur
Eine Geschichte sind, wie auch das Christentum nur Eines ist
selbst für den gemeinen Sinn. Für die Kenntniß des Christentums ist daher sein weiterer Verlauf ein eben so wichtiger und
nothwendiger Gegenstand wie seine Urgeschichte. --Dieß ist die
katholische Ansicht von der historischen Theologie."

[22] Drey's interest in historical questions is evident in
his Journals, where he shows a critical sense in judging questions of history and exegesis. His earliest published works
were concerned with historical questions: "Observata quaedam
ad illustrandam Justini martyris de regno millenario sententiam" (Gamundiae: Typis Joann. Georg. Ritter, 1814) and "Dissertatio historico-theologica originem ac vicissitudines exomologeseos in ecclesia catholica ex documentis ecclesiasticis
illustrans" (Ellwangen: Typis Joann. Georg. Ritter, 1815).
The former is a very short (8 pp.) but careful and perceptive
interpretation of the Greek texts of Justin. The latter draws

Writing in 1819, Drey delineated the various tasks of
Scripture study with a remarkably modern awareness of the
critical-historical method.[23] What he saw as the fruit of such
study, however, is consonant with his general view of Christianity as the work of the divine Spirit. Since this Spirit is
bringing about a "system" of divine Ideas for the instruction
of mankind in His purposes, one must look for at least the
basis or "germ" of this system in Scripture.

> The compilation of the teaching of Christ and his
> apostles forms "biblical theology" for the Christian. The
> main thing in this part of bible study is the correct
> understanding of these doctrines individually, and the
> penetration into their spirit as a whole. Both are neces-
> sary, in order to reach an exact knowledge of the Christian
> religion as an objectively given system [altered in the
> margin to "whole"] of Ideas. And the biblical-historical
> knowledge of this system is the condition and basis for the
> scientific treatment and presentation of it. . . . Biblical
> theology must, therefore, be regarded as the basis of the
> entire science.[24]

Although Drey thus attributes a foundational significance
to Scripture, he does not think that theology is based solely

---

upon texts of Tertullian, Origen, and Cyprian to establish the
origins and development of the Church's discipline of penance.
Drey also published a lengthy study of the "Apostolic Constitu-
tions" in ThQ 11 (1829):397-477, 609-723, which was later
published as a book: Neue Untersuchungen über die Constitutiones
und Kanones der Apostel: Ein historisch. kritischer Beitrag zur
Literatur der Kirchengeschichte u. des Kirchenrechts (Tübingen:
Laupp, 1832). Hefele, the Church historian, praised this work
lavishly in his obituary for Drey. Cf. ThQ 35 (1853):347.

[23]KE §§ 107-73, pp. 73-117.

[24]KE § 115, p. 78: "Die Zusammenstellung der Lehre Christi
und seiner Apostel bildet die biblische Theologie für den
Christen. Die Hauptsache in diesem Theile des Bibelstudiums
ist das richtige Verständniß dieser Lehren im Einzelnen, das
Eindringen in ihren Geist im Ganzen. Beydes ist nothwendig, um
von der christlichen Religion als einem objectiv gegebenen
System [Ganzen] von Ideen eine genaue Kenntniß zu erlangen; und
die biblisch-historische Kenntniß dieses Systems ist die
Bedingung und Grundlage der wissenschaftlichen Verarbeitung und
Darstellung desselben . . . Die biblische Theologie muß also
als die Grundlage der gesammten Wissenschaft betrachtet werden."
Drey notes, as an "Anmerkung" to this paragraph, that a study
of the doctrinal content of the Old Testament is also essential
to the understanding of Christ's teaching in the New Testament.

on Scripture. For the reality of Christianity as God's work in
history continues to grow and unfold from the events of origin
which Scripture reflects. Drey saw this distinction as the
fundamental difference between Catholic and Protestant theology:

> If Scripture alone is taken as the medium for the
> handing-on of the ideas of religious faith, then [histor-
> ical] "construction" is the interpretation of Scripture,
> and all of theology is exegesis. But if (along with
> Scripture . . .) there exists and is generally recognized
> a living, objective phenomenon as continuation of the
> original fact, as its truest handing-on, then the historical
> demonstration takes place with respect to it. Such a
> phenomenon is the Church.[25]

The entire history of the Church (not merely the first
stage, represented by Scripture) becomes theologically significant for Drey, because he views this history as guided and
ruled by the same Spirit who initiated it.[26]

There are two aspects to this history: the "outer history,"
which is made up of Christianity's impact upon the world, its
interaction with non-Christian institutions and forces; and the
"inner history," which is the authentic self-expression of what

---

[25]KE § 47, p. 29: "Wird als Überlieferungsmittel der
Ideen des religiösen Glaubens bloße Schrift angenommen, so ist
die Construction Schrift-Auslegung, die ganze Theologie Exegese.
Besteht aber (neben der Schrift . . .) und wird allegemein
anerkannt eine lebendige objective Erscheinung als Fortsetzung
der ursprünglichen Thatsache, als ihre eigentlichste Überlieferung, so geschieht die historische Nachweisung an ihr und
durch sie. Eine solche Erscheinung ist die Kirche."

[26]He speaks of this process in romantic language, invok-
ing both the "higher concept of history" and the Christian
faith in the guidance of the Holy Spirit, to account for the
phenomenon of Christianity (KE § 175, p. 118): "In Beziehung
auf die Grundansicht aller hieher gehörigen Erscheinungen
nöthigt schon der höhere Begriff der Geschichte sie als das
Streben und Weben eines einigen Princips, eines Geistes anzusehen, der unter den Geistern der Zeit hervorbricht, sich seine
eigene zu gestalten, der aus sich herauswirkend alles in seinen
Kreis zieht, das Bildsame nach sich bildend, das Widerstrebende
zerstörend. Alle grossen Erscheinungen der Geschichte müssen
so betrachtet werden. Noch mehr aber hat das Christentum diese
Ansicht von sich selbst aufgestellt, indem es den Geist, aus
welchem es seine Entwickelungen alle ableitet, genau und
buchstäblich bezeichnet . . . Jede geschichtliche Auffassung
und Darstellung der Erscheinungen des Christentums aus einem
andern Princip als aus dem bezeichneten widerspricht dem
Christentum, ist unchristlich und untheologisch."

is distinctive in Christianity--both in doctrine and in practice.[27] Both these aspects are relevant to historical theology,
for it is one and the same Spirit who is discernible in both.
And Christianity's impact upon human institutions, as well as
its own internal life and discipline are intimately related to
its doctrines, or "ideas."

Doctrinal Development

What is of primary importance to the systematic Theologian, however, is the doctrinal development of Christianity.
Scripture represents, in a sense, the earliest stage of the one,
divinely guided formation of a coherent system of dogmas. The
later stages, however, are equally relevant to the empirical-
historical task of attending to the divinely given revelation.

Hence, Drey includes the history of dogma ("Geschichte
des Lehrbegriffs") as a prominent part of the "historische
Propädeutik." Moreover, his "higher viewpoint" on this history[28] does not make him blind to the human factors involved.
He demands a careful account of the "external influences and
stimuli" in the development of the Christian ideas.[29] Foremost
among these are: (1) sacred Scripture insofar as it was something external to the "living tradition" of the Church. Bible
study has modified the Christian "Lehrbegriff." (2) The ideas
of the various cultures through which Christianity has lived.
The stimulus of philosophical and "scientific" ideas has led to
developments of Christian dogma.[30] To take account of the
external influences on the development of dogma leads inescapably to a dialectical view of this development.

-----

[27]KE §§ 176-79, pp. 118-21.

[28]Cf. "Ideen zur Geschichte des katholischen Dogmensystems," GdChr, pp. 241-47.

[29]KE § 191, p. 129.

[30]Drey does not see such influence as leading necessarily
to a "corruption" of Christian doctrine. Not only is such
influence historically inevitable. The main thing is "ob jene
philosophische Ideen im Geiste des Christenthums sind, und mit
ihm harmonisiren. Nur wenn sie es nicht sind, kann Corruption
entstehen." And he concludes his observation by pointing
toward his own ideal of theology: "Die Ausbildung der Christlichen Lehren zu Ideen überhaupt, ist nicht Corruption, sondern
eben die Aufgabe der Wissenschaft" (KE § 192, Anmerkung,
pp. 130-31).

The expression "external influence" is used in contrast
to a postulated "inner regularity in the development."[31]   In
the "Ideen zur Geschichte des katholischen Dogmensystems," Drey
had used the romantic metaphor of organic growth from a seed or
germ, in order to affirm the intelligible unity of the system
of dogmas.[32]

On the other hand, the actual history of doctrinal development cannot readily be viewed as such a smooth, organic process. There has been conflict and division. Interpretations
of the faith maintained by individuals and groups have been
rejected by official decisions of Church councils.

Drey takes account of this historical reality by viewing
the "heresies" as false developments that were recognized as
such and rejected by the Spirit guiding the Church's organic
development. Nevertheless, all these developments--whether
they are to be judged "true" or "false"--belong to the history
of dogma.[33]

Evaluation and Judgment of Doctrinal Developments

Drey is aware that a dialectical ordering and judging of
these historical developments is essential to the theological
enterprise, as a whole. But the "sifting out" of true from
false developments is not the historian's task. The historian
has only to recover and document the actual developments from
the relevant sources. It is for the dogmatic theologian to
evaluate and judge the historically given facts.[34]

---

[31]KE § 191, p. 129.

[32]GdChr, pp. 239-40: "eine Entwicklung aus einem Kern und
Keim . . ."

[33]KE § 193, p. 131. Geiselmann comments on Drey's notion
of the "necessity" of heretical oppositions in the divinely-
guided development of the Church's system of dogmas, and sees
Hegel's influence in this dialectical understanding of the
development. Drey's pupils, Kuhn and Staudenmaier, were to
work further along these lines. Cf. Geiselmann, "Die Glaubenswissenschaft der katholischen Tübinger Schule," ThQ 111 (1930):
101-3.

[34]KE § 193, Anmerkung, p. 131.

It seems that there are two distinct ways of going about this evaluative task. And even though this is to anticipate the treatment of "wissenschaftliche Theologie," it seems worthwhile to identify and distinguish these, in the present context.

The first way might be called "extrinsic," insofar as it relies on an historical criterion. In many cases, there has been a formal "judicium ecclesiae," which has set the limits for what may or may not be affirmed about some point of doctrine. In the "Praemonita" to the third version of his Dogmatics lectures, Drey demands such an explicit official judgment of the Church as a condition for calling a doctrine "dogma."[35]

From this point of view, history itself provides the evidence for evaluating at least some doctrinal developments as "true" or "authentic" or "guided by the Spirit." And, even though it is not the business of the historian to make such value judgments, he does provide the dogmatic theologian with the reliable, documented evidence of "judicia ecclesiae" which enable the latter to determine the authentic, divinely-guided doctrinal development.

It seems evident in Drey's "Ideen zur Geschichte des katholischen Dogmensystems" that he relies on the Church's judgment to provide him with an ordered _system_ of dogmas, which he is willing to regard as the work of the divine Spirit.

He takes a somewhat different approach to the problem of judging doctrinal development in KE §§ 249-51, pp. 166-68. It is not that he denies his fundamental principle of divine agency in this development.[36] But he looks, rather, to an "intrinsic" criterion for authentic development. Supposing that the "master Idea" of Christianity has been identified in the scientific "Grundlegung" of theology (Apologetics), the scientific dogmatic theologian must examine all the empirically given doctrines of Christianity's long history, to see how well they express the essential ideas which are involved in the one highest idea.[37]

---

[35]PD III 4-6.

[36]In KE § 190, p. 128, he affirms this in language very similar to the "Ideen" MS.

[37]KE § 250, p. 167.

In this testing of the individual, historically given
concepts with respect to the Idea (or the Ideas) of Christianity, it cannot fail that some things are found to be
historically true which do not correspond to the Christian
Idea to which they are supposed to correspond. Such a
concept appears, therefore, as a malformation in the development of Christianity, it must be identified as an error
or blunder, and expelled from the system.[38]

What results, positively, from such a testing of the historically given doctrines is the discovery of "the inner--not
historical--truth of the entire Christian system . . ."[39] This
"inner truth" is the business of theology as "Wissenschaft," to
which we are about to turn our attention.

There is, however, a danger in this second way of judging
doctrinal development, which Drey does not comment on, but
which the logic of his entire method suggests. The kind of
testing of the historically given which he speaks about here
seems very close to a philosophical critique of received
Christian doctrines. Only that is to be affirmed as authentic
Christian doctrine which can be perceived to be in accord with
some philosophically determined Idea of the essence of Christianity.

It is, however, quite clear that he did not wish to adopt
this last position. In the 1819 ThQ article already cited, he
rejects as "gnosis" all versions of Christianity which are
primarily speculative, and which either reject altogether the
historical or value it only as "Andeutung der Ideen."[40] The
priority of the "positive" and historical is basic to Drey's
method in theology.

What must be taken into account here is Drey's conviction
that the "master Idea" of Christianity--congenial as it is to
human reason--does not arise out of philosophical speculation,

---

[38]KE § 251, pp. 167-68: "Bey jener Prüfung der einzelnen
historischgegebenen Begriffe an der Idee (oder den Ideen) des
Christentums kann es dann nicht fehlen, daß manches historisch
Wahre gefunden werden muß, was der christlichen Idee nicht entspricht, der es entsprechen soll. Ein solches erscheint
alsdann als Mißbildung in der Entwickelung des Christentums, es
muß als Irtum oder Fehlgriff ausgezeichnet, und aus dem Systeme
ausgestossen werden.

[39]KE § 250, p. 167: ". . . die innere--nicht historische
--Wahrheit des ganzen christlichen Systems . . ."

[40]GdChr, p. 201.

but is itself historically _given_ as the central content of
revelation. Hence, the authenticity of doctrinal developments
is actually to be judged in terms of their consistency and
coherence with this divinely given Idea. Only in this way can
their intrinsic relationship to the entire divinely-guided
system of dogmas be perceived.

Having distinguished these two ways of judging doctrinal
development, we can now suggest how they might be correlated.
The material basis for making any such judgments must, of
course, be provided by the historian. The judging, however,
belongs to the province of dogmatic theology. Judging according to the "extrinsic" criterion of the _judicium ecclesiae_
provides a system of dogmas resting on the authority of the
Church. Drey would take this as the normatively given material
for the work of speculative theology. This might be called the
"positive part of dogmatics."[41] But this does not yet provide
an adequate understanding of the intrinsic intelligibility and
coherence of the system of dogmas. This can only be achieved
by looking at the dialectical development of dogma in relation
to the central Idea of Christianity (the Kingdom of God). This
is the "speculative part of dogmatics."[42]

The speculative viewpoint does provide an insight into
the intrinsic consistency and coherence of the Church's system
of dogmas, such that false developments of the past can be
recognized as such. But it does not seem that Drey attributed
to this "wissenschaftliche" Dogmatics the first and only dis-
crimination of true from false developments of dogma. For it
is clear that he took as normative the Catholic Church's system
of dogmas, which he viewed as the work of the Holy Spirit. And
this is the matter of "positive" Dogmatics--the historically
given, which has yet to be grasped speculatively.

Hence, we might say that the full intellectual appropriation of the divinely given system of dogmas can only be achieved
by examining the entire dialectical process of this system's
development (including all its "oppositions" and inauthentic
formations), in relation to the master Idea of _Reich Gottes_.
For only such a study of the historical material can eliminate

_____

[41]Geiselmann in _ThQ_ 111 (1930):107.   [42]Ibid.

the impression of the accidental and arbitrary, and can discover the intrinsic necessity of the actual judicia ecclesiae
which rejected false developments and gradually established the
Church's system of dogmas.

We acknowledged above that this entire discussion of how
to judge the development of dogma would lead us beyond historical theology into the domain of "scientific" theology. This
points up the "dynamic" of Drey's method. Since he regards the
historical as the work of divine Mind, there is a drive towards
the speculative grasp of the historically given. And, even
though he distinguishes clearly between the various tasks of
theology, it is finally impossible for him to judge the historical properly without reaching to the viewpoint of the "Ideas."

The Importance of Historical Theology

In assessing the place of historical theology in Drey's
method, we may say that it is primary and, at the same time,
only preliminary. It is primary, because it discovers and
orders the divinely given facts and doctrines which are to be
understood. It is only preliminary, because its mode of knowing is the empirical-historical. Once the empirical reality of
Christianity has been attained historically, there is a further
task which is properly philosophical.

In the "Praemonita" to the third version of his Dogmatics,
Drey distinguishes three functions of reason in theology: the
"historical," the "logical," and the "philosophical." So far,
we have been considering the first two of these, whose task is
the recovery and orderly presentation of the historically given.
More specifically--for the purposes of dogmatic theology--their
work is to establish reliably the historically given body of
Christian doctrines (which Drey often calls the "Lehrbegriff").

This kind of theological activity may be called "historical construction." We have shown why it is primary for Christian theology, and have noted that Drey meant for it to be done
in a rigorous, critical-historical fashion. The fruit of this
labor is to be a systematic presentation of the entirety of
Christian doctrines, documented carefully from their sources
(Scripture and the later writings of the Church's development),
and explicated in such a way that they are seen to form a
logically inter-related whole.

This "historical construction" of Christian doctrines is
the primary and indispensable task of the theologian. Because
of the rigor demanded both in the critical-historical work and
in the logical systematizing, Drey is willing to call this
"scientific, in a sense."[43]

The _properly_ scientific task of theology, of course, is
the "more important but also more difficult 'inner construction.'"[44] This is the third function of reason in theology:
the "philosophical." Drey values this most highly, and the
whole thrust of his method--as we have noted--is toward this.
But before turning our attention to this "Theologie als Wissenschaft," it is important to assess fairly the value of the
merely historical treatment of Christianity, as Drey saw it.

Historical Theology as
Primary for Christian Life

First of all, the historical is _normative_ for Christian
faith and theology because of the divine authority of a revelation which is "positively," historically given.[45] There is no
other access to the divinely given truth except the empirical-
historical way, and "Christian theology is--both in its beginning and in its basis--likewise positive and historical (a
positive _Wissenschaft_) . . ."[46]

Moreover, the very nature of Christianity is so insepar-
ably bound to historical persons and events that it _ought_ to be
viewed primarily as a history rather than as a system of ideas.
He observes in his Journal:

> Christianity has announced itself not as a speculative
> system, but rather as part of the great Kingdom of God, as
> a part of the historical Providence and its plan, as the
> fulfillment of the ages, even as a necessary age. The

---

[43]KE § 310, p. 208: ". . . in einem Sinne wissenschaftlich . . ."

[44]KE § 312, p. 209: "Wichtiger ist allerdings, aber auch
schwieriger, die innere Construction."

[45]Cf. _Apol_ I, "Einleitung" § 1, p. 1.

[46]_Apol_ I, "Einleitung" § 3, p. 3: ". . . die christliche
Theologie ist, ihrem Gegenstand entsprechend, in ihrem Anfang
und in ihrer Grundlage ebenfalls positiv und historisch (eine
positive Wissenschaft) . . ."

speculative idea which it has, it did not link to reason
as an abstraction, but rather to persons, actions and
consequently to purely historical objects, and especially
made this idea dependent on one person; hence, even though
--for speculative treatment--the ideas can again, in part,
be separated from the history, for instruction of the
people and in a practical context, they can never be
separated from it.[47]

Hence, the historical form of Christianity's doctrines is
the ordinary way in which most people can and should assimilate
the divinely given revelation. On the one hand, a philosophical insight into the intrinsic truth and necessity of the
Christian ideas is possible only for a relatively few minds.[48]
On the other hand, the merely historical knowledge and appropriation of Christianity is sufficient for the practical purpose of revelation: to affect the attitudes and behavior of
human beings in relation to God.[49]

Drey, therefore, for all his emphasis on "philosophical
construction," carefully limits this to the academic setting,
thus relativizing the role of speculative theology for Church
life in general.[50] He observes, too, that Jesus himself did
not develop a speculative system, precisely "because of the
universality of his mission, which was for the world. What is

---

[47]Tagebucher II, 134-35, in GdChr, pp. 127-28: "Das
Christentum selbst hat sich nicht als ein spekulatives System,
sondern als Teil des grossen Gottesreiches, als ein Teil der
historischen Providenz und ihres Planes, als Erfüllung der
Zeiten, selbst als notwendige Zeit angekündet. Es hat seine
spekulative Idee, die es hat, nicht an die Vernunft als ein
Abstraktum, sondern an Personen, Handlungen und folglich an
lauter historische Gegenstände angeknüpft, und namentlich von
Einer Person abhängig gemacht, so daß, wenn für die spekulative
Behandlung die Ideen wieder davon zum Teil abgetrennt werden,
sie im Volksunterricht und in praktischer Beziehung nie davon
getrennt werden können." Cf. also KE § 50, p. 31: "Indessen
verbreitete sich und wurzelte der christlich-religiöse Glaube
in der Form, in der das Christentum selbst gegeben wurde, das
heißt in der Form einer Geschichte."

[48]KE § 309, p. 208.

[49]Apol I, "Einleitung" § 3, pp. 3-4.

[50]ThQ 1 (1819):237. "Wann werden es doch die Theologen
begreifen, daß alle das Construiren des Christenthums durch was
immer für ein philosophisches System nur für die Schule, und
für die Theologen selbst nur insoferne sey, als sie der Schule
angehören . . . ?"

received in the School does not penetrate the world."[51]

Historical Theology as Preliminary
to "Scientific" Theology

It remains, nevertheless, true that historical theology
is only preliminary in the whole enterprise of Dogmatics. To
see why this is so--and to become oriented towards the task of
"wissenschaftliche Theologie"--we need to consider, finally,
the limitation of a merely historical view of Christianity and
its doctrines, as Drey saw it.

This limitation can best be appreciated by noticing the
ambiguity of the word "positive," so often used by Drey to
characterize Christianity. In one sense, the word refers to
that which is "posited" or constituted through particular
events in history. It may thus be contrasted with the "natural":
i.e., that which is everywhere and always the case.[52] Used in
this sense, "positive" seems to be linked with "accidental"
(zufällig): what "happens to be the case." The opposite of
"accidental," of course, is "necessary" (nothwendig). Drey
remarks: "It is one and the same opposition: that of the accidental and the necessary, and that of the positive and the
natural . . ."[53]

On the other hand, Drey uses the word "positive" to
affirm the divine origin and authority of Christianity. In
this sense, the word refers to God's creative activity, which
"posits" the events of revelation. And, since God does not act
accidentally or arbitrarily,[54] to call Christianity "positive"
in this sense is to affirm that it is not accidental, i.e., not
merely the result of human initiatives or fortuitous historical
forces, but indeed necessary insofar as caused by God's own
action.[55]

---

[51]GdChr, p. 264: ". . . wegen der Universalität seiner
Sendung, die für die Welt war. Was in der Schule empfangen
ist, durchdringt die Welt nicht."

[52]KE § 315, p. 211.

[53]KE § 315, p. 212: "Denn es ist ein und derselbe Gegensatz, der des Zufälligen und Nothwendigen, und jener des Positiven und Natürlichen . . ."

[54]Apologetik I § 12, p. 148.

[55]Apologetik I, "Einleitung" § 2, p. 2.

The limitation of a merely historical account of Christianity, therefore, is its inability to show the intelligible
necessity of what has, as a matter of fact, happened. For,
even though this historical phenomenon be attributed to God's
action, it still has the appearance of the accidental. To move
beyond this kind of knowledge of Christianity demands a higher
intellectual process. The goal is

> . . . to snatch the given Christianity away from the form
> of "accidentality" in which it appears (like everything
> which is "given," in the ordinary way of looking at history),
> and to raise it, as a whole, to a viewpoint from which it
> is grasped as a necessary phenomenon.[56]

He is careful to point out that he is not referring to a
deterministic kind of "historical construction," which would
simply explain Christianity as necessary in terms of "preceding
or co-existing phenomena." He is asking, rather, for a "truly
scientific" viewpoint, and a "construction" of Christianity
"from pure Ideas."[57]

"Theologie als Wissenschaft"

The Ideal of "Scientific Knowing"

What Drey is demanding--above and beyond the merely
historical account of Christianity--can only be explained in
terms of his ideal of scientific knowing. He requires that
theology be done in a way that corresponds to the generally
recognized norms for a true "Wissenschaft."

> . . . we hold that the notion which our age has more
> correctly and carefully defined for every kind of science
> is also valid for theology. If, indeed, theology wishes

---

[56]KE § 312, p. 209: ". . . daß man das gegebene Christentum der Form der Zufälligkeit, in der es wie alles Gegebene in
der gemeinen Geschichtsanschauung erscheint, zu entreissen, und
es im Ganzen auf einen Standpunct der Betrachtung zu erheben
weiß, auf welchem es als eine nothwendige Erscheinung begriffen
wird."

[57]KE § 312, pp. 209-10: ". . . eine wahrhaft wissenschaftliche Betrachtungsweise . . . . . . die Construktion des
Christentums nicht etwa . . . aus den ihm vorhergegangenen oder
coexistirenden Erscheinungen, . . . sie muß aus reinen Ideen
geschehen."

to be considered worthy of the dignity and name of science,
it must conform to common principles.[58]

Drey's ideal of "Wissenschaft" is derived from contemporary German philosophy, as he explicitly acknowledges.[59] But he
does not identify himself formally with any one system.[60] He
takes for granted that there is a commonly accepted standard
for scientific knowing,[61] and proceeds to specify just how this
notion of Wissenschaft is to be verified in the case of theology.

Our purpose, therefore, is simply to show what is distinctive about Drey's own ideal of scientific knowing in theology,
without attempting to relate it to the entire context of contemporary German philosophy. Nevertheless, the points of contact
with Schelling's thought will become apparent, and the earlier,
detailed presentation of the early Schelling's point of view
will provide a helpful background

Discovering the "Necessity" of the Given

The best place to begin is with the contrast noted above
between "accidental" (zufällig) and "necessary" (nothwendig).
The distinctive characteristic of rigorously scientific knowing
is the insight into the necessity of what, at first, seemed
merely factual. Hence, what is demanded of the beginning

---

[58]PD III 42: ". . . statuimus, eam notionem, quam de omni
scientiarum genere aetas nostra rectius ac curatius definivit,
in theologiam quoque valere, atque hanc ipsam ad principia
communia conformari debere, siquidem scientiae honore et
nomine digna haberi velit."

[59]In KE § 308, p. 207, he refers to philosophy as the
norm for what is to be considered "wissenschaftlich": ". . .
was zu dieser [der wissenschaftlichen Methode] im allgemeinen
gehört, das bestimmt die Philosophie, in so fern sie formale
Wissenschaftslehre ist." Cf. also KE § 94, p. 63, where he
expects the student of theology to derive from philosophy the
very concept of "Wissenschaft," as well as the concept of his
own discipline as a "Wissenschaft" in relation to the others.

[60]Cf. Apologetik I, Vorrede, pp. xi-xii.

[61]Cf. KE § 56, p. 34: "Der Geist unserer Zeit ist ein
streng wissenschaftlicher . . ." And in PD III 17 he refers
to the demands of the "praesens scientiarum conditio."

practitioner of any <u>Wissenschaft</u> is to learn "to grasp what is accidentally given, as something necessary."[62]

In the opening pages of the <u>Apologetik</u>, Drey gave clear expression to this ideal of scientific knowing which had been prominent in all his writings, from the beginning:

> . . . the law of knowing in general . . . is this: only that is truly known which—no matter how it may originally be given or found—is recognized from within itself as true and necessary. From this law it follows that if something historically given, or the cognizance of what is thus given, is to be raised to a knowing, in addition to this given there must be found the principles from which it is grasped as something necessary and, therefore, in itself true.[63]

What he means by these "principles" in the case of theology will become apparent, as we examine closely just how the move from historical theology to scientific theology is to be made.

We should recall that history is primary for Drey because of his concept of revelation. He views universal history as the work of divine providence, guided infallibly by the never-ceasing divine creative activity, so as to achieve God's purposes for the human race. The particular history of revelation is viewed as God's education of mankind to recognize His

---

[62]KE § 315, pp. 211-12: ". . . das zufällig Gegebene als ein Nothwendiges zu begreifen."

[63]<u>Apologetik</u> I, "Einleitung" § 4, pp. 4-5: ". . . das Gesetz des <u>Wissens</u> überhaupt . . . ist, daß nur dasjenige wahrhaft gewußt wird, was, wie es auch ursprünglich gegeben oder gefunden seyn mag, aus ihm selbst heraus als wahr und nothwendig erkannt wird. Aus diesem Gesetz folgt, daß wenn ein historisch Gegebenes, oder die Kenntniß des so Gegebenen zu einem Wissen erhoben werden soll, zu diesem Gegebenen die Prinzipien gefunden werden müssen, aus welchen es als ein Nothwendiges und darum in sich Wahres begriffen wird." Cf. PD III 37: ". . . cum nihil verae exactaeque scientiae rationem habere possit, nisi quod vel necessario esse vel necessario cogitari certis rationis principiis intelligatur, sive si cum scholis hodiernis loquamur, quod <u>ideae</u> alicuius <u>necessariae</u> rationem habeat; ad has ideas rerum certas et immutabiles revocare notiones omnes, atque tali ratione scientiam perfecte construere oportebit." Menke thinks that the <u>Apologetik</u> text just cited shows Drey's adherence to Kant's concept of <u>Wissenschaft</u>. Cf. Menke, "Der Begriff 'Dogma' im Werke J. S. Dreys," <u>Theologie und Philosophie</u> 52 (1977):209.

purposes and to conform freely to them. This history is made
up of "facts": persons and events, the social reality of Church,
etc. It also includes ideas and doctrines, which develop gradually within this history.

Recognizing the Divine
"Ideas" in History

It is crucial to appreciate that Drey considers this
history--both the "facts" and the "ideas" (the "real" and the
"ideal")--not only to be "worked" by God as Agent, but also to
be the consequence of divine Mind. What God has done and is
doing (i.e., history) is according to His own Ideas, His
"decrees" (which are the "eternal acts of the divine intellect
and will"[64]).

These divine Ideas are, so to speak, "within" history, in
the sense that history is wrought by God to be the realization
of them. But the divine Ideas are not immediately apparent to
the human mind, as it views history. They can only be discovered from a "higher viewpoint," which is both religious and
speculative.[65]

Historical theology, as we have seen, presents the "given"
reality of Christianity. This, which can only be known empirically and historically, is the "material basis" for scientific
theology. The further step in theological method, therefore,
is to rise to the higher viewpoint from which the divine Ideas
ruling this history can be recognized and taken as the "principles" for a truly "scientific construction" of the empirically
given.

The Unifying Idea of the "Kingdom
of God" as Historically Revealed

Drey thinks that the master Idea, from which such a construction can be attempted, has been historically revealed by
God as the central content of Jesus' preaching. It is the idea

---

[64]Apologetik I § 29, p. 242: ". . . die ewigen Akte des
göttlichen Verstandes und Willens . . ."

[65]Drey's higher viewpoint on history is manifestly parallel to Schelling's. Cf. Chapter IV, pp. 96-97. The difference
between the two has to do with Drey's theistic, creationist
understanding of God. See below, pp. 168-70, 173-74.

of "the Kingdom of God."[66] He sees a gradual development and
clarification of this idea in the experience of Israel. In its
earlier stages, the idea was formulated in terms of a Jewish
theocracy, and even its later widening to take in the gentile
nations was still bound up with earthly and political expecta-
tions (the messianic hope).[67] The full purification of the
idea came only with Christ. "He refined that material idea of
an earthly kingdom of God and world-state to the purity and
universality of a Kingdom of Heaven, a moral Kingdom in the
universe."[68]

This transfigured idea became a way of viewing all of
history as the gradual realization of the harmonious relationship of all men to God (the stages of God's education of the
human race). It became a unifying idea by which all of history
could be viewed as the work of divine providence, climaxing and
centering in Jesus:

> This, therefore, is the Idea of the Kingdom of God, in
> Christ's sense: the decrees of God concerning mankind and
> the world, to be thought of as eternal in His Spirit,
> revealed and making themselves real in the sacred history,
> but only gradually, and hence still hidden from the mind
> of men, until the fullness of time--and, with it, Christ--
> appeared, who now clarified those decrees, expressed them
> in particular concepts, and linked them to his own
> history.[69]

----

[66]The term Reich Gottes is used by Drey with various
nuances of meaning in different contexts. See Chapter VI for a
full treatment of these related meanings.

[67]KE § 58, pp. 36-37.

[68]KE § 59, p. 37: "Er läuterte jene sinnliche Idee von
einem irdischen Reiche Gottes und Weltbürgertum zu jener Reinheit und Allgemeinheit eines Himmelreiches, eines moralischen
Reiches im Universum."

[69]KE § 59, p. 37: "Dieß also ist die Idee vom Reiche
Gottes im Sinne Christi: Die Ratschlüsse Gottes über die
Menschen und die Welt, von Ewigkeit zu denken in seinem Geiste,
geoffenbart und sich verwirklichend in der heiligen Geschichte,
aber nur allmählig und daher noch verborgen vor dem Sinne der
Menschen, bis die Fülle der Zeit und mit ihr Christus erschien,
der nun jene Ratschlüsse aufklärte, sie in bestimmten Begriffen
aussprach, und diese wieder an seine eigene Geschichte
knüpfte."

It is worth stressing that Drey considers this Idea of
the Kingdom of God to be divinely, historically _given_ to the
human mind. Looking at the "positive" reality of Christianity
(which springs from Jesus and his teaching), Drey judges that
the Idea of the Kingdom of God is manifestly the central concept
of Christianity and, indeed, the "highest" concept, under which
all other doctrines and concepts can be ordered.[70]

"Kingdom of God" as an Idea
Proper to Human Reason

Hence, the key to a properly scientific construction of
Christianity has been given to man by divine revelation.
Nevertheless, although divinely given, the Idea of the Kingdom
of God is simultaneously an idea proper to human reason. Its
validity and truth can be grasped by the human mind.[71] Hence,
to the extent that all particular facts and doctrines of
Christianity can be viewed in their intrinsic relationship to
this great Idea, one is able to achieve a true "knowing" of the
entire historically given reality of Christianity.

The following text sums up this perspective so well that
it deserves to be quoted in full:

> . . . the empirical-historical knowledge [Kenntniß] of
> Christianity is raised to a proper science [Wissenschaft]
> when its content is brought back to an Idea and is pre-
> sented from this Idea in appropriate deduction. We have
> designated this Idea in §§ 58-61. It has, indeed, first
> been given and made known through Christianity itself; but
> it is grounded in reason, a true Idea of reason, which--
> like all other Ideas--was first awakened to a free emer-
> gence by the extrinsic, inciting ray of educative revel-
> ation. Because of the absolute necessity and truth which
> this Idea of the Kingdom of God has for reason, the same
> character of necessity and truth is achieved by all the
> appearances of this Kingdom in the history of mankind, and
> by all the doctrines of Christianity, which uncover and
> explain the mysteries (the plan and organization of the
> Kingdom) in this same history. Just as Christ himself
> evidently re-cast the entire history of the former time
> into Ideas (and his apostles did the same), so also
> scientific theology re-casts the history of Christ himself

---

[70]KE § 60, p. 38. Cf. PD III 46.

[71]More will be said about this below.

into pure Ideas, and so binds together both the former and the latter history into a whole.[72]

This text expresses Drey's peculiar way of seeking the synthesis of the historical and the speculative in theology. What he is trying to understand, of course, is historically given in the facts and ideas of Christianity. But, because this historical reality is the work of divine Mind, it all has a systematic, necessary relationship to God's own master Idea. This highest Idea--once made known to mankind--has a compelling validity for the human mind. Hence, the goal of theology as Wissenschaft must be to "deduce" all the actual events and historically shaped doctrines of Christianity from this one great Idea, by seeing how everything must develop as it does, in order to be the realization or the expression of this one Idea of God. The intelligible necessity which the master Idea has for the mind will then be seen to extend to all the concrete details of this Idea's realization.

The theologian's attention, therefore, is directed to a this-worldly reality, visible in historical events. (Theology is a "positive Wissenschaft.")[73] What he ambitions is a grasp

---

[72]KE § 65, p. 41: ". . . zur eigentlichen Wissenschaft erhebt sich die empirisch-historische Kenntniß des Christenthums, wenn sein Inhalt auf eine Idee zurückgebracht, und aus dieser in gehöriger Deduction des Einzelnen dargestellt wird. Diese Idee haben wir §§.58-61 bezeichnet. Sie ist zwar durch das Christentum selbst erst gegeben und bekannt gemacht worden; sie ist aber in der Vernunft gegründet, eine wahre Vernunftidee, die wie alle andern erst durch den von außen anregenden Strahl der erziehenden Offenbarung zum freyen Hervortreten in der Vernunft geweckt wurde. Durch die absolute Nothwendigkeit und Wahrheit, die die Idee eines Reiches Gottes vor der Vernunft hat, erlangen auch alle Erscheinungen desselben in der Geschichte der Menschheit, alle Lehren des Christenthums, welche die Geheimnisse (der Plan und die Organisation des Reiches) in derselben Geschichte aufdecken und erklären, den gleichen Charakter von Nothwendigkeit und Wahrheit. Wie Christus selbst die ganze Geschichte der Vorzeit offenbar in Ideen umgewandelt hat, und seine Apostel dasselbe thaten, so wandelt die wissenschaftliche Theologie hinwieder die Geschichte Christi selbst in lauter Ideen um, und verbindet diese und jene zu einem Ganzen."

[73]Cf. Apologetik I, "Einleitung" § 3, p. 3, cited above. Cf. Schelling's conception of theology as a "real Wissenschaft," Chapter IV, pp. 100ff.

of this phenomenon from the perspective of the divinely given
Idea which actually rules it. But the reality comes first.
And even the very idea of the "Kingdom of God" is given through
an historical development, and continues to be clarified and
perfected through the development of doctrine and theology.[74]
Hence, attentiveness to the given is the first principle of
theology, as of all other knowing.[75]

Discovering the "Necessity" of the Given by Perceiving the "Idea"

The distinguishing feature of "scientific knowing," however, is the discovery of "necessity" in the material which is
being considered. How is it that the theologian can find this
"necessity" in the empirical shape of history?

For Drey (as for Schelling), the human mind can only
discover necessity by perceiving the Idea which is manifested
in a particular object of knowledge; or, turning it around the
other way, by perceiving the object in its Idea.[76] Drey
remarks: ". . . to perceive a thing in Idea is to perceive that
which is eternally simple and of one kind and of such a quality
as it is."[77]

Now, what the scientific theologian is attempting to
grasp "in the Idea" is the entire sequence of events and

---

[74]The doctrines of Christianity are the "ideal" expression of God's decrees, and these decrees find their highest
unity in the Kingdom-of-God Idea. Cf. GdChr, p. 245: ". . .
das ganze dogmatische Christentum [ist] nichts anderes als die
ewigen Ideen Gottes über die Erziehung des Menschengeschlechtes
. . ."; and GdChr, p. 251: ". . . die Geschichte des christlichen Dogmensystems [ist] nichts anderes als die Geschichte
der Entwickelung jener Ratschlüsse [Gottes] für das
Erkenntnisvermögen der Menschen . . ."

[75]Apologetik I § 35, p. 306.

[76]Cf. Chapter IV, pp. 88-91. Geiselmann comments on
Drey's similarity to Schelling, with regard to the intellectual
intuition of Ideas, in "Die Glaubenswissenschaft," ThQ 111
(1930):105: "Wie kommt . . . Vernunft zu dieser Idee [des
Reiches Gottes]? Drey geht hier ganz mit Schellings ästheti-
schem Idealismus, wenn er der Vernunft das Vermögen unmittelbarer Anschauung der Ideen und zwar an dem empirisch Gegebenen
zuschreibt."

[77]PD III 43: ". . . id enim est rem cernere in idea, cum
cernitur id, quod semper est simplex et uniusmodi et tale,
quale est."

doctrinal formulations which historical theology presents him
with. The Idea which is discoverable in all this is, as a
matter of fact, divinely revealed. But it cannot function in
the process of "scientific knowing" unless it is able to be
appropriated by the human mind as its own Idea. Only if this
is so, can there be the requisite "necessity."

What is at stake here is really the intelligibility of
divine revelation. If the master Idea ruling God's guidance of
history--which God has made known to mankind as the central
content of His educative revelation--can be appropriated by the
human mind and recognized as an eternally valid idea, then a
truly scientific knowing of the divinely guided history is
possible. Then, a "scientific construction" of Christianity's
doctrines is possible, so that their intrinsic truth and intelligible necessity are apparent. Obviously, Drey thinks that
this is the case. "We maintain that this notion [Kingdom of
God] is such as to be received and reverenced by human reason
as its own idea."[78]

To appreciate fully Drey's reasons for making this judgment, one would have to examine the content of the Kingdom-of-
God idea, as he unfolds it. But to do this would far exceed
the limits of the present discussion, since the Kingdom-of-God
Idea embraces in a unity the entire plan of God for mankind.

> This kingdom and rule . . . is the very governance of
> this world and of all things, under God's direction, and
> the unified cooperation of all things with one another and
> with God and His divine decrees towards a definite end, in
> spite of all appearances to the contrary.[79]

Thus, the Kingdom-of-God idea is equivalent to the notion
of divine providence.[80] Hence, one can and must distinguish

---

[78]PD III 57: "Porro hanc ipsam notionem talem esse
contendimus, ut eam ratio humana ad instar ideae propriae
suscipere et revereri debeat."

[79]PD III 46-47: "Est enim illud regnum et regimen . . .
ipsa mundi hujus rerumque omnium moderante Deo gubernatio,
atque cum inter se tum cum Deo divinisque consiliis, haud
obstante contraria specie, ad certum finem conspiratio."

[80]Ibid.: ". . . regnum divinum ipsa est providentiae idea
ad captum hominum expressa."

between the formal aspect of this idea and its material content. The latter embraces the entire pattern of events which God decrees and guides. To examine this in detail and to show how it is all intelligibly related to God's highest purpose for mankind is precisely the work of systematic, "scientific" theology.[81]

The focus of the present discussion is necessarily limited to the formal aspect of the Kingdom-of-God idea. What Drey says about his treatment of the topic "providence" is applicable to our present treatment of "Kingdom of God":

> . . . here we will be speaking only in general, and we are to consider more that God rules this world, rather than how or by what decrees, since the work of all of exoteric theology is devoted to the detailed explication of the decrees of divine providence.[82]

It is this formal aspect of the Kingdom-of-God idea which is congenial to the human mind. The full content is present to God's mind alone in its totality, and what we can see or experience is only a partial manifestation of this divine Idea. Nevertheless, what imperfect sense of the divine decrees we have leads us naturally to believe in a divine order or providence. And it is this natural inclination of the human mind which makes the revealed idea of Kingdom of God so apt that it can be recognized and appropriated as human reason's own idea.

> The Kingdom of God--true and entire and such as it really is--is eternal, it is placed in the divine mind and decrees by which He rules this entire world. Of these decrees we have some sense and understanding, either from the very order of this world or from our own mind. Hence, we believe naturally that there is a providence and a

----

[81]Cf. PD I 103-4ff. Chapter VI will be devoted to Drey's way of organizing the themes of dogmatic theology from the perspective of this master Idea of divine providence (the "Kingdom of God")--a perspective which is simultaneously historical and philosophical.

[82]PD I 109: ". . . in genere tantum noster hic loci sermo versabitur, magisque quod Deus, quam quomodo, quibusve consiliis hunc mundum regat, expendendum erit, quoniam explicandis fuse divinae providentiae consiliis universae theologiae exotericae labor est dedicatus." (By the phrase "exoteric theology" Drey appears to be referring to the treatment of the "economy" of salvation, in contrast to the treatment of God in Himself.)

divine law. And this is the reason why this notion of the
Kingdom of God can be said to be intrinsic to us or an idea
of human reason.[83]

Drey does not wish to deny the divine givenness of the
Idea.[84] So, perhaps what he is saying could be formulated in
this way: it is an intrinsic possibility for the human mind to
conceive the world and its development as ruled by God's
decrees. Moreover, there is an inclination to see things this
way. Hence, when the Idea of the Kingdom of God is presented
in its explicitness and clarity by divine revelation, the human
mind is able to recognize its truth and validity, since it
corresponds so well to the mind's expectation.[85]

The Notion of "Necessity"

More needs to be said, at this point, about the kind of
"necessity" which can be discovered by referring all things to
this master Idea. Light is thrown on Drey's notion of necessity by a text referred to earlier. In KE § 315, he says that
the beginner in Wissenschaft must understand properly the
opposition between the "positive" and the "natural," or rather
must see that this is only an apparent opposition. As we noted
in the earlier reference to this text, "positive" is linked
with "accidental" and "natural" with "necessary." The quest,
therefore, for the necessity of what is positively given, must
lead to the discovery of how this given is related to man's
essential nature.

---

[83]PD III 58: "Verum et integrum et tale quale est, regnum
Dei aeternum est, in mente consiliisque positum, quibus omnem
hunc mundum regit; quorum vel ex ipso hujus mundi ordine vel ex
mente nostra sensum aliquem et intelligentiam habemus, unde et
providentiam omnium rerum legemque divinam esse naturaliter
credimus. Atque haec est causa, ob quam notio illa regni
divini nobis insita sive rationis humanae idea dici potest."

[84]Cf. Drey's Tagebücher V 54-55. Commenting there on a
contemporary Catholic theologian's effort to utilize the Kingdom
-of-God idea, Drey insists that this idea is not already present
in human reason, but is given to it by revelation: ". . . es ist
unrichtig gesprochen, daß sich das Reich Gottes in uns vorfinde,
daß es in uns sey, usw. Die idee eines Reiches Gottes ist uns
und unserer Vernunft, wenigstens in der Reinheit, Umfassung und
Genauigkeit zuerst durch Christus, also von außen in göttlicher
Offenbarung gegeben worden."

[85]Cf. Apol I § 35, p. 298 and p. 300. See above, p. 66.

> . . . the positivity of the positive in religion can only
> be related to its origin and its given-ness; but the neces-
> sity of the positive can only be related to the nature of
> man and his natural relationship to God.[86]

From this point of view, necessity is perceived whenever
some phenomenon or fact of history is seen to be intrinsically
related to man's universal nature and condition.[87]

The idealist perspective on the "nature of man" is
clearly expressed in another context, where Drey refers to
Schleiermacher's notion of "Ethics" as "the general Wissenschaft
of the principles, according to which the necessary Ideas in
the nature of man take shape in history and form societies and
mores . . ."[88] The "necessity" of the natural is thus conceived in terms of the eternally necessary Ideas being manifested or realized. This point of view is familiar from
Schelling.

For Drey, however, man's essential nature is inconceivable apart from the relationship to God which is grounded in
the mystery of creation. This is why he mentions, as the
correlative of "necessity," not only "the nature of man" but
also "his natural relationship to God." The discovery of
intelligible necessity in the events and doctrines of revelation, therefore, consists in seeing how these things are
intrinsically related to man's needs as creature of God. Whatever reveals and makes explicit this relatedness to God, and

---

[86]KE § 315, p. 212: ". . . indem die Positivität des
Positiven in der Religion sich eben nur auf seinen Ursprung und
sein Gegebenseyn, die Nothwendigkeit desselben aber sich auf
die Natur des Menschen und sein natürliches Verhältniß zu Gott
beziehen kann."

[87]Ruf points out that the German word Notwendigkeit has
the root meaning of "turning aside a need." "Notwendig ist,
was eine Not wenden, also einem Bedürfnis entspricht . . ."
Hence, he interprets the Idealist notion of "necessity" as a
relative necessity which consists in the correspondence of the
thing in question to some need, purpose, or ideal. In this
sense, notwendig may be equated with sinnvoll ("meaningful,"
"intelligible"). Cf. Ruf, J. S. von Dreys System der Theologie,
p. 58.

[88]KE § 383, p. 251: ". . . die allgemeine Wissenschaft
der Prinzipien, wie sich nothwendige in der Natur des Menschen
liegende Ideen in der Geschichte gestalten, Gesellschaften und
Sitten bilden . . ."

whatever is seen to be required for the development and/or restoration of this relationship, can be grasped as "necessary."

The highest idea, which takes in the entire historical process of God's action upon man for the sake of his education and development, is "the Kingdom of God." To "construct" history from the perspective of this Idea is to grasp the appropriateness of actual historical developments to the intelligible nature of man in relationship to God. In such a "scientific construction" of the given, the mind rises above the apparent opposition of the "positive" and the "natural," and is able to see how God's "positive" arrangements (the divinely guided history of revelation) actually correspond to man's "nature" and its requirements. Hence, all semblance of accidentality in the positive is removed, and the necessity requisite to strictly scientific knowing is achieved.[89]

Two Views of the Economy of Salvation: Historical and "Scientific"

Because the decrees of God for the development of mankind (the divine Ideas, unified as the Idea of "Kingdom of God") are only gradually realized through the process of history, it is possible to regard God's plan of salvation in two different ways.[90] That is, if one takes the religious view of history as the work of divine providence, it is possible to regard it primarily as a story or drama, with its periods and turning-points. This biblical viewpoint is the most natural way of looking at it, and is well suited to "the popular mind." This is the _fact_ of providence, viewed as a divinely ruled history. On the other hand, the "economy" of the Kingdom of God may be regarded

> as it was arranged from eternity in the mind of God, enclosed in the decrees by which He determined and ordained

---

[89]For an example of such a "scientific construction," cf. Apol I §§ 8-9, pp. 127-33, where Drey establishes the "scientific concept of revelation." See above, pp. 51-56.

[90]PD III 64-65.

that the world should exist and how it should exist both in
the order of its destinies and in their outcome.[91]

This way of regarding the "economy" perceives the intelligibility of providence. To use Idealist terminology, it would be
the "ideal" aspect of providence, in contrast to the "real"
(the story or drama of historical events).

The historical perspective discovers what Drey calls the
"phainomenē oeconomia." This is the viewpoint of historical
theology. The other perspective discovers what he calls the
"nooumenē oeconomia." This is the viewpoint of scientific
theology.

> And this indeed is the method of considering [the
> economy of the Kingdom of God] which is proper to theology:
> not merely because it should avoid the common error of
> supposing that God must make his decrees in temporal
> sequence, in the manner of men, but rather, because the
> method of history is different from the method of science.
> The former consists in searching out and connecting facts
> and phenomena; the latter seeks out not the immediate and
> apparent causes of these facts but rather their true and
> ultimate causes--in their very Ideas. And to philosophize
> in theology is really this: to rise from that which
> presents itself to us in the appearance of facts, to the
> nooumena, i.e., to the divine decrees, in which are con-
> tained the ultimate causes of things and their true forms
> or Ideas.[92]

What comes through unmistakably in Drey's conception of
this "highest task of the theologian" is the Idealist conviction that reality is the consequence of Mind. The reality in
question is the given shape of history, especially the sacred

---

[91]PD III 65: ". . . prouti ab aeterno fuit in mente Dei
disposita, ipsis nimirum consiliis inclusa, quibus ut mundus
esset, et qualis cum in fatorum suorum ordine tum in horum
exitu sit futurus, decrevit Deus et sanxit . . ."

[92]PD III 65: "Et haec quidem considerandi ratio theologiae propria est, non tantum quia vitare debet vulgarem
errorem, quasi Deus ad instar hominum consilia sua ex tempore
capiat; sed quia alia est historiae ratio alia scientiae. Illa
enim in investigandis connectendisque factis et phaenomenis
versatur; haec omnium factorum causas non proximas tantum et
adparentes sed veras et ultimas in ipsis nimirum ideis anquirit.
Et hoc quidem est philosophari in theologia, cum ab iis, quae
factorum specie se nobis offerunt, ad nooumena adscenditur, ad
consilia nimirum divina, quibus ipsae rerum causae ultimae et
verae demum species sive ideae continentur."

history of revelation. "But these phenomena originate not from
blind chance, but rather from supreme Mind."[93] The intelligibility of the phenomena, therefore, is to be sought from the
perspective of the divine Ideas which govern this history.

> These things occur in their own time, but they are
> determined beforehand; and they are ruled not by human
> purposes but by divine ones; and they are not fully under-
> stood from the form in which they appear, but must be
> explained from those eternal purposes. Hence, the contem-
> plation of those phenomena must turn from the senses to the
> mind, from history to the secret and true meaning of
> things.[94]

Since Drey views history as God's work, and considers Him
to be the Agent hidden behind the seemingly random and arbitrary activities of men, what he is seeking is to recognize the
divine Mind which rules the divine activity. This quest of
scientific theology for the rationality of the historically
given is postulated in terms of the Idealist notion of Wissenschaft, and Drey admits that many people think it impossible to
carry this out in the case of "revealed truths." But he judges
that such a quest for intelligibility is actually enjoined by
this very divine revelation, since the central content of what
God reveals is His own great Idea: the Kingdom of God.[95] In
this sense, God Himself provides the human mind with the
pattern of intelligibility according to which the divinely
ruled events of history are to be grasped as necessary.

Looking at the doctrines of Christianity, which are the
primary concern of the dogmatic theologian, Drey thinks that

---

[93]PD III 47: ". . . verum ea ipsa phaenomena non caeca
forte sed summa mente prognata . . ."

[94]Ibid.: ". . . temporibus quidem suis accidunt, ante
tamen sunt definita; neque consiliis humanis sed divinis regun-
tur; neque et specie sua, qua videntur, plene intelliguntur,
sed ex sempiternis istis consiliis explicari debent; unde illo-
rum contemplatio a sensibus ad mentem, ab historia ad arcanum
verumque rerum sensum convertitur.

[95]PD III 37: "Quae constructio, licet, ut in veritatibus
revelatis, impossibilis videatur multis, re tamen vera non
solum possibilem judicamus, sed sacris literis quodammodo prae-
ceptam; quandoquidem omnes notiones christianas, manadata etiam,
imo facta ipsa et historias ad supremam aliquam, regni nimirum
divini sive coelestis notionem referre jubemur; haec autem
notio, siqua alia, certissimam ideae rationem habet." Drey
also defends the possibility of "scientific construction" of
the divinely given revelation in KE § 56, p. 34.

they may be regarded as the articulation of the divine intelligibility of history. Although given authoritatively by revelation ("positive"), these doctrines can nevertheless be understood in their intrinsic intelligibility as eternally valid
truths.[96] And, as such, they provide a systematic view of the
intelligible necessity of the actual historical shape of divine
providence.

> . . . the innate force and significance of the revealed
> doctrines is to be searched out. For those doctrines, if
> you consider their source, are first given to us by the
> divine author and are drawn from without by education. But,
> if you consider their nature, they are, at the same time,
> eternal truths which explain the intelligible relationships
> of things human and divine, which place before our eyes the
> forms and arrangements of a truer and changeless world,
> which open up the secrets of the divine mind, which explain
> the laws and successions of the ages in which those secrets
> are unfolded, which--finally--explain, as though on a map,
> the ways and trajectories of the entire divine providence
> which weaves together this whole progression of visible
> things.[97]

The Legitimacy of Speculative Theology

Drey is quite clear that such a handling of Christian
doctrines requires a philosophical mind, and is aware of the
danger inherent in such a philosophical formulation of Christian truth. Nevertheless, he considers this speculative form
of theologizing to be both legitimate and necessary. What is
crucial is the relationship of the speculative to the historical.

> There is a purely philosophical treatment of Dogmatics
> --for those who desire it and can understand it--but it

---

[96]Such an understanding of Christian doctrines is possible, to be sure, only for a mind which has the habitus of
"Wissenschaft," and can grasp the "necessity" of these doctrines by referring them to the "nature of man and man's
natural relationship to God."

[97]PD III 42-43: ". . . innata doctrinarum revelatarum vis
et significatio indaganda est. Sunt enim doctrinae istae, si
originem spectes, ab auctore divino primum nobis traditae et
extrinsecus hauriuntur institutione; at simul sunt, si naturam
spectes, veritates aeternae, quibus rerum divinarum humanarum-
que rationes explicantur, mundi verioris et immutabilis species
habitusque ponuntur ob oculos, divinae mentis aracana panduntur,
temporum, quibus illa evolvuntur leges et successiones, totius
denique providentiae, omnem hanc rerum apparentium seriem
texentis, modi et circuli veluti in charta explicantur."

presupposes an exact historical knowledge; it must not
supplant this historical knowledge, but can only be joined
to it.[98]

The consequence of a one-sidedly speculative method in
theology is the loss of Christianity's specific content.

> Conceived in a one-sided way, [the purely philosophical
> treatment of Dogmatics] can easily take a direction opposed
> to positive Christianity and positive, historical theology,
> and place itself in contradiction to historical Christian-
> ity . . . It thus becomes a formalism.[99]

It is interesting that Drey--for all his emphasis on
Wissenschaft--saw clearly the deficiency of an excessively
formal philosophical re-casting of Christianity. Looking at
the history of theology, he distinguished two different ways of
doing theology in the philosophical mode.

It is possible, he observes, to transform philosophy into
Christianity, ". . . if the entire religious, Christian view of
reality is made the basis of the true philosophy, and the doc-
trines of Christianity are handled formally as philosophy."[100]
This is characteristic, he thought, of "the Fathers, and of
Scholastics, old and new."[101]

On the other hand, it is possible to transform Christianity into philosophy, ". . . if the metaphysics of some philosophical system is taken as the basis, and its doctrines are
presented as the dogmas of Christianity."[102] As examples of

----

[98]PD III 42, marginal notation: "Es giebt eine rein
philosophische Behandlung der D. -- für solche die sie wünschen
und verstehen können--aber sie setzt die genaue historische
Kenntnis voraus, darf also diese nicht verdrängen, kann sich
nur an die anschließen."

[99]PD III 43, marginal notation: "Einseitig aufgefaßt kann
sie leicht eine Richtung gegen das positive Christentum u. die
positive historische Theologie nehmen, und sich in Widerspruch
mit dem hist. Christentum setzen . . . So wird es ein Formal-
ismus."

[100]PD III 44, marginal notation: ". . . wenn die ganze
christlich religiöse Weltanschauung als die wahre Philosophie
zu Grund gelegt, und die Lehren des Christenthums der Form nach
als Phil. behandelt werden."

[101]Ibid.: "Patres und Scholastiker alte u. neue."

[102]Ibid.: ". . . wenn die Metaphysik irgend eines philosophischen Systems zu Grunde gelegt, u. die Lehren desselben
als Dogmen des Christenthums dargestellt werden."

this method, he cites Zimmer, Schleiermacher, Daub, and
Marheineke, and characterizes the results thus:

> Christianity as the doctrine of the Absolute and its
> development [Zimmer, following Schelling], as the develop-
> ment of the religious feeling and consciousness [Schleier-
> macher], as the movement of God in man to the concept
> [Marheineke, following Hegel].[103]

Drey's manifestly negative judgment on such attempts to
use philosophy in theology does not imply his rejection of
philosophy.[104] The problem, as he sees it, is to find the
proper way to _integrate_ Christianity (the historical) and
philosophy (the speculative).[105] His own way of attempting
this has been sketched out in the preceding pages. As already
noted, the crucial consideration is not to neglect the historical. This is the distinguishing feature of Drey's proposal
for a scientific theology of the historically given. "A
philosophical treatment of Dogmatics . . . is possible . . .
But it must not supplant its basis, positive Dogmatics. Hence
my method."[106]

Relationship of Historical
and Speculative Theology

Finally, therefore, Drey remains strikingly oriented
towards the historical and the "positive." Since this provides
the indispensable _object_ of theology, it remains, for him, the
basis of all further thinking.[107] The distinction, therefore,

---

[103]Ibid.: "Christenthum als die Lehre vom Absoluten u.
seiner Entwickelung, als die Entwickelung des religiösen
Gefühls u. Bewußtseyns, als die Bewegung Gottes im Menschen zum
Begriffe."

[104]Cf. KE §§ 96-97, pp. 64-65.

[105]PD III 42, marginal notation: "Wie im Collegium?"

[106]PD III 45, marginal notation: "Es ist eine philosophische Behandlung der Dogmat . . . möglich . . . Aber sie darf
ihre Grundlage die positive Dogmatik nicht verdrängen. Hieraus
meine Methode."

[107]Cf. _Apologetik_ I § 1, p. 79: "Von einer Thatsache muß
jede auch spekulative Untersuchung ausgehen, von ihr nur kann
sie zum Begriffe fortschreiten, die Genesis des Begriffes
selbst ist nichts anderes als die genaue und getreue Ausein-
anderlegung der Thatsache im Denken."

between historical and scientific theology must be made according to the differing formality of their respective ways of
knowing this one divinely given object.

> From this, then, the mutual relationship of these two
> main branches of theology becomes clear. It is not so much
> the material which distinguishes them, but rather the form
> of knowing. For the same thing which is first found by way
> of historical studies, is now brought into a system by way
> of scientific construction--the same Christianity. Hence,
> they can never be truly separated from each other, but can
> only be distinguished; historical knowing--or rather, its
> result--runs through the entire science (Wissenschaft).
> They are, therefore, related to each other as the historical
> propaedeutic to the science (Wissenschaft) itself.[108]

Because of this orientation towards the historical, Drey
is realistically modest about the extent to which a strictly
scientific construction of Christianity may be possible. First
of all, of course, he recognizes that such a high-level intellectual activity is not possible for all theologians, since it
demands a special talent for philosophical thinking.[109] For
this reason alone, a systematic, logically ordered historical
construction is the most (and the least!) that can be demanded
of many theologians.[110] But even for those capable of strictly
scientific construction, it will not be possible to grasp all
the details of empirical, historical Christianity in a deductive

---

[108]KE § 66, pp. 41-42: "Hieraus erhellt denn auch das
Verhältniß dieser beyden Hauptzweige der Theologie zu einander.
Es ist nicht so fast der Stoff, als vielmehr die Form des
Wissens, was sie unterscheidet; denn dasselbe, was zuerst auf
dem Wege geschichtlicher Studien gefunden wird, wird hier auf
dem Wege wissenschaftlicher Construction in ein System gebracht,
dasselbe Christentum. --Daher können sie auch nie wahrhaft von
einander getrennt, sondern nur unterschieden seyn; das geschichtliche Wissen oder vielmehr sein Resultat lauft durch die ganze
Wissenschaft hin. Sie verhalten sich daher zu einander wie die
historische Propädeutik zu der Wissenschaft selbst."

[109]KE § 309, p. 208: ". . . ein wahrhaft wissenschaft-
liches Begreifen des Inhalts der christlichen Theologie [ist]
nicht Jedermanns Sache . . . Den Prüfstein für seine Kräfte
wird der Einzelne darin finden, wenn es ihm gelingt, jeden
gegebenen Lehrsatz der historischen Theologie als etwas
Nothwendiges vor seiner Vernunft zu begreifen."

[110]KE § 316, § 310.

way, from the master Idea of Kingdom of God. Hence much of
Christianity can only be known in the historical mode.[111]

The Importance of "Wissen-
schaftliche Theologie"

In conclusion, therefore, it is instructive to consider
just why Drey laid such emphasis on "wissenschaftliche Theologie" in his overall view of the theological enterprise. The
answer is to be found, I think, in his dominantly apologetic
interest. For Drey's life-work was devoted to the rational
vindication of Christianity's claim to be a divinely revealed
religion. This is why the concept "revelation" was central to
his theologizing. But he judged that the divine "positivity"
of Christianity could not be made evident to human reason from
a merely empirical perspective on history. It was not adequate
merely to argue from the historical evidence of some kind of
perceptibly divine intervention in the affairs of men (miracles,
prophecy).[112]

The merely empirical, historical view of Christianity
could not avoid the semblance of arbitrariness or "accidentality." No matter how many indications there might be of a
genuine divine agency in Christianity's history, the content of
Christianity could not be commended to the human mind as true
and valid unless one could achieve the insight into the intelligible "necessity" of this history and of these doctrines. In
other words, it was not enough to show historically the factual-
ity of the divine revelatory activity ("Positivität"). One had
also to discover the intelligibility of this activity and of
its content ("innere Wahrheit" or "Vernunftgemäßheit"). Since

---

[111]KE § 64, p. 40: "Alles, was einer Construction aus
Ideen nicht fähig ist (und vieles, was der Theolog zu wissen
braucht, ist von dieser Art), alles, was er nicht in der Form
der Wissenschaft, sondern als reinen Gegenstand der Geschichte,
oder als gelehrte Kenntniß besitzt, fällt als eigentlicher
Gegenstand der historischen Theologie,--besser, dem historischen
Studium der Theologie--anheim."

[112]Although not sufficient, this kind of argumentation
was, nevertheless, demanded. Drey followed this historical
approach in Vol. 2 of his Apologetik. But--even if successful--
this could only show the divine "givenness" of Christianity,
which is to be carefully distinguished from its intelligible
truth for the human mind.

revelation has its source in the divine Mind and is given _for_
the human mind, Drey expects that there is a system and intelligibility about it which can and must be discovered. And he
assigns this discovery of the intelligibility of revelation to
the philosophical function of the human mind. This is the
level of "Wissenschaft."

> But if--after all this--someone should still wish to
> ask what philosophy can have to do with a revealed theology,
> we answer (in addition to what was already said in § 56):
> Every revelation, conceived by the eternal absolute Reason
> in God, has gone forth from this Reason and therefore can-
> not be altogether alien to human reason, in which the
> divine Reason itself is revealed; the purpose of all reve-
> lation can be none other than the education of the human
> race by God, and consequently, there must be, in its
> history and in its doctrines, a plan, order and system; to
> discover and to determine this system precisely is not only
> a need of the believer, but it is not possible in any other
> way [i.e., other than the way of philosophy]; the sense and
> significance of every revelation--even of a true and genu-
> ine one--is lost for science [für die Wissenschaft] with
> the lapse of time, unless all the facts and doctrines
> bearing upon this revelation are brought back to changeless
> Ideas of reason, and thus snatched away from the accidental-
> ity which alone can make their true source doubtful or
> suspicious.[113]

The failure to provide this scientific construction of
the historically given revelation would make Christianity unintelligible to the contemporary mind. As Drey understood the

---

[113]KE § 97, p. 65: "Wenn aber Jemand nach dem allem noch
fragen möchte, was denn die Philosophie mit einer geoffenbarten
Theologie zu thun haben könne?--dem antworten wir--außer dem
§ 56 bereits gesagten: daß jede Offenbarung von der ewigen
absoluten Vernunft in Gott empfangen, von dieser ausgegangen
ist, und darum der menschlichen Vernunft, in welcher sich die
göttliche überhaupt offenbart, nicht durchaus fremd seyn kann;
daß der zweck aller Offenbarung kein anderer seyn kann als
Erziehung des Menschengeschlechts durch Gott, daß folglich
darum in ihrer Geschichte und in ihren Lehren Plan, Ordnung und
System seyn muß, welche zu entdecken und genau zu bestimmen
nicht nur Bedürfniß für den gläubigen Menschen, sondern auch
auf einem andern Wege gar nicht möglich ist; daß der Sinn und
die Bedeutung jeder auch wahren und wirklichen Offenbarung für
die Wissenschaft mit dem Laufe der Zeiten verloren geht, wenn
nicht alle sich darauf beziehenden Thatsachen und Lehren auf
unwandelbare Ideen der Vernunft zurückgebracht, und so der
Zufälligkeit entrissen werden, die allein ihren wahren Ursprung
zweifelhaft oder verdächtig machen kann."

mentality of his day, it was characterized by the "rigorously
scientific spirit" which "seeks everywhere the highest unity
[of concepts] in Ideas through 'construction'"[114]

   To such a mentality, the truth of Christianity could only
be demonstrated if its doctrines could be grasped in a unity on
the level of Ideas. This is why Drey thought that theology had
to be attempted as a "Wissenschaft." The standard for genuine
knowing was set by the general state of intellectual culture in
his day. If Christianity's doctrines were to be recognized as
true, then the established mode of rigorous knowing must be
followed in theology as well. In this way, Drey consciously
formulated his method for theology so as to meet the mentality
and legitimate intellectual demands of his cultural situation.[115]

   On the other hand, Drey had an intrinsic theological
reason for advocating theology as "Wissenschaft." It was his
conviction that revelation as God's education of the human race
must be intelligible to its recipients. Granting that revelation's purpose is eminently practical--to bring mankind to the
free acknowledgment of its relationship to God--Drey insists
that this practical purpose cannot be achieved unless the
content of revelation is proportioned to the human mind. God's
revealed truths could not move mankind to "piety" and holy
living

> . . . if they were in no way accessible to our knowledge,
> nor related [cognata] to our mind, nor connected with the
> highest and most important judgments which are in us, but
> rather were altogether at odds with them and were alien and
> distant from our nature.[116]

   We have seen that Drey sought an understanding of the
divinely ruled events and doctrines of the history of revelation
precisely in terms of their appropriateness to man's universal

---

[114]KE § 56, p. 34: ". . . der streng wissenschaftlicher
[Geist] . . . er sucht überall ihre höchste Einheit in Ideen
durch Construction." Cf. above, pp. 138-39.

[115]KE § 226, p. 152.

[116]PD III 44: ". . . si nulla ratione cognitioni nostrae
pervia, nec menti nostrae cognata, nec cum summis gravissim-
isque, quae nobis insunt, judiciis connexa, sed cum his omnino
pugnantia, remota a natura nostra et peregrina forent."

nature as creature of God. He expected this to be possible
because revelation was the action of the same God who was
responsible, as Creator, for man's rational nature. And even
though the divine Ideas communicated in revelation were, indeed,
above man's empirical intelligence (Verstand), God had also
given to man as his natural endowment the power of intuitive
intelligence (Vernunft), which was capable of recognizing and
appropriating these Ideas as its own.[117]

Because of the intelligible, "ideal" character of divine
revelation--proportioned to man's power of intuitive intelli-
gence--Drey expected that the divinely "given" truths of
revelation could, in principle, be both appropriated by the
human mind and integrated with its own natural knowing. The
result would be a unified, "scientific" understanding of world
and man in relationship to God and His eternal purposes for the
human race's development. In this sense, theology would truly
be a "rerum divinarum scientia."[118]

Drey's confidence in the intelligibility of revelation is
manifestly formed and expressed in the perspectives of German
Idealism. Reality--including the events and doctrines of
revelation--is felt to be "menti nostrae cognata"[119] because
this reality is first and foremost "summa mente prognata."[120]
It is divine Mind[121] which is primary. It is expected that
what springs from this absolute Mind will be proportioned to

----

[117]Cf. PD III 45: ". . . hanc ipsam rationem a conditore
Deo menti nostrae insitam fuisse, quae caelestia et divina,
semota ab oculis, contemplaretur, ut quemadmodum homo his
inclusus compagibus corporis duobus oculis videt, ita duo simul
haberet lumina mentis, quorum altero intellectus res sensibus
perceptas discernat, altero rationis quae remota sunt a sensibus percipiat et dijudicet."

[118]PD III 45: "Quam ob rem defendimus, rerum quae supra
sensus sunt cognitionem propriam esse rationi, cujus sit etiam
revelationis divinae doctrinas non solum percipere, verum cum
iis etiam, quae ipsa naturaliter detegit, conferre, componere,
atque inde unum quemdam omnium judiciorum apparatum adornare,
qui de argumento rerum divinarum scientia dici possit."

[119]PD III 44.   [120]PD III 47.

[121]"Die ewige, absolute Vernunft" (KE § 97, p. 65).

the human mind, since the former is manifested in the latter.[122]

Drey's Affinities and Tensions with Schelling's Early Thought

We are now in a position to point up the features of Drey's theological method which seem closely akin to the early Schelling's version of Idealism. At the same time, it will be possible to designate the distinctive elements in Drey's thought which do not fit at all comfortably with Schelling's perspective.

The Concept of "Wissenschaft"

The principal affinity is undoubtedly to be found in the general conception of "Wissenschaft" which Drey takes as also valid for theology. It does not seem that he followed Schelling closely in a formal, explicit way. Drey did not adopt any one philosophical system as the formal framework of his thought. Rather, he tried to take account of what he regarded as the commonly accepted standards of rigorous knowing in the contemporary intellectual culture.

Without, therefore, attempting to demonstrate any direct influence of Schelling's writings on Drey's methodology, we wish only to identify certain key features of his ideal of "Wissenschaft" which, as a matter of fact, are prominent in Schelling's thought. Although these notions may well have gained a more general acceptance by 1819 (the date of the KE's publication), they can be documented in Schelling's early writings. Hence, it seems legitimate to look there for the background of Drey's proposal, especially since he refers explicitly to Schelling's Lectures on Academic Study with regard to "Wissenschaft."[123]

Perhaps the most striking feature of Drey's thought is his constant search for the intelligible "necessity" of what is otherwise apprehended as merely factual or "accidental." We have seen that the discovery of this necessity is a matter of perceiving the "Idea" which is exemplified or realized in

---

[122]". . . die menschliche Vernunft, in welcher sich die göttliche überhaupt offenbart" (KE § 97, p. 65).

[123]KE § 84, p. 57. See above, p. 73.

the empirically given.[124] This intellectual operation is
referred to as "philosophical" or "scientific construction."[125]
The faculty which is capable of such knowing is called
"Vernunft," in contrast to "Verstand," which is limited to the
empirical in its causal interrelationships.

Now, this whole way of talking is familiar from our close
examination of Schelling in the previous chapter. What is
clearly operative in both Drey and Schelling is the conviction
that the empirically given reality of what we apprehend follows
with intelligible necessity from a prior pattern of rationality.
To discover this pattern is to rise to a higher way of knowing
the empirically given, so that the semblance of "accidentality"
is removed.

The similarity of outlook is illustrated by a parallel
between an observation in Drey's Journal and an early text of
Schelling. Drey notes that the difference between "analytic"
and "synthetic" judgments depends on whether we perceive
"necessity":

> In general, we can judge synthetically only about
> things which we regard as accidental, since for that very
> reason we do not perceive why this or that predicate is
> attributed; as soon as we think of a certain being as
> necessary, all judgments are only analytic. . . . It is the
> task of all science [Wissenschaft] or speculation to
> transform synthetic, i.e. empirical, judgments into
> analytic ones, or to show that all the predicates (asser-
> tions) which are attributed to the subject on an empirical
> basis, belong to it necessarily or according to its
> nature.[126]

---

[124]Cf. Apologetik I, "Einleitung" § 6, p. 7: ". . . die
Idee selbst . . . ist das Ewige, in dem Thatsächlichen und
Zeitlichen sich realisirende, das in sich selbst Eine und
Gleiche, in der Erscheinung aber sich zur Mannichfaltigkeit
gestaltende, sie kann daher nur aus ihr selbst begriffen und
beurtheilt werden."

[125]Cf. KE § 46, p. 28.

[126]Tagebücher III 18-19; 21 (1812-15): "Überhaupt können
wir synthetisch nur von Dingen urteilen, die wir für zufällig
halten, denn deswegen sehen wir eben nicht ein, warum dieses
oder jenes Prädicat beigelegt werde; sobald wir uns ein ge-
wisses Wesen als nothwendig denken, so sind alle Urteile nur
mehr analytische. . . . Es ist die Aufgabe aller Wissenschaft
oder Speculation die synthetischen, d.h. empirischen Urteile in
analytische zu verwandeln oder zu zeigen, daß alle Prädicate
(Behauptungen) die aus einem empirischen Grunde dem Subject

There is an interesting parallel in Schelling's observation about the difference between a posteriori and a priori knowing of nature. He envisions a speculative knowing of nature "through the derivation of all natural phenomena from an absolute presupposition."[127] This would be "eine Wissenschaft der Natur a priori."[128] But he is at pains to affirm the indispensability of experience. The point of his method for a "purely speculative physics" is to rise to the discovery of the necessity of what is first apprehended empirically.

> . . . we know originally nothing at all except through experience, and to this extent all our knowing consists in propositions of experience. These propositions become a priori propositions only when one becomes aware of them as necessary; and so every proposition, regardless of its content, can be raised to that dignity, since the distinction between a priori and a posteriori propositions is not . . . a distinction which inheres originally in the propositions themselves. Rather, it is a distinction which is made merely with respect to our knowing and the way we know these propositions. Hence, every proposition which is, for me, merely historical is a proposition of experience; but the same proposition, as soon as I attain immediately or mediately to the insight into its inner necessity, becomes an a priori proposition.[129]

Theology and the "Higher View" of History

This shared perspective on the difference between (merely) empirical knowing and absolute or scientific knowing is, of

---

beigelegt werden, diesem notwendig oder seiner Natur nach zukommen."

[127] Schellings Werke 2:278. "Durch diese Ableitung aller Naturerscheinungen eben aus einer absoluten Voraussetzung . . . ."

[128] Ibid.

[129] Ibid. ("Einleitung zu dem Entwurf eines Systems der Naturphilosophie," 1799): ". . . wir wissen ursprünglich überhaupt nichts als durch Erfahrung, und insofern besteht unser ganzes Wissen aus Erfahrungssätzen. Zu Sätzen a priori werden diese Sätze nur dadurch, daß man sich ihrer als nothwendiger bewußt wird, und so kann jeder Satz, sein Inhalt sey übrigens welcher er wolle, zu jener Dignität erhoben werden, da der Unterschied zwischen Sätzen a priori und a posteriori nicht etwa . . . ein ursprünglich an den Sätzen selbst haftender Unterschied, sondern ein Unterschied ist, der bloß in Absicht auf unser Wissen und die Art unseres Wissens von diesen Sätzen gemacht wird, so daß jeder Satz, der für mich bloß historisch ist, ein Erfahrungssatz, derselbe aber, sobald ich unmittelbar oder mittelbar die Einsicht in seine innere Nothwendigkeit erlange, ein Satz a priori wird."

course, most significant in Drey's view of history. His effort
to know scientifically the actual, given shape of history is
governed by this Idealist perspective. ". . . if philosophy is
the Wissenschaft of the Ideas, history is the realization of
the Ideas; and the true conception of history is the knowledge
of the Ideas in their realization . . ."[130]

It is a matter of relinquishing the ordinary way of seeing
things, in order to perceive in a deductive way the logical
necessity of the Ideas' realization:

> . . . the philosophical view . . . sublates the sensibly
> given reality of all being and all history, in order to
> construct both from their Ideas, and to let them come to
> be a second time for the higher perception.[131]

It is from this general perspective, too, that Drey is
able to conceive theology as a true Wissenschaft of the positively given. He would, in this sense, be able to locate
theology--along with Schelling--among the Wissenschaften of the
"real."[132]

The indispensable requirement for such a conception of
theology is, of course, a "higher viewpoint" on history. One
must not regard history in a merely empirical way as if it were
solely the result of arbitrary human choices. Rather, it is
"the work of an eternal necessity, which the religious man
calls providence."[133] Thus, the similarity between Drey's and

------

[130]Apologetik I, "Einleitung" § 14, p. 28: ". . . sey die
Philosophie die Wissenschaft der Ideen, so ist die Geschichte
die Verwirklichung der Ideen und die wahre Auffassung der
Geschichte die Erkenntnis der Ideen in ihrer Verwirklichung . . ."

[131]Tagebücher V 77 (1816-17), in GdChr, p. 151: ". . . zu
der philosophischen Ansicht . . . , die die sinnlich gegebene
Realität alles Seins und aller Geschichte aufhebt, um beide aus
ihren Ideen zu konstruiren und für die höhere Anschauung zum
zweiten Male werden zu lassen."

[132]See above, pp. 98-101.

[133]"Revision des gegenwärtigen Zustandes der Theologie,"
in Schupp, Revision von Kirche und Theologie, p. 21: ". . . die
Geschichte . . . als das Werk einer ewigen Nothwendigkeit, die
der religiöse Mensch Vorsehung nennt . . ."

Schelling's views of history is overwhelmingly evident.[134]

The God-World Relationship

What we must now examine closely, however, is the conception of the God-world relationship which underlies Schelling's
theory of _Wissenschaft_ and his view of history. For it is here
that the chief tension is found between Schelling and Drey.

Schelling's general perspective, in common with all German idealism, might be simply expressed by saying: reality is
the consequence of Mind. Drey appears to share this fully.
But the difference between them lies in the _way_ in which
reality is thought to follow from Mind.

We have tried to understand Schelling's early thought
from his apparent feeling for the ineffable oneness of reality.
What appears as diverse and separate is to be understood as the
finite differentiation of an ultimate, undifferentiated Identity of Thought and Being. This is a way of conceiving the key
issue of all Idealist thought: the relationship of the finite
and the Infinite.

Drey found a deep affinity in Schelling's way of conceiving all finite reality as merely the manifestation of God. He
judged this to be a philosophical system which was congenial to
Christianity because it was religious in its very basis.[135]
Schelling himself criticized the dominant mentality of his day
as "irreligious" because it placed God outside the world and
the human self.[136]

We saw in the previous chapter that the indispensable
entry into the higher perspective of "Wissenschaft," in Schelling's view, is the "intellectual intuition" of the Absolute.
This is the basis of Schelling's system, which Drey characterized as religious. Schelling himself says explicitly that this

---

[134]Geiselmann comments on this, and notes the detailed
echoes of Schelling's 8th and 9th _Lectures on Academic Study_
in Drey's earliest published article, "Revision des gegenwärtigen Zustandes der Theologie" (1812). Cf. Geiselmann, "Die
Glaubenswissenschaft der katholischen Tübinger Schule," _ThQ_ 111
(1930):54-55; 61-64.

[135]KE § 96, p. 64. See above, pp. 28-30.

[136]_Werke_ 3:528-29.

immediate intuition of the Absolute must be at the very beginning of any true philosophy. It is in this sense that philosophy must be religious "in its very principle."[137]

"Mysticism" and "Wissenschaft"

We remarked earlier that Schelling calls this fundamental
intuition of the Infinite in the finite "mysticism."[138] There
is an instructive parallel in Drey's Journal, where he is contrasting "Verstand" and "Vernunft," with reference to Kant.[139]

Drey agrees with Kant that "the concept of the Infinite
is a completely alien concept for the Verstand."[140] On the
other hand, the Vernunft has the Idea of the Infinite by virtue
of intuition, and presents this idea to the Verstand. These
two intellectual capacities of the human mind are in tension,
therefore. The empirical intelligence which is limited to the
finite and particular is "autonomous, unassailable and invinci-
ble in its own territory."[141] The intuitive intelligence is
equally so, with its Ideas. "Only faith, i.e., a free decision,
can make the Verstand captive to the Vernunft."[142] Such a submission of empirical intelligence to the intuitive can lead,
however, to an extreme which Drey calls "the one-sided mysticism, which declares everything finite to be merely illusion."[143]
This is the annihilation of the Verstand. The opposite is the
one-sidedness of "the Enlightenment, which considers the finite
to be all that is true and certain."[144]

---

[137]Werke 3:536. See above, p. 28, note 13, and pp. 79-80.

[138]See above, p. 110. Cf. Werke 3:538; 1:722-23; 3:327.

[139]Tägebucher II 97-99 (1812-15), printed in GdChr,
pp. 121-23.

[140]GdChr, p. 122: ". . . der Begriff des Unendlichen ist
dem Verstand ein Allerdings ganz fremder Begriff . . ."

[141]GdChr, p. 122: ". . . der Verstand [ist] auf seinem
Gebiete selbständig, unangreiflich, unüberwindlich . . ."

[142]Ibid.: ". . . nur der Glaube, d.h. ein freiwilliger
Entschluß [kann] den Verstand unter die Vernunft gefangen
machen . . ."

[143]Ibid.: "Die . . . einseitige Mystik . . . erklärt
alles Endliche für eine bloße Täuschung . . ."

[144]Ibid.: ". . . die Aufklärung hält dies [alles End-
liche] für das einzig Wahre und Gewisse."

Drey thinks that there is a mean between these two
extremes. "Speculation and Wissenschaft stands between the two
and grants to each its rights."[145] Drey thus links Wissenschaft
closely with the intuitive sense of the Infinite. Without the
latter, one has the one-sided, exclusive dominance of the
Verstand, which is unable to perceive any Ideas in the finite
objects of its knowing.[146] On the other hand, Wissenschaft
seeks to penetrate and clarify rationally the relationship of
the finite to the Infinite. "It subordinates the concept to
the Idea."[147] An extreme, irrational form of mysticism, in
contrast, simply denies the reality of the finite.

In another place, Drey says that a "mysticism which
understands itself is at the same time philosophy."[148] And,
further, "Mysticism . . . which has raised itself above mere
feeling . . . [is] the highest knowing . . ."[149]

What is noticeable in this linkage of mysticism and
speculative, "scientific" knowing is the overriding demand to
conceive the finite in relationship to the Infinite. This is
what Drey shares with Schelling. True knowing--which perceives
the necessity of the empirically given--is possible only if one
can rise to the intuition of the Infinite in the finite. This
is a religious perception, closely akin to mysticism. It
transcends the merely empirical, finite apprehension of particular objects, in order to grasp God and world in a close
unity and congruence. It is able to understand the finite as
the consequence of the Infinite, the real as the consequence of
divine Mind (what Schelling calls the "absolut-Ideal").

---

[145]Ibid.: "Die Spekulation und Wissenschaft steht
zwischen beiden und gewährt jeder ihre Rechte."

[146]Cf. Apologetik I § 32, p. 269.

[147]GdChr, p. 123: ". . . sie subordinirt . . . den
Begriff der Idee . . ."

[148]"Über das Verhältnis des Mystizismus zum Katholizismus," ThQ 6 (1824), reprinted in Franz Schupp, Revision von
Kirche und Theologie, p. 29: ". . . die Mystik die sich selbst
versteht, ist auch zugleich Philosophie . . ."

[149]Ibid., p. 30: ". . . die Mystik . . . die sich von der
blossen Empfindung . . . erhoben hat . . . [ist] das höchste
Wissen . . ."

Drey's Stress on Creation

There is, nevertheless, a significant difference between Schelling and Drey in the way of conceiving the God-world relationship. This difference can be identified by recalling the central importance of creation in Drey's thought. In conscious continuity with the Christian tradition, Drey conceives creation as the gratuitous calling-into-being of all things by the inconceivable act of an utterly transcendent God.[150] This divine initiative, "God's act of creating," is a "transcendent fact" which cannot be grasped or explained.[151]

Moreover, Drey does not limit God's creative activity to a "moment" of origin. As we have seen, he conceives God as continually active in guiding and "re-creating" the world which is His "work and possession." This is especially relevant to Drey's theory of revelation and his valuation of history as the manifestation of God's purposes for mankind.

In contrast to this, the early Schelling tends to conceive the world as the spontaneous, inevitable self-objectification of the Absolute. There is no operative notion of a personal, transcendent creator nor of creation in the traditional sense. The world is the finite appearance and expression of the Infinite.[152]

God's "Decrees" vs. Divine "Ideas"

This basic difference is noticeable in Drey's use of the term "Ideas." In Schelling's early writings, as we saw, the "Ideenlehre" is added to the "Identitätsphilosophie" as a kind of bridge between the Absolute and particular, finite things.[153]

---

[150]Cf. Apologetik I § 21, p. 182. Cf. above, pp. 33-34.

[151]Apologetik I § 33, p. 284: ". . . wer darf sagen, daß er die transcendente Thatsache, den Schöpfungsakt Gottes, begriffen oder erklärt habe?"

[152]Schelling's later speculation did, it is true, move in the direction of a personal God, as a subject with will and love, arising out of a pre-personal "ground." But even in this speculative view of divine personality, creation appears to be a kind of necessity for His full development. This is still quite different from Drey's view.

[153]See above, pp. 85-87.

But there is scarcely any sense of a personal, transcendent
Subject of the Ideas. Rather, the Ideas seem to be the first
self-objectification of the undifferentiated Identity of
Subject and Object. The event of such self-objectification
seems to be as spontaneous and inevitable as is the further
event of the realization of the Ideas in the finite order.

For Drey, on the other hand, the Ideas are equated with
God's decrees or purposes. While recognizing the validity of
the Idealist view of reality, Drey nevertheless affirms explicitly a theistic conception of God's relationship to the world:

> For what is that which we call the real in nature and
> history, what is it but the manifestation of that which is
> per se, the temporal appearance of the eternally true, the
> accomplishment of the Ideas from and in themselves? This
> is how reason expresses itself, which does its work in
> abstraction; but religious reason, which sees the Ideal and
> the Real equally in God, recognizes in the Ideas only the
> eternal acts of the divine intellect and will, which the
> Bible calls the decrees of God, and it sees in all that is
> real the accomplishment of these decrees.[154]

The notion of God's decrees plays a prominent part in
Drey's theology. The "economy" of the Kingdom of God may be
viewed as the sum total of these decrees--in other words, the
specific content of divine providence. As we have seen, Drey
expects to find an intelligible system in these decrees, since
they arise from divine Mind and are intrinsically related to
the requirements of human nature in relationship to God. It is
in this sense that he equates them with the "Ideas" perceived
by philosophical reason.

But there is a tension in Drey's thought, which is perceptible in this equating of "Ideas" and "decrees." The former
term has its place in the Idealist view of reality as the
consequence of Mind. The intelligibility of the real is found

---

[154]Apologetik I § 29, pp. 242-43: "Denn was ist das, was
wir das Wirkliche nennen in Natur und Geschichte, was ist es
anders als das Offenbarwerden dessen, was an sich ist, die
zeitliche Erscheinung des ewig wahren, die Vollziehung der
Ideen aus und an ihnen selbst? So drückt sich die Vernunft
aus, die an der Abstraktion ihre Arbeit hat, die religiöse
Vernunft aber, die das Ideale und Reale gleicherweise in Gott
sieht, erkennt in den Ideen nur die ewigen Akte des göttlichen
Verstandes und Willens, welche die Bibel die Rathschlüsse
Gottes nennt, in allem Wirklichen aber die Vollziehung dieser
Rathschlüsse . . ."

in the eternally valid archetypes of the divine Mind (which
Schelling calls the "modi" of the "Urwissen").[155] On the other
hand, the term "decrees" has its place in a theistic, creationist view of the God-world relationship. God is conceived as
personal Agent, calling reality into existence by His creative
will and guiding history according to His purposes. Now, it is
clear enough that the latter view is dominant in Drey's theology. On the other hand, his method for "scientific" theology
is based on the former (Idealist) view of reality.

What is at stake, for Drey, is the postulated intelligibility of the historically given. Unless the positively given
revelation is proportionate to the human mind, there can be no
theology as Wissenschaft of the "real." Since Drey's standard
for genuine knowing is established by Idealism, he must, therefore, seek the eternally valid Ideas in the empirically given
reality of Christianity.

When this requirement is joined to the theistic notion of
God's creation and guidance of the world, there is the tension
between "Ideas" and "decrees." If God is transcendent Agent,
how can one be sure of intelligibility in what He decides to do
(in His "decrees")? On the other hand, if the reality of
history is the consequence of eternal Ideas, how can one consider God to be a free, personal Agent?

In other words, intelligibility is so closely linked to
necessity in the Idealist perspective that a divine guidance of
the world according to Ideas is hard to reconcile with divine
freedom. The tendency to see reality (with Schelling) as an
inevitable "unfolding" of the Absolute is difficult to resist.[156]

---

[155]See above, p. 84.

[156]When this perspective controls an interpretation of
Christianity, what is lost is precisely the sense of divine
freedom, the sense of the utter gratuitousness of the economy
of salvation. Karl Barth notes approvingly that Schleiermacher
resisted this trend of his Idealist contemporaries, Schelling
and Hegel: "In ihm [Schleiermacher] protestiert etwas zu
gunsten der Eigenart und Unableitbarkeit gerade dieser Sätze
[die Sätze der Theologie], gegen die Allgewalt der Deduktion
im Denken jener seiner Zeitgenossen, gegen die Verwischung der
'hohen Willkür', die jedenfalls von einer Seite der Schlüssel
des Christentums sein mochte, wie er sich gegen Schelling
(Briefe IV, 586) ausgedrückt hat" (Die Protestantische Theologie im 19. Jahrhundert [Zürich: Zollikon, 3d ed. 1960], p. 400).

Drey's Trinitarian Modification
of the Idealist Perspective

Drey's way of trying to reconcile intelligible necessity
with divine freedom is to be found in his doctrine of the
Trinity. First of all, the intelligibility of the divine
"decrees" is located within the divine essence. That is, God's
free activity is not arbitrary, but is, so to speak, patterned
by His very nature.[157] This way of speaking could, however, be
taken in a sense which is quite close to Schelling's notion of
an absolute Urwissen making itself manifest according to its
intrinsic rationality.[158] But what clearly differentiates Drey
from any view of creation as a necessary unfolding of the
divine essence is his doctrine of the Trinity. The full and
detailed treatment of this is reserved for the following chapter. Here, it is sufficient to indicate its relevance to the
difficulty under discussion.

Drey locates the "Ideas" or "decrees" which govern the
world and its history not merely within a divine essence
considered abstractly. Rather, these decrees as the "apices"
of the entire economy of the Kingdom of God are located within
the divine Persons of the Son and the Spirit.[159] The very
possibility and intelligibility of a created world order is
given within God and, moreover, within a relationship of divine
Persons. The deterministic inevitability of a divine essence
manifesting itself in the finite is avoided by locating the
intelligible patterns of the finite, so to speak, within the
personal differentiation of the Godhead. Creation, therefore,
can be conceived as a free act because of the interpersonal
character of the Trinity. But if God chooses to create, He

---

[157]Cf. Tagebücher V 82: "In Beziehung auf Gott ist Regel
und Motiv [des Handelns] seine eigene Natur; Gott ist heilig,
indem er seinen Willen seiner Natur unterordnet, dieß ist seine
Freyheit." And cf. PD I 33: "In Deo non dari libertatem eo
sensu, quo homines ista [libertate] gaudent; sed Deum aliquo
modo necessitari a natura sua, statuendum est."

[158]Cf. Rief, Reich Gottes und Gesellschaft, p. 96, where
he relates Drey's notion of God's "omniscientia" to Schelling's
"Urwissen."

[159]PD III 187a.

does so according to the pattern of intelligibility already
embodied in the Son and Spirit.

Thus far, we have identified the affinity of Drey's
thought with the Schellingian Idealist perspective, but have
also pointed out the tension caused by Drey's theistic, creationist view of the God-world relationship. There are other
differences from Schelling, which are closely related to this
principal difference.

Drey's Concept of Religion

Drey's concept of religion is noticeably different from
the early Schelling's. As we saw in the previous chapter, what
is religious about the "higher viewpoint" of Schelling's intellectual intuition is exclusively aesthetic and speculative. It
is the perception of the ultimate, divine oneness of reality--
above all apparent duality. It is the intuition of the Infinite in the finite.

For Drey, on the other hand, there is an important dimension of moral and personal submission to God's dominion. Like
Schelling, he finds "reconciliation" (Versöhnung) to be a good
characterization of the philosophical significance of Christianity. But this is not exclusively a matter of intellectual
intuition. What is demanded is obedience.[160] What is dia-
metrically opposed to this free acknowledgment of one's
relationship of subordination to God is a kind of egotism and
self-will.[161] This is man's refusal to belong to God as
creature in the harmonious, divinely intended order of the
"Kingdom of God."

The most basic feature of religion, therefore, is an
attitude of heart which is willing to give up the illusion of

---

[160]Cf. KE § 10, p. 6: ". . . Anforderung zu einer freiwilligen Unterordnung." And KE § 29, p. 17: ". . . wo der
Mensch . . . die vollkommene Herrschaft Gottes über sich . . .
anerkennt; sich freiwillig der göttlichen Ordnung unterwirft
. . ."

[161]"Eigenwille" (KE § 10, p. 6 and § 12, p. 8); ". . .
den Menschen im Wahne seiner Selbstheit" (KE § 26, p. 14);
"Herrschaft des Egoismus" (KE § 32, p. 19); ". . . der Egoismus
in allen seinen Gestalten, als Eigenwille, Eigenliebe, Eigen-
dünkel, Eigennutz, usw . . ." ("Vom Geist und Wesen des
Katholizismus," in GdChr, p. 209).

self-sufficiency and belong utterly to the Other who is
Creator and Lord of His creation. Drey calls this "humility,"
and finds it at the root of both faith and love.

> Faith and love--the two principles of Christianity--
> have a common character. It is the quality of being tender,
> soft, supple, malleable; it is abandonment to God. And the
> true basis of all this, sought out in the heart (Gemüt)
> itself as a type of attitude (Mut) is humility (Demut).
> This is the deepest in religion, deeper than faith and love.
> Only through humility is it possible for man, in a free
> decision, to surrender his intellect to the service of
> faith and his will to the service of love.162

The Other to whom man surrenders in humility is, for Drey, the
transcendent, personal Creator. Hence, this concept of religion is in contrast to the aesthetic monism of the early
Schelling.163

Drey's Valuation of the Historical
as the Locus of Revelation

Drey's contrasting view of the God-world relationship is
also decisive for his valuation of history. As noted earlier,
of course, Drey shared Schelling's vision of history as the work
of necessity, as the great drama of divine providence. Yet, as
Geiselmann points out, Drey envisioned this divine quality of
history in a way consonant with his theistic conception of God.
He saw history as guided by the divine Spirit, according to
His eternal purposes.164

162"Vom Geist und Wesen des Katholizismus," in GdChr,
pp. 204-5: "Glaube und Liebe--oder beide Prinzipien des
Christentums haben daher einen gemeinsamen Charakter. Es ist
das Zarte, Weiche, Biegsame, Geschmeidige, es ist die Hingebung
an Gott; und der rechte Grund von dem allem im Gemüte selbst
aufgesucht als eine Spezies von Mut, als Demut. Sie ist das
tiefste in der Religion, tiefer als Glauben und Liebe; nur
durch sie wird es dem Menschen möglich, seinen Verstand zum
Dienste des Glaubens, seinen Willen zum Dienste der Liebe aus
freier Entschließung hinzugeben."

163Schelling's later thought, of course, turned increasingly towards a concept of God as personal. Cf. Schellings
Werke 5:746-53, especially p. 748. But this move from "negative" to "positive" philosophy was a departure from the
Identitätsphilosophie which influenced Drey.

164Cf. Geiselmann, "Die Glaubenswissenschaft der katholischen Tübinger Schule," ThQ 111 (1930):56. "Was ihn [Drey] von
aller idealistischen Geschichtsphilosophie dem Wesen nach unterscheidet ist die Tatsache, daß bei ihm die Entwicklung unter
der Leitung des göttlichen Geistes steht."

Moreover, Drey considered certain features of this divinely ruled history to be uniquely revelatory of God's purposes for mankind. And he thought that the divine "positivity" of these persons and events could be discovered by an attentive and objective examination of the evidence.

In all this, Drey was in contrast to Schelling, who did not think that any empirical events or persons could be recognized as divine.[165] Schelling was willing to consider Christianity as divine only from the higher viewpoint which discovers the divine necessity in the totality of history.[166] No particular event can be regarded as the revelation of God. It is only the (not-yet-complete) totality of history which would be the adequate manifestation of God.[167]

Closely related to this valuation of history is Schelling's emphasis on the speculative "Idea" of Christianity as uniquely significant. He contrasts this inner truth (the "esoteric") with the outward, empirical forms of Christian doctrine and practice (the "exoteric"). The latter is to be transcended insofar as the former is finally grasped.[168] In this sense, history can be left behind by the theologian.

In sharp contrast to this, Drey considers the "fact" of revelation to be abidingly significant and normative for both Christian faith and theology, even for those few who are capable of perceiving the Ideas which are embodied in or carried by this fact (or series of facts).[169]

Drey's View of Church as the Basis of Theology

Moreover, Drey's concept of revelation (based on the "anti-deist" view of God's never-ceasing presence and influence upon His creation) leads him to regard the Church as the continuing embodiment and development of this revelation. This has important consequences for his theological method.

Far from transcending the empirical shape of Christianity's history, Drey values this history as the divinely guided development and continuation of the great "fact" of revelation.

---

[165]Werke 3:324.   [166]Werke 3:325.   [167]Werke 2:600-603.

[168]See above, pp. 105ff.   [169]See above, pp. 69-70.

Christianity is a social and historical reality, a great
"objective phenomenon" created and ruled by the Holy Spirit.

Hence, the primary object of the theologian's study must
be this phenomenon in history--not merely the beginning, but
the entire, ongoing development. For this is where the divine
Ideas are being made real (and also, of course, where their
"ideal" content is more and more clearly understood--in the
doctrinal development of the Church's system of dogmas).

One sees here the empirical orientation of Drey towards
the given, historical reality of the Church. This reality is
theologically significant for him because he views it as the
work of the ever-active creative Spirit, and hence expects it
to show the intelligibility of the divine Ideas which rule this
temporal development.

If the theologian, whose task is "a purely intellectual
occupation with the Ideas of Christianity,"[170] must be oriented
towards the Church as the "given" of his science (in the sense
just explained), he must also be oriented towards the life of
the Church as the purpose and justification of his purely
intellectual task. For his intellectual grasp of Christianity's Ideas is to be directed to the practical end of the
fuller actualization of these Ideas in the Church. Because of
this two-fold relationship of theology to Church, Drey finds an
analogy in both jurisprudence and medicine. In both cases,
there is a "positive" reality--indeed, an "organism"--which is
both the object to be known and the purpose of the science's
exercise.

> . . . the Church is the true basis of all theological know-
> ing. It is from the Church and through it that the
> theologian receives the empirically given matter of this
> theological knowing. It is by relation to the Church that
> all his concepts must first attain reality; otherwise they
> end up in airy, groundless speculation. It is the Church
> into which his knowing must flow practically; otherwise, it
> remains an idle, aimless movement of the mind. The Church
> is for the theologian what the State is for jurisprudence,
> what the animal organism is for the science of medicine:

---

[170]KE § 37, p. 22: ". . . eine bloß intellectuelle
Beschäftigung mit den Ideen . . . des Christentums."

the concrete expression of the science itself, that by
which each science becomes positive.[171]

In his orientation towards the historical and, in particular, towards the Church, Drey is governed by considerations
other than Schelling's ideal of <u>Wissenschaft</u>. Specifically, it
is Drey's anti-deist, creationist (and trinitarian) understanding of the God-world relationship which is dominant.

Nevertheless, Schelling's influence is unmistakable in
the whole project of "wissenschaftliche Theologie." Against
the background of Chapter IV it has been possible to see this
affinity but at the same time to notice the tension between
Schelling's and Drey's underlying views of the God-world
relationship.

----

[171]KE § 54, p. 33: ". . . die Kirche ist die wahre Basis
alles theologischen Wissens. Von ihr und durch sie erhält der
Theolog den empirisch gegebenen Stoff desselben; durch die
Beziehung auf sie müssen alle seine Begriffe erst Realität
gewinnen, außerdem laufen sie in luftige, haltungslose Speculation aus; in sie muß sein Wissen sich wieder praktisch
ergiessen, sonst bleibt es müßiges, zweckloses Umhertreiben.
Die Kirche ist für den Theologen dasselbe, was für die
Rechtswissenschaft der Staat, für die Arzneywissenschaft der
thierische organismus; der concrete Ausdruck der Wissenschaft
selbst, das, wodurch eine jede positiv wird."

CHAPTER VI

SYSTEM IN DREY'S DOGMATICS

Introduction

The preceding chapters have been directed to one
principal purpose: to make clear Drey's methodological viewpoint on the task of theology. This provides the perspective
needed, in order to appreciate the system in his Dogmatics,
since--as Rief observes--it is this formal aspect which makes
Drey's theology distinctive.[1] Before addressing the Dogmatics,
however, it may be helpful to recall briefly how the earlier
chapters have contributed to an understanding of Drey's
approach to theology.

As we saw in Chapter V, he is oriented to a concrete
history as the object of theological understanding. In order
to account for this, we began in Chapters II and III with his
theory of revelation. In opposition to deistic naturalism and
rationalism, Drey conceives the world to be intimately related
to an ever-active God who creates and re-creates it to be the
"Kingdom of God." History, in this view, is shaped and guided
by a constant divine influence upon human subjectivity which
awakens and promotes the religious development of mankind. The
culmination and center of this "education of the human race" is

---

[1]Rief, "Johann Sebastian von Drey," pp. 36-37: "Johann
Sebastian von Dreys Theologie muß vom Systemgedanken her, der
ihr zugrunde liegt, beurteilt werden. Alle Versuche, die
Eigenart dieser Theologie vom Inhalt her zu bestimmen, etwa
anhand der Frage, wie von Drey das Verhältnis zwischen Natur
und Gnade gesehen wird, müssen als verfehlt gelten. Denn das
Spezifische seiner Theologie ist nicht der Inhalt, sondern die
Form. Als die eigentliche Leistung des Dogmatikers ist die
'Begründung des Ganzen' anzusehen; das Einzelne wird nach Drey
ohnehin nur gefunden."

the divinely caused phenomenon of Christianity, which provides
the key for interpreting the entirety of mankind's history.
Because of the "divine positivity" of Christianity, therefore,
what the theologian is to understand is given in the form of a
history. Hence, theology must always begin as historical
investigation and must remain oriented to the one, unbroken,
continuing history which is the Church.

On the other hand, the goal of theology as a "science" is
to grasp the intelligibility of this divinely given history.
In order to appreciate Drey's notion of theology as "Wissenschaft," we devoted Chapter IV to the German Idealist background of his thought, as exemplified in the early writings of
Schelling. This enabled us, in Chapter V, to see why Drey
seeks a "higher viewpoint" on history which can discover the
divine Ideas being made real in the finite order. Since the
finite is the consequence of divine Mind, its patterns of
intelligibility (the Ideas) are in principle accessible to the
human mind (which is the finite, partial manifestation of
divine Mind). The task of "scientific theology," therefore, is
to "construct" the divinely given history with reference to
these divine Ideas--above all, with reference to the highest,
unifying Idea of Reich Gottes.

Against this background, the present chapter is devoted
to Drey's unpublished Dogmatics, with the purpose of documenting and interpreting just how his formal viewpoint on theology
is actually operative in his systematic treatment of the
traditional material of Dogmatics.

Sources

Although Drey lectured on Dogmatics for some twenty-five
years, he was never able to put this material into a form suitable for publication. The principal source for his Dogmatics,
therefore, is the collection of his own rough lecture notes
preserved in the library of the Wilhelmsstift in Tübingen.[2]

---

[2]In addition to Drey's own manuscripts, there are extant
several sets of student notes from his Dogmatics lectures.
(See Bibliography.) For a brief assessment of the nature and
value of these notes, see Ruf, J. S. von Dreys System der
Theologie, pp. 23-25. Apart from a few pages published by
Geiselmann, I make no use of this material. There are two
reasons for this: (a) intrinsic: Drey's own writings must be

Originally in the form of loose pages, they were bound together
sometime after 1918 into three volumes, and entitled collectively "Praelectiones Dogmaticae."[3] The arrangement into three
volumes corresponds to the nature of the MSS, which contain
three successive versions of his Dogmatics--the earliest dating
from 1815 (in Ellwangen), the second drafted around 1818, and
the third in the early 1820's (with additions going to around
1834).[4]

    These notes are written in Latin, with marginal notations
in German.[5] In no sense may they be taken as a complete, final
presentation of Drey's Dogmatics. They appear to have been
simply the basis from which he lectured. The terse, summary
treatment in the Latin notes was presumably expanded at greater
length in the German oral presentation.[6] There is abundant
evidence of continual reworking and improvement in the form of
insertions, revisions, and marginal notations in the continuous
sections. There is also supplementary material bound together

----

the primary source for documenting his thought; student notes
could only have a secondary value, to further enrich and con-
firm our knowledge of Drey's teaching, but have no independent
value; (b) extrinsic: it is nearly impossible for an
"Ausländer" to decipher the handwriting of these student notes.
The already sufficiently difficult antique German handwriting
is rendered yet more difficult by the hasty scrawl of a student
hurrying to keep up with the lecturer. Hence, not without
regret, I leave the utilization of these MSS to some German
scholar with excellent eyesight and great patience.

[3]Ruf (p. 23) points out that the newspapers used in the
bindings of the three PD volumes date from World War I.

[4]For a more detailed description of these MSS, see Ruf,
pp. 21-23. The third version, written on only one column of
each page in a different hand (presumably a student's) differs
very little from the second, but Drey crossed out many sections
and wrote a different version on the blank half-page opposite.

[5]Drey's use of Latin in these notes remains a puzzle,
since there is little doubt that the lectures in Tübingen were
given in German. It seems that (at least in the early Ellwangen
years, and perhaps also later in Tübingen) the basic theses were
read in Latin before a detailed presentation was given in
German. At any rate, Drey cast his thought somewhat laboriously
into a neo-Latin which is clear enough, if not always graceful.

[6]This may be indicated by the apparently greater length
of the student notes on Drey's Dogmatics course, in contrast to
Drey's own lecture notes. Cf. Bibliography.

with the third version--"annotations" to particular paragraphs
(containing scriptural and historical material), as well as
disparate treatises on various themes.

The most important and instructive section of these notes
is the methodological preface to the third version, entitled
"Praemonita."[7] This is a coherent, unified essay on the
method and divisions of dogmatic theology, which lays out the
master idea and framework of Drey's Dogmatics. In very brief
compass, it sets forth his distinctive way of conceiving the
systematic unity of the doctrines to be treated.

Method of Presentation

The nature of this material obviously presents problems
for the interpreter. It is quite evident from the manuscripts
that Drey came nowhere near a completely worked-out, consistent
"construction" of the positive data from his speculative viewpoint. The preponderant content of these notes is drawn from
Scripture and tradition.[8]

On the other hand, there are clear indications of his
speculative viewpoint: first of all, his whole way of setting
up the method and framework of Dogmatics in the "Praemonita" to
PD III; and secondly, the observations made here and there
throughout the text of the three versions, which betray a
consistent point of view.

Our chief interest in this material, as already noted, is
the formal aspect. We are concerned to document the characteristic "architectonic" of Drey's thought, his way of discovering

---

[7]PD III 1-69. The latter part of the "Praemonita" (69-
96) contains a history of theology from its beginnings up to
Drey's own time. Ruf (p. 22) dates this text around 1820-21,
on the basis of the works cited in this latter section. Written in Drey's own hand, it stands as a unit which may or may not
have belonged originally with the later material in Vol. 3 of
the "Praelectiones."

[8]This presumably reflects the situation in which Drey
composed his Dogmatics lectures. He had to communicate to his
students each year the essential content of the Christian
tradition. There was undoubtedly not enough leisure to work
out a consistent speculative interpretation of Christianity.
Judging from the character of Drey's published works, if he had
published a Dogmatics, it would probably have been much more
rigorously systematic in a philosophical, speculative way.

system in the historically given events and doctrines of
Christianity. Our attention, therefore, is directed to particular doctrines only insofar as Drey's treatment of them discloses his systematizing bent.

Hence, the key text to be interpreted is the "Praemonita"
section which is prefaced to the third version of the Dogmatics
lectures. What is distinctive and interesting about Drey's
treatment of Dogmatics is to be found here. Taking this as the
framework, therefore, we can draw upon relevant texts in all
three versions of the lecture notes in order to illustrate
certain key points in Drey's system.[9] We can likewise cite
parallel texts from the published works which clarify and supplement the thought of the Dogmatics.

A word of caution is appropriate about this way of interpreting such material. It is the effort to explicate an overall conception which appears to be present only in a sketchy
way. The limitations thus imposed by the condition of the
Dogmatics notes obviously demand of the interpreter considerable
sensitivity and restraint, so as not to attribute to Drey a
fullness and completeness of thought which he did not actually
achieve. On the other hand, it seems worthwhile to articulate
as explicitly as possible the logic which is only partially
expressed in Drey's treatment of the themes of Dogmatics.

The primary requisite of fidelity to his thought is to be
safeguarded by relating this interpretation of the manuscripts
to the characteristic ideas which are clearly enunciated in the
published works. Hence, the examination of the Dogmatics comes
only after the lengthy preceding exposition of Drey's whole
point of view.

The order of presentation will be the following:

First of all, it will be helpful to account for Drey's
arrangement of topics in terms of his fundamental conception of
the God-world relationship. This will involve a close look at

---

[9]Another especially helpful text is PD I 16-20, dated 18
and 19 February, 1818, where Drey gives a succinct sketch of
the proper "Divisio Dogmaticae." Since this overview of Dogmatics is substantially the same as the longer treatment in the
"Praemonita" text, it will be used to clarify Drey's systematic
viewpoint.

his doctrine of the Trinity, which was alluded to at the end of
the preceding chapter.

With this context established, the principal task will be
to lay out the structure of the Dogmatics, following Drey's
conception of the "phases" and "turning-points" of the historical development of the Reich Gottes. At certain points in
this development, we will shift the focus from a general
overview to a somewhat more detailed examination of a particular topic--in order to show its relevance to his systematic
viewpoint.

Finally, by way of a supplementary excursus, we will
indicate briefly the significance of the Church in Drey's
system of theology. Although the topic of Church is not
treated as a distinct section in the Dogmatics notes,[10] some
mention of it in this chapter is appropriate, in order to show
its importance in the overall scheme of Drey's thought.

A Trinitarian View of the
God-World Relationship

The Two Major Parts
of Dogmatics

The large structure of the Dogmatics divides all the
material to be treated into two major sections: (1) "Theologia"
(God "in Himself") and (2) "Oeconomia" (the world in relationship to God).[11] The former section treats of the divine nature
and attributes, and concludes with the doctrine of Trinity.
Drey's treatment of the divine attributes is largely traditional, and will not be examined here. What is of interest is
his concern to show the intrinsic connection between the two
major parts of Dogmatics. He does this by means of his highest
unifying concept, Reich Gottes, and by interpreting the doctrine of Trinity in a way which roots the created order within
the very Being of God.[12]

---

[10]The explanation of this omission is to be found in
Drey's limitation of the subject matter of Dogmatics to the
"ideal" side of Christianity, whereas the Church is the making-
real of these ideas. See below.

[11]PD I 17; PD III 56, 61.

[12]For a perceptive analysis and evaluation of Drey's
Trinitätslehre, see Rief, Reich Gottes und Gesellschaft,
pp. 106-19.

As we have seen, Drey conceives God and the world in the
closest possible intrinsic relationship. The world cannot
properly be conceived apart from God, since God belongs to the
very definition of created reality. On the other hand, God
cannot properly be thought of apart from the world which He
creates, since He can be known only in and through the mediation of the world of objects.

Hence, the large division of Drey's Dogmatics would be
misleading if it were taken to imply that the theologian could
first talk about God in Himself, in isolation from the world
and without reference to it, before proceeding to talk about
the world as created and redeemed by God. The division is made
for the sake of clarity, but Drey explicitly acknowledges that
all discourse about God "in Himself" actually derives from the
created world in which God's activity and being are manifest.[13]

The apparent separation between God and world implied in
the division of the Dogmatics material is to be overcome by
paying attention to the master idea of Drey's theology, Reich
Gottes. This idea was adumbrated in the previous chapter
principally in terms of the divinely conceived and divinely
ruled order of the finite and temporal, i.e., as divine providence. But Drey regards this created order as the manifestation of the very Being of God. Hence, the concept of Reich
Gottes unites God and world in a single intuition.[14] To call
this finite, temporal world the Reich Gottes is to perceive its

_____

[13]PD III 61-62: ". . . ut quidquid ejus [naturae divinae]
cognoscimus, id nonnisi ex opere ejus aliquo, specieque externa
cognoscamus . . . Quam ob rem . . . quaecumque etiam de Deo
enuncientur, semper rationes ejus ad mundum in istis enuncientur. Adeo in illo disserendi genere, in quo scientiae causa
Deum ab omni ejus opere sejungimus, alter cum altero manet
conjunctus, ut cogitando solum divelli possit." Cf. Drey's
review of Dobmayer in ThQ 1 (1819):420-21, "Recensent hält . . .
keine andere Erkenntniß Gottes für möglich . . . als unter der
Vermittelung seiner Beziehungen und seiner Wirkungen auf die
Welt."

[14]PD III 58: "Nihil enim magis universale, nihil omnino
esse supra eam cogitationem puto, quae Deum et quaecumque sunt
praeter ipsum una meditatione unoque quasi obtutu constringit."
PD III 61: ". . . Deum ipsum . . . in idea cum mundo conjunctum cogitamus . . ."

divine quality, to recognize it as that which belongs utterly
to God as the form of His self-manifestation.

Drey postulates, therefore, that the Reich Gottes must--
in some sense--already exist within the divine Being, if it is
to be manifested and realized in the created order.[15] This way
of thinking seems closely akin to the Identitätsphilosophie of
Schelling. What seems to be in the background is the notion of
the Absolute (the Urwissen) objectifying and specifying itself
as the finite Universe of particular beings.[16]

This way of conceiving the God-world relationship verges
on pantheism, insofar as finite beings tend to be regarded as
modes of the one divine Being. Although Drey avoids pantheism
by stressing that the finite world is the manifestation of the
divine in that which is not divine,[17] the dynamic of this way
of thinking still tends towards a conception of creation/self-
manifestation as a necessary, spontaneous, and inevitable event
of the divine Being.

The Relevance of the Doctrine of Trinity

Drey's interest in the doctrine of Trinity is focussed
precisely on this difficult issue of how to understand the
created world in its historical development as related to the
very Being of God. If the temporal unfolding and realization
of the Reich Gottes is, at the same time, the self-
manifestation of God, how is this "economy" rooted in the very
reality of God?

He expresses his concern in an early reflection in the
Journals on the proper arrangement of the material of dogmatic
theology. After observing that Dogmatics must present "a
sacred history from the perspective of the Idea,"[18] he notes

---

[15] See below.

[16] Cf. Rief, Reich Gottes und Gesellschaft, pp. 95-96.

[17] KE § 16, p. 10.

[18] Tagebücher V 50 (GdChr, p. 145): ". . . die Dogmatik
. . . eine positive Wissenschaft, die . . . eine heilige
Geschichte aus der Idee darstellt . . ." Cf. Schupp, Die
Evidenz der Geschichte, p. 22, n. 112, where the correct reading of this text is established. Geiselmann had incorrectly
printed "gewisse" instead of "positive."

that a philosophical arrangement of the material must view the
totality according to this idea (Reich Gottes). But this
composite idea is unthinkable without the idea of God Himself;
hence, the first treatise must be about the Being and proper-
ties of God. The consideration of God's Kingdom must, then,
properly begin by thinking of this Kingdom--prior to its
created realization--as in God. The Idealist mentality is
manifest in this text, which stresses the relevance of Trinity
for conceiving how the Reich Gottes is in God:

> The Kingdom of God originally was and must be thought of--
> like everything--in God. It was in Him from eternity and
> before it could appear in the finite; as it is in Him, so
> it appears gradually here and develops. It is only through
> its Idea in God that the real is possible and conceivable.
> The question, therefore, arises: how the Kingdom of God is
> and was in God before all appearance. Or--which comes to
> the same thing--how all things, the entire Universe, is in
> God, according to the doctrine of the Bible. The answer to
> this is contained in the doctrine of Trinity, which
> explains how, within God, anything distinct from Him arises,
> how anything outside Him can be.[19]

This text expresses the profound sense of the "rootedness"
of finite reality in God which seems basic to all of Drey's
theologizing. The traditional Christian belief in God as
Creator of the finite order is here expressed in Idealist
language. "It is only through its Idea in God that the real is
possible and conceivable." What actually comes to be must
somehow pre-exist "in" God. The problem is how this finite
order of things is to be conceived as already "in" God before
its appearance.

We have already noticed the tension between the Idealist
thought-frame and the Christian belief in a personal, transcendent, free Creator. For Schelling, as we saw, the finite world

----

[19]Tagebücher V 50-53 (GdChr, p. 146): "Das Reich Gottes
aber war ursprünglich und muß ursprünglich gedacht werden--wie
alles überhaupt--in Gott. In ihm war es von Ewigkeit und ehe
als es im Endlichen erscheinen konnte: wie es in ihm ist, so
erscheint es allmählich hier und entwickelt sich. Durch seine
Idee in Gott ist das Wirkliche einzig möglich und begreiflich.
Es entsteht also die Frage: wie das Reich Gottes in Gott ist
und war vor aller Erscheinung? Oder was eins ist, wie alle
Dinge, das ganze Universum in Gott ist nach der Lehre der
Bibel? Die Antwort hierauf enthält die Trinitätslehre, welche
erklärt, wie überhaupt in Gott etwas von ihm Verschiedenes
entstehe und überhaupt etwas außer ihm sein könne."

is the outward expression of the eternal Ideas, i.e., of the
"modes" of that primal knowing which the Absolute is. The
expression of these Ideas is a spontaneous, inevitable "unfolding" of the undifferentiated Absolute. Since Drey wishes to
maintain that God creates freely and gratuitously as the
transcendent Author of the finite order, he cannot adopt the
Idealist thought-frame without some modification.

After asking, in the text just cited, "how the entire
Universe is in God," Drey says that the answer is to be found
in the doctrine of Trinity. The significance of this passing
remark in the Journals is made sufficiently clear in the
Dogmatics lectures, where Drey's treatment of Trinity is
directed to the God-world relationship, rather than to the
processions and relations within the Trinity.

He presents scriptural material on the three Persons, and
reports on the doctrinal development of the early centuries.
He does not, however, go into the history of Scholastic speculation on the interrelationships of Father, Son, and Spirit
within the "immanent" Trinity. His approach is rather what has
come to be called today "heilsökonomisch." His interest is not
so much in the "inner life" of God as in the relationship of
the revealed mystery of Trinity to the whole plan of salvation.[20]

We may distinguish two principal aspects of his utilization of the doctrine of Trinity: (1) to account for the radical
relatedness of the created order to God, and (2) to account for
the actual historical shape of salvation in terms of the differentiation of divine Persons acting in this history.

How the World is "in God"

The first aspect is basic, and corresponds to the question of "how the entire Universe is in God." Drey focuses on
the distinction between Father and Son in the Godhead, first

---

[20]Cf. Tagebücher V 50-53 (GdChr, p. 146): "Es muß hier so
stark als möglich bemerklich gemacht werden, daß sowohl die
Bibel, als die alten Kirchenlehrer die Trinitätslehre weniger
auf das Wesen Gottes als auf die Welt und das Reich Gottes
beziehen, weniger daraus das Wesen Gottes als den Plan seines
Reiches erklären." Cf. ThQ 1 (1819): 424, ". . . den Zusammenhang der Trinitätslehre mit der ganzen Ökonomie des Reiches
Gottes zu zeigen . . ."

revealed in Jesus Christ. He notes that the word "Father" in
the New Testament manifestly refers to God, but that Jesus' way
of attributing his own origin to this same God opens up "an
altogether new relationship in the very nature of God, hitherto
unknown: the relationship, namely, of God as Father to Christ
the son, altogether distinct from that relationship which exists
between God and created things."[21] And he further specifies
this relationship as "of God Himself to Himself."[22]

It is from this new perspective on the Being of God that
Drey formulates his conception of the entire created universe
as "within" God. In the following text, he conceives the Son
as the perfect self-expression of the divine essence (of the
Father as "ground" of the Trinity)[23] and--in this sense--as the
cause and "prototype" of the created world.

> The Son of God, therefore, . . . is a substance or person
> of some sort, eternal, intimately joined to God, His first
> and properly unique offspring, intermediate between God
> Himself and created things, the proximate cause, from which
> the origin of all things and their relationship to God is
> known. For it is in His Son, as cause and prototype, that
> God brought forth all that is; and by the love with which
> He loved this Son, He embraced simultaneously all things as
> founded in Him from all eternity, before they had come
> forth from within and became manifest.[24]

---

[21]PD II 81-82: ". . . nova omnino exsurgit in ipsa Dei
natura relatio, hucusque non cognita; relatio nimirum Dei ceu
Patris ad Christum filium, atque ab eo habitu prorsus distincta,
qui Deum inter et res creatas intercedit."

[22]PD II 82, marginal notation: ". . . ostenditur specia-
tim, relationem hujus filii ad divinum patrem et vice versa
diversam esse ab omnibus relationibus jam explicatis, et con-
sistere non jam in relatione Dei ad quasnam res creatas et
mundanas, sed in relatione Dei supernaturali et sui ipsius ad
se."

[23]Cf. PD I 47-48, cited below.

[24]PD III 168a-169a: "Est itaque Filius Dei . . . substan-
tia sive persona quaedam aeterna, intime conjuncta Deo, ejusque
prima et proprie unica soboles, media inter ipsum et res
creatas causaque proxima, ex qua rerum omnium origo relatioque
ad Deum cognoscitur. In filio nimirum suo, tanquam causa et
prototypo, Deus produxit omnia quae sunt; et amore quo hunc
amavit, complexus est simul omnia in ipso ab aeterno recondita;
antequam intus prodiissent et in mundo fierent conspicua . . ."

Drey's reasons for formulating the world's relationship to
God in these terms (and the Idealist background of this thought)
become more evident, when he comments on the above statement:

> This biblical doctrine satisfies human reason, which cannot
> think of God as ever idle or alone, nor of this world as
> eternal; nor does it contemplate in this world an altogether
> perfect image of God, similar to Him, and, therefore, it
> seeks such an image beyond the limits and ages of this
> world.[25]

What glimmers through this remark is the Idealist conception of God as objectifying Himself in a creative, productive
act of Selbstbestimmung. If human reason is truly unwilling to
conceive the finite world itself as this self-manifestation of
the Absolute (as Schelling does), then it must look to some kind
of self-objectification within the divine Being. And Drey
interprets the eternal Son as this perfectly adequate image of
the divine Ground or Father. This is even clearer in the
following text:

> Christian revelation presents God as the creator of all
> things. But God, insofar as he is not in time, does not
> beget or produce in time, nor is it thinkable that God pro-
> duce directly something finite or limited. Hence, according
> to the principles of reason, God is to be thought of as
> producing and generating from eternity, and one must admit
> of a kind of ideal, eternal, infinite and divine world.
> And this is the Son of God, who was in the bosom of the
> Father from eternity, through whom and to whose image all
> things have been created. Thus it is certain that God
> cannot be a Creator God, unless He is at the same time
> Father and has a Son from eternity.[26]

------

[25]PD III 169a: "Satisfecit doctrina haec biblica rationi
humanae, quae Deum neque otiosum unquam aut solum, neque mundum
hunc aeternum cogitare potest; neque in hoc ipso perfectam
omnino Deique similem imaginem contemplatur, adeoque talem extra
mundi fines et tempora quaerit."

[26]PD I 68-69: "Revelatio christiana Deum ut conditorem
omnium rerum repraesentat; Deus autem prouti non est in tempore,
ita nec in tempore gignit vel producit, neque etiam cogitabile
est, Deum aliquid finiti aut limitati producere immediate:
quare secundum principia rationis Deus ab aeterno producens et
generans cogitandus est, et admittendus mundus quidam idealis
aeternus, infinitus atque divinus: Atque hic filius Dei, qui in
sinu Patris fuit ab aeterno, per quem et ad cujus imaginem condita sunt universa. Proinde certum est, Deum esse non posse
Deum conditorem, nisi simul Pater sit et filium habeat ab
aeterno." For a parallel text, cf. Apologetik II § 65, pp. 244-
45: ". . . Gott ist ewig, er hat aber von Ewigkeit her ein ihm
vollkommen ähnliches Wesen, den Theilhaber aller seiner

It is clear enough that this "ideal, eternal . . . world"
is posited as a self-manifestation of the divine Being. The
actual finite, created world is only secondarily such a manifestation, insofar as it reproduces, in that which is not God, the
divine Being of the eternal prototype.[27] It is from this point
of view that Drey can insist on the importance of the eternal
Son's relationship to the world, in order to explain how the
world is related to God. In the following text, Drey is commenting in a book review on the Dogmatics of Marianus Dobmayer:

> . . . the author's presentation of the Son of God is also
> dogmatically incomplete, since it lacks what is both neces-
> sary from a scientific standpoint and biblically founded:
> namely, a demonstration of the relation of the Son of God
> to the world; it is only through this relation that the
> entire relationship of the world to God, its being from and
> outside of God, and God's view of it are mediated. The Son
> of God is the eternal Type of the temporal world, He is the
> world itself, insofar as it stands before God as the eter-
> nal revelation of God to the outside.[28]

This way of conceiving the Son of God affects one's way
of regarding and valuing the created world, as Drey notes in a
strikingly parallel text of the Apologetik. Referring to
Christ's teaching and revelation of the inner mystery of God,
he says:

> . . . our view of the world and its relation to God has
> also become different; although temporal in its becoming,
> enduring, and passing away, the world was nevertheless from
> all eternity the object of the divine love and providence,
> the goal of His eternal decrees, through its relation to

Eigenschaften, den Abglanz seiner Herrlichkeit bei sich; woher
kann dieses ewige gottgleiche Wesen anders seyn, als nur aus
Gott? . . . Gott, wie er von Ewigkeit sich vor sich selbst in
der Vollkommenheit seines Wesens in seinem Sohne geoffenbaret
. . . . . . jenes ewige übersinnliche Verhältniß Gottes zu dem
Producte seiner Selbstoffenbarung . . ."

[27]Cf. above, pp. 85-86, for the parallel to Schelling's
thought.

[28]ThQ 1 (1819) 424: "Des Verfassers Darstellung vom Sohne
Gottes ist auch dogmatisch unvollständig, denn es fehlt ihr die
in wissenschaftlicher Hinsicht eben so nothwendige als biblisch-
gegründete Nachweisung der Beziehung des Sohnes Gottes zur Welt,
einer Beziehung, durch welche allein das ganze Verhältniß der
Welt zu Gott, ihr Seyn aus und außer Gott und die Anschauung
Gottes von ihr vermittelt ist. Der Sohn Gottes ist der ewige
Typus der zeitlichen Welt, die Welt selbst, inwieferne sie als
ewige Offenbarung Gottes nach außen vor ihm steht."

the Son, through whom He has not only created everything,
but in whom He has also loved the world from eternity . . .
through whom He has also determined to restore everything
. . . in whom He has chosen us before the foundation of the
world . . . and has foreseen, predestined and called us to
become conformed to him . . .[29]

The explicit mention of the divine love in this context[30]
seems significant. For this introduces a personal category into
what might otherwise seem to be a purely intellectual conception
of how the pattern of the finite world pre-exists as an aspect
of the divine Being. Drey "locates" the created world within
the divine Being, so to speak, not only to account for its pre-
existence in the "ideal" order, but also to account for God's
love of this created world. It is the eternal Son whom the
Father loves. The created world is loved "in the Son," who is
its eternal Prototype.[31]

Thus, Drey says that the notion of the Son of God implies
"the representation of the world before God, such as He sees
it"[32] and goes on to say:

Therefore, the Son of God is the Prototype not only of the
Son of Man, such as he afterwards appears on this earth,

---

[29]Apologetik II § 68, p. 253: ". . . unsere Ansicht von
der Welt und ihrer Beziehung zu Gott ist eine andere geworden;
wenn auch zeitlich in ihrem Werden, Bestehen und Vergehen, war
sie doch von Ewigkeit Gegenstand der göttlichen Liebe und
Vorsehung, Zweck seiner ewigen Rathschlüsse durch ihre Beziehung zu dem Sohne, durch welchen er nicht nur alles geschaffen,
in welchem er auch die Welt von Ewigkeit geliebt . . . durch
welchen er auch alles wiederherzustellen beschlossen . . . in
welchem er uns vor der Welt Gründung auserwählt . . . und
vorhergesehen, vorherbestimmt und berufen hat ihm gleichförmig
zu werden . . ."

[30]Cf. also PD III 168a-169a, cited above.

[31]Cf. Rief's comment on this, Reich Gottes und Gesellschaft, p. 112. To say, however, as Rief does, that God loves
the Son in view of the world to be created is misleading insofar as it implies that this created world is the ultimate
object of His love, and that the Son is lovable only insofar as
He is the prototype of this to-be-created finite world. Actually, Drey's thought seems to be just the reverse: the finite
world is lovable insofar as it is an imperfect realization of
the eternal Prototype which the Son is.

[32]PD II 88, marginal notation: "Notio filii Dei duo
importat: repraesentatio amoris Dei ipsius coram hominibus,
qualem hi capere possent, et repraesentatio mundi coram Deo,
qualem hic videt."

but is the Prototype of the world itself and of all the
ages, such as God regarded it from eternity and ought to
have regarded it. Nor is he some kind of empty or imagin-
ary prototype, like the ones which are in us, but rather
the living and true one, in whom the Father embraced with
an eternal love both Himself and all things which were at
some time to be, and also brought forth all things.[33]

To conceive the finite world's relationship to the Infinite in these trinitarian categories is not merely to overcome
the deistic separation of the world from an extrinsic Maker; it
is to place the world within the interpersonal dynamic of the
divine Being. Drey comments on this explicitly in the Apologetik, just after the text cited above:

Through these ideas, man and the world are not merely
brought close to God, but are, to a certain extent, moved
into the Godhead; with His eternal wisdom and love He bore
them in Himself, determined from eternity their relationship to Himself, the relationships of every individual
thing to the whole, the special ends and the final end of
everything. Through His omnipotence, whose visible bearer
the Son is, He let them come forth from Himself, guides
them and holds them together in their temporal unfolding
according to the plan of His eternal predestination.[34]

The texts already cited show sufficiently the first aspect
of Drey's trinitarian doctrine: to account for the radical
relatedness of the created order to God. I have called this
basic to his theology, because it links together God and world
intrinsically (and thus links together the two major parts of
dogmatic theology).

---

[33] PD II 88-89: "Est itaque Filius Dei Prototypon non solum
Filii hominis, qualis postea in his terris comparuit, sed
Prototypon mundi ipsius et saeculorum omnium quale Deus ab
aeterno intuitus est et intueri debuit; nec inane aliquod et
imaginarium prototypon, qualia in nobis sunt, sed vivum et
verum, in quo et se ipsum et omnes res aliquando futuras amore
aeterno Pater complexus est, et cuncta etiam produxit."

[34] Apologetik II § 68, p. 253: "Durch diese Ideen wird der
Mensch und die Welt Gott nicht blos nahe gebracht, sondern
gewissermaßen in die Gottheit hineingerückt; mit seiner ewigen
Weisheit und Liebe trug er sie in sich, bestimmte von Ewigkeit
ihr Verhältniß zu ihm, die Verhältnisse alles Einzelnen zum
Ganzen, die besondern Zwecke und den Endzweck von Allem; durch
seine Allmacht, deren sichtbarer Träger der Sohn ist, ließ er
sie aus sich hervorgehen, leitet sie und hält sie in ihrer
zeitlichen Entfaltung zusammen nach dem Plane seiner ewigen
Vorherbestimmung."

Moreover, while clearly moving in the ambience of Idealism,
Drey's thought is able to avoid the consequence of having to
conceive the finite order itself as the spontaneous, inevitable
unfolding of the Absolute.[35] It is not the finite world which
is the <u>necessary</u> imaging-forth of the divine, but rather the
eternal Son, conceived according to the tradition as both con-
substantial with the Father and personal. Within this Son, so
to speak, the entire created order is known and loved eternally.
The self-differentiation within the Godhead is conceived as a
pre-condition for creating a finite order, but such creation is
not perceived as necessary to the perfect self-manifestation of
God to Himself.

Trinity and the "Economy" of Salvation

There is a second aspect to Drey's utilization of the
doctrine of Trinity: to account for the actual historical shape
of salvation in terms of the differentiation of divine Persons
acting in this history.

We have already noted that Drey's interest in Trinity is
primarily its relevance to the "economy" of salvation--under-
standing this "economy" to begin with and to be rooted in the
very relationship of created world to Creator God. That there
should be a created order at all is to be explained--as we have
just seen--in terms of the eternal differentiation, within the
Godhead, of Father and Son. But this created order is to be
conceived dynamically as a process in time, by which God's
eternal purposes (<u>consilia</u>) are achieved. The entire second
part of dogmatic theology is to present this history in a way
which shows its intelligibility as the making-real of an Idea.
Drey refers to this as the "economy of the Kingdom of God."

We noted in Chapter V that Drey equates the "Ideas" of
philosophy (united in the highest Idea: <u>Reich Gottes</u>) with the
"decrees" of God. Every created being and every event of
temporal process is known and willed eternally by God before
its realization in time. Obviously enough, a detailed knowledge of these divine decrees is impossible for the human mind.[36]

---

[35]Contrast with Schelling, pp. 106-7, above.

[36]Cf. PD III 216-18.

But Drey thinks that the "capita" or chief features of God's
plan of providence can be recognized, under the tutelage of
divine revelation. It is these "capita" which he sketches out
in §§ XIII-XVIII of the "Praemonita" text (PD III, 56; 61-69)
as the chief phases and turning-points of the Kingdom of God in
its coming-to-be. This is the framework which we are about to
examine in the latter part of this chapter. It is the schema
by which Drey attempts to unify the traditional themes of
dogmatic theology in terms of his systematizing concept.

Having given this overview in the "Praemonita," he
attempts in the Trinity section to indicate the foundational
relevance of Trinity to a proper interpretation of the "economy."
The "decrees" are to be viewed in their intrinsic relationship
to the differentiation of Persons within the Godhead, so as to
see these divine Persons as the source and summit of the dynamic
which is being wrought out in time and created reality.

> . . . these decrees--embracing the entire economy of the
> Kingdom of God-- . . . are either altogether rooted in the
> most sacred Persons of the Son and the Holy Spirit, or are
> related to them by christian doctrine, or finally, cannot
> be conceived or worthily presented by a proper theologian
> without these divine Persons. Therefore, besides God the
> Father--author of all the decrees--the Son and Holy Spirit
> are, as it were, the heads and apices of the entire divine
> economy, and they have, carry, and sustain this very econ-
> omy, so to speak, within themselves . . .[37]

The Son and Holy Spirit seem to be viewed as the bearers
and agents of the "economy," whereas the Father is conceived as
the ultimate Source and Ground both of Son and Spirit, and of
created reality.[38] To call God "Father" seems to express the

---

[37]PD III 187a: ". . . illa [decreta] . . . omnem regni
divini oeconomiam complexa . . . vel omnino inhaerent sanctis-
simis Filii et Spiritus Sancti personis, vel ad easdem a doctrina christiana referuntur, vel denique sine his concipi
digneque exhiberi a Theologo justo non possunt. Sunt itaque
praeter Deum Patrem consiliorum omnium auctorem Filius et
Spiritus S. quasi capita et apices omnis oeconomiae divinae,
atque hanc ipsam quasi intus inclusam in se habent, portant et
sustinent."

[38]PD I 47-48: "Divini Patris tam crebra est in sacris
literis mentio, tam reverens Augusti hujus nominis commendatio,
ut eo sacrum designari Numen nemo negaverit. Atque cum hic
idem non solum mundi hujus atque generis nostri auctor et
parens, verum et reliquorum, qui Sacra Trinitate censentur,
filii nimirum et Spiritus Sancti fons et origo dicatur, Patris

mystery of Origin, of ungenerated Source of all things.[39] Moreover, this term involves the correlative name of Son, so that
the fundamental differentiation of the Godhead into unoriginate
Source and perfect self-expression is affirmed as the condition
of possibility for there being a finite, created order distinct
from God.[40]

What he goes on to say about Son and Spirit is said in
terms of their "missions." For he observes that Scripture
gives no information about the manner of generation of Son or
Spirit from the Father, but speaks only of their being sent to
do something in the world.[41]

The Son

The function of the Son--to redeem mankind--is intimately
bound up with His very Being in relation to the Father:

---

nomine ipsam substantiam divinam indivisam aeternam atque omnia
generantem absque ulla reprehensione intelligimus."

[39]PD II 82: "Dicitur autem solus Pater nec visus ulli nec
videndus, nec ab aliquo esse, nec alicui inesse, sed vitam
habere in semetipso, quibus utique descriptionibus investiga-
bilis et summa atque ex omni parte independens Dei majestas
indicatur."

[40]Cf. PD I 68-69, cited above.

[41]Cf. PD I 61. This should not, however, be taken to
imply that Drey was doubtful about the "threeness" of the
"immanent Trinity." Quite the reverse: because he conceived
the created world--in its historical development--as the very
manifestation of the Being of God, he judged that the God who
is manifest as threefold in the economy must also be threefold
in Himself. In this sense, Drey anticipated Rahner's thesis
that the "economic Trinity is the immanent Trinity." Cf. Karl
Rahner, The Trinity (New York: Herder & Herder, 1970). PD I
66: "Si deus non est trinus in se, etiam id esse non potest ad
extra, sive erga nos." PD I 68: ". . . id quod Deus est erga
genus nostrum spectatis his consiliis divinis, esse non posset,
nisi esset multiplex etiam et pluriformis in se; quae multipli-
citas dei in se conditio est sine qua non, simulque causa
illius multiplicitatis externae ad nos." PD III 183a, marginal
notation: ". . . wir gehen nun über zur Betrachtung Gottes in
seinem Außersichseyn, d.h. seinen Verhältnissen zur Welt u.
umgekehrt. Wenn aber in diesen eine wahre Offenbarung des
göttlichen Wesens nach außen erkannt wird, so muß das Insich-
seyn Gottes auch in seinem Außersichseyn sich wieder darstellen
. . . d.h. es muß auch die Dreieinigkeit Gottes in seinen
Verhältnissen zur Welt offenbar werden, und das Ganze von jenen
auf dieser ruhen."

It will be shown in its proper place that the role of the
Son, who appeared on this earth, is to educate our race, to
heal it once it has been educated, to render God benevolent
and friendly towards it once it is healed, and thus in
every way to save it and make it happy. And this decree of
the eternal Father concerning the salvation of mankind is
so joined together with the person of the Son, that it
resides intimately within Him.[42]

Moreover, in accord with his way of conceiving the finite
world as eternally known and loved by the Father in the Son,
Drey includes "within the Son" all that leads up to the actual
redemption, beginning with the creation of the world:

But those things which, in the ordinary way of thinking,
precede that decree, are not separate from Him [the Son]:
namely, the very creation of things, the Fall, and the
remedies employed beforehand; those things too are related
to the Son in such a way that the world is said to have
been created in Him, the Fall itself is said to have been
allowed as the cause of a more excellent salvation, and the
remedies of the earlier time are said to have been types
and prophecies of the final work to be achieved by the Son.[43]

A closer look at the Son's redemptive work will be provided in the latter part of this chapter. The point of the
brief characterization given here is to stress the "eternity"
and divine "ideality" of the entire historically achieved plan
of salvation. This is very important for Drey's conception of
the intelligibility to be found by the theologian in the
historically given shape of God's revelation. Although regarding this revelation as a process achieved in time, he must rise
to the perspective from which the entire history may be appreciated as the realization of God's eternal Idea. Moreover, by

---

[42]PD III 187a: "Eas esse Filii, qui in his terris comparuit, partes, ut genus nostrum erudiret, eruditum sanaret,
sanato placabilem Deum et amicum redderet, atque sic omni modo
sospitaret bearetque; multis suo tempore ostendetur. Atque hoc
quidem aeterni Patris de hominum salute placitum ita cum Filii
persona conjunctum est, ut huic penitus insit atque insideat."

[43]PD III 187a-188a: "Verum nec remotiora ab eo sunt, quae pro
pro communi cogitandi modo illud ipsum placitum antecedunt,
rerum ipsarum creatio, lapsus, et curationes ante adhibitae;
quare et illa sic ad Filium referuntur, ut mundus in ipso
conditus, lapsus ipse insignioris salutis causa concessus,
curationes autem anteriores opis postremae a Filio afferendae
typi dicantur fuisse et praesagia."

his trinitarian emphasis, Drey wishes to identify the intelligible pattern of creation and salvation with the very Person of
the Son. In this way, the very historical shape of the created
world is "located" within the interpersonal Being of God. What
has happened and is happening may not, therefore, be regarded
merely in terms of human ideas or purposes, but must be interpreted as the manifestation of divine purposes which are
finally inseparable from the divine Persons of the Trinity.

Referring to the sentence quoted just above, Drey goes on
to say:

> But how can all those things be worthily explained in their
> proper places by the theologian, unless this doctrine of
> the Holy Trinity which we have given provide a light? Will
> he be able to speak worthily of all those things, and remove
> from the divine purposes (consilia) the appearance of human
> purposes, unless he conceives those things--even though
> made manifest through the course of time--nevertheless as
> eternal, fixed, and unalterable in the Son?[44]

The Holy Spirit

To appreciate what Drey says, in this context, about the
Holy Spirit, one must take into account the dimension of time
and becoming. Part of the romantic thought-world in which Drey
lived was a strong sense of growth and development. The Holy
Spirit is invoked as the Principle and Agent of the process of
salvation which was begun and enabled by Christ but which must
become actual over a long period of time, in many individual
lives and in social, visible form.

> Since, however, the salvation of those who have been saved
> must be brought to fulfilment not in a single moment, so to
> speak, but rather by certain stages, and because the huge
> difference between God's majesty and the human condition is
> able--not indeed to be removed--but to be reduced and
> diminished only over long intervals of time, God estab-
> lished to this end special helps in His Holy Spirit.
> According to the doctrine of the gospels, it is the Spirit's

---

[44]PD III 188a: "Quomodo vero ista omnia a Theologo suis
locis digne explicari poterunt, nisi facem praeferat haec, quam
dedimus, S. Trinitatis doctrina? Poteritne de omnibus istis
digne loqui, atque a consiliis divinis consiliorum humanorum
speciem avertere, nisi ista, quamvis temporum decursu patefacta,
aeterna tamen ac rata atque firma in Filio cogitet?"

task to bring to completion the work begun by the
Redeemer.[45]

As we shall see, the Holy Spirit is the Agent in the
process of "sanctification," by which individuals are justified
so as to become partakers of the relationship to God made known
and established by Christ. Moreover, the Spirit is the Principle of the new social reality arising out of Christ, the Church.
Since the "economy" which has been eternally known and willed
in the Son can only gradually be made actual in the created
order by the agency of the Spirit, it is evident that a large
sector of the divine purposes is inseparable from and intimately
identified with the Person of the Spirit.

> We perceive that to the Spirit has been entrusted this
> office in the economy of the divine kingdom: to take up the
> person of Christ upon his departure from this earth, to act
> in his place, to carry on and bring to completion his work.
> . . . We understand, therefore, that a great part of the
> divine decrees has been located in this very Spirit . . .[46]

This temporal process, guided and worked by the Holy
Spirit, is at the same time rooted and, so to speak, prefigured
in the very inner dynamic of the divine Being. For the end
result of the process, as Drey conceives it, is the perfect
union of created being with God through the free acknowledgment
by mankind of God's perfect dominion over them. This will be
the end-state of the Kingdom of God. Since the created world
is already known and loved by the Father in the eternal Son,
Drey is able to conceive the union of Father and Son as a
prefiguration, in some sense, of the ultimately-to-be-achieved
union of the created world with God. And it is from this
exalted perspective that the role of the Holy Spirit is properly
appreciated. Since it is He who unites Father and Son, it is
also He who actualizes in the order of finite, created being
the intended union of this created world with God.

---

[45]PD I 67: "Simul autem cum servatorum etiam salus non
uno quasi momento, sed stadiis quibusdam perfici debeat, et
quod inter Dei majestatem ac humanam conditionem intercedit dis-
crimen ingens, longis solum ac diuturnis intervallis non quidem
tolli sed elevari possit et imminui, ad hunc finem specialia
nobis auxilia in spiritu suo sancto constituit, cujus est ex
doctrina evangelica, opus a redemtore inceptum perficere."

[46]PD III 188a-189a: "Huic [Spiritui Sancto] enim demanda-
tam in regni divini oeconomia provinciam cernimus, ut Christi

Our union with God is the end and destiny of our present
condition after Christ. This condition is prefigured
through the union of Father and Son from eternity. (The
Son of Man, from the mouth of Christ, is the eternal man,
humanity as Idea in the divine intellect.) This union is
made real by the Holy Spirit who unites us with God in the
same way that He unites Father with Son.[47]

This last text shows how much Drey's trinitarian view of
the "economy" reflects the traditional exitus-reditus pattern.
Created reality "comes forth" from God, within whose interpersonal differentiation it was known and loved eternally. Its
destiny is to be united by free choice with the Source of its
being--a union prefigured in the eternal union of Son with
Father. But the process whereby this ultimate union is achieved
takes the form of a temporal development, a history. The ideal
pattern for this development is already contained in the eternal
Son. But the making-real of this ideal pattern is the "work"
of Son and Spirit in their missions. The Son's work, although
decisive, is limited in time and place. The Spirit continues
the Son's work in time, achieving the sanctification of individuals and the growth of the great social reality of the Kingdom
of God. The end-state is envisioned as a "return" to God the
Father, a union of created reality with God in the Son by the
agency of the Spirit.

The "Economy": Part II of the Dogmatics

The preceding section on the Trinity was directed to the
principal interest of this chapter: how Drey's "formal" viewpoint governs his systematic treatment of Dogmatics. His trinitarian conception of how the finite world is related to God
and how the "economy" of salvation is rooted in the tri-personal
Being of God is basic to his effort to understand God and world

---

ex his terris egressi personam suscipiat, locum sustineat, opus
gerat et perficiat. . . . Magnam itaque consiliorum divinorum
partem in hoc ipso Spiritu repositam deprehendimus . . ."

[47]PD I 69: "Nostra enim cum Deo conjunctio finis est et
destinatio conditionis praesentis post Christum. Haec conditio
praefigurata per unitionem patris et filii ab aeterno (Filius
hominis ex ore Christi est homo aeternus, humanitas ceu Idea in
intellectu divino) realis efficitur per spir. S. qui nos, eodem
modo unit cum Deo, quomodo unit Patrem cum filio."

in unity. What remains to be examined now is the way Drey
organizes the contents of the second major part of Dogmatics,
the "economy."

It is here that the distinctive concern of Drey to grasp
the "ideal" intelligibility of an historically given process
finds expression. For the economy of salvation embraces an
historical development of mankind under divine influence. Both
Scripture and popular piety regard this simply as history which
is ruled by God. But the scientific theologian seeks to understand this history from the perspective of Ideas. Hence, the
way in which Drey sets up the divisions of his material reflects
his governing Idea of the Reich Gottes.

In one way, he seems to be following a temporal sequence--
beginning with creation and the "original" condition of world
and man, then following through the event of the Fall and the
ensuing divine remedies for man's sinful condition, culminating
in Christ, then showing the continuation and expansion of this
salvific event in the form of the Spirit-guided Church where
individuals are sanctified.

On the other hand, his intention is to employ the concept
Reich Gottes as a systematizing category of interpretation for
these temporally achieved events. It has already been explained, in Chapter V, that Drey claims for this concept the status
of an "Idea" which --although presented to mankind in its full
clarity only by divine revelation--nevertheless has a compelling
validity for the human mind. Hence, to the extent that the
temporally achieved phases of mankind's relationship to God may
be interpreted as permutations of the eternal Idea of Reich
Gottes, the systematic theologian can achieve his purpose of
discovering necessity in the seemingly fortuitous. Theology
can then become a true "Wissenschaft" of the "real," to speak
in Schelling's categories.[48]

As we saw in Chapter V, Drey's distinction of the merely
historical view of the divinely ruled history (which he calls
"phaenomenological") from the properly scientific and speculative view of that same history (which he calls "noumenologi-
cal")[49] is of foundational importance for his method in theology.

---

[48]Cf. above, pp. 98-105.   [49]PD I 19.

Up until now, we have had to speak of this in a rather formal
way, since we were following Drey's own discussion of method.
But we have the opportunity now to see how the formal distinction actually functions in Drey's treatment of the content of
Christian doctrines.

The term Reich Gottes--as Drey explicitly acknowledges--
is a unifying concept which attempts to think God and world in
one thought. Hence, it is laden with all the tensions of that
mysterious juxtaposition: finite-Infinite, creature-Creator,
temporal-eternal. Drey's usage of the term betrays various
nuances of meaning, reflecting these tensions. We must begin,
therefore, by attempting to name and distinguish the various
senses and functions of the term Reich Gottes.[50] This work of
clarification will provide the framework for Drey's "scientific
construction" of the history of salvation--the system in his
Dogmatics.

Senses of "Reich Gottes"
1. Abstract, mystical,
trans-historical

The most profound level of meaning has to do with the
very God-world relationship itself, as this is constituted
unalterably by the transcendent "fact" of the divine creative
activity. At this level, as we have seen, the concept functions
abstractly to unite Creator and created in a single intuition.
In considering Reich Gottes (in this sense) as the highest idea
possible to the human mind, Drey affirms both that God cannot
be known apart from the world and that the world cannot be
conceived in isolation from God.

Not only does the world "belong" utterly and completely
to the Creator, so that it is appropriately called His "Reich,"
that is, the area of His dominion, mastery, indeed ownership.[51]
Even more profoundly, created being is intrinsically related to
the Creator by being the very manifestation of the divine Being.

------

[50]For a thorough treatment of the historical background of
this idea and the various sources from which Drey may have
drawn, see Rief, Reich Gottes und Gesellschaft, pp. 11-15, 19-
21, 26-69. My concern is simply to clarify the senses in which
Drey himself uses the term in his MSS and published works.

[51]KE § 18, p. 10: ". . . das Universum . . . rein als
Werk und Eigentum Gottes betrachtet . . ."

In this sense, calling the world the Reich Gottes is equivalent
to affirming that this finite, created realm--perceived correctly[52]--is God Himself as manifested in that which is not God:

> The end of creation is the Kingdom of God, that is, the
> external manifestation of the divine perfections in a
> system of things which are not divine, but which can repre-
> sent those [divine] properties and can make the finite
> beings happy.--The transposition of the Ideal in God into a
> Real.[53]

This rather mystical way of regarding world and God in
one intuition is, of course, further qualified by Drey's trinitarian thought, as we saw above. And it is this trinitarian
aspect of the God-world relationship (in addition to his creationist view) which appears to distinguish Drey's thought from
Schelling's. A further brief comment on this will help to move
us into the other operative senses of the term Reich Gottes.

The intimacy of relationship between Creator and created
world is to be understood not merely from the fact that the
latter is a manifestation of the former. There is, indeed,
what Drey calls an "eternal relationship" constituted by the
very creative action of God. But this is to be understood as
"rooted," so to speak, within the personal differentiation of
the very divine Being, as we have seen.

The totality of created being, referred to as the Reich
Gottes, is already known and loved by the Father "in the Son."
The eternal relationship of creature to uncreated Source is
thus, in principle, one of intimacy and union, since it is
grounded in the Father-Son relationship within the Godhead.
From this perspective, the "Bestimmung" (purpose and destiny)
of the created world is to belong utterly to the uncreated
Source in a personal relationship characterized by love.

---

[52]Man's failure to perceive the world this way is the
consequence of his radical sin: absolutizing his own sense of
self. Cf. KE §§ 7-12, pp. 3-8 and § 18, pp. 10-11.

[53]PD I 74, marginal notation: "Finis creationis est regnum Dei sive perfectionum divinarum manifestatio ad extra in
systemate rerum non divinarum, quod tamen illas proprietates
referre et res finitas beare possit. -- Die Übersetzung des
Ideals in Gott in ein Reales." Cf. Rief, Reich Gottes und
Gesellschaft, pp. 98-99.

2. Concrete, historical, developmental

This destiny of the created world, however, can only be achieved through a temporal process,[54] in the course of which mankind (the conscious, free portion of created reality) comes to acknowledge freely the eternal relationship to God which was established "in principle" by the very act of creation. This developmental perspective involves a more concrete, historical sense of Reich Gottes.

There is a close relationship and interplay in Drey's thought between senses (1) and (2) of Reich Gottes. Sense (1) is obviously fundamental, since it determines the very essence of the human from the mystical perspective of the finite's rootedness in the Infinite. At the same time, Drey views man historically and developmentally. That is, he supposes that man was created in a state analogous to childhood, and could only gradually develop towards the intended perfection of free relatedness to God. Moreover, as we saw in Chapter III, God's revelatory influence upon the human spirit is conceived as intrinsic to the human condition. Religion must develop, as man's rational consciousness develops, under the stimulating effect of God's educative activity in and through history.

This religion which develops gradually under the influence of divine revelation is conceived as man's subjective acknowledgment and affirmation of the objective "state of affairs" constituted by creation. This "original" relationship of everything to God is what is meant by Reich Gottes in sense (1). Hence, the mystical sense of Reich Gottes is the normative context for Drey's conception of man's "Bestimmung" in relation to God. Man is conceived as integral part of this

---

[54]The transition from the mystical perspective to the historical perspective is a problematic feature of Drey's thought. The former perspective, so closely akin to Schelling's view, tends to see man's relationship to God as eternal--in a sense, transcending any particular historical events. On the other hand, Drey has a strongly romantic sense of development which governs his view of the "economy" of salvation as a history. There is a tension between these two views which seems intrinsic to Drey's method of seeking the intelligibility of the historical from the "higher viewpoint" which is, at once, mystical and speculative.

finite order, the totality of which is oriented towards God as
eternal Ground and Center. The uniqueness of man is his capacity to acknowledge consciously and freely the radical relationship which is constituted by creation. This acknowledgment is
"religion": the subjective exercise in a human mode of the
objective relatedness which is ontologically constituted prior
to man's freedom.

The concrete, historical sense of Reich Gottes refers,
therefore, to a gradually realized, ever more perfect relationship of created freedom to God in a harmonious unity of men
with one another and with Him. How this might have taken place
if man had not sinned remains a moot point. For the temporal
development of the Reich Gottes has been profoundly affected by
mankind's refusal--from the beginning of consciousness--to
acknowledge the primal relatedness to God. Hence, the actual
history of revelation has had to take on the form of "recalling"
mankind from its sinful self-absolutizing to the "original"
truth of its relationship to God.[55] In other words, God's
revelatory influence upon human reason[56] has taken on the form
of "redemption," to overcome the evil of sin. The history of
mankind, therefore, is guided and ruled by the divine Agency in
such a way as to realize God's purposes, in spite of man's sin,[57]
and to bring His Kingdom into being through the free response
of mankind.

"Reich Gottes" as equivalent to divine providence.--It is
from this point of view that the term Reich Gottes is equivalent to divine providence, the divinely ruled order of events
in time.[58] This perspective is not so much "ontological" (the

---

[55]Cf. above, pp. 41-43; KE §§ 18-22, pp. 10-12.

[56]This revelatory influence would have been a constant
feature of human existence, even without sin. Cf. Chapter III.

[57]There is an ambiguity about the place of sin in Drey's
Idealist-inspired view of the economy of salvation. On the one
hand, he sees sin as a disturbance of the divine plan, which
must be overcome by God's revelatory activity. On the other
hand, the Idealist influence is evident in his tendency to see
sin as "included" in the divine plan, as a way in which the
divinely intended realization of the Idea Reich Gottes is
advanced. See below.

[58]See above, pp. 146-47.

eternal relationship grounded in creation) as historical. In
other words, the realm of created being which is utterly subject
to the will of the Creator is viewed explicitly as a temporal
process involving human freedom. To call this the <u>Reich Gottes</u>
is to affirm the sovereignty and infallible efficacy of God's
will in the affairs of men.

To find intelligibility in God's sovereign guidance of
history (the task of "scientific" theology) is, therefore, a
matter of seeing how this sequence of events brings about a
realization in the mode of human freedom of that primal relationship of creature to Creator constituted eternally by the creative will of God.

The intelligible necessity of this Idea is grounded in
the mystical intuition of man's essential relatedness to God,
insofar as created. The actual shape of the temporal realization of this relationship in freedom is a matter of history--
what has happened and what is happening. Since the crucial
condition of man's achieving his destiny is the free submission
to God's dominion in a life lived in harmony with the divine
will, it is possible to relate the concrete, historical pattern
of the God-given salvation to the trans-historical Idea of man
in essential relatedness to God.

<u>"Reich Gottes" as a social reality</u>.--In his concrete view
of mankind, moreover, Drey is aware not only of the temporal,
developmental character of human existence, but even more of
its social character. His account of salvation takes a very
broad universal-historical perspective, in order to appreciate
the social context of mankind's growing submission to God's
rule.

We need, therefore, to distinguish (within the concrete,
historical sense of <u>Reich Gottes</u>) yet another sense in which
the term functions. And this will enable us to appreciate
better how Drey thought that this master Idea could function as
a <u>Leitmotiv</u> for the interpretation of history. For it is not a
totally formal concept which merely affirms divine guidance of
history ("providence") without at all specifying what actual
shape that guidance is bringing about.

Looking at the history of God's revelatory influence upon
the human race, Drey sees in the Jewish ideal of a theocracy

which is ultimately to embrace even the Gentiles a foreshadow-
ing of the divine Idea of <u>Reich Gottes</u>.[59] The form in which
the human race's acknowledgment of God's dominion over them is
to find expression is conceived as a great <u>social</u> reality, a
union of all men which transcends racial and cultural differences.[60] In this sense, the term <u>Reich Gottes</u> was adapted by
Christ and given a new spiritual and moral meaning which went
far beyond the ethnic and political ideal of the Jewish messianic hopes:

> . . . it is . . . a purely spiritual and ethical Kingdom,
> which recognizes no other Lord than God and His Son, whom
> He has sent and destined not to destroy the kingdoms of
> this world but to ennoble them through his religious and
> ethical spirit, and not to subjugate the peoples of the
> earth to one (favorite) nation, but rather to unite them
> all through the bond of love into one people of God under
> the dominion of the Father of men and the King of Kings.[61]

The unity envisioned here, although spiritual, is not
conceived as invisible. Drey's Catholic identity finds

---

[59]<u>Apologetik</u> II § 40, p. 167: ". . . die Idee der mosai-
schen Theokratie ist die Anticipation der erst im Christenthum
hervortretenden Idee vom Reiche Gottes als eines ethischen
Gottesstaates, welche der alten Welt und Bildung nur unter
dieser Hülle eines sinnlichen Weltstaates zugänglich und begreiflich gemacht werden konnte." Cf. KE §§ 58-59, pp. 36-37.

[60]Drey seems clearly influenced by Herder's vision of the
widely differing human possibilities realized in the many
<u>Völker</u> of the earth. He takes this variety into account in his
survey of the world religions in <u>Apologetik</u> II. His conception
of God's Kingdom postulates a spiritual unity which is to be
not ethnic or political, but "rein menschlich." Cf. <u>Apologetik</u>
I § 3, pp. 96-97; II § 56, p. 215; II § 68, pp. 257-59; III §
27, p. 149; KE § 27, p. 15; § 187, p. 126; § 228, p. 153, § 301,
p. 203; <u>Tagebücher</u> IV 81-82; 128. Drey thus seems to anticipate today's ideal of a "world Church" which could unite quite
diverse cultural embodiments of Christianity in an overarching
spiritual communion. Cf. Karl Rahner, "Towards a Fundamental
Theological Interpretation of Vatican II," <u>Theological Studies</u>
40 (1979):716-27.

[61]<u>Apologetik</u> II § 56, p. 212: ". . . es ist . . . ein rein
geistiges und sittliches Reich, welches keinen andern Herrn
anerkennt als Gott und seinen Sohn, den er gesandt hat,
bestimmt die Reiche dieser Welt nicht aufzuheben, sondern durch
seinen religiösen und sittlichen Geist zu veredeln, und die
Völker der Erde nicht einem (Lieblings-)Volke zu unterwerfen,
sondern alle durch das Band der Liebe zu vereinigen zu Einem
Volke Gottes unter der Herrschaft des Vaters der Menschen und
des Königs der Könige."

expression in his conception of the visible Church as the
partial, incipient manifestation of the ideal Reich Gottes. It
is the spread of Christianity among the peoples of the earth
which is to bring about the divinely intended unification.
That this is the pattern of God's purposes is indicated already,
Drey thinks, by the fact that the origin of Christianity
occurred at the time when the Roman Empire had succeeded in
perhaps the widest possible unification of diverse races and
nations under a single political rule.[62]

3. Eschatological

What is basic to Drey's conception of the social unification of mankind is, of course, the religious attitude of
acknowledging God's dominion. Since this is never complete and
perfect at any stage of the world's history, there is a final
sense of the term Reich Gottes which points beyond history to
the eschatological fulfillment.

The end-state of God's Kingdom will be the unity of all
those who have been saved and sanctified in one perfect society
with God and Christ.[63] Only in this final, eternal condition
of the world will the Idea of Reich Gottes finally be actualized completely. Although this can only be an object of hope
during this present age, it is nevertheless in continuity with
what is already visible as Church.

This end-state is the perfect achievement of the divinely
intended union of all mankind with God in freedom. It is
"beyond history" in a different way than sense (1) above. For,
since it is the making-real in human freedom of the essential
relatedness of creature to Creator (the Idea), it is the culmination of an actual historical process, without which it
could not come about. What begins and progresses as history
reaches the finality and perfection of eternity.[64]

---

[62]Cf. Apologetik I § 19, p. 177.

[63]PD III, end pages, p. 50: "Sancti . . . in unam atque
individuam societatem cum Deo et Christo collecti regni divini
perfectam formam effingent . . ."

[64]This eschatological dimension of Drey's thought places
him, to some extent, in relation to present-day theologies of
hope. Although his conviction that Church is the form of mankind's unification would not be affirmed so confidently today,

The "Phases" and "Turning-Points"
of the "Reich Gottes"

The content of the second major part of the Dogmatics has
to do with the concrete, developmental sense of the Reich
Gottes--the historical process in which this divine Idea is
made real. The formal aspect, however, from which this history
is interpreted seems to be provided by the abstract, mystical
sense of the term.

The task, as Drey sees it, is to interpret a process
which embraces the entire history of mankind. Hence, he must
follow a temporal sequence in interpreting the content of
Christian faith. On the other hand, he views this process in a
somewhat abstract way--not only because of the manifest impossibility of treating universal history in its concrete details,
but even more because of the historically given "key" to the
meaning of history: the divine Idea of the Reich Gottes, made
known explicitly (as he thinks) in the teaching and career of
Jesus. The temporal development is to be presented in terms of
this Idea. The themes of Dogmatics are, therefore, treated in
the framework of the successive "phases" and "turning-points"
of the Reich Gottes.

Creation: The "First Phase"
of the Kingdom of God

In accord with this divinely revealed Idea, Drey conceives
the destiny and direction of mankind's development in its
intrinsic intelligibility. That is, he considers it in terms
of the essential relationship of world to God (Ursprungsverhältnis) established by the creative act of God. This is not
only constitutive of the very essence of being creature, but is
also first in the temporal sequence. It is the "Urzustand" of
world and of man. As such, it may be regarded as the initial
condition of the Reich Gottes, the "first phase" of its development.

The "Relation of Origin"

Drey views this not merely as a temporal beginning, but
more profoundly as the establishment of the radical relationship

---

his sense of universal history as a process leading towards a
hoped-for fulfillment does seem contemporary.

of finite to Infinite. The doctrine of creation is concerned
with the "relatio originis" which characterizes the very being
of all created reality:

> The first thing to be considered in the economy of the
> kingdom of God--which ought to be called its beginning and
> principle--is the originating manifestation of the kingdom
> in the world itself, and the relation of all things to God
> arising out of this manifestation, that is, the relation
> of origin . . .[65]

In this way, the mystery of creation establishes the
primal condition of the Reich Gottes--a totality of finite
beings harmoniously interrelated to one another and oriented
radically to their Ground and Center. As we saw in Chapter II,
Drey's romantic sense of development envisions a gradual
bringing-into-being of this finite order, under continuing and
renewed divine creative agency. Hence, there is a process
taking its beginning from the initial creative moment. And, in
this sense, the initial creation of the finite as the Reich
Gottes is only the first phase of a development which must
unfold in time. On the other hand, there is something about
this primal state of the created world which Drey conceives as
the normative, abiding reality willed by the Creator. This way
of thinking shows up in his characteristic phrase: "die ewigen
Verhältnisse," which is used interchangeably with "die
Ursprungsverhältnisse."[66]

In other words, there is an ambiguity about the word
"origin" (Ursprung). Since its direct and ordinary sense
refers to temporal beginning, when it is applied to the doctrine of creation it seems to refer to the point of beginning,
how the world "began." On the other hand, meditation on the
"whence" of the finite world drives the mind to an intuition of
the abiding, radical relationship of ontological dependence on
the Creator.[67] It is this more profound sense of "origin"

---

[65]PD III 189: "Primum, quod in oeconomia regni divini
considerandum venit, hujusque caput dici debet et principium,
originaria est regni hujus in mundo ipso manifestatio, relatioque omnium rerum ad Deum ex hac manifestatione orta, relatio
nimirum originis . . ."

[66]Cf. KE § 26, p. 14; § 32, p. 19; § 36, p. 21.

[67]Cf. above, pp. 33-35.

which is normative for Drey's conception of the God-world relationship. This intuition of the world as "rooted" in the
eternal Ground leads Drey to speak of the finite world itself
as "the Kingdom of God."

In treating explicitly the doctrine of creation, therefore, he is not merely accounting for the temporal beginning of
the world. He is also characterizing the essential nature of
this world as belonging utterly to God, so that it is ruled by
His will and is the manifestation of His very Being. This is
the status of created reality in its primal condition, as it is
willed by the Creator. It is called "Ursprungsverhältnis"
("relation of origin") not only because it began this way, but
--even more--because this beginning characterizes its permanent
and unchangeable ontological status. The created world is the
totality of that whose being is forever received from and
oriented towards its Source and Center. It is this relationship which constitutes the very essence of being creature--a
relationship of "being originated."

This "relation of origin" establishes the finite world as
Reich Gottes. We have seen, however, that this realm of created
being has a history. Although initially constituted by God's
creative will, it must develop through temporal process to the
full actualization of God's eternal Idea.

Man's Destiny in the Development
of the "Reich Gottes"

The way in which this development is to take place can
only be appreciated by considering the unique status of man
within the totality of the Reich Gottes. This is characterized
most fully in Drey's treatment of "religion" in the opening
pages of the KE and in Vol. 1 of the Apologetik.[68] The same
view of man's nature and destiny is also evident in the Dogmatics lectures, where it becomes the key to Drey's conception
of both sin and redemption.

Drey begins the KE with a sketch of what he considers to
be the objective basis of man's subjective feeling of religion.[69]

_____

[68]See above, pp. 48-51.

[69]KE §§ 1-11, pp. 1-7.

It is a vision of finite reality as the Kingdom of God, rooted
in the eternal Ground and abidingly oriented towards this
Source and Center. Man, as integral part of this universe,
shares in the common condition of being radically dependent
upon and oriented towards God. But the distinctively human
condition of self-awareness and freedom makes possible a distinctively human way of actualizing the fundamental "relation
of origin." This takes the form of "religion" as an impulse
and direction of the human spirit, leading man spontaneously to
surrender to God in love. This is the uniquely human way of
being part of the great Reich Gottes: a free, personal
acknowledgment and ratification of the relationship of belonging utterly to God (the "relation of origin" which characterizes the essence of created reality as such).

    Further insight into the paradoxical condition of man as
free creature can be gained by looking once again at Drey's
treatment of the "rise of consciousness" in Vol. 1 of the
Apologetik, which was examined earlier in the context of
"religion."[70] This phrase refers to the emergence of a distinctively human way of being, consisting in self-awareness and
self-possession as a subject over against the Other.

    As we saw in Chapter III, Drey maintains that this ini-
tial awareness of self is inseparable from a primal sense of
God as the Other. His effort to account for this leads him to
a meditation on the mystery of man's primal oneness with God in
the moment of being created. A closer look at this will help
to clarify the "Bestimmung" (purpose and destiny) of man, as
this is operative in Drey's Dogmatics.

    The basic perspective may be stated simply as follows:
Man as creature is one with God in the moment of being created.
This accounts for the awareness of God which arises with the
emergence of human self-awareness itself. As soon as man has
an awareness of self as distinct from Other, he is also aware
of God as the Other to whom he belongs but from whom he is
separate.

    In the time in which man finds himself, in which he
    achieves awareness of himself--and in this awareness of

---

[70]See above, pp. 50-51. Cf. Apol I § 5, pp. 109-13.

himself--God and man separate from one another; the latter
finds himself or his ego, and closes off this ego in itself
as his own proper personality. He also finds God, but as
something other, different from his own ego, as a second
and higher personality. The first and immediate impression
of this higher personality upon him in that very self-
awareness generates the feeling of dependence, by which he
recognizes himself as simultaneously bound indissolubly to
God, and yet different from Him and--by that difference--
separated from Him.[71]

To say that the rise of distinctively human consciousness
leads to a separation from God clearly implies a prior state of
oneness with God. And Drey goes on to make this explicit. He
notes that the concept of creation includes the notion that
Creator and creature are one in the moment of creating:

> . . . In the act of creating, the Creator and the creature,
> in this case God and man, touch one another, and the will
> of the Creator permeates the creature. . . . It has always
> been implied in the concept of creation that there is a
> being-in-one-another of Creator and creature, as the condi-
> tion of their going apart from one another in temporal
> appearance.[72]

This prior oneness, however, is manifestly pre-personal insofar
as there is not yet a distinct human subject, possessing itself
in freedom, which could relate consciously to God.[73]

---

[71]Apologetik I § 5, pp. 109-10: "In der Zeit, in welcher
der Mensch sich selbst findet, zum Bewußtseyn seiner selbst
gelangt, und in diesem Bewußtseyn von sich selbst, treten Gott
und der Mensch auseinander, der letztere findet sich oder sein
Ich, und schließt es ab in sich als eigene Persönlichkeit; er
findet auch Gott, aber als etwas anderes, von seinem Ich verschiedenes, als eine zweite und höhere Persönlichkeit, deren
erster und unmittelbarer Eindruck auf ihn in ebenjenem Selbstbewußtseyn das Gefühl der Abhängigkeit erzeugt, wodurch er sich
zugleich unauflößlich an Gott gebunden, wie von ihm verschieden
und durch Verschiedenheit getrennt erkennt."

[72]Apologetik I § 5, p. 111: ". . . daß in jenem Akte [dem
Schöpfungsakt] der Schöpfer und das Geschöpf, hier Gott und der
Mensch, sich berühren, daß in demselben der Wille des Schöpfers
das Geschöpf durchdringt . . . ein Ineinanderseyn des Schöpfers
und des Geschöpfes, als Bedingung ihres Auseinandergehens in
der zeitlichen Erscheinung, ist im Begriffe der Schöpfung immer
gedacht worden . . ."

[73]One could conceive this kind of oneness with God as a
state of innocence, and correspondingly, could conceive the
emergence of distinct subjects as a kind of "fall," a breaking-
off from the primal unity. This kind of thought was current in
Drey's day, deriving from the "esoteric" mediaeval tradition of
neo-Platonic thought and expressed in the influential writings

Thus, if there is ever to be a personal oneness with God--
realized through free human choice--there must first be a separation and differentiation of man from God. It is the sense of.
separation and otherness generated in the rise of self-awareness
which allows for an entirely new possibility in the creature-
Creator relationship: a relatedness chosen freely and exercised
in love.

At the same time, the radical "relation of origin" remains
--for man, as well as for all other created beings--as the
normative determinant of his existence. What is made possible
by the rise of human consciousness is really, therefore, a
transposition of the meaning of Reich Gottes from the level of
the pre-personal to that of the personal. For man, what is at
stake is not merely the ontological relatedness by which all
things are God's Kingdom by virtue of being created. For man,
there is the invitation to a personal relatedness to God in
freedom, a living-out of the "relation of origin" in a distinctively human mode.[74]

A Divinely Established
Direction of Development

The movement from the pre-personal oneness with God (in
the act of being created) to the personal oneness in conscious
freedom characterizes the unique destiny of man. But this is
not thought of as an instantaneous event, to be achieved in a
single act of the will. To be human at all is to be inchoative-
ly religious, as we have seen. But this initial obscure
impulse towards God must develop gradually, as man's rational
nature develops, under the constant educative influence of

---

of Jakob Boehme. Schelling, among others, picked up elements
from this tradition. Cf. M. H. Abrams, Natural Supernaturalism
(New York: W. W. Norton & Co., 1971), pp. 220-25, 295. But
this is not the view of Drey. It is not the emergence of distinct finite selves which is the Fall, in his thought. The
emergence of self-awareness is the condition of possibility for
either the free participation of man in the Kingdom of God, or
the sinful refusal to do so. Only the latter is considered to
be the Fall.

[74]The deepest grounding of this possibility is in Drey's
trinitarian conception of the created world's relationship to
God. It is in the Son that the world is known and loved by the
Father, and destined for personal union with Him. See above.

divine revelation. Drey expresses his strongly romantic sense
of development in the following text from the Apologetik:

> The law of the finite is Becoming, by means of its
> progressive opening-up of itself in time, and the unfolding
> into appearance of the germ hidden in its particularity.
> In the same way, although man is originally and--so to
> speak--germinally already religious, he can only become
> religious actually through an unfolding in time. Thereby
> revelation, too, which incites and sustains the religious
> unfolding of man, enters together with it into time . . .[75]

It is thus clear that Drey does not conceive of man's
primal condition before God as static. He supposes a movement
from undeveloped, child-like relatedness to God[76] to an increasingly mature, conscious choice to be related to God. Hence, as
we try to characterize the initial state of the Kingdom of God
(and of man as part of it), it seems that we must think of a
divinely established direction of development, which is to
follow from the normative relation of origin. This perspective
is well illustrated by a remark recorded in one of the extant
sets of student's notes on Drey's Dogmatics lectures: ". . .
the purpose of all creatures lies in this, to develop in a
harmonious way that original condition in which they were
created."[77]

It seems, therefore, that--however much Drey harks back
to the "eternal relationship of origin"--he is not supposing a
static state of perfection in primal innocence. There was to

---

[75]Apologetik I § 19, p. 173: "Das Gesetz des Endlichen
ist das Werden vermittelst der fortschreitenden Aufschließung
seiner selbst in der Zeit, und der Entfaltung des in der
Besonderheit verborgenen Keims in die Erscheinung; nicht anders
wird auch der Mensch, wiewohl ursprünglich und gleichsam in
seinem Keime schon religiös, dieses wirklich außer durch
Entfaltung in der Zeit. Dadurch tritt auch die Offenbarung,
welche die religiöse Entfaltung des Menschen anregt und unterhält, mit dieser selbst in die Zeit . . ." Cf. ThQ 8 (1826):
264-65: ". . . die Offenbarung konnte das Gesetz einer all-
mäligen stufenweisen Entwickelung nicht aufheben."

[76]Cf. ThQ 8 (1826):264.

[77]Fuchs MS of Drey's Dogmatics lectures, § 13, printed in
Geiselmann's Die Katholische Tübinger Schule, p. 219: ". . .
daß der Zweck aller Geschöpfe darin liege, jenen ursprünglichen
Zustand, in dem sie geschaffen worden, auf harmonische Weise
auszubilden . . ."

have been development, even if man had not sinned. Hence, what
man falls away from is not an already established paradisaical
state, but rather a divinely intended direction of development.

> . . . the history of the world "falls" (i.e., falls away
> from God) after its origin, and so also does the history of
> mankind. It shows us not a progression in the condition of
> origin, not a development and cultivation of it, but rather
> a departure from this condition, and a direction which is
> directly opposed to the direction which is posited for us
> by God.[78]

The same understanding is expressed in the Apologetik,
where Drey is speaking of the need of sinful man for a form of
revelation that will remedy the false and "abnormal" direction
which he has given to his development by sinning:

> . . . It is above all necessary for him [man], that this
> abnormal direction should be abolished, and that he should
> be put back into his normal condition, in order to continue
> his development again from the original standpoint, after
> this interruption.[79]

Sin: The First "Turning-Point"

From the perspective established in the previous section,
the fact of sin must be regarded as a great disorder in the
divinely established relationship of all things to their eternal Ground. What is created to belong utterly to God now
refuses to be in that relationship, refuses to develop in the
direction intended by the Creator. Drey characterizes this in
his Journal as "the defection of things--or the self-assertion
of things with its consequences as the entanglement or the knot
of the drama."[80]

---

[78]Fuchs MS, § 13, in Geiselmann's Die Katholische Tübinger Schule, p. 219: ". . . die Geschichte der Welt 'fällt' (d.h.
von Gott abfällt) nach ihrem Ursprunge und so auch die
Geschichte der Menschheit. Sie zeigt uns nicht ein Fortschreiten im ursprünglichen Zustande, nicht eine Entwicklung
und Ausbildung desselben, sondern ein Heraustreten aus demselben
und eine Richtung, welche derjenigen, die uns von Gott gesetzt
ist, gerade entgegensteht."

[79]Apologetik I § 18, p. 170: ". . . Für ihn ist es daher
vor Allem nöthig, daß diese abnorme Richtung aufgehoben, und er
selbst in den normalen Zustand zurückversetzt werde, um nach
diesem Abbrechen seine Entwicklung vom ursprünglichen Standpunkt aus wieder fortzusetzen."

[80]Tagebücher V 50-53, GdChr, p. 146: "Der Abfall der
Dinge--oder die Eigenmacht der Dinge mit seinen Folgen als die
Verflechtung, der Knoten des Dramas."

What is of interest in Drey's treatment of sin in the
Dogmatics (as in all the other topics treated) is his systematic,
unifying perspective on the Reich Gottes. This is indicated by
his location of sin as the first turning-point in the development of the Kingdom of God. But his actual treatment of the
material is mainly biblical and traditional, so that his
speculative viewpoint is to be discovered only in certain
revealing phrases which reflect his general understanding of
man's place in the Reich Gottes. Hence, it is especially necessary in this section to begin with his published works, in
order to establish and clarify the larger context of meaning
within which the relevant remarks in the Dogmatics notes become
intelligible.

Sin as Disavowal of the "Relation of Origin"

What needs to be understood is the way in which Drey
considers sin to be opposed to the Kingdom of God. His conception of sin is closely correlated with his governing intuition
of the "relation of origin" (the deepest level of meaning of
the term Reich Gottes).

The peculiar nature of sin is to be perceived by considering again the "moment" in which distinctively human consciousness arises. We observed above that it is in this moment that
the possibility of a freely willed relationship of creature to
Creator is first given. But this moment of self-possession
also gives man the possibility of disregarding and ignoring the
foundational relationship to God.

This possibility is inherent in the very structure of
human consciousness as a "self-positing." The sense of self-
possession (what Drey calls "man gaining mastery of his I-ness")
is capable of being falsely absolutized, so that man does not
understand himself as belonging completely to God the Creator.
To the extent that this happens, man is subjectively disavowing
the objective relatedness which we have characterized as the
"relation of origin."[81]

---

[81]KE § 12, p. 7: ". . . mit demjenigen Acte, durch den
der Mensch seines Ichs, und seiner Ichheit Meister wird, ist
für ihn die Möglichkeit gegeben, wenn schon nicht objectiv,
doch subjectiv aus jenen Verhältnissen herauszutreten . . ."

Culpable ignorance of the "Reich Gottes."--The consequence
of such a false choice, as we have seen, is a fundamentally non-
religious perception of the world itself.[82] The religious view
of the finite--for Drey, as well as for Schelling--intuits "the
universe purely as revelation, purely as the work and possession
of God."[83] With the rise of self-awareness and freedom in man,
however, this primal and almost instinctive impulse of religion
must be either freely chosen and lived out in obedience or else
refused and repudiated.

> It [human self-awareness in freedom] can now--in self-
> possession and self-determination--follow further the
> direction which originally announced itself and to this
> extent was posited both for instinct and for the will. But
> it can also, by a blunder . . . elevate itself as self-will
> above and against the will of God expressed in the relation-
> ships of the universe . . .[84]

The actual and universal choice by mankind of the latter
alternative has brought about a disturbance of the divinely
willed Reich Gottes and the need of mankind for a revelation
which will recall them to the truth of their relationship to
God. It is characteristic of Drey's whole point of view that
he links the false choice of absolute autonomy to a false perception of the world and of man's place within it.[85]

> For, as man has placed himself on this latter stand-
> point [self-positing in freedom against the will of God]--
> and everyone places himself there--God's entire revelation
> falls into man's hand and will; it becomes his--man's--work.
> He himself, originally God's work, posits himself as free,

---

[82]See above, pp. 42-43.

[83]KE § 18, p. 10. See above, p. 42.

[84]KE § 12, p. 8: "Es [Selbstbewußtseyn im freyen Wollen]
kann die ursprüngliche sich ankündigende, und insofern wie dem
Instinct, so dem Willen gesetzte Richtung nun besonnen und mit
Selbstbestimmung ferner verfolgen; es kann aber auch durch
einen Mißgriff . . . als Eigenwille über und gegen den in den
Verhältnissen des Universums ausgesprochenen Willen Gottes sich
erheben . . ."

[85]Drey's understanding of his intellectual context in
terms of naturalism and rationalism is based on this same fundamental point. The root error and sin, as he sees it, is for
man to posit himself as quite autonomous and the world as quite
self-sufficient and self-contained.

> self-sufficient being . . . What is originally divine
> becomes man's work, with which he operates as his own
> Master.[86]

The anomaly of this wilful mis-perception of reality is
only possible because of the unique position of man within
God's creation, as we saw above. Only a creature which, in
some sense, possesses itself is capable of a free, personal
choice to be in the "relation of origin" which constitutes all
pre-personal finite reality on the ontological level. Since
God's intention for mankind is that they should freely choose
to be part of his Reich, they must have the kind of self-
possession which is capable of false self-absolutizing.

The paradox and pathos of human existence is thus strikingly illustrated in the text just cited. Man himself, in Drey's
view, is "in his origin God's work." Like everything else, he
is posited by God. Yet, he must also posit himself in order to
have the self-possession in freedom which constitutes distinctively human existence. And in that moment of self-positing,
he makes the fatal mistake of denying the God-relationship
which is actually the deepest level of truth about what he is.[87]

The world itself, consequently, is mis-perceived in a
similar fashion. Recalling the earlier analysis of Drey's key
idea of Reich Gottes, one can see the whole problematic of sin
in the last sentence of the above text: "Das ursprünglich
Göttliche wird des Menschen Werk, womit er schaltet als eigener
Herr."

The world itself (including man) is essentially God's.
(The word ursprünglich must be taken not merely in a temporal
sense but in the sense of "in principle," as we saw above.)
This is another way of saying that the world itself is the
domain of God's rule, of His absolute dominion and Lordship.

---

[86]KE § 19, p. 11: "Denn wie sich der Mensch auf diesen
letztern Standpunct gestellt hat;--und jeder stellt sich darauf,
--fällt Gottes ganze Offenbarung in des Menschen Hand und
Willen, wird sein--des Menschen--Werk. Er selbst, ursprünglich
Gottes Werk, setzt sich selbst als freyes, selbständiges Wesen
. . . Das ursprünglich Göttliche wird des Menschen Werk, womit
er schaltet als eigener Herr."

[87]Cf. above, p. 48.

On the other hand, the "blunder" of self-absolutizing leads man
to a way of perceiving and acting which takes the world for
granted as the domain of his own Lordship. Both his own being
and operations--and "nature" as over against him--are taken as
absolutes in themselves, without attending to the "relation of
origin."[88] In this way, man ceases to perceive or acknowledge
"his true relationship in the universe to God, the perfect
dominion of God over himself."[89] In other words, he lives out
the exact opposite of his divinely intended destiny.

This seems to be a frustration of God's purposes, a disturbance or disruption of the Reich Gottes. But Drey distinguishes carefully between the eternally constituted relationship of being created, and the human subjective acknowledgment
or refusal of that eternal relation of origin.[90] Thus, he sums
up the content of the sin-section of his Dogmatics in the
following way:

> . . . it treats of the disturbances of the kingdom of God
> arising out of the ignorance and the fall of creatures--
> not, indeed, intrinsic or objective disturbances (since the
> decrees and acts of God cannot be disturbed by human
> counsels), but extrinsic and subjective, or related to

---

[88]KE § 19, p. 11: ". . . jenes innere Regen und Ziehen,
ursprünglich Gottes Kraft und Geist, es ist jetzt sein eigener
Wille, der sich bestimmt dafür oder dagegen, wie es ihm beliebt;
alle Vorstellungen werden nun seine Gedanken, die er sich
gemacht hat; selbst der lauteste Ruf der Offenbarung, das
Gewissen in des Menschen Brust, es ist das Gesetz, welches er
sich selbst giebt." KE § 20, p. 11: "So mit der Offenbarung
Gottes in der Natur. Mit demselben Act, durch den der Mensch
sich selbst setzt als ein Ich, setzt er auch die Außenwelt als
ein solches, in Beziehung auf ihn zwar ein NichtIch, in ihr
selbst aber auch ein Ich, das besteht in sich . . ."

[89]KE § 29, p. 17: ". . . sein wahres Verhältniß im
Universum zu Gott, die vollkommne Herrschaft Gottes über sich
. . ."

[90]Cf. Apol I § 31, pp. 250-51: ". . . die durch den
Schöpfungsakt gegründeten Verhältnisse sind ewig und unveränderlich. -- Auch dadurch ändert sich an diesen Verhältnissen
nichts, daß der Mensch durch die Sünde versucht hat und versucht, aus denselben herauszutreten, und sich von seiner
Abhängigkeit von Gott zu befreien; denn das Bestreben des
Sünders ist, objektiv betrachtet, eitel und nichtig, subjektiv
aber angesehen, ein ungeheurer Irrthum und Frevel zugleich."
Cf. also KE § 7, pp. 3-4, and KE § 36, pp. 21-22.

human beings, who began from that time more and more <u>to be ignorant of and to disdain</u> both God and His kingdom . . .[91]

Drey's understanding of sin is thus closely correlated with his unifying intuition of created reality as the <u>Reich Gottes</u>. To make the fateful choice of self-absolutizing alienates human subjectivity from this most profound truth about the human condition. There is ignorance of the Kingdom of God. But this is not a simple lack of knowledge. It is, rather, a refusal to recognize God's absolute dominion, a culpable disregard of the God-relationship of created reality (including oneself).[92]

There seems to be a dialectical relationship between sin and ignorance. Sin, because of the very nature of a spiritual being, can only be possible as <u>error</u>, as a mis-reading of reality. On the other hand, sin seems to have as an effect the darkening of the mind, so that human reason mis-perceives reality.[93]

<u>Evil as an "unreal nature."</u>--Because of his governing sense of the Creator-creature relationship, Drey has a highly metaphysical conception of the essence of moral evil. There is a paradoxical character in this evil, which resists understanding. For God is regarded as the author of all that is. How, then, can there be moral evil which is manifestly contrary to the divinely willed order?

---

[91]PD I 17: ". . . agit de perturbationibus regni divini ex ignorantia et lapsu creaturarum ortis, non quidem internis illis seu objectivis--cum decreta et acta divina humanis consiliis perturbari non possint--sed externis et subjectivis, seu relate ad homines, qui ex illo tempore Deum ejusque regnum magis magisque <u>ignorare et spernere</u> coeperunt . . ." (emphasis added).

[92]Cf. PD III 46: ". . . divini illius imperii vestigia in mundi hujus phaenomenis et in genere humano manifesta quidem semper, verum <u>neque satis cognita neque reverita</u> ab hominibus fuisse . . ." (emphasis added). Cf. KE § 32, p. 19: ". . . die ursprünglich im Universum ausgedrückte, dem ersten religiösen Gefühle zu Grund liegende, <u>während der Herrschaft des Egoismus verkannte</u> Idee eines Reiches Gottes . . ." (emphasis added).

[93]Cf. <u>Apol</u> I § 18, p. 171: ". . . wie nämlich dem Bösen überall in seinem Ursprunge der Abfall von der Wahrheit,--der Irrthum zu Grunde liegt, und es nach der Natur eines Geistes nicht anders seyn kann, so hängt sich im Zustande des gefallenen Menschen überall der Irrthum an die Erkenntniß der Wahrheit . . ."

Drey regards the moral choice of evil as the irrational
and futile attempt of created freedom to get absolute possession
of itself.[94] Sin is thus the absurd attempt of a nature created
utterly by God to "generate itself" in opposition to the order
created and ruled by God. It is an attempt to posit something
"this side of the efficacy of God." Since, however, the only
basis of being and activity is that which God has created and
sustains, evil has the character of an inferior, unreal "nature"
which falls away into nothingness. The history which follows
from sin is a kind of pseudo-kingdom in opposition to the real
Kingdom of God. Despite all efforts to the contrary, this
"kingdom of Satan" actually serves the purposes of God (who can
bring good out of perverse moral choices) and is thus sublated
into the consilia of His Kingdom.[95]

The Ambiguity of Sin
in Drey's System

The origin and fact of evil is, nevertheless, difficult
for Drey to integrate into his system. The radical absurdity
of sin poses a basic problem for his theological method. Since
a properly "wissenschaftliche" account of the phases of the
Reich Gottes seeks the intelligible necessity of what has
happened, it must view all the features of this process in

---

[94]Apol I § 18, p. 170: ". . . die Freiheit selbst, der es
in ihrer eigenen Entwickelung einfallen kann (ich sage nicht,
einfallen muß), auch einmal nach dem Bösen zu greifen, in der
Meinung, daß sie nur so ihrer selbst ganz habhaft werden könne,
was der dem Bösen zu Grund liegende Irrthum ist." Cf. the
material cited above. Also Apol II § 61, p. 237: ". . . Selbstsucht . . ." And Apol I § 14, p. 15: "sich selbst als Mittel-
punkt setzend . . ."

[95]PD II 120: ". . . certum est, quidquid sit vel fiat
mali moralis in hoc mundo, et inter homines praecipue, id ad
regnum Satanae, non ad regnum Dei pertinere, hoc est, non esse
illius naturae et illius ordinis, cui Deus auctor praesidet,
sed alterius cujusdam naturae et ordinis, quae citra Dei effi-
caciam propria quadam mentis creatae agitatione, propriore con-
silio exoritur, et quasi se ipsam generat; haec ipsa natura,
cum verae solidaeque existentiae fundamentum unicum natura est
a Deo condita, Deoque obtemperans, fundamento caret, atque in
se ipsum corruat et emoriatur necesse est. Nullam proin exis-
tentiam habet, nisi caducam, nec finem suum quem intendit,
unquam attingit, sed Deo nolens etiam et reluctans servit,
ejusque regnum ipsis infestationibus promovet; quare a Deo non
tolerari solum sed et in consilia regni sui adscisci potuit."
Cf. KE & 29, pp. 17-18.

terms of the realization of God's great Idea. Since sin (the
Fall) is the first "turning-point" in the process, which introduces the second "phase" of the Kingdom of God, sin would seem
to be "necessary." If it is not, how can it be understood
"scientifically" as part of the great divinely ruled process?
There seems to be an inconsistency in Drey's view of this
problem.

On the one hand, he acknowledges that sin must be regarded
as "Zufall," rather than as essential and intrinsic to the
human condition. For the latter view would attribute the
origin of sin to God the Creator--clearly an unacceptable position.[96] Hence, the "scientific" concept of revelation is to be
correlated not with man's accidental condition of sinfulness,
but rather with his "original, pure nature," which is logically
prior to the event of the Fall.[97]

On the other hand, Drey is unwilling to regard sin as an
exception to the universal scope of divine providence, as something not included in God's eternal plan for created reality.
Hence, he says explicitly: "The Fall is to be regarded as one
of the great divine decrees, by which God educates mankind in
His Kingdom."[98] Moreover, he clearly attributes to the event

---

[96]Apol I § 10, pp. 139-40: ". . . sodann darf doch wohl
nicht behauptet werden, daß der Sündenfall als Thatsache ein
inneres Verhältniß der Nothwendigkeit ausdrücke, an sich und
schlechthin nothwendig sey oder war . . . Denn unter dieser
Voraussetzung müßten wir die Natur des Menschen als schlechthin
zum Bösen geneigt, folglich als schlechthin bös setzen, und es
könnte Niemand anders seyn, der ihr diese Neigung zum Bösen
gegeben hätte, als Gott der Schöpfer selbst. Lassen wir aber,
wie wir auch noch aus andern Gründen müssen, dem Sündenfall
seinen Ursprung aus der Freiheit und insofern einen zufälligen
Ursprung . . ."

[97]Apol I § 10, p. 140: ". . . so müssen wir . . . uns
über den Sündenfall erheben, und bis zu den Anfängen des
Menschen, zu seiner ursprünglichen reinen Natur zurückgehen
. . ."

[98]PD I 128, marginal notation: "Der Sündenfall ist als
einer der großen göttlichen Rathschlüße zu betrachten, durch
die Gott die Menschen in seinem Reiche erzieht." Cf. PD III 67:
"Nos autem instructi idea regni divini ita in hac quaestione
versabimur, ut quantum etiam distare a natura et efficientia
Dei omne genus mali contendamus, tantum simul affirmemus, ipsos
creaturarum lapsus et hominum praecipue vitia ad consilia
illius imperii divini pertinere, quod efficit, ut malo etiam
bonum insit, quidquid autem mali naturam habet, continuo
elidatur destruaturque."

of sin a significant influence upon the further development of
the Reich Gottes in accordance with the divine decrees.[99]

Drey appeals to the mysterious ability of God to bring
good out of evil, in order to affirm that even sin is somehow
made to serve the divine purposes.[100] This may well be the
most that can be said to reconcile the fact of evil with the
belief in a universal divine providence. But the difficulty
remains obvious, given Drey's overall viewpoint.

Insofar as Drey tends to equate the divine "decrees" with
eternal Ideas, in order to find intelligibility in the given
shape of the divinely ruled history, the fact of sin confronts
his system with an embarrassing dilemma. Is sin to be considered as part of the divine essence's self-manifestation in
finite reality? (This is clearly unacceptable to Christian
theology.) If sin is not so regarded, does it not stand outside the intelligibility of the divine Ideas, whose realization
the finite order is thought to be? In the latter case, how can
sin consistently be regarded as a turning-point of the Reich-
Gottes Idea's unfolding in time?

This difficulty seems inherent in the attempt to utilize
the Idealist model of intelligibility for Christian theology.
Hence, it points to a fundamental criticism of Drey's Schelling-

---

[99]Cf. Drey's observation in a review of Dobmayer's
Dogmatics, ThQ 7 (1825):129, "Der Sündenfall und seine Folgen
gehören daher mit zu den Planen des Reiches Gottes, bilden in
seiner Geschichte eine besondere Periode, an welche sich die
Periode Christi anschließt, nicht um das in der vorigen verloren gegangene Reich Gottes wieder herzustellen, sondern um
die durch jene eigenthümliche Wendung vorbereitete neue Entwickelung anzufangen und fortzüfuhren." Cf. also Drey's review
of Thanner, ThQ 1 (1819):31, "Nach Paulus . . . (Röm. XI, 32;
Gal. III, 22) hat Gott alles unter Unglauben und Sünde
beschlossen, um allen sein Erbarmen und seine freye Gnade zu
beweisen. Der Sündenfall selbst gehört mit in den Plan seines
Reiches . . ."

[100]Cf. PD III 67, cited above. Cf. ThQ 7 (1825):129-30,
"Das eben ist der Triumph der Theodicee und die Beschämung
menschlicher Weisheit . . . daß das Böse als Erscheinung in der
Welt das Reich Gottes gerade so fördert, wie das Gute; dasjenige
aber, was im Bösen eigentlich das Böse ist, der verkehrte Sinn
und Willen der Einzelnen, ewig außer der Welt und dem Reiche
Gottes ist, d.h. aller Wahrheit und wahren Wirklichkeit erman-
gelt."

inspired view of the rationality of the real.[101] If the real
is intractably existential and historical (seen most clearly,
perhaps, in the case of sin), then it is not to be grasped as
the consequence of Mind.

A World in Sin: The "Second Phase" of the Kingdom of God

The new state of affairs resulting from the Fall has to
do with man's subjective alienation from the reality of God's
rule. This does not change man's foundational relationship to
God as part of the great Reich Gottes.[102] But the universal
fact of man's sinfulness does put man in an abnormal subjective
state, in which his nature seems distorted and perversely
oriented towards evil.[103]

Drey regards this "proclivity toward evil" as intrinsic
to the human nature which results from the Fall. Although the
consequence of free choice, this perversion of human subjectivity becomes a constant accompanying feature of the human
nature inherited by each generation.[104]

From this perspective, Drey considers that sin (the per-
verted human subjectivity which disregards the rule of God) has

---

[101]Cf. Rief, Reich Gottes und Gesellschaft, p. 96, commenting on Drey's notion of God's omniscience, against the background of Schelling's Urwissen. If God knows all finite particulars by first of all knowing His own essence, then the free
choices of creatures (sinful or otherwise) would seem to be
necessary manifestations of the divine Being.

[102]Cf. Apol I § 18, p. 172: ". . . der ursprüngliche
Zustand des Menschen [hat] . . . sich in den der Sündhaftigkeit
umgesetzt . . . aber dieser selbst [ist] nur ein zeitlicher
. . . , und durch dieses zeitliche Verhältniß des Menschen
[wird] sein ursprüngliches und ewiges, seine wahre Bestimmung
nicht aufgehoben . . . [bleibt] vielmehr als von Gott gesetzt
unveränderlich . . ."

[103]PD I 131: "Constat enim inesse generi humanae communem
quandam vitiositatem, . . . quae in spontanea et universali pro-
clivitate ad malum posita . . . est."

[104]PD I 136: "Ante omnia id oportet assumere: quaecumque
sit causa illius vitiositatis, communem eam esse omnibus hominibus atque ad omnes pertinentem. . . . Unde etiam . . . conse-
quitur, hanc ipsam . . . causam cum ipsis hominum originibus,
adeoque cum natura hominum ipsa, qualis nunc est, conjunctam
esse, neque nasci quem posse, qui ab eadem immunis existat."

become so intimately united with human nature that it must be
regarded as a kind of "second nature." Consequently, the overcoming of sin will have to take the form of a kind of re-
creation or re-birth of human nature.[105]

The plight of mankind in the second phase of the Reich
Gottes may be characterized as "the power of sin, and ignorance."[106] There is, in fact, a close intrinsic relationship
between the two.[107] As we pointed out above, Drey tends to
link sin with a mis-reading of reality. The deepest level of
sinful man's alienation from reality is his disregard of the
"relation of origin," his mis-perception of the world and himself as absolutely autonomous. In other words, sin is inseparable from "ignorance" of the Reich Gottes.

The history of the second phase of the Kingdom is, therefore, a matter of mankind's growing estrangement from the truth
of the Reich Gottes, as the power of sin works itself out and
spreads through all parts of the human race.[108] At the same
time, this period includes the divine initiative which continues to recall man to the truth of his relationship to God.[109]
Drey sees this as one consistent pattern of revelation--opera-
tive both in the unique history of Israel and in the various
religious traditions of the "nations."[110] It is characteristic
of Drey's universal-historical perspective that he sees the

---

[105]PD II 129-30: (Speaking of St. Paul's view of sin as a
principle or force which invades the world . . .) ". . . et
nunc . . . cum natura hominis quasi concreta sit, imo quasi
altera natura priori divinae ita cohaereat et dominetur, ut non
aliter, nisi nova per Christum regeneratione haec expelli, et
prior restitui natura possit."

[106]PD I 151: ". . . malorum vero nostrorum summam peccati
vis et ignorantia efficiebant . . ."

[107]PD I 157-58: "Die Summe des alten Zustandes concen-
trirt sich in den zwey Übeln - Unwissenheit und Sünde - oder
Sünde und aus ihr hervorgehende Unwissenheit."

[108]Cf. KE §§ 12-15, pp. 7-9; Apol II §§ 2-9, pp. 8-30.

[109]Cf. KE §§ 25-26, pp. 13-14.

[110]Cf. KE § 27, pp. 14-15. "Ein fester und consequenter
Plan Gottes lauft . . . durch das Ganze dieser besondern
Leitungen und Offenbarungen hin . . . (p. 15).

divine influence at work in all Völker (not merely in Israel),
preparing them for the fullness of revelation which is to result
from the particular history of Israel.[111]

God's education of the erring human race is conceived as
a long, patient preparation of mankind for the coming of
Christ.[112] Hence, the divine initiative which is to bring
about the restoration of the human race actually precedes the
decisive turning-point of the whole process, which is to ini-
tiate a new phase of the Reich Gottes.

Christ: The Second "Turning-Point" of the "Reich Gottes"

The significance of Christ in Drey's system is certainly
to be understood in the large context of his interpretation of
the unity of history. The unifying Idea of Reich Gottes provides the over-arching meaning of the entire process of God's
revelatory activity, beginning with the transcendent fact of
creation itself. Hence, the coming of Christ is viewed as the
crucial turning-point in the development of the world to become
what God intends.

The Restoration of Human Nature

Since Drey's foundational understanding of the Reich
Gottes springs from his mystical sense of the world in relation
to the Creator-reality of God, the work of Christ is regarded
as a re-creation and restoration of human nature so as to
acknowledge this radical "relation of origin."[113] Hence,

---

[111]This perspective is evident in Apologetik II, which
surveys the religious development of mankind. It is also
expressed in PD I 19-20 and PD III 257; 264-65. Drey even
regards the sages and spiritual leaders of the "nations" as
similar to the prophets of Israel, and considers them to have
been inspired by the Holy Spirit ("divino quodam spiritu
afflati," PD III 265). Cf. also the Fuchs MS of Drey's Dogmatics lectures, § 16, in Geiselmann's Die Katholische Tübinger
Schule, pp. 222-23. Drey seems strikingly modern in his demand
that Christian theology take into account "den Gang Gottes mit
den Heiden" (ThQ 1 [1819]:429).

[112]Cf. PD III 67-68.

[113]This way of conceiving redemption is thus closely
correlated with Drey's understanding of "religion." In common
with Schleiermacher and others, Drey rooted religion in a certain quality of "consciousness" (Bewußtsein). Sin, as we have
seen, is thought to be inseparable from a distortion of man's

the section of the Dogmatics which treats of redemption is
entitled "De generis humani restitutione."[114]   In the overview
of Dogmatics which Drey sketched out in 1818, he entitled this
whole section "Palingenesia" or "Palingenesis,"[115] and remarked
that "the salient point of Christology is the palingenesis of
all things."[116]

Drey's reason for so conceiving the point of Christology
has been indicated in the preceding section on sin. The Fall
led to a distortion of human nature, a perverse orientation
towards evil which is inseparable from the disavowal of the
"relation of origin." This culpable ignorance of the Reich
Gottes has become so intimately conjoined with the fallen condition of human nature that the overcoming of it is conceived
as a creative, spritual re-fashioning of mankind.[117] This is
what Christ brings about.

Drey's treatment of Christ in the Dogmatics is strongly
traditional and scriptural. As in the Apologetik, he affirms
the Chalcedonian understanding of the God-man. In his treatment of the redemptive work of Christ, he marshals the

---

consciousness, so that he no longer perceives or acknowledges
his true relationship to God. Hence, Drey's view of redemption
seems closely akin to the general tendency of his time to
interpret the work of Christ as the initiation of a new kind of
"consciousness" of man's eternal relationship to God. For Drey,
however, the alteration or "re-creation" of human nature which
Christ brings about is not limited to a new kind of consciousness, but must find its full expression in a new quality of
life. See below.

[114]PD I 146; PD III 256.

[115]PD I 16; 18. This is preceded by "Ctiseologia" (the
creation of all things) and "Hamartologia" (the origin and
progress of sin).

[116]PD I 20: "Punctum saliens Christologiae est Palingenesis omnium rerum."

[117]PD I 151: ". . . cum hominem ex tam gravi casu integrum restituere idem prorsus erat, ac ejus naturam immutare,
illud opus non minus arduum fuit, quam ipsa creatio; vires itaque divinas, auctoremque divinum exigebat, qui in has terras
descenderet, opus suum perfecturus." PD I 158: "Die Begründung
eines neuen Zustandes mit entschiedener Richtung zu Gott ist
eine wahre Schöpfung - also Gottes Werk - vermittelst eines
eigenen Princips des neuen Lebens - daher sie auch Wiedergeburt,
neuer Mensch gennant wird." For parallel texts, cf. Apol II
§ 61, pp. 237-38; II § 73, p. 279; III § 26, p. 142.

scriptural data without providing a clear speculative unification of this material. There are, however, a number of indications of his speculative viewpoint.

In order to bring out the logic which is implicit in
Drey's location of Christology in the overall scheme of his
Dogmatics, it is necessary to have recourse to his published
works. Once the characteristic perspective on Christ as a
turning-point of the Reich Gottes has been clarified from this
source, it will be possible to point out the indications of this
in the Dogmatics notes. We can, then, conclude by commenting on
the incompleteness of Drey's speculative treatment of Christ in
the Dogmatics.

Drey views Christ in the context of the single, unified
history of revelation. As we have seen, revelation is thought
to be intrinsic to the religious development of mankind.
"Redemption" is simply the form which revelation had to take,
given the fact of sin. The long history of God's revelatory
influence upon the human spirit has, as its purpose, to recall
mankind from its subjective disregard of the highest truth
about its condition: that the finite world (including mankind)
is God's Kingdom.

Free and Conscious Union with God

The acknowledgment of the Idea Reich Gottes is not, however, merely a matter of cognition. The truth of this Idea can
only be appreciated in the personal surrender of the human
subject to the objective reality of God's perfect dominion over
all finite reality (including him/herself).[118]

From this latter perspective, the purpose of revelation
may be seen as the achievement of the free and conscious union
of mankind with God.[119] Drey views this as the restoration of

----

[118]Cf. KE § 29, p. 17.

[119]Cf. KE § 32, p. 19: "Die Offenbarung auf ihrem Gipfel,
also auch an ihrem Ziele gedacht, kann nichts anderes bewirkt
haben als die Wiederherstellung der ursprünglichen Einheits-
Verhältnisse in der Form einer freiwilligen und bewußten Einigung . . ." Cf. Apol II § 55, p. 207: ". . . durch die
Erlösung wieder zurück zu Gott in der Wiedervereinigung, als
der mit Bewußtseyn hergestellten ursprünglichen Einheit."

the "Ursprungsverhältnis" which was constituted, in principle,
by God's transcendent act of creating. But the end-state is
more than the primal oneness, since it is achieved through the
free response of the creature. Hence, the recognition and
acknowledgment of the Idea Reich Gottes is inseparable from the
creature's renunciation of its mistaken egotism in the free
choice to relate to God in mutual love.[120]

The coming of Christ is, therefore, regarded as the
culmination of the entire process of revelation, which brings
about the acknowledgment of the Reich Gottes and the free,
conscious union of mankind with God.

The "Work" of Christ: Over-
coming Ignorance and Sin

This general view of the significance of Christ seems to
be operative in the Dogmatics notes, even though it is not
developed systematically. The redemptive work of Christ is
treated in correlation with the preceding account of sin. What
is needed, as we have seen, is a radical alteration of human
subjectivity, replacing the distorted "second nature" which has
resulted from man's refusal to acknowledge the Reich Gottes.
Man's need for redemption had been characterized in terms of
"the power of sin, and ignorance." The work of Christ, therefore, is conceived as overcoming both ignorance and sin.

The redemptive work of Christ is treated in terms of
three functions. He is "teacher, reconciler, and sanctifier."[121]

---

[120]Cf. KE § 32, p. 19: "In jener und durch jene Einigung ist
die ursprünglich im Universum ausgedrückte, dem ersten religiösen Gefühle zu Grund liegende, während der Herrschaft des
Egoismus verkannte Idee eines Reiches Gottes wieder anerkannt,
sowohl theoretisch als praktisch." Cf. PD I 181, where Drey
equates the "regni divini ideam" with "mutua Deum inter et
homines conjunctione et amore mutuo." Cf. the Fuchs MS, in
Geiselmann's Die Katholische Tübinger Schule, p. 214: "Die
Absicht bei der Gründung des Reiches Gottes in der Schöpfung
war: reine innige Verbindung des Menschen mit Gott. Diese ist
durch den Sündenfall und noch mehr durch die wachsende
Verschlimmerung aufgehoben, wird aber durch die Erscheinung
Christi und sein Werk wiederhergestellt, und zwar auf einer
höheren Stufe, indem die ursprüngliche Unschuld eine bloß aner-
schaffene, die wiedererrungene aber das Werk der Freiheit und
des freien Bestrebens der Menschheit ist . . . ."

[121]PD I 153: ". . . ut inde ostendamus, quomodo eadem
persona divina triplici suo munere functus est, magistri scilicet doctoris, reconciliatoris ac sanctificatoris."

The office of teacher is obviously correlated with the "ignorance" which is characteristic of man's sinful condition. To
overcome this, Jesus makes known to mankind the truth of their
eternal relationship to God by teaching them above all the Idea
of the Kingdom of God. The office of reconciler is directed to
the overcoming of mankind's perverse choice of evil and the
consequent estrangement from God's holiness and justice. Drey's
treatment of this is quite traditional. The third function of
sanctifier is concerned with mankind's positive growth in
holiness of life. While Drey considers Christ to be the Agent
in this process of sanctification, he stresses the need for a
divine, _interior_ principle of the new life. Christ, therefore,
seems to be sanctifier insofar as he sends the Holy Spirit as
the enabling power which governs the new life both of individuals and of the Church.[122]

This three-fold office of Christ has as its purpose the
re-creation of mankind, after the distortion of human nature
occasioned by the Fall. This can, in general, be correlated
with Drey's overall conception of Christ's significance in the
"economy" of the Reich Gottes: to achieve the conscious unification of man with God by recalling man to the truth of the
Reich-Gottes Idea. This specifies, to some extent, how Christ
is the second turning-point in the development of the Kingdom
of God.

Drey's Failure to Develop a
Speculative Account
of Redemption

Nevertheless, Drey's detailed treatment of Christ in the
Dogmatics notes does not exploit his systematic viewpoint at all
clearly or consistently. His unifying concept of Reich Gottes
is, to be sure, mentioned as the chief content of Jesus' teaching. But the full implications of this--as indicated here--are

---

[122]Whereas the first two functions of Christ seem to constitute the "objective redemption," the third function seems to
be directed to mankind's subjective appropriation of this redemption. Perhaps for this reason, Drey's treatment of Christ
as sanctifier is relatively brief, and leads into the topic of
the "application of salvation" (PD I 221), which is called in
the later versions "Soteriologia, sive de ordine salutis conse-
quendae a singulis" (PD II 156, PD III 288). This will be
treated below.

not spelled out in the notes. Moreover, the _way_ in which
Christ achieves mankind's reconciliation with God (his second
office) is treated merely by presenting the various scriptural
themes, without attempting to relate them to a unifying
speculative concept.

This latter failure is all the more disappointing,
against the background of Drey's trinitarian doctrine and his
conception of the essence of sin. He could readily utilize the
concept of Incarnation in order to understand how the whole
finite order (pre-existent "ideally" in the eternal Son) is
brought through the created freedom of the Incarnate Christ to
personal union with the Father in mutual love (the destiny pre-
established for the created world in the eternal union of Father
and Son).[123] Furthermore, the theme of obedience[124] could be
developed as the reversal of man's sinful self-absolutizing
which has made him blind to the truth of the _Reich Gottes._

This suggestion of how the missing development in Drey's
Dogmatics might be filled out in accord with his own systematic
viewpoint is not altogether without support in his published
works. For example, he remarks in a book review that if the
reconciling power of Christ's death is to be explained "aus der
reinen Idee," it must be "the Idea of the Son of God as the
eternal representative of the world and of mankind before
God."[125] Moreover, he regards Jesus' entire life (not merely
his death) as salvific[126] and even mentions "obedience" as the

---

[123]In his discussion of the mode of redemption, Drey does
mention the theme of Incarnation as "quam maxime accomodatum"
(PD I 198), but does not relate this to his systematic viewpoint.

[124]This, too, is merely mentioned (PD I 198; 200) but not
utilized as a unifying concept.

[125]ThQ 1 (1819):435, ". . . so ist es die Idee vom Sohne
Gottes als dem ewigen Repräsentanten der Welt und der Menschheit vor Gott . . ."

[126]ThQ 1 (1819):434, ". . . die an sich klare und ein-
leuchtende Idee, daß zu unserer Erlösung die ganze Erscheinung
Christi auf Erde mitgewirkt, in seinem Tode aber die ganze
Kraft und Bedeutung seines Lebens sich herausgestellt habe."

significant feature of this life.[127] In the Apologetik, he
reflects the trinitarian concept of Christ as the archetype of
what man is destined to be, and sees His Incarnation as the
full realization of that archetype, so that it may be realized
more easily by all men.[128] And, in speaking of Christ's unique
inner relationship with the Father, he stresses Ergebenheit
(surrender) as the essential attitude which marks his earthly
life and allows us to regard him as "religion personified."[129]

The Christian Order of Sanctification:
"Third Phase" of the Kingdom

This portion of the Dogmatics continues the general theme
of "Palingenesis" or the restoration of the human race. This
restoration is viewed by Drey as an historical process, which
was prepared by the revelatory influence of God throughout the
"second phase" and was definitively established by the redemptive work of Christ, which initiated a new phase of the Kingdom's
development. In this "third phase," the salvation which Christ
has brought into world history is to be extended to all individual human beings. In this way, the complete restoration of the
human race is gradually to be brought about, as all human

---

[127]ThQ 8 (1826):538, "[die Schrift] . . . knüpft darum
selbst diese [die Sündenvergebung] nicht ausschließlich, wenn
schon größtentheils an den Tod Jesu, sondern bald an das Ganze
seines Kommens und Wirkens in der Welt, bald an seinen vollkommenen Gehorsam, d.h. seine sittliche Vollkommenheit u.s.w."

[128]Apol I § 18, p. 172: ". . . welches Bild [des Sohnes
Gottes] selbst kein anderes ist als dasjenige, wornach der
Mensch ursprünglich geschaffen ward, was dieser selbst ursprüng-
lich in sich ausbilden sollte, und weil er es nicht that, der
Erstgeborene des Vaters in seiner menschlichen Erscheinung voll-
kommen ausgeprägt darstellte, damit den übrigen dieselbe
Ausprägung ihrerseits erleichtert würde."

[129]Apol II § 70, p. 266: ". . . sein inniges Verhältniß
zu dem Vater . . . erfüllt nun auch sein menschlich-irdisches
Bewußtseyn . . . und dieses . . . Bewußtseyn verbunden mit dem
seiner irdischen Sendung, erzeugt und unterhält in ihm die
Empfindungen der innigsten Ehrfurcht, der zartesten Liebe, der
vollkommensten Ergebenheit; einer Ergebenheit, welche macht,
daß er seinen Willen ganz in den Willen seines Vaters versenkt
. . . Nennen wir nun das lebendige und durchgängige Bestimmtseyn
des Menschen durch das Gottesbewußtseyn--Religion, so erscheint
in Christus nicht blos die höchste Religiosität, er selbst ist
die personificirte Religion."

beings are drawn into the divinely established order of
sanctification.

Church Not an Explicit Theme

The logic of Drey's thought would lead naturally at this
point to a consideration of Church as the new "form" of the
Reich Gottes, for it is in the context of this new social
reality that individuals become partakers of the new life.[130]
In the Apologetik, Drey includes in the purposes of Christ's
work the founding of a great new Religionsgemeinschaft, as well
as the moral re-creation of mankind and a general forgiveness
of sins.[131] He sees the unity of these three purposes as "the
unification of mankind in a great Kingdom of God,"[132] and says
that "the founding of a great religious community was to give
this Kingdom its ethical form."[133]

The Process of "Justification"

In the Dogmatics, however, Drey's attention is directed
primarily to the "order of salvation," that is, the process
through which individuals come to appropriate the salvation
achieved by Christ.[134] Church is taken for granted as the
context of this process, but is not made an explicit theme of
Dogmatics.[135]

---

[130]Cf. Apol III § 26, p. 142: ". . . zur Unterhaltung des
Prozesses der Erlösung und Heiligung in den Individuen hat
Christus seine Kirche gegründet und dieser Bestimmung gemäß
ausgestattet, weil die gedachten Zwecke nur in einer solchen
Anstalt erreicht werden konnten, wie wir § . 15. gezeigt haben.
Der Kirche liegt also die individuelle Zuwendung der Erlösungs-
und Heilsmittel an die Menschen ob . . ."

[131]Apol II § 73, pp. 278-80.

[132]Ibid., p. 280: ". . . die Menschheit in einem großen
Reiche Gottes zu vereinigen . . ."

[133]Ibid., p. 281: "Diesem Reiche sollte die Stiftung
einer großen Religionsgemeinschaft die ethische Form geben . . ."

[134]PD I 221-22, marginal notation: "Diese vierte Sect.
[De applicatione salutis per J. Chr. partae] ist die letzte der
chr. Dogmatik, nach dem strengen Systeme der Wissenschaft. Sie
enthält die Lehre des Xtums über die Art und Weise, wie Gott
beschlossen hat, die Einzelnen an der Wohlthat der Wiederherstellung durch Christus Theil nehmen zu lassen."

[135]Drey acknowledges that one could readily integrate a
treatise on Church at this point. (PD I 221-22: "Zwar könnte

The process of the "regeneration" of individuals corresponds to the pattern established by the redemptive work of
Christ.[136] In his three-fold office, Christ has overcome mankind's ignorance by his teaching, has brought about the forgiveness of sins by his reconciling function, and has provided the
means for rebirth into a new life by sending the Holy Spirit as
his agent of sanctification. The "objective" benefits of Christ
are, therefore, characterized succinctly as "teaching, forgiveness of sins, and sanctification."[137]

Drey interprets the traditional notion of "justification"
as the entire process by which the individual comes to appropriate subjectively these objective benefits of Christ.[138] He
regards this process on the one hand as enabled by the immediate
influence of the Holy Spirit upon the human subject. Hence, he
treats the topic of "grace" as part of this section. On the
other hand, he simultaneously understands the process in terms
of the attitudes and behavior of the human individual who is
being "justified" or "sanctified."[139]

The stages of justification correspond to the three objective benefits of Christ. First of all, "faith" is the individual's way of appropriating the teaching of Christ, so that the

---

hier die Lehre von der Kirche und den Sakramenten geradezu ein-
geflochten werden . . .") And in his overview of Dogmatics of
20 February 1818, he even envisaged a separate section on
Church (PD I 20). He did not, however, carry out this projec-
tion in any of the versions of the PD. See below for an
explanation of his methodological reason for this omission.

[136]PD I 20: "In genere salutis ordo circa singulos idem
est, ac in restitutione universi generis humani."

[137]PD I 223: "Quare . . . ista beneficia tribus potissimum capitibus constare vidimus, doctrina scilicet, venia
peccatorum, et sanctificatione . . ."

[138]Cf. ThQ 2 (1820):53, ". . . er [referring to himself
as the author of this book review] würde . . . die Rechtfertigung selbst aber als Heilsordnung begreifen, d.h. als nähere
Bestimmung, wie der einzelne Mensch subjektiv und für sich der
Heilswerke theilhaftig werde, welche Christus objectiv und für
das ganze Geschlecht geltend vollbracht hat."

[139]Geiselmann presents a detailed report on Drey's doctrine of justification and grace, as contained in the Fuchs MS
of Drey's Dogmatics lectures of 1828-29. See Die Katholische
Tübinger Schule, pp. 450-503.

human subject accepts and affirms as true what Christ has made
known about man's relationship to God. Secondly, a radical
change of heart ("resipiscentia" or "Sinnesänderung") is the
requisite for appropriating the forgiveness of sins made possible by Christ. Finally, the sanctification which Christ enables
through the agency of his Spirit can only be appropriated by a
corresponding transformation of the individual's whole way of
life ("vita honesta" or "gute Werke").[140]

Drey regards these three aspects of the human subject's
transformation not as preliminary dispositions for "justification," but rather as the very structure and pattern of justification itself.[141]

The Role of the Holy Spirit

Drey attributes to the Holy Spirit the internal, immediate
divine influence upon the human spirit which enables the entire
process of justification.[142] This immediate divine Agency is

---

[140]PD I 223: ". . . facile est intelligere, doctrinam
Christi utpote summam credendorum fide praecipue stare et per-
suasione; veniam autem peccatorum absque animi mutatione sive
resipiscentia non esse possibilem, ipsam vero sanctitatem in
vita honesta atque actionibus bonis fieri perspicuam. Atque
haec sunt quae ex parte hominis tanquam conditiones necessariae
requiruntur, ut quis beneficiorum Christi particeps revera dici
aut fieri possit; fides scilicet, resipiscentia, et opera bona."
Cf. ThQ 2 (1820):53, "Dieser Heilswerke [Christi] sind aber
drey: die seligmachende Lehre, die der Mensch nur ergreifen
kann durch den Glauben; die Versöhnung mit Gott durch den Tod
Christi, die dem Menschen als wirkliche Sündenvergebung zuge-
wendet wird in der Sinnesänderung oder Buße; die eigentliche
Heiligung im engern Sinne als Frucht und Wirkung des lebendigen
Glaubens und der wahren Buße, die wo sie im Menschen vorhanden
ist, sich nothwendig äußern muß in einem christlichen Leben,
oder nach dem Sprachgebrauche der katholischen Dogmatik, in
guten Werken."

[141]ThQ 2 (1820):53, "So bildeten der Glaube, die Sinnesänderung und die guten Werke--nicht die bloße Vorbereitung zur
Rechtfertigung, sondern wirkliche Theile derselben, gleichsam
ihre Stufenordnung, in welcher sie vollendet wird." Cf. ThQ 8
(1826):540, ". . . im Glauben, in der Sinnesänderung . . . und
in der guten Gesinnung liege eben die Rechtfertigung selbst,
ungefähr so wie die Hebung der Krankheit nicht eine bloße Dis-
position zum Gesundwerden ist, sondern das Gesundwerden selbst."

[142]PD I 166-67: ". . . benevolam Dei actionem in animum
hominis, occultam illam quidem, prorsus individualem et imme-
diatam, qua fit ut animus inde excitatus atque alacer bonum
quodvis arripiat, adminiculis etiam externis utatur et consen-
tiat, atque sic salutis Xnae vere demum et perfectae [sic]

distinguished sharply from all exterior means of grace, including the historical fact of Christ.[143] Moreover, while this
Spirit is regarded as God Himself, He is distinguished from
Christ in terms of His role in the "economy": as internal principle of sanctification, in contrast to the external.[144]

At the same time, the Spirit is linked closely with
Christ as the principle of mankind's sanctification. This is
most evident in the fact that Drey's treatment of the Holy
Spirit's role in this process occurs in the section which deals
with the third function of Christ, as "sanctifier."[145] As
noted above, Christ appears to exercise this function insofar
as he sends into the world the Holy Spirit. Although distinct
from Christ, the Spirit is regarded as his Spirit, whose function is to carry out Christ's work of the regeneration and
sanctification of all human beings.[146]

The Spirit is, therefore, the divine principle which rules
the new phase of the Kingdom of God initiated by Christ.[147]
Drey's treatment of the Spirit, in this context, is concerned
primarily with the Spirit's role in the sanctification of
individuals.[148] This role is, however, clearly inseparable

---

particeps fiat . . ." Ibid., 167-68: ". . . speciale principium
occultae illius actionis in animos hominum constitutum videmus,
Spiritum Sanctum videlicet, tanquam primariam fontem operatio-
num, et largitorem gratiarum omnium."

[143]PD I 168: "Distinguitur autem hic Spiritus ab omni
gratiae medio, quod per sensus adlabitur, ab evangelio et omni
opere Christi externo . . ."

[144]PD III 407: "Distingui Spiritum a Filio, et actionem
Spiritus ab actione Christi ut internum quid ab externo. Joh.
XIV, 16.17; XV, 26, XVI, 13.14."

[145]PD II 149-53; PD III 284-88.

[146]PD II 153: "quamvis a Christi persona distinguatur,
tamen quia ab ipso venit, et ejus nomine agit, ejus etiam est,
adeoque nos integrum restitutionis beneficium per omnes ejus
partes Christo in acceptis referimus." PD II 149: "Hoc . . .
spiritu ceu administratore suo Christus homines sanctificat."

[147]PD II 149: ". . . novi temporis a [Christo] . . .
inchoati manifestum rectorem et quasi quemdam principem . . ."
PD II 151: ". . . novi rerum ordinis ducem et promotorem . . ."

[148]PD I 218: ". . . peculiare . . . est et maxime recur-
rens negotium ipsius, ut homines ad sanctitatem ducat."

from the Spirit's function of creating, guiding, and ruling the
Church. His abiding presence to all individuals is likewise a
presence to the community.[149] This role of the Spirit as life-
principle of the Church's development in history is a central
theme in Drey's theology, even though it is not developed in
the Dogmatics.[150]

Sacraments as the Means of Sanctification

Drey includes the treatise on Sacraments in this section,
even though he has no treatise on the Church as such. His
treatment of this topic is traditional, and does not merit
closer inspection here. He regards the Sacraments as the means
instituted by Christ for individual human beings to undergo the
process of justification in the Church, under the enabling
influence of the Holy Spirit. Drey's inclusion of Sacraments
in his Dogmatics is to be explained in terms of the needs of
his students, rather than from his methodological viewpoint
(which would assign this material not to Dogmatics, but to a
separate discipline that would treat of the Church as the
making-real of the Ideas of Christianity).

Eschatological Fulfillment: Third "Turning-Point" and "Final Phase"

In Drey's universal-historical perspective, the progressive realization of the Idea Reich Gottes is to culminate in a
final, perfect state of restored mankind in relationship to the
eternal Ground of their being.

His treatment of the "last things" is primarily scriptural
and traditional. Hence, the third "turning-point" which
initiates the fourth and final "phase" of the Kingdom is
equated with the second coming of Christ,[151] but no further

---

[149]PD I 220-21: ". . . semper praesens hominum generi, et
quidem . . . duplici ratione: scilicet et universam conciliat
rempublicam Christianam, dirigit atque perficit; et singulis
adest fidelibus ut fons et auctor immediatus sanctificationis
nostrae." PD II 152: ". . . perennem et stabilem hominum sanc-
tificandorum praesidem . . . atque in ecclesia Christi perpetuo
praesentem, semper agentem, optima quaevis potenter promoventem
. . ."

[150]Cf. KE § 175, p. 118, cited in Chapter V, p. 128.
Cf. also Apol I §§ 54-55, pp. 398-409.

[151]PD III 456.

speculative interpretation of this event is offered. The
themes of the resurrection of the dead, the last judgment, and
the state of both the just and the unjust after death are
likewise presented in a traditional manner.

Perfect Union with God
through Obedience

Drey's distinctive systematic viewpoint is, however, discernible in certain features of this "end-state" of the Kingdom
of God. In accord with his basic conception of the Reich
Gottes, Drey envisions its fulfillment as "the perfect uniting
of all things with God."[152] As we have seen, the destiny of
man is to reach this unity with God through freedom and love
(the perfection of "religion"). Hence, the final perfection of
the Kingdom will be achieved insofar as everything "which is
now opposed and hostile to God and the divine decrees will
disappear utterly and be removed."[153] This is a matter of the
free obedience of mankind, which is the condition for the full
and final presence of the Kingdom of God.[154]

It is the function of Christ to bring all nations and
individual human beings into this attitude of perfect obedience
to the Father. Drey's strong "theocentrism" is evident in his
utilization of the scriptural theme of Christ's "handing over"
the Kingdom to the Father.[155] Referring to Christ's status and
function as risen, Drey says:

> This new condition of Christ in heaven differs from
> that condition which he enjoyed with God from the beginning

---

[152]PD III 68: "Die vollkommene Vereinigung aller Dinge
mit Gott."

[153]PD III 69: ". . . disparebit penitus atque auferetur a
medio, . . . quidquid nunc undecunque Deo divinisque consiliis
contrarium est et inimicum . . ."

[154]PD III 69: ". . . tum vero cunctis Deo sponte parenti-
bus regnum ejus praesentissimum aeternumque comparebit."

[155]Cf. ThQ 2 (1820):40, ". . . [die Bibel] lehrt, daß
das Reich und die Herrschaft jetzt nur sichtbar von dem Vater
an Christus übertragen ist, wie dieser es jenem am Schlusse
der gegenwärtigen Periode eben so sichtbar wieder zurückstellen
wird."

> . . . most of all because that heavenly rule (imperium)
> which the Father has held from all eternity, destined for
> the Son, has now truly been transferred to Christ. And
> Christ now exercises this rule in such a way that . . . he
> is gradually uniting all nations with himself in his reli-
> gion, is making them obedient to himself and to the Father,
> and thus is forming his church on earth; but whatever is
> hostile and rebellious he is breaking and diminishing until
> finally--when all this has been completed--he may restore
> the dominion (imperium), now absolute and fully purified,
> to the Father.156

This text is another indication of the kind of speculative
integration of his Christology into the systematic viewpoint of
the Reich Gottes which Drey might have done, if he had been more
explicit and consistent.

It is, at any rate, fairly clear that the ultimate state
of the Kingdom--though brought about by Christ--is conceived
finally as God's Kingdom. The essential and eternal relationship of created being to the Creator is realized in the mode of
human freedom, insofar as all human beings are united with the
Father in the obedience which Christ brings about.157

A Social Fulfillment in
Continuity with Church

The above text also indicates clearly the social character
of the fulfillment. It is in the form of a perfect social
union of all nations and individuals in Christ that mankind is
to reach its destiny of union with God.158 Hence, the

156PD I 174: "Differt autem haec nova Christi in coelis
conditio ab ipsa qua fruitus est ab initio apud Deum . . .
maxime quia imperium illud coeleste, quod Pater ab aeterno ten-
uit, olim jam filio destinatum, nunc revera ad Christum trans-
latum est. Atque hoc quidem imperio Christus nunc ita defungi-
tur, ut . . . omnes paulatim gentes religione sua sibi conciliet,
sibi atque Patri oboedientes efficiat, atque sic ecclesiam suam
in his terris exornat, quidquid autem est virium adversarum et
rebellium, frangat et comminuat, donec tandem his omnibus per-
fectis imperium absolutum jam et plene purgatum Patri restituat."

157Drey does not, however, suppose that all will necessarily be saved. Those who resist God's rule will finally be
excluded from the harmonious, perfect unity of the Kingdom of
God.

158PD III, end-pages, p. 50: "Sancti . . . tum demum in
unam atque individuam societatem cum Deo et Christo collecti
regni divini perfectam formam effingent . . ." PD III 340-41:
". . . Christus asseverat, idemque repetunt apostoli . . . omne
hoc quod nunc currit aevum, explicando et augendo regno divino,

fulfillment of the Reich Gottes, although it transcends all
temporal process in the perfect, unchanging stability of
"eternity,"[159] is nevertheless thought to be in continuity with
the historical development of the Reich Gottes in this present
"third phase." That is, the Church is regarded as the incipient, progressive realization of the Idea,[160] so that the
final state may be equated with "the perfection of the Church
of Christ and the communion of saints."[161]

In a certain sense, therefore, Drey's Dogmatics concludes
with a vision of Church--not, to be sure, the imperfect realization of God's Idea which we now experience, but the perfect
actualization of God's intention for mankind.[162] Hence, this
survey of the Dogmatics can appropriately include a brief
supplement on Drey's view of the Church, even though this is
not treated as a separate theme in the Dogmatics notes.

The Place of the Church in
Drey's Theology

Not a Topic for Dogmatics

As Rief remarks, Drey attributes to the Church "a significance which is scarcely surpassable," insofar as he considers

---

divulgando nimirum ejus nuncio, contrahendis in tam beatam cum
Deo societatem hominibus, et hac ipsa societate ad omnem per-
fectionem excolendis esse destinatum."

[159]PD III, end-pages, p. 49: "Erit autem hic ordo . . .
in genere aeternus. Quo utique vocabulo praeprimis illud
indicatur, eundem ordinem a praesenti, qui quidem varius est et
mutabilis et incertus, non solum diversum esse, sed huic prorsus oppositum."

[160]PD I 20: ". . . cum in . . . ecclesia, quatenus in
dies increscit et perficitur, generis nostri restitutio continuo magis completa, salus universim propagata, gratia Christi
victrix, et regnum coelorum jam proximum compareat . . ."

[161]PD III, end-pages, p. 47: ". . . ecclesia Christi con-
summata, et communione sanctorum perfecta . . ."

[162]Cf. ThQ 7 (1825):132, "Denn was nothwendig herauskommt,
wenn alle Gläubigen das uns durch Christus gewordene Heil leben-
dig ergreifen, d.h. wenn alle vom höhern Geist aus Christus,
und durch ihn von Glauben und Liebe durchdrungen werden und in
dieser Gesinnung handeln, das ist die Kirche, die glorreiche,
die da ist ohne Fleck und Runzel, und allen Fehl der Art,
sondern heilig und untadelig . . ."

it to be the manifestation of the <u>Reich Gottes</u>, the continuing
presence in history of the originating fact of revelation, hence
"the basis of all theological knowledge."[163] In view of the
prominence of the Church in Drey's whole conception of the
subject matter and method of Christian theology,[164] it must be
puzzling at first to find that he does not include a distinct
treatise "de ecclesia" in his Dogmatics notes.

We shall, therefore, first account for this omission in
terms of Drey's peculiar methodological viewpoint. Then, for
the sake of completeness, we shall provide a very brief overview of Drey's principal ideas on the Church, referring the
reader to the relevant <u>loci</u> in Drey's writings and the places
in the secondary literature where the theme of Church is
examined.

Drey's conception of theology limits Dogmatics to the
treatment of the "Lehrbegriff," that is, of the "Ideas" of
Christianity--which are equated with the "decrees" of God
governing the entire process of world history. In accord with
his Idealist perspective, Drey regards this as the "ideal side"
of Christianity. In contrast to this, the "real side" com-
prises the historical phenomena in which these divine Ideas are
actualized. The Church--as the incipient realization of the
<u>Reich Gottes</u>--belongs to this "real side." Hence, it is not to
be treated as one of the topics of Dogmatics, but rather in a

---

[163]Rief, "Johann Sebastian von Drey," p. 33, cites KE §
54, p. 33: "Denn die Kirche ist die wahre Basis alles theologischen Wissens." (See Chapter V, p. 176, for the full citation
of this text.) He also cites Drey's "Ideen zur Geschichte des
katholischen Dogmensystems," <u>GdChr</u> 246: ". . . postulieren wir
eine Kirche als die äußere wohlorganisierte Erscheinung der
religiösen Providenz oder des Reiches Gottes . . . , als Organ
der göttlichen Offenbarung, als ein verkörpertes System, das
sich fortwährend von innen heraus durch die Regung eines un-
sichtbaren Geistes bildet und gestaltet." Rief then observes:
". . . in Äußerungen solcher Art [wird] der Kirche eine kaum
überbietbare Bedeutung zugeschrieben . . ."

[164]Cf. Rief, "Johann Sebastian von Drey," pp. 32-35;
Schupp, <u>Die Evidenz der Geschichte</u>, pp. 66-67. See Chapter V,
pp. 123, 174-76.

separate discipline called "the theory of the Christian
Church."[165]

Church as Living Embodiment
of Revelation

Although the Church is not treated as a topic in Dogmatics,
the reality of Church is clearly presupposed as the condition
for doing Dogmatics at all. This is because Drey regards the
Church primarily as the ongoing embodiment of revelation, "die
lebendige Selbstüberlieferung der Offenbarung."[166]

Because Drey links the Church so closely with the concept
of revelation, his most extensive treatment of the Church occurs
in the Apologetik, where he is concerned with the continuity
and extension through time of the original, decisive revelation
of Christ.[167] This same understanding of the Church is to be
found in Drey's Journals[168] and in his early published works.
It is expressed in strongly romantic language in his article
"Vom Geist und Wesen des Katholizismus," which stresses the
need for an ever-present "objective" phenomenon in relation to
which individual human beings can encounter the divine initiative and come to a living faith.[169]

Drey's notion of the Church as the living continuation
and embodiment of revelation is probably the best-known portion

---

[165]KE § 71, pp. 44-45. Cf. also KE § 268, p. 181; § 275,
p. 186. Cf. PD III 58: "Hic adnotatio singularis exponit, regnum Dei in idea argumentum dogmatices esse, cum regnum Dei in
realitate propriam disciplinam exposcat." This same point of
view is expressed clearly in Drey's reviews of Dobmayer's Dogmatics. Cf. ThQ 1 (1819):435, 437-38; ThQ 7 (1825):132. Cf.
also Tagebücher V 46: "Die Lehre von der Kirche und von den
Sacramenten . . . gehört als eine praktische nicht eigentlich
mehr zur Dogmatik, da sie praktisch ist, und das ganze
theoretisch-dogmatische System des Christentums in demselben
praktisch wird. Hier gehen die Ideen des Christentums nicht
mehr in den Begriff über wie in der Dogmatik, alle Begriffe,
die Ideen selbst gehen im Glauben auf."

[166]Apol I § 49, p. 382.

[167]Cf. Apol I §§ 49-56, pp. 380-410, esp. pp. 398-404.
Cf. Apol III §§ 1-3, pp. 1-17.

[168]Cf. Tagebucher V 181-82, GdChr, pp. 187-88.

[169]"Vom Geist und Wesen des Katholizismus," ThQ 1 (1819),
reprinted in GdChr, pp. 195-234. See especially GdChr, pp.
195-96, 205-7.

of his thought, thanks to the exhaustive treatment of this by
Geiselmann.[170]

Church as Context for Individual's
Faith and Sanctification

Closely related to this is Drey's conviction that the
context for the individual's subjective appropriation of God's
salvation is the Church as the guardian and guarantor of the
means of salvation.[171] The Church is conceived as an organism
ruled by the one divine life-principle of the Holy Spirit.[172]
Christ is thought to have initiated and established this great
new "Religionsgemeinschaft"[173] so that all men and women can
come to share in the new, restored relationship with God which
he has brought about. The process of "justification" or sanctification, as we have seen above, is enabled by the Holy Spirit
acting in the community and is structured by the sacraments as
the channels of grace. Although he gives full weight to the
institutional element of this religious community,[174] Drey
conceives its importance for the individual primarily in terms
of a context of life, a great "objective phenomenon" transcending individual life-times and finding embodiment in doctrine,
worship, ethical ideals, and life-style.[175] It is in this

---

[170]Cf. Geiselmann, Lebendiger Glaube aus geheiligter
Überlieferung, pp. 120-298. Cf. also Schupp, Die Evidenz der
Geschichte, pp. 66-73; and Menke, "Der Begriff 'Dogma' im Werke
J. S. von Dreys," Theologie und Philosophie 52 (1977):48-56.

[171]Cf. Apol III §§ 13-16, pp. 71-87. Cf. KE § 324,
pp. 217-18. Cf. also Drey's article "Über den Satz von der
allein seligmachenden Kirche," in Der Apologet des Katholizismus, ed. A. Gratz (Mainz: 1822), Heft 5, pp. 39-85; reprinted
in GdChr, pp. 333-57.

[172]Cf. "Ideen zur Geschichte des katholischen Dogmensystems," GdChr, pp. 245-46; KE § 175, p. 118.

[173]Cf. Apol III § 73, pp. 278-80; III §§ 18-23, pp. 89-126.

[174]Cf. his lengthy treatment of the structure and offices
of the Church in Apol III §§ 29-56, pp. 163-275.

[175]Cf. Tagebücher IV 80-81: ". . . das zeitliche Element
[des Reiches Gottes], wie es unter den Menschen hervortritt,
muß ihnen einen bestimmten Charakter . . . , eine gleiche Sitte
geben . . . nicht das politische, nicht das bürgerliche, sondern das rein menschliche (in religiöser und sittlicher
Hinsicht--in Andacht, Gerechtigkeit, Liebe--) ist ihr Zweck . . ."

sense that he can view the Church as the "Selbstüberlieferung"
of the originating salvific, revelatory event of Christ.

Church as Realization of
the "Reich Gottes"

Finally, as we have seen, Drey regards the Church--devel-
oping and spreading through all cultures--as the growing realization of the divinely intended Reich Gottes. In this way of
speaking, both of the previously named aspects of the Church
come together in a universal-historical perspective. The
Church is the living continuation of revelation not in an
extrinsic way--by merely preserving and handing-on the memory
of what once happened--but rather in an intrinsic way, by
becoming an ever more perfect embodiment of what God is bringing about through His revelatory influence upon the human
spirit. This realization of God's "Idea" occurs insofar as all
the nations and all individual human beings take on the new
quality of life made possible by Christ and awakened by the
ever-present and ever-active Spirit. The Church is conceived
as a changing, developing social reality, because its destiny
is to unite the diverse cultures and races of the earth into a
society which transcends the ethnic and the political.[176]

"Society" as the Condition
for Love

Rief has examined in great detail Drey's understanding of
the societal character of the Church.[177] One of the features
of this understanding is the conception of "society as the
condition of love."[178] This is an appropriate note on which to

---

[176]Cf. KE § 27, p. 15. See above, pp. 203-6. Cf. also
Drey's articles "Von der Landesreligion und der Weltreligion,"
ThQ 9 (1827):234-74; 391-435; and "Der katholische Lehrsatz von
der Gemeinschaft der Heiligen," ThQ 4 (1822):587-634, reprinted
in GdChr, pp. 359-88.

[177]Cf. Rief, Reich Gottes und Gesellschaft, pp. 244-345.
Important texts of Drey in this regard are Apol III, "Vorrede,"
pp. III-VIII; §§ 1-3, pp. 1-17; § 16, pp. 85-87.

[178]Rief, Reich Gottes und Gesellschaft, pp. 245-47:
"Gesellschaft als Bedingung der Liebe." The key text of Drey
is "Vom Geist und Wesen des Katholizismus," GdChr, pp. 209-12.
On this same text, cf. Rief, p. 128.

conclude this brief survey of Drey's views on the Church, because it connects with his foundational understanding of the Reich Gottes.

As we have seen, the condition for taking part in the Reich Gottes is the acknowledgment of the "relation of origin." This can only happen as the overcoming of the "egotism" which is characteristic of man's sinful self-absolutizing in disregard of God's absolute dominion. Hence, Drey considers "love" to be the mode of man's participation in the Reich Gottes, since this is the way in which the individual transcends his intrinsic egotism and "loses himself" in the great harmonious whole of God's Kingdom. This movement away from self-sufficiency into a greater whole is only possible in the attitude of "humility" (Demut), which Drey considers to be "the deepest in religion, deeper than faith and love."[179] Love, as well as the underlying attitude of humility, is fostered and made possible only in the great fellowship of the Church. The individual overcomes his egotism by surrendering not merely to the greater life of the community but, ultimately, to the God whose Kingdom this is.

---

[179]"Vom Geist und Wesen des Katholizismus," GdChr, pp. 204-5. For the citation of this text, see Chapter V, p. 173.

CHAPTER VII

CRITICAL ASSESSMENT

The earlier chapters have examined the texts of Drey,
both published and unpublished, in an effort to discover and
communicate the "specificity" of his thought. This final
chapter will pull together the results of this investigation,
in order to make some critical and appreciative judgments on
his theology.

The first section presents a summarizing review of Drey's
thought, as it has been interpreted in this study. Against
this background, the second section offers a critique of Drey's
theological project, both in terms of his own intentions and in
the light of later intellectual developments. Finally, the
third section surveys those features of Drey's contribution
which seem especially relevant to the continuing task of
contemporary theology.

Review: Drey's Dominant Concern

Perhaps the best way of summarizing my interpretation of
Drey is to address the question: what is his dominant concern?
Without trying to oversimplify his thought, one can nevertheless appreciate the actual unity of his theological project by
noticing how it springs from a characteristic concern.

It may reasonably be taken as significant that Drey's
major published work is a three-volume Apologetics. Confronted
by radical challenges to traditional Catholic faith, at a time
when the "coordinate system" of Christian theology was changing
drastically,[1] he needed to re-think the very basis of the

---

[1]Cf. Schupp, Revision von Kirche und Theologie (Darmstadt:
Wissenschaftliche Buchgesellschaft, 1971), pp. VII-VIII.

theological enterprise. Hence, his dominant concern is clearly
apologetic, in the sense of refashioning a rational account of
Christian faith in a way which could commend its truth to the
mentality of his time. We can best appreciate the creative and
integrative power of Drey's mind if we consider briefly both
the challenges he perceived and the intellectual resources
which he found for his apologetic task.

Challenges

There were two prominent features of Catholic faith (as
Drey understood it) which were rendered implausible by the
dominant mentality of the Enlightenment in late eighteenth-
century Germany: (1) the orientation of faith towards an
historically mediated divine revelation, and (2) the valuation
of Church as the divinely instituted, reliable context for
relating authentically to that revelation.

Both these attitudes were undercut by the deistic naturalist view of the God-world relationship, which ruled out any
particular divine initiatives within the course of nature and
history. Furthermore, the rationalist idea of a universal
"natural religion" of reason made the postulate of a divinely
given, particular revelation seem quite unnecessary.

A further challenge to Drey's form of faith was presented
by the mainly Protestant historical-critical examination of the
origins and later development of Christianity. This had only
begun in the latter part of the eighteenth century, but its
relativizing effect on both doctrine and Church institutions
was felt already in Drey's lifetime. Hence, he was confronted
with the problem of change and development in Church doctrine
and life.

The Apologetic Task

For Drey, therefore, the indispensable first task of
theology was to ground and defend the "revelation-character" of
Christianity as a unique, "positive" religion springing from
the divine initiative in history.[2] At the same time, this
foundational account of revelation had to show the intrinsic
relationship of the divine initiative to the universal

---

[2]Cf. Apol I, "Vorrede," pp. V-VII, and "Einleitung"
§§ 1-2, pp. 1-3.

phenomenon of religion in mankind.[3] Moreover, in order to
defend his Catholic valuation of Church, Drey needed to show
the logical and necessary connection between the divinely given
revelation and the social, historical reality of Church.[4]

Resources

Drey found in the intellectual movements of the early
nineteenth century a number of elements which seemed promising
for his apologetic enterprise.

The newly emergent philosophy of religion, especially in
Schleiermacher, offered a new kind of philosophical anthropology which seemed to transcend the shallow rationalism of the
Enlightenment. By distinguishing religion sharply from both
metaphysical speculation and ethical thought, it located the
individual's felt relationship with the Infinite in a certain
kind of immediate intuition.

The new philosophy of German Idealism (especially in the
early writings of Schelling), with its sense of the intimate
unity of finite and Infinite, seemed to offer an alternative to
the deist isolation of the world from God. Moreover, despite
its tendency to reduce Christianity to a kind of timeless
speculative system, this new philosophy appeared to offer a
model for discovering the intelligible unity of the empirically
given. In particular, Schelling's view of history as the
"identity" of freedom and necessity appealed to Drey as a
perspective for interpreting Christianity in the context of a
divinely ruled universal history.[5]

---

[3]Cf. Apol I, "Einleitung" § 14, p. 27.

[4]Cf. Apol I § 49, pp. 380-82; §§ 54-55, pp. 398-410.

[5]It is a curious fact that Drey shows no sign of being
influenced by Hegel's writings. The period in which Drey
studied German philosophy intensively (1801-6) was, of course,
before Hegel's prominence, and the Hegelian influence in the
Protestant faculty of Tübingen dates from the arrival of
Ferdinand Christian Baur in 1826. By the early 1820's, Drey
had already established his own characteristic line of thought,
oriented to the early Schelling's form of Idealism, and he
remained remarkably consistent throughout his career in the
basic orientation and direction of his theology. Drey's few
references to Hegel occur in passing, mainly in book reviews.
Drey's failure to react significantly to Hegel's thought is
surprising, in view of the striking parallels to Hegel in his
own work (cf. Hünermann, "Der Reflex des deutschen Idealismus,"

Drey's concern to take seriously the "positive," historical character of Christianity found support in the new Romantic
sensibility which valued above all the concrete, particular,
"given" phenomena of history (in contrast to the abstract,
universal aspects of human nature). The new interest in
history was accompanied by a new appreciation of growth and
development, of the continuity of human life through the mediation of social groups and institutions. Especially the Romantic metaphor of the "organism" and the tendency to think of a
social group in history as a kind of person with the unity of a
unique "spirit" (Volksgeist) were well-suited to Drey's effort
to understand the Church as bearer of revelation.

The newly emergent interest in world religions offered a
wider context for valuing Christianity as a positive, historical religion. The fascination with universal history, inspired
by Herder's comprehensive view of the diverse Völker of the
earth, provided a further dimension for the location and esti-
mation of Christianity. Finally, Lessing's idea of revelation
as the education of the human race gave Drey a valuable perspective for unifying his interpretation of religion, revelation, and Christianity in the context of universal history.

Drey's way of integrating these diverse elements into an
apologetic interpretation of Christianity has been presented in
the expository chapters of this study. The chief features of
his thought are now to be touched upon again, in the following
overview.

The Apologetic Concern: "Divine
Positivity" and Rationality

The proper task of Apologetics as a distinct discipline,
Drey thinks, is to establish and vindicate the quality of
"divine positivity" which attaches to the entire historical
phenomenon of Christianity. Without such a grounding, it is
impossible to construct a theology oriented to an historically
given revelation.

On the one hand, this task involves the historical examination of the actual shape of mankind's development, so as to

_____

Philosophisches Jahrbuch 73 [1965-66]:59-61). In particular,
Hegel's concern to do justice to "positivity" and take it up
into "ideality" seems much closer to Drey's project than the
"Identitätsphilosophie" of the early Schelling.

show the divine initiative at work in that history. In this
connection, it is significant that Drey considers the entire
history of mankind to be relevant, not merely that portion of it
which embraces the particular origin and development of
Christianity. He is concerned to situate Christianity in the
widest possible context of the religious development of mankind,
so that it may be viewed as the climax and fulfillment of the
one revelation which embraces and influences all times and
places.

This historical task, although required for the grounding
of Christianity as the work of God, is not sufficient. Equally
necessary is a properly philosophical account of religion, so
as to establish a valid concept of revelation as intrinsically
related to the very nature of man. Without such a "scientific
concept" of revelation, the historically established evidence
of divine initiative can only appear as an arbitrary, fortuitous,
and unintelligible phenomenon. In other words, the _fact_ of
revelation (established historically) must be appreciated in
its quality of intelligible _necessity_.

Christianity, Drey thinks, cannot be commended to the
human mind unless its apparent quality of "accidentality" is
subsumed into a higher viewpoint which can appreciate its
"necessity." Thus, the "locating" of Christianity may not be
limited to the merely historical perspective. Beyond that, the
theologian must intuit the intelligible necessity of the entire
historical development (of which Christianity is the center and
fulfillment), by discovering how this development corresponds
to the essential nature of man in relation to God.

Apologetics is thus the "Grundlegung" of the whole enterprise of "scientific theology," insofar as it establishes the
fundamental character of Christianity as a _divinely given_
phenomenon (the "revelation-character" of Christianity), and
shows the intrinsic relationship of this "positive" phenomenon
to the essential nature of man as created spirit. But it is
not the task of Apologetics to treat the doctrinal content of
Christian faith.[6] The latter task is for Dogmatics.

---

[6]Drey's earlier conception of Apologetics, influenced by
Schleiermacher, assigned to that discipline the task of clarifying the intelligible "essence" of Christianity in terms of

The full intelligibility of the divine initiative in the
religious development of mankind can only be appreciated
through the "scientific construction" of the historically given
doctrines of Christianity. And this cannot be done without a
properly "scientific" or philosophical "construction" of universal history from the perspective of the divinely given Idea
which provides the key to understanding that history as a unity.
Thus, the effort to vindicate Christianity before the bar of
reason[7] leads from the foundational discipline of Apologetics
through historical theology to the crowning discipline of
"wissenschaftliche Theologie."

We have shown in some detail that Drey's demand for a
Wissenschaft of theology finds its meaning only in the Idealist
context of Schelling's early writings. But this involves a
peculiar perspective on the finite-Infinite relationship.
Hence, Drey's apologetic concern to ground the divine givenness
of Christianity and to commend its truth to the human mind by
"wissenschaftliche Konstruktion" leads inescapably to a more
profound theme: the nature of the God-world relationship.

The God-World Relationship

There seems to be two distinguishable contexts in which
the God-world relationship becomes crucial for Drey's theology.
The one--just indicated--is the Idealist model of intelligibility: the finite is taken to be the manifestation of the
Infinite, the making-real (in the sense of self-manifesting) of
divine Ideas. The other context is Drey's philosophy of revelation, which attempts to conceive revelation as a continuation
of God's eternal creative activity in and upon the world which
originates from His creative act.

In both of these contexts, Drey is following his apologetic concern. The creationist account of God's activity upon
His world is essential for his effort to transcend the

---

its master Idea. (KE §§ 221-26, pp. 149-52; § 230, pp. 154-55)
In his own Apologetics, however, Drey came to a different view
of that discipline's proper task. It is concerned not with the
content of Christianity's Ideas, but rather with the basic
character of the historical phenomenon of Christianity as
divinely given. Cf. Apol I, "Vorrede," pp. IV-V.

[7]Cf. KE § 226, p. 152.

naturalist/supernaturalist impasse and establish a valid concept
of revelation. Without this he cannot argue for the divine
positivity of Christianity. The Idealist view of the finite-
Infinite relationship, on the other hand, is essential for
Drey's model of intelligibility. He cannot discover the intelligible necessity of what God has done (and is doing) unless
the whole realm of finite reality is taken to be the consequence
of divine Mind, the making-real of divine Ideas. Thus, both
the characteristics of Christianity which Drey is attempting to
defend and synthesize--"positivity" and "rationality"--imply
particular conceptions of the God-world relationship.[8]

Hence, my interpretation of Drey's thought has taken the
God-world relationship as the most radical and characteristic
theme which is operative in his theology. This is not to deny
that the apologetic concern is the dominant formal feature of
his thought. But Drey's apologetic project finds its deepest
grounding in his distinctive way of conceiving the finite world
in relationship to its divine Source. In order to clarify and
support this assertion, we need only recall the results of the
earlier detailed examinations of Drey's account of revelation
(Chapters II and III), of his ideal of "Theologie als Wissenschaft" (Chapters IV and V), and of his systematic viewpoint in
the Dogmatics (Chapter VI).

Revelation as Creative Activity

Chapters II and III made sufficiently clear how and why
an account of revelation is foundational for Drey's theology.
His alternative to the deist view stresses the constant,
ongoing presence and activity of God in and upon the world
which He creates. It is only because Drey grounds the very
God-world relationship itself in the mystery of creation that
he is able to conceptualize revelation as continuing, renewed
creative activity of God.

The eternal creative activity of God is the "transcendent
fact" which not only constitutes the "relation of origin," but

---

[8]These two views coexist in uneasy combination in Drey's
thought. This must be a chief point in the critical assessment
of his project. See below.

which continues to characterize the relationship.[9] Because God
is always Creator, the world may be conceived as utterly subject to His Will, guided by His providence, "open" to His
ongoing, renewed initiatives which shape and reshape the religious development of mankind. It is from this point of view
that he is able to conceive "revelation" as ongoing, ever-
renewed creative activity of God upon both the world of nature
and the human spirit.

Since the creative activity called "revelation" is essentially identical with the originating creative activity of God,
Drey can also conceive "revelation" as a continuation of
"creation." In other words, the renewed divine initiatives are
not fortuitous interruptions of an originally established
course of the world. They are rather the continuation of this
world process. The "extraordinary" nature of the further
divine creations is accounted for in terms of mankind's refusal
to acknowledge and respond to the original creation/revelation.
Thus, the "form" of the further creation is different from that
of the original creation, but not its essential nature and
purpose.

The importance of creation for Drey's thought does not
seem to have been examined previously in as much depth and
detail as in this essay.[10] But it clearly deserves a prominent
place in any account of Drey's system, precisely because it is
the necessary theoretical grounding for and first stage of his
vision of universal history, as guided and ruled by God's
constant accompanying influence.

"Theologie als Wissenschaft"

On the other hand, Drey's quest for the intelligibility
of what this divine influence has brought about involves a
somewhat different perspective on the God-world relationship.

---

[9]Cf. above, pp. 200-201, 207-9.

[10]Schupp, Die Evidenz der Geschichte, p. 12, points out
that "für Drey Theologie grundsätzlich Theologie der Schöpfung
ist, und zwar nicht derselben als eines bestimmten den Beginn
setzenden Aktes, sondern als der von Gott abhängigen ganzen
Wirklichkeit." Geiselmann, in Die Katholische Tübinger Schule,
pp. 426-43, reports on the material which I examined in Chapter
II. But neither of these authors shows the implications of
this for Drey's foundational understanding of Reich Gottes, as
this concept is operative in the Dogmatics.

For the divine initiative (creating and recreating) is, in
Drey's view, not arbitrary. It is rather the making-real of
eternal divine "decrees" which a properly "scientific" theology
must appreciate in their quality as "Ideas."[11] But this way of
seeking the intelligibility of history is rooted in the Idealist
view of the finite-Infinite relationship, as Chapters IV and V
have made sufficiently clear.[12]

"Reich Gottes"

The Idealist view of the God-world relationship is, however, qualified in a distinctive way by Drey's characteristic
idea of Reich Gottes. It is in this key concept that his
thought is both closely akin to the Idealist mentality and—at
the same time—significantly divergent from it.

The affinity with Idealist thought is manifest. Drey
considers the notion of Reich Gottes to be the highest unifying
Idea which allows all the subordinate divine Ideas to be seen
in their speculative inter-relationship, so that the unity of
history may be appreciated from this highest viewpoint. All
this is clearly in the context of the Idealist model of
"scientific knowing." Moreover, the most profound level of
meaning for this master Idea seems to derive from Drey's
"mystical" feeling for the intimate unity of finite and
Infinite. This, too, he has in common with Schelling and the
other German Idealists.

On the other hand, Drey's systematic use of the Reich-
Gottes idea diverges from Schellingian Idealism in several
respects. The doctrine of creation is clearly basic to the
deepest meaning of finite reality as Reich Gottes. Moreover,
Drey's conception of man's "Bestimmung" as part of the great
Reich Gottes involves an interpersonal, developmental view of
the human-divine relationship. Finally, there is Drey's

---

[11]Cf. above, pp. 168-70.

[12]It is this affinity of Drey's thought with the Idealist
mentality which gave his account of Christianity its particular
apologetic force for his day and age. At the same time, it
caused problems and tensions with the Christian substance
which he wished to defend, and must remain for us the most
questionable feature of his theology. See below.

peculiar way of "locating" the Reich Gottes "within" the
interpersonal differentiation of the Godhead (his trinitarian
conception), which attempts to reconcile the creationist view
of man's destiny with the Idealist mentality.

Man is to participate in the Reich Gottes in a free,
interpersonal way through surrender in love. The destiny of
mankind is conceived as the free choice to be in the "relation
of origin" which is constituted ontologically by the divine act
of creation. This destiny is to be realized through a temporal,
historical process. Hence, it is not a timeless relationship
which is envisioned by the term Reich Gottes, but rather a
movement of growth and development--under the influence of
divine revelation--towards the intended perfection of free
relatedness to and union with God, the Ground and Center of His
Kingdom.

To conceive man's destiny in relation to God as a matter
of personal surrender in love is not easily reconcilable with
the kind of monism which is evident in the early writings of
Schelling. Hence, Drey's way of conceiving mankind's participation in the Reich Gottes involves a further differentiation
in his view of the God-world relationship. This differentiation becomes apparent in Drey's trinitarian modification of the
Ideal-Real polarity.

Trinitarian Perspective

The entire finite order "pre-exists" in a certain not
easily specifiable sense in the divine Person of the Son.
God's "self-objectification" is thought to take place "within"
the dynamic of the eternal, tri-personal divine Being, so that
the production of the created world is not regarded as the
spontaneous, inevitable unfolding of the Infinite as the finite.
In this way, the creation of the world may be regarded, with
the tradition, as a free act of God--even though the "Ideal"
pattern for this created world is pre-established, so to speak,
in the "internal" self-objectification of the divine Being.
Moreover, since the Son is loved eternally by the Father as the
"prototype" of the created world, and the Father and Son are
united eternally by the Spirit, the "Bestimmung" of the created
world may be interpreted as the achievement in created freedom
of the eternal interpersonal unity of the Son with the Father

in the Spirit.

Summary

We may sum up this interpretation of the unity in Drey's
thought in the following way:

His concern is to vindicate the "divine positivity" of
the historically given fact of Christianity by locating Christianity in the widest possible context. This context takes in
the entirety of universal history, conceived as the religious
development of mankind under the never-failing revelatory
influence of God. By introducing and defending the concept of
"revelation" (in his peculiar sense), Drey goes beyond the
history and philosophy of religion, to affirm the most profound
and ultimate "context" for Christianity: the ineffable relationship of finite to Infinite.

On the one hand, this relationship is grounded in the
mystery of God's unceasing creative activity. Hence, the world
is utterly "open" to God's influence, so that history may be
viewed as the result of God's revelatory enabling of mankind's
religious development. Thus, the "divine positivity" of the
historical phenomenon is made thinkable.

On the other hand, the relationship of finite to Infinite
is conceived as the making-real of the Ideal, i.e., of the
eternal divine Ideas which are inseparable from the Person of
the Son. Since the historically given reality is thus a consequence of divine Mind, it is inherently intelligible (even
though only "after the fact"), and the human mind which is
capable of rising to the viewpoint of the Ideas can appreciate
the intelligible necessity of the entire divinely willed
process. In this way, the "rationality" of the historically
given is discoverable, so that Christianity finds its most complete vindication for reason in the context of the intelligible
unity of history.

Other Views of Drey's
Dominant Concern

Because of the richness and diversity of Drey's thought,
it is possible to single out various features which may seem
important from one or another point of view. Hence, before
concluding this resume of my own interpretation of Drey, it

will be helpful to correlate it with what other interpreters
have seen as most important.

Through the work of Geiselmann, Drey's concept of "living
tradition" has been clarified and evaluated. In this context,
what can seem most important as the central concern of his
theology is the Romantic vision of the unbroken, organic
continuity of Church as the extension and objective continuation of the originating "fact" of revelation.

Both Geiselmann and Rief single out a phrase from Drey's
earliest published work, to characterize this concern: ". . .
the indivisible unity of Christianity and its history . . ."[13]
Rief, in a passing remark, judges that this "must undoubtedly
count as the basic thought of Drey's theology which governs
everything."[14] Geiselmann is less exclusive in his judgment on
this idea: ". . . [it] becomes one of the basic thoughts by
which the Tübinger's theology is governed."[15]

The centrality of this thought in Drey's theology is
unquestionable, but it needs to be put in a somewhat larger
context. Schupp, who has provided the most balanced and comprehensive over-all account of Drey's enterprise, points out
correctly that it is "the possibility of grasping history as a
whole" which "becomes the central problem of Drey's theology."[16]
Schupp stresses the unity of history as Drey's dominant concern,
because of Drey's epistemology. In the quest for true _Wissen_,

---

[13]"Revision des gegenwärtigen Zustandes der Theologie"
(1812), reprinted in Franz Schupp's libellus Revision von
Kirche und Theologie (Darmstadt: Wissenschaftliche Buchgesellschaft, 1971), p. 19: ". . . die untheilbare Einheit des
Christenthums und seiner Geschichte . . ."

[14]Rief, Reich Gottes und Gesellschaft, p. 266: ". . . die
zweifellos als der alles beherrschende Grundgedanke der Theologie Dreys zu gelten hat."

[15]Geiselmann, Lebendiger Glaube aus geheiligter Überlieferung, p. 143: ". . . wird so zu einem der Grundgedanken, von
der [sic] die Theologie des Tübingers beherrscht wird."

[16]Schupp, Die Evidenz der Geschichte, p. 94: ". . . muß
die Möglichkeit, die Geschichte als ganze zu begreifen, zum
Zentralproblem der Theologie Dreys werden" (emphasis in text).

all particulars must be known from the higher viewpoint of the
whole (das Ganze). Hence, theology as Wissenschaft is possible
only if history can be grasped in its speculative unity. This
point of view is familiar, in the light of Chapters IV and V.

Schupp, of course, concedes the correctness of Geiselmann's
interpretation of "living tradition" in Drey's thought, but
judges that this concept is merely an element in a larger and
more basic concern: namely, to grasp the intelligible unity of
history itself (not merely of Christianity), in order to ground
the Wissenschaft of theology.[17]

Drey, to be sure, thinks that the phenomenon of Christianity provides the key to the speculative understanding of
history's unity.   "The Christian theologian . . . makes
[Christianity] the center of all the historical phenomena of
religion."[18] The perspective on universal history is thus
decidedly "theonomous," in the sense that history is thought to
be ruled by a great, comprehensive plan of divine providence.
Christianity, in this view, is not simply one empirical
phenomenon among many others, but is the shape in which God's
purposes for all mankind and for universal history are made
manifest and--as Church--are realized.[19]

This thought is clearly expressed in the same early
article cited by Geiselmann and Rief:

> . . . the more exalted view of Christianity as a great
> decree of God embracing the entire history of mankind . . .
> also the concept of the Church as the endlessly progressing
> realization of this decree . . .[20]

---

[17]Schupp, Die Evidenz der Geschichte, p. 94: "Die Frage
ist nur, was hier das eigentliche Anliegen Dreys war, ob er
also mit den Mitteln der romantischen und idealistischen
Geschichtsauffassung den Begriff der lebendigen Selbstüberlieferung entwickelte, oder ob dieser nicht bloß ein Element war
innerhalb der grundlegenderen Frage nach der Einheit und Form
der Geschichte überhaupt in ihrer Funktion zur Begründung der
Theologie."

[18]KE § 107, p. 73: "Der christliche Theolog . . . macht es
[das Christentum] zum Mittelpunct aller geschichtlichen
Ercheinungen der Religion."

[19]Cf. Chapter V, pp. 122-23.

[20]Drey, "Revision . . . ," Schupp edition, p. 18: ". . .
die erhabnere Auffassung des Christenthums als eines großen die
ganze Geschichte der Menschheit umfassenden Rathschlusses

Drey's dominant apologetic concern, therefore, finds full
expression not merely in a theory of the Church as the developing continuation of the primal fact of revelation. His way of
conceiving Church is part of a much larger view of reality,
which seeks the speculative unity of history itself as a great
whole. But this quest for the unity of history is, in turn,
governed by a perspective on the God-world relationship which
is simultaneously "mystical" and philosophical.[21]

Hence, in my interpretation of Drey's project, I have
pushed repeatedly to this level of the God-world relationship,
in order to clarify and criticize the metaphysical and epistemological grounding of Drey's apologetic account of Christianity.
It is only on this level that one can finally appreciate and
judge his distinctive way of attempting the synthesis of
history and speculation, of "positivity" and "rationality," of
faith and knowing.

Critical Assessment

The most problematic feature of Drey's thought is
undoubtedly its Idealist intellectual context. The difficulties
and embarrassments which this caused for Drey in his interpretation of Christianity can be noticed and assessed, first of
all, in terms of his own understanding of his task. There is
an internal critique to be made. Beyond this, however, it is
possible and necessary to criticize Drey's thought from the
perspective of later developments which challenge and relativize
the Idealist thought-frame.

Gottes . . . auch der Begriff von der Kirche als von der ins
Unendliche fortschreitenden Realisirung dieses Rathschlusses
. . ." For a striking echo of this in Möhler, cf. the latter's
"Einleitung in die Kirchengeschichte," Gesammelte Schriften und
Aüfsatze, edited by Döllinger, Vol. 2 (Regensburg: Manz, 1840),
pp. 268-69: "Der christliche Philosoph Malebranche hat einen
großen Gedanken ausgesprochen, wenn er sagte: 'Der Zweck der
Schöpfung ist die Gründung der christlichen Kirche.' . . . Ja,
einen Tempel für Gott zu erbauen, in welchem ihm in Christo
ewiges Lob und ewiger Preis dargebracht wird, das ist die
Aufgabe der ganzen Geschichte. Aus allen Völkern werden
Materialien zu diesem Baue gesammelt . . ."

[21]Cf. above, pp. 96, 110ff., and 166-67.

Internal Critique

The Historical and the Speculative

Drey's intellectual context was not only powerfully and profoundly affected by German Idealism, but also included the Romantic awareness of the historicity of Christianity. Hence, the problem which he faced was how to value the unique, particular, historically given, while seeking its intelligibility in an Idealist frame of reference.

As we have seen, it was the entire phenomenon of empirical Christianity (in the larger context of the universal history of religion) which Drey wanted to take seriously as the object of theology. At the same time, he sought a speculative "construction" of this historically given reality, so as to discover its intelligibility from the highest viewpoint of the "Idea" Reich Gottes.

There is, therefore, an inescapable tension in Drey's project between the two values of "positivity" and "rationality." What is perhaps most striking and characteristic in his thought is the explicit formulation of this opposition, along with a self-conscious effort to transcend it in a "higher viewpoint" which would reconcile the two concerns. It must finally be asked, however, whether Drey succeeded in this purpose. Did he, in fact, come down on one or other side of the opposition? Or did he simply oscillate between the two, without being able to integrate them?

At times, it seems that Drey's dominant concern is with "positivity." He polemicizes against "gnosis," by which he means the abandonment of the empirical and historical in order to convert Christianity into a speculative system. In contrast to this, he demands attention to history as the source and abiding basis of theology. (What he means by "history," of course, is not merely the beginning of Christianity but its entire ongoing development as the Spirit's creation of the Reich Gottes.) This emphasis in Drey's thought--if taken alone and absolutized--would be a kind of "right-wing" reaction against the rationalism of both the Enlightenment and German Idealism.

On the other hand, Drey is unmistakably under the spell of German Idealism in his insistence that this positive

Christianity can and must be understood speculatively from the
highest viewpoint of the "Ideas." This is possible, to be
sure, for only a few minds, but the project of "wissenschaftliche Theologie" must be undertaken in order to vindicate the
intrinsic truth of Christianity before the bar of reason. For,
even if the "divine positivity" of Christianity as historically
given revelation is vindicated (against the challenge of naturalism), one also needs to remove the semblance of "accidentality" which would still make Christianity unacceptable to the
contemporary mind. This feature of Drey's thought--if taken
alone and absolutized--would be a kind of "left-wing" interpretation of Christianity. It seems that Zimmer and Thanner came
close to this in their efforts to utilize Schelling for
Catholic theology.[22]

It cannot be said that Drey came down decisively or
exclusively in either one of these two extreme positions. His
writings show <u>both</u> a striking and impressive openness for the
factual in the history of religion (including Christianity),
<u>and</u> a constant rigorous search for the intelligible unity of
all these phenomena. Nevertheless, it is apparent that Drey's
success in integrating satisfactorily the two emphases of his
thought was very incomplete.

He was able to show a certain intelligibility of the
positively given by situating Christianity in the widest
possible context of meaning, provided by the philosophy of
religion and the history of religions. He could thus show the
"appropriateness" of what he considered a divinely given
revelation to man's essential nature in relation to God. This
attempt makes Drey's <u>Apologetik</u> a significant landmark in the
development of a modern Catholic fundamental theology.

On the other hand, the incompleteness of his achievement
can be judged in two ways. First of all, in formal terms, one
can examine the presuppositions of his method, so as to notice
the underlying, unresolved tension between two contrasting
views of the God-world relationship. Secondly, one can
consider the actual execution of his project in the Dogmatics,

---

[22]Cf. Geiselmann, <u>ThQ</u> 111 (1930):109.

where his goal of a speculative "construction" of the doctrines
of Christianity is realized only in a sketchy and fragmentary
fashion.

Two Irreconcilable Views of
the God-World Relationship

Looking at Drey's system as system, one must recognize the
chief problem which is inherent in his utilization of Idealist
categories for the interpretation of Christianity. As already
pointed out, there are two quite different conceptions of the
God-world relationship underlying Drey's proposal for the method
of theology. These two views are not readily reconcilable, so
that there is a tension in Drey's thought which remains
unresolved.

On the one hand, his concern for positivity leads him to
conceive the world as the freely willed creation and continuing
re-creation of a transcendent, personal Creator. The kind of
divine activity in and upon the world which Drey envisions (his
anti-deist view) is thinkable only from his creationist account
of the God-world relationship. This perspective is indispensable for Drey's interpretation of Christianity as a unified,
divinely guided process of development.

On the other hand, his concern for rationality is expressed in terms of the Schelling-inspired ideal of "Wissenschaft."
As we have shown, this epistemology involves an Idealist view
of the finite-infinite relationship. This perspective is
indispensable for the kind of intelligibility which Drey seeks
in the seemingly accidental course of history.

The point of criticism is that these two views of the God-
world relationship are in very uneasy juxtaposition in Drey's
system. It is not at all apparent that they can be integrated
successfully into one coherent view.[23] The closest that Drey
comes to such an integration is in his doctrine of the Trinity.

The Problem of Freedom

Even in his trinitarian modification of the Idealist view,
however, Drey does not avoid altogether the fundamental embarrassment of not being able to give full value to freedom. This

_____

[23]Cf. above, pp. 168-70.

difficulty pertains both to the freedom of God and to the
freedom of man.

In Drey's view, to be sure, God is not thought to produce
a finite world as the necessary and inevitable act of self-
objectification. But the "pattern" or "prototype" of the finite
world is eternally established as the Son, the perfect self-
objectification of the divine Being. In Drey's conception, not
merely "nature" is contained in this prototype, but the entire
course of history.

Thus, what God does, by creating a finite world and by
guiding infallibly the historical development of this world, is
already established with the necessity of God's own being quite
prior (i.e., ontologically prior) to the finite realization of
this divine Idea (or complex of Ideas). In this sense, the
stress is so one-sidedly on the divine essence as "Ideal" that
little room is left for the affirmation of the divine freedom
as the sovereign principle of all created being.

Likewise, it is very difficult in this conception to give
full value to the freedom of human beings. The characteristic
of history, as even Schelling remarks, is that it is not pre-
dictable before the event, since it is the outcome of what
human beings do with their freedom.[24] Yet Drey conceives
history as already "contained" in the Person of the Son, i.e.,
in the divine Being as self-objectified eternally. In other
words, the paradoxical assertion is being made that what human
beings do freely is the consequence of divine Mind, the making-
real of the eternal pattern or prototype of the finite order.

The Problem of Sin

This inescapably Idealist conception of the God-world
relationship finds its greatest embarrassment in the effort to
understand sin as part of the eternal divine decrees. As we
have seen in Chapter VI, Drey wavers in his interpretation of
sin. In a way, it seems to be the unavoidable case of "Zufall,"

_____

[24]Cf. Schellings Werke 2:589 ("System des transzendentalen Idealismus," 1800): "Der Mensch hat nur deßwegen Geschichte, weil, was er thun wird, sich nach keiner Theorie zum
voraus berechnen läßt. Die Willkür ist insofern die Göttin der
Geschichte."

a surd which resists all efforts to show its necessity and
intrinsic connection with the great whole which God intends.
Yet, Drey's search for a speculative "construction" of what has
actually happened leads him to assert that sin must be understood as included, in some sense, in God's "decrees."

As we noted in Chapter V, Drey's use of the term "decrees"
has its proper place in the theistic, creationist view of the
God-world relationship, where it is correlated with the divine
freedom. In that context, sin could be regarded as a contingency which God foresees, so to speak, and overcomes through His
sovereign action. But this way of understanding sin is not
allowable in the Idealist thought-frame (which speaks rather of
eternal "Ideas"). In the latter view, all finite being
(including the misuse of human freedom) must be regarded as the
consequence of divine Mind, as the self-manifestation of divine
Being. The fundamental flaw of any Idealist interpretation of
Christianity is thus also disclosed in Drey's thought: the
aporia of having to interpret absurdity, irrationality, and
evil as the self-manifestation of God.

The difficulty is perhaps most evident in the case of sin
as the radically unintelligible misuse of created freedom. But
the same difficulty is really also contained in affirming the
value of the correct use of created freedom. Drey wishes to
value this as the condition for the realization of the Reich
Gottes. But it is certainly difficult to assign this value to
created freedom if it is viewed as the necessary making-real of
the Ideal.[25]

Drey's Incomplete Execution
of His Proposed Method

Up to this point, the internal critique of Drey's system
has been undertaken from the formal aspect of his method as an
effort to reconcile "positivity" and "rationality." But there

---

[25]In view of the difficulties which seem intrinsic to the
use of Idealist categories in Christian theology, it is striking that Drey nowhere engages in a critical reflection on the
limitations of the Idealist mentality for his own project. He
seems rather to share this mentality in an unselfconscious way,
so that he fully expects to be able to formulate the truth of
Christian faith in the language and thought-form of his day
(cf. Schupp, Die Evidenz der Geschichte, p. 24). This failure
to examine more reflectively his theological language and

is a further consideration, as one looks at his over-all
achievement, and in particular his own incomplete Dogmatics.
To what extent did he actually carry out the speculative
"construction" of empirical Christianity which he demanded as
the proper task of a "scientific theology?"

On the one hand, he undeniably has a unifying perspective
on the "story" of God's dealings with man. But the close study
of his Dogmatics manuscripts reveals unmistakably that he was
unable to present the detailed positive content of the Christian tradition in such a way as to show the "intelligible
necessity" of every part. In his Dogmatics lectures, Drey did
not achieve what he prescribed in the Kurze Einleitung as the
test for a successful practitioner of "wissenschaftliche Theologie": "to grasp every given doctrinal proposition of historical theology as something necessary for his reason."[26] His own
effort thus illustrates the truth of what he realistically
conceded, that not everything in empirical Christianity is such
as to be grasped scientifically through "Konstruktion aus
Ideen."[27]

There are, of course, extrinsic factors to account for
the incomplete and imperfect state of his Dogmatics. But one
must raise the question of an intrinsic factor: the inherent
difficulty (or, indeed, impossibility) of integrating all the
data of Christian theology into one unified interpretation "von
der Idee her." This is not a matter of ungenerous quibbling
over the extent of Drey's success. It is rather an indication
of the fundamental problem raised by Drey's ideal of synthesiz-
ing the historical and the speculative. This problem continued

---

conceptuality results in the unresolved tensions which we have
noticed in his conception of the God-world relationship.

[26]KE § 309, p. 208: ". . . jeden gegebenen Lehrsatz der
historischen Theologie als etwas Nothwendiges vor seiner
Vernunft zu begreifen" (emphasis added). In Drey's view, historical theology documents and orders logically the divinely
created system of dogmas which has been formed gradually. Cf.
above, pp. 134-35. It is for "scientific" theology to grasp
the inner truth of each of these doctrines by relating it to
the highest unifying "Idea." Cf. above, pp. 133-34, 143-45.

[27]KE § 64, p. 40. Cf. above, pp. 156-57.

to exercise his successors in the Catholic Tübingen School and
remains, in a way, a perennial challenge for every theology
which attempts a rational account of Christian faith.

What is actually exemplified in Drey's Dogmatics notes is
his conviction that history is primary as the source and object
of Christian theology. The dominant quality of his treatment
of Dogmatics is "positive," rather than speculative, as he
marshals and interprets perceptively the themes of Scripture
and the Church's doctrinal tradition.

His systematic, speculative viewpoint finds expression
properly only in the arrangement of topics and in his essay on
the method and parts of Dogmatics in the "Praemonita" to PD III.
Thus, the properly "wissenschaftliche" element is to be found
in this formal perspective on his material, which is an overview of the "story" or "economy" of salvation in terms of the
Idea Reich Gottes.

In Chapter VI, I have attempted to explicate the logic of
this formal perspective, as it integrates the major themes of
his Dogmatics. In the detailed treatment of his material, however, Drey does not carry through his speculative viewpoint in
an explicit, systematic fashion. Hence, my clarifying inter-
pretation--though faithful to the over-all conception which
Drey sketches in the "Praemonita"--should not be taken as the
exposition of a system which Drey worked out in satisfying
completeness. What Drey might have achieved in this direction
if he had been able to bring his Dogmatics notes into a version
suitable for publication must remain unknowable.[28]

What Drey does offer in the Dogmatics notes, however, is
a "concept," a speculative vision of the mystery of mankind in
relation to God, which allows him to find a profound meaning in
the "empirical" doctrines of Christianity. In this vision, the

---

[28]Merely on the basis of the Dogmatics notes, one would
have to say that Drey was not a systematic theologian of the
first rank. His forte was rather "Apologetics," which he conceived and executed as "fundamental theology." In this, he
prepared the way for a truly modern Catholic theology by
attempting to establish the categories for understanding the
whole Christian dispensation in correlation with the universal
human phenomenon of religion. Cf. Apologetik I, "Einleitung"
§ 14, p. 27, referred to above, p. 48, note 5.

"Idea" is certainly predominant. Yet it would not be true to
say that he expounds the Idea in complete abstraction from the
historical progress of Christianity from its origin in Jesus.
The subject matter of Dogmatics remains the "story"--but
regarded, as far as possible, from the unifying perspective of
the Idea Reich Gottes.

It is certainly difficult to sustain Drey's claim that
this ruling idea is simply "given" to the human mind in the
historical career and teaching of Jesus. In the light of
modern exegesis, we are aware rather of the immense distance
between the New Testament meaning of basileia tou theou and the
various meanings of Reich Gottes in German theologians of the
early 19th century.[29] Hence, Drey's systematizing concept is
seen not to be an historically revealed "Idea" (as he thought),
but rather an intuition of his own creative mind, reflecting
both philosophically and religiously on the radical mystery of
the God-world relationship.[30] In this respect, Drey is like so
many other systematic theologians who have sought a speculative
unification of Christian truth from some persuasive and compelling insight of their own intellectual culture.

From a contemporary point of view, the use of such a
unifying insight in systematic theology does not seem inappro-
priate, even if it is not derivable from the teaching of Jesus.
The problem in Drey's effort to "construct" history does not
lie in the provenance of his unifying idea, but rather in the
very concept of history which such a "construction" implies.

Drey shared the Romantic conviction that history can be
understood as the organic unfolding of a germinal "Idea." Not

---

[29]Cf. Rief, Reich Gottes und Gesellschaft, pp. 60-69.

[30]One might, however, see in Drey's thought a kind of
intuitive affinity with the historical content of Jesus' preaching of the Kingdom of God, insofar as Drey is concerned with
the absolute dominion of God in relation to created reality.
Cf. Walter Kasper's interpretation of Jesus' message, in Jesus
der Christus (Mainz: Matthias Grünewald, 1974), pp. 83-103; ET:
Jesus the Christ (New York: Paulist, 1976), pp. 72-88. It is
noteworthy that Kasper uses some of Drey's favorite expressions
to characterize man's sinful estrangement from God's rule:
"Egoismus, Selbstsucht, Eigenwillen, Eigennutz, Eigensinn"
(Jesus der Christus, p. 102).

only does such a view of history tend to result in an unduly
abstract, oversimplifying treatment of the complexities of
individual historical developments.[31] More importantly, such
a view does not appreciate history in its distinctive quality
of freedom and unpredictability. It supposes that history is
really governed by a kind of a priori, an intelligible idea
that must work itself out.

The New Valuation of History
in Drey's Students
        At the end of this internal critique of Drey's thought,
we need, therefore, to take account briefly of the way in which
his stress on history continued to echo in his students, particularly in Johann Adam Möhler and Franz Anton Staudenmaier. For
their way of valuing history really leads beyond the method of
Drey towards a more contemporary view of the problematic, and
so points us into a critique of Drey from the viewpoint of
later developments.
        It is a peculiarity of Drey's rich and balanced thought
that one can easily misrepresent him by stressing one or other
of the themes which he is constantly interweaving and striving
to reconcile. The exposition of his Idealist thought-frame and
his speculative enthusiasm can lead to a characterization of
him as a rationalist or at least "semi-rationalist."[32] An
exclusive interest in his theory of living tradition can make
him appear strikingly oriented towards the unique, historical
shape of revelation. In fact, Drey's thought eludes a simple,
unambiguous characterization.
        While recognizing this, one can nevertheless judge that
his lasting influence upon his successors lay more in his
historical orientation than in his speculative bent. When one

─────────────

[31]This fault is discernible not only in Drey, but equally
so in his most famous student, Möhler, who is sometimes praised
for his more historical orientation. Cf. Vermeil's critical
observation on the work of the Catholic Tübingen School in
general: "Son oeuvre implique fatalement, à l'égard d'un passé
singulièrement riche, édulcoration et appauvrissement" (Jean-
Adam Möhler et l'école catholique de Tubingue, p. xii).

[32]Cf. Karl Adam, "Die katholische Tübinger Schule,"
Hochland 24 (1926/27):594.

looks at Drey's entire life-work, one must recognize that--for
all his magisterial emphasis on "strenge Wissenschaftlichkeit"--
he really operates in a way that is remarkably open to the
positive data of historical research.[33] This is evident in his
wide perspective on the religious development of mankind in the
Apologetik, as well as his detailed interest in and knowledge
of the dogmatic tradition of Christianity.

Moreover, Drey thought that the dogmatic theologian had
to take as his subject matter a history, a dynamic process. Of
course, Drey was convinced that this history could be grasped
in its unity, by rising to the perspective of the Ideas. It is
here that his Idealist thought-frame is obtrusive, and his project seems unrealizable. But the orientation of systematic
theology towards a concrete history remains as an immensely
valuable legacy of the Catholic Tübingen School. The fact that
this legacy was submerged and forgotten for a century, in the
Catholic Church's flight from historicity and modernity, only
makes the contribution of Drey and the others appear more
significant today.

The recognition of the distinctive character of history
came, however, as a transcending of the strict Idealist categories to which Drey remained bound.[34] In general terms, it
was a matter of attributing more importance to the irreducible
individuality, freedom, and contingency of the human agents in
the great process of history, while at the same time recognizing
the sovereign freedom of God as the ultimate principle of
history.

This development began to be evident in Möhler, who
expressed reservations about the ideal of "philosophical construction" as the proper method of dogmatic theology[35] and

---

[33]This kind of attention to the data of historical
research is, of course, actually closer to what would today (in
contrast to the German Idealist period) be regarded as "Wissenschaftlichkeit."

[34]Cf. Walter Kasper's very perceptive essay, "Verständnis
der Theologie damals und heute," in Glaube und Geschichte (Mainz:
Matthias Grünewald Verlag, 1970), esp. pp. 14-18.

[35]Cf. Möhler's review of A. Gengler in ThQ 9 (1827):516.
"Dieses historische in der Dogmatik ist darum das Wichtigste.
Die philosophische Konstruktion der christlichen Ideen ist, wenn

stressed the freedom of divine providence ruling history as the
proper viewpoint for Christian theology.[36] But it was Franz
Anton Staudenmaier who gave systematic expression, especially
in his later writings, to this new way of valuing history for
theology.[37]

Drey, along with Schelling, regarded history as the
consequence of divine Mind, as the "work of eternal necessity."[38]
Staudenmaier came increasingly to view history rather as the
work of divine freedom. His concept of "positivity" was rooted
in the mystery of sovereign divine initiative as the principle
of all reality. The logic of this view led to a transcending
of the Idealist philosophy of nature and spirit, and a recognition of history as the proper category for interpreting all
reality.

If reality is regarded as radically historical, and at
the same time as the result of the incalculable "positing" of
unique facts and events by divine freedom, then any a priori
"construction" of reality is excluded. If there is a logic
and intelligibility in this historical reality, it can only be
appreciated a posteriori. From such a perspective, the proper
mode of knowing in theology becomes a "higher kind of

---

sie gelingt, eine schöne Zugabe, unter manchen Umständen, und
gerade nach den vorwaltenden Bedürfnissen, und dem Stande der
Wissenschaft, nothwendig. Aber das nothwendigste ist sie
nicht . . ." Cf. Geiselmann on this text, ThQ 111 (1930):117.

[36]Cf. Möhler's lectures, "Einleitung in die Kirchenge-
schichte," printed posthumously in Gesammelte Schriften und
Aufsätze, 2:261-71 ("Von dem christlichen Begriffe der
Geschichte"), edited by Joh. Jos. Ign. Döllinger (Regensburg:
Manz, 1840).

[37]Cf. Peter Hünermann, "Der Reflex des deutschen Idealismus in der Theologie der katholischen Tübinger Schule,"
Philosophisches Jahrbuch 73 (1965-66):63-74; also Bernhard
Casper, "Der Systemgedanke in der späten Tübinger Schule und in
der deutschen Neuscholastik," Philosophisches Jahrbuch 72
(1964-65):164-72; and Bernhard Welte, "Beobachtungen zum Systemgedanken in der Tübinger katholischen Schule," ThQ 147 (1967):
48-53. These authors provide abundant references to the relevant texts of Staudenmaier.

[38]Drey, "Revision des gegenwärtigen Zustandes der Theologie" reprinted in Schupp, Revision von Kirche und Theologie,
p. 21.

experience."[39]

The difference between Drey and Staudenmaier should not, however, obscure the underlying similarity and continuity. On the one hand, Drey also emphasizes the priority of the "given," of the Tatsache. The shift comes in Staudenmaier's resolute abandonment of the effort to "construct" this given in a deductive, a priori fashion. This is a significant departure from the mentality of "high Idealism." Nevertheless, the insistent demand of Drey that theology find the unity of history continues to govern Staudenmaier's enterprise. Just as much as Drey, he strives for system, and expects to find a system in the history which God creates.

There is, therefore, considerable tension in Staudenmaier's thought between the new valuation of history and the old ideal of intelligible unity. To attempt to discover a "system of freedom" is strongly paradoxical.[40] The fact that Staudenmaier strains his systematizing thought to the breaking-point shows the power of the Idealist legacy of Drey. The radical turn to history as the proper thought-form for Christian theology is accompanied by the persistent conviction that truth is only to be grasped by finding the deeper unity of seemingly disparate facts.[41]

Welte traces a progressive loosening and weakening of the "Systemgedanke" in the progression from Drey through Staudenmaier to Kuhn. It seems that the more seriously history was taken as the unforeseeable outcome of divine initiative interacting with human freedom, the less optimism there was about constructing a system of theology which could grasp the unity of this history in Ideas.

Hence, Kasper sees in the late Tübingen School (Staudenmaier and Kuhn) an approximation to the modern perception of

---

[39]Kasper, Glaube und Geschichte, p. 18: "Für Staudenmaier wird jetzt alles theologische Erkennen zu einer höhern Art der Erfahrung; Freiheit ist letztlich unableitbar, sie kann nur erfahren werden, wenn sie sich in der Geschichte offenbart."

[40]Cf. Hünermann, Philosophisches Jahrbuch 73 (1965-66):71.

[41]Cf. ibid., p. 65; Welte, ThQ 147 (1967):49.

the "problem of history" for theology, and thinks that some
helpful points of contact might be found between their thought
and contemporary efforts to interpret history in a theological
way.

There is, however, no question of simply returning to the
thought-world of even the later Tübingen theologians. Despite
their contribution to a new appreciation of history, these
thinkers remained in the context of German Idealism. What
separates us from them, as well as from Drey, are the later
developments which radically challenge and relativize the
entire Idealist way of thinking about God and man.

External Critique: Inadequacy of
the Idealist Thought-Frame

Kierkegaard's Protest Against
Speculative Christianity

Perhaps the most radical _religious_ protest against all
speculative interpretations of Christianity (especially of the
Idealist type) came in Drey's own life-time, although its full
influence upon Christian theology was not felt until the
twentieth century. Søren Kierkegaard's passionate witness to
"subjectivity" as the generating context of all God-talk and
his stress on "paradox" as the proper form of such seemingly
objective discourse provide a significant counterposition to
the speculative enthusiasm of Drey's theology.[42] In particular,
it is Drey's ambition to move from faith to knowing[43] which
seems most problematical, in the light of Kierkegaard's existential thought. The latter's challenge to Hegel (and, indeed,
to all speculative "constructions" of Christianity) also
strikes Drey.

Kierkegaard insists that the truth of the creature-
Creator relationship is only to be appropriated in the
"existential dialectic" of the individual human being, who
experiences alternately the fascinating attraction of the
Mystery and yet his alienation from it in guilt. In this

---

[42]Cf. Emanuel Hirsch, _Geschichte der neuern evangelischen
Theologie_, vol. 5 (Gütersloh: C. Bertelsmann Verlag, 1954), esp.
pp. 447-53 and 456-59, for a concise and perceptive treatment
of these themes in Kierkegaard.

[43]See above, pp. 68-72.

"wrestling with God," the human subject is always on the
perilous divide between belief and unbelief, confronted with the
alternatives of either surrendering in a faith which is worship
or else of taking offense at the absurdity of the Mystery in a
refusal to believe.

Because the very relationship itself of man to God is
profoundly paradoxical and dialectical, it is impossible to
formulate it in objective language which would reconcile the
terms of the relationship in a unified speculative view. Hence,
the proper form for theological discourse is "paradox," which
is not satisfying to the human mind but rather points it back
to "subjectivity" and "inwardness," and thus indicates the only
possible context in which the truth about God can be discovered:
the "existential dialectic" of the individual human being who
lives out the Mystery in ethical-religious earnestness.

Donald Baillie, in his book God Was in Christ, has an
illuminating section on the pervasiveness of paradox in Christian thought.[44] To account for this paradoxical character of
Christian theology, Baillie draws upon both Kierkegaard and
Martin Buber:

> . . . God can be known only in a direct personal relation-
> ship, an 'I-and-Thou' intercourse . . . we cannot know God
> by studying Him as an object, of which we can speak in the
> third person, in an 'I-it' relationship, from a spectator-
> attitude. He eludes all our words and categories. We
> cannot objectify or conceptualize Him. When we try, we
> fall immediately into contradiction. Our thought gets
> diffracted, broken up into statements which it seems impos-
> sible to reconcile with each other. . . . When we "objec-
> tify" [the divine reality] . . . all our judgments are in
> some measure falsified, and the higher truth which recon-
> ciles them cannot be fully expressed in words, though it is
> experienced and lived in the 'I-and-Thou' relationship of
> faith towards God.[45]

In a way, this is only a modern expression of what the
greatest theologians have always known. But it is particularly
relevant to a critique of the Idealist type of theology, which

---

[44]D. M. Baillie, God Was In Christ: An Essay on Incarnation and Atonement (New York: Charles Scribner's Sons, 1955;
first published in 1948), pp. 106-18.

[45]Ibid., pp. 108-9.

is so optimistic about constructing a speculative system that
would grasp God, world, and man in a higher unity. If one
recognizes the trans-rational character of all human relationship to God, and the existential, religious context out of
which all theological discourse is generated, then one must also
recognize the impossibility of a merely objective, speculative
account of God and man.

The Importance of "Subjectivity"

The speculative approach to Christian theology, in the
mode of Idealist thought, is thus defective insofar as it does
not take sufficient account of the "subjectivity" of the
existing thinker. Kierkegaard characterizes this as the lived
surrender to the Mystery in the antinomy of faith. Bernard
Lonergan, in his own way, also takes this into account by
stressing "authentic subjectivity" as the condition for objective knowledge of any kind, and by specifying "religious
conversion" as the decisive feature of subjectivity for the
enterprise of theology.[46]

What is to be said, from this viewpoint, about Drey's
theological project? It would not be accurate to say that Drey
in no way takes religious subjectivity into account.[47] To
judge this matter fairly, one should perhaps distinguish between
his formal view of theological method and his predominant style
of theological discourse.

In his account of method, Drey--like Schleiermacher--
considers religion to be the fundamental reality preceding and
grounding theology. Since the inarticulate sense of God which
begins as feeling in the Gemüt eventually penetrates and qualifies all human faculties and operations, it also finds rational
expression as theological thought.[48] Theology is thus generated
out of religious feeling.

One should also recall that Drey links man's sinful
refusal to surrender to the Creator-reality of God with a fateful misperception of the God-world relationship. Likewise, he

---

[46]Method in Theology (New York: Herder and Herder, 1972).

[47]See above, pp. 26-28.

[48]Cf. KE §§ 38-40, pp. 23-24. Cf. Schupp, Die Evidenz
der Geschichte, pp. 7-11.

supposes that a rational appropriation of the truths of faith
involves the practical dimension of letting one's life and
conduct be guided by them.

There are, therefore, points of contact in Drey's thought
with the later existential emphasis of Kierkegaard-inspired
theology. Nevertheless, Drey's concern is to penetrate and
clarify rationally the obscurely felt relationship to God with
which religion begins. For him (in contrast to Schleiermacher),
religion does not remain in the domain of the trans-rational,
but finds expression ultimately in a rational, speculative
account of the God-world relationship (as well as in a
religious-ethical life).[49] Theology is thus the legitimate
intellectual activity of grasping in rational form a truth
which is indeed discoverable only in lived religion, but which
also needs to find expression as thought.

Hence, the style of Drey's theology is strongly rational
and "scientific," proceeding always to establish clear concepts
and construct rigorous arguments. The source of this careful
thought in the depths of religious experience is only occasionally discernible, for example, in his treatment of nature's
origin from God[50] or in the remarks on humility as the deepest
in religion.[51] The grounding of theology in religious subjectivity, although affirmed as a methodological principle, is
only occasionally made thematic in his actual treatment of the
material of theology. For this reason, it is possible to over-
look the ways in which his seemingly quite speculative account
of Christian truth is actually rooted in what must be called a
mystical sensibility.

What is to be said, however, about Drey's ambition to
pass from (mere) faith to knowledge in the strict sense? If
one concedes the point made by Kierkegaard and Baillie about
the irreducibly paradoxical character of theology, this goal of
Drey's must seem impossible. If the truth about man in relation
to God can only be discovered in a life lived, then all

-----

[49]In this respect, whether he knew it or not, he sided
with Hegel against Schleiermacher in the crucial disagreement
between the two.

[50]See above, pp. 33-34.   [51]See above, pp. 172-73.

seemingly objective accounts of that relationship cannot be
regarded as the adequate speculative "domination" of that truth
from some higher viewpoint. Rather, the inescapable paradoxes
of theology point the thinker back into the proper originating
context of his assertions: the authentic subjectivity of the
individual, existing human being. Kierkegaard's protest
against all speculative accounts of Christianity is thus
undoubtedly a salutary corrective to Drey's optimism about
moving from Glauben to Wissen.

Kierkegaard's position, however, is so extreme that it
cannot finally be taken as an adequate basis for a theology
which strives to give a rational account of Christian faith.
If one eliminates completely the apologetic "moment" (so
important for Drey), Christianity is in danger of becoming
wholly non-rational and private. Being Christian then seems to
be possible only as a kind of subjective removal from the
world-view of contemporary culture, a dramatic and unintelligible protest against it. This provides no basis for a
Christian view of culture, nor does it provide a rational basis
for Christian ethics.[52]

In contrast to this, Drey's apologetic approach to
theology can be seen as a consistent expression of the traditional Catholic conviction that theology is a "science," in
which reason has a limited but legitimate function. From this
perspective, Drey is not to be faulted for attempting to do
theology in a manner which was coherent with the other ways of
human knowledge available to him. The criticism to be made is,
rather, that the form of his project was governed by an
Idealist thought-frame which today must be judged inadequate
for a number of reasons. The reference to Kierkegaard has
served to challenge this thought-frame by pointing up the
decisive importance of "subjectivity" for the method of
theology.

The Contemporary Worldview

When we regard Drey's Idealist mentality from the vantage-
point of the present, however, there are still other

---

[52]The contrast between Drey and Kierkegaard thus inevita-
bly calls to mind the fundamental and perennial tension in all
Christian thought which H. Richard Niebuhr has analyzed in
Christ and Culture (New York: Harper & Row, 1951).

considerations which relativize his way of attempting Christian
theology. This critique of his thought must, therefore,
conclude with a brief mention of some obvious features of our
contemporary intellectual situation which compel us to view the
task of theology somewhat differently.[53]

First of all, it is impossible today to think of "constructing" reality deductively from the unifying perspective of
an idea. The growth of the positive sciences has provided such
a detailed and differentiated knowledge of both "nature" and
the specifically human that the ambition of finding a speculative unity of all this "from the Idea" can only seem chimaer-
ical. The shift from the Romantic worldview to the more
positive, empirical mode of thought is discernible around the
middle of the nineteenth century.[54] It is a great watershed of
intellectual history which makes the speculative enthusiasm of
early nineteenth-century Germany seem very remote.

Another major feature of our contemporary worldview is
the evolutionary perspective on the human species within the
great cosmic process. Chance is seen to be such a prominent
feature of this process that it is once again illusionary to
think of "constructing" the complex development from a speculative viewpoint.

Moreover, the growth of history as a major intellectual
discipline, although inspired by the Romantic vision of history,
has actually relativized that vision in a twofold way.
"Historicity" in the sense of historical relativity has been
seen to characterize all things human--including all human ways
of thinking. Hence, the hope--shared by Drey--of finding an
"eternal Idea" as the principle of intelligible unity for
interpreting universal history must be recognized as deceptive.
Secondly, our more detailed and nuanced knowledge of the past--
together with our own experience of the unforeseeable

[53]Cf. Kasper, Glaube und Geschichte, pp. 11-12, 18-19.

[54]Cf. Bernhard Welte's essay "Zum Strukturwandel der
katholischen Theologie im 19. Jahrhundert," pp. 380-409 in his
Auf der Spur des Ewigen (Freiburg: Herder, 1965). Welte points
up the contrast between the mentality of the early nineteenth
century and that of the later period, as this affected
Catholic theology.

irrationality of human events--has made us profoundly skeptical
about any attempt to discover a pattern of "intelligible
necessity" in what has happened and is happening.

History, on the other hand, is increasingly regarded as a
process which human intelligence and freedom is capable of
creating and shaping. In a way, all of reality is viewed as--
at least potentially--the work of our hands, as our own creation, insofar as our exploding technology gives us the power to
modify "nature" and re-order it to suit human purposes, and
insofar as our philosophies themselves are believed to be
social constructs. From this perspective, Marx's challenge to
merely speculative philosophy adds another immensely significant factor to our contemporary intellectual situation.
Instead of supposing that one can grasp speculatively a "given"
order of things, we are concerned to transform both "nature"
and human society in a way that will humanize it.

This orientation towards reality, taken together with
today's increasingly sophisticated understanding of social,
economic, and political structures, has had a profound effect
on Christian theology which also separates us from Drey's
Idealist model of intelligibility. Kierkegaard had protested
against speculation which is not rooted in existence. In a
certain sense, the Marxist perspective in theology is simply an
expansion of this protest from an individual to a social and
political context. Christian "knowledge" is seen to be a
product of Christian action. The praxis which is the indispensable context for thinking and talking about God is seen to
be the involvement of the thinker in the political task of
transforming the world.[55]

These summary observations may suffice to indicate how
unrealizable the Idealist model of "scientific knowing" must
appear today. To this extent, Drey's conception of "Theologie
als Wissenschaft" likewise seems dated and unrealizable in its
formal speculative principles.

---

[55]This perspective is prominent not only in Latin American
liberation theology, but also in European and North American
political theology of various types.

The critical assessment of Drey's achievement must
recognize a number of inadequacies and questionable features.
If his creative synthesis nevertheless continues to be of
interest, it is because of his remarkably clear-sighted perception of many of the problems posed for Catholic theology by
"modernity." Hence, we turn our attention in the final section
of this chapter to Drey's continuing relevance for theology.

Drey's Contribution to Theology

Interest in historical material is, no doubt, always
guided in some way by contemporary concerns. This study is no
exception. Drey and the Catholic Tübingen School have a special
relationship to the enterprise of Catholic theology today,
since they constitute a significant portion of its own past.

Drey worked at a time of major change in the intellectual
context of Christian faith, which may rightly be considered the
beginning of an era in which we are still living. His greatness
was in his ability to recognize and delineate the tasks of a
truly modern Catholic theology, open to history and contemporary
culture, while faithful to the "living tradition" of the Church.
He thus represents a promising turning-point in the development
of Catholic theology, when an honest confrontation with the
modern world was begun and carried forward with considerable
intellectual power.

In the continuing ferment and confusion of the post-
conciliar period of the Catholic Church, knowledge of these
creative beginnings of modern Catholic theology provides a much-
needed perspective. In the concluding section, therefore, we
turn explicitly to this contemporary concern, and address the
contribution of Drey's thought to the ongoing task of Catholic
theology. From today's ecumenical perspective, the concern is
to appreciate how Drey's style of theology might stimulate and
enrich the Catholic community's current effort to re-think the
truth of Christianity for the world.

The Apologetic Concern

The first in order of importance is surely Drey's
apologetic concern to commend the truth of Christianity to the
human mind in a form which corresponds to the contemporary
intellectual situation. Although the particular form which

Drey's own effort took is now dated and can only be appreciated
historically, the project remains valid and, indeed, urgent.
Any truly contemporary theology must find categories for relating the Christian message to a given generation's overall
perception of reality. Hence, it must be grounded in some
foundational account of the human condition.[56]

The University Setting

It is significant that the apologetic style of theology
characteristic of the Catholic Tübingen School developed in a
University setting, where theology was considered to be an
academic discipline ("Wissenschaft") that must find its place
in an organic totality of human knowledge. As a result, their
theology was remarkably open to a wide range of data, both
historical and philosophical.

Only such intellectual openness and breadth of culture
can create a theology which is a persuasive interpretation of
reality, rather than merely the reiteration of familiar scriptural and doctrinal formulas. The need for such an "open"
intellectual treatment of Christianity, in dialogue with
contemporary culture, is all the more acute today because of
the widespread resurgence of various forms of fundamentalism.

The Ecclesial Context

The rigorously academic theology of the Tübingen thinkers
was, at the same time, guided and informed by a striking eccle-
sial identity and loyalty. Drey attributed a methodological
significance to the Church by recognizing it as not merely the
context but the very basis of the theologian's intellectual
activity.

Drey's conception of the Church as the divinely created
perpetuation and development of the originating "fact" of
revelation is, no doubt, open to criticism from a more empirical viewpoint. The use of the "organic metaphor," in particular, can lead to an illegitimate identification of the Church

---

[56]This is recognized, in their own ways, by such widely
differing Catholic theologians as Karl Rahner and Hans Küng.
It is especially prominent in David Tracy's recent effort to
present Christianity's view of reality as the needed grounding
of the secular mind's most cherished values. Cf. The Analogical Imagination (New York: Crossroad, 1981).

with Christ, so that the human dimension of inconsistency, sin, and historical relativity is not given sufficient weight.[57]

Nevertheless, Drey's view of the Church as a "living tradition" which mediates the truth of Christianity in a social form is a helpful perspective for understanding the role of theology. It gives full value to the social-historical context of human knowledge, which has become so evident today. It is also in striking accord with the insight of modern hermeneutical theory that the full meaning of an event or text becomes apparent only in the history which follows from it.[58] Finally, it assigns to theology an important role in promoting the continuity of living witness by criticizing all Church beliefs and practices in the light of a normative understanding of revelation.

Development

This view of Church, moreover, presupposes continual change and development as the condition for the full unfolding of the originating event. Drey clearly anticipated Newman in recognizing the importance of development as a basic principle for understanding Christianity.[59] Since he regarded theology as a life-function of the Church, he was likewise realistic about the historical and developmental character of this

---

[57] Cf. Kasper, Glaube und Geschichte, pp. 24-25; and Karl Barth, Kirchliche Dogmatik I/2 (Zurich: Zollikon, 1938), pp. 622-27.

[58] Drey thus anticipates the modern notion of "Wirkungs-geschichte." Cf. "Vom Geist und Wesen des Katholizismus," GdChr, p. 195: "Aber keine Tatsache ist momentan, d.h. keine erlischt und verschwindet in dem Augenblicke wieder, in dem sie entstand; sie greift vielmehr ein in die Reihe und das Zusammenwirken aller übrigen, breitet sich aus und hemmt oder beschleunigt, oder ändert ab ihre gemeinsame Wirkung in engeren oder weiteren Kreisen; dadurch erlangt sie ihre eigene Geschichte."

[59] Cf. Tagebücher IV 95-96, GdChr, pp. 141-42: "Die fortschreitende Entwicklung des Christentums nach allen seinen Beziehungen, als ein Grundprinzip des Katholischen Kirchen- und Glaubenssystems . . ." Cf. Geiselmann's comment on this in Die Katholische Tübinger Schule, p. 23.

discipline.[60] It was this awareness which made him resolute
in seeking a contemporary form for theology which departed
drastically from the inherited categories of scholastic
thought.[61]

Universal History as Object of Theology

Drey's concern to find the intelligible unity of history
from a religious perspective led him to situate Christianity in
relation to the wider context of "God's way with the pagans,"
so as to show a single, unified plan of revelation which
embraced all the diverse cultural traditions of the human race.[62]
This orientation to universal history as the object of theological understanding makes Drey strikingly modern.

As Schupp points out, those theologians who try today to
take the course of world history seriously as an object of
theology must relate Christ (and Christianity) to the history
of other religions and to the general phenomenon of religion in
mankind.[63] It remains, therefore, an outstanding achievement
of Drey to have attempted such an interpretation of Christianity

---

[60]Cf. KE § 40, p. 24: ". . . wie sich seine [des Menschen]
geistige oder intellectuelle Cultur ändert, so ändert sich auch
seine Theologie . . ." It is especially the various philosophies which affect the development of theology: KE § 95,
pp. 63-64 and § 261, pp. 173-74. Drey's own view of the history of theology is found in his programmatic article,
"Revision des gegenwärtigen Zustandes der Theologie," in
Schupp, Revision von Kirche und Theologie, pp. 1-24, and in the
"Praemonita" text of PD III, pp. 69-94: "Historia theologiae
potissimum dogmaticae."

[61]There is, no doubt, some inconsistency in his adopting
the categories of an Idealist thought-frame which supposed that
the human mind could attain absolute "Ideas." But he was willing to admit the relativity of all philosophical systems, and
expected an indefinite progression of theologies. Cf. ThQ 17
(1835):194.

[62]His treatment of world religions in Vol. 2 of the
Apologetik, though not examined in this study, should be kept
in mind.

[63]In this respect, Schupp sees a significant parallel
between Drey and such contemporary theologians as Tillich,
Rahner, Pannenberg, and von Balthasar. Cf. "Die Geschichtsauffassung am Beginn der Tübinger Schule," Zeitschrift für
katholische Theologie 91 (1969):167.

at a time when Catholic theology was about to retreat from
history into a timeless version of medieval thought. Only
recently have Catholic theologians again reached the height of
Drey's perspective on the object and task of theology.

"Kingdom of God"

Drey's unifying concept for interpreting history also has
contemporary relevance, since it expresses a hope for the
transformation of this world in a social-historical way. Drey's
conviction that the Church is the form in which all human beings
are to be gathered into a new social relationship is, of course,
not so confidently shared by contemporary theology. But the
term "Kingdom of God" has become central as a symbol for the
graced transformation of the entire social-political order.
There is, thus, a noticeable affinity between Drey's Reich-
Gottes theology and the more politically oriented present-day
theologies of hope inspired by Ernst Bloch.[64]

In this connection, Drey's integration of the mystical and
the social-historical also appears relevant today, when Christianity is often polarized between political activists and
religious enthusiasts. In Drey's conception, the hoped-for
harmonious world order can only come about through the religious surrender of created freedom to God's absolute Rule.
Self-transcendence in "humility" is what allows the individual
to take part in the great Whole which God is shaping in history.
To speak in contemporary terms, there is thus a kind of synthesis of the mystical and political in Drey's thought.

Synthesis of Natural and Supernatural

Because Drey views the economy of salvation from the
perspective of creation (the "relation of origin"), he has a
unified conception of a single, divinely willed order of
reality, which is a synthesis of natural and supernatural.
Man's orientation toward union with God is already established
in the very creation of the "natural" order, since this created

---

[64]Cf. Max Seckler, "Reich Gottes als Thema des Denkens:
Ein philosophisches und ein theologisches Modell (E. Bloch und
J. S. Drey)," in Heribert Gauly et al. (ed.), Im Gespräch: der
Mensch (Düsseldorf: Patmos Verlag, 1981), pp. 53-62.

world is intrinsically related to the supernatural reality of
God.

In this respect, Drey's thought is parallel to today's
avoidance of the dualism of natural and supernatural by the
concept of universal grace operative in and through the structures of life in this world. This position, especially as
articulated by Karl Rahner, has won general acceptance in
contemporary Catholic theology, and is taken for granted in
liberation theology's political interpretation of the shape of
salvation.

The advantage of such a position is its ability to take
seriously the secular reality of life in this world, while
still recognizing the hidden mystery of the divine at work in
every situation and circumstance. This allows for an apologetic
interpretation of Christian faith which corresponds to the
human in all its features. It is precisely in this respect
that Drey's project is parallel to contemporary theology,
despite the considerable differences in material treatment.

This perspective, however, can present a problem in
interpreting the unique salvific significance of Christ. Does
it allow for the traditional Christian conviction that there is
an absolute "newness" about the eschatological event of
Christ's life, death, and resurrection which "elevates" human
possibilities into a new order?

Divine Freedom
and "the New"

This question points beyond Drey's Idealist mentality to
the later Tübingen School's view of history as the work of
divine freedom. This theme arises from Drey's legacy of attention to history, as it took a transmuted form in Staudenmaier's
thought.

Staudenmaier, as we have seen, departed from the Idealist
conviction that reality is the necessary realization of an Idea,
and postulated divine freedom as the ultimate principle of all
reality. This clearly sets limits to the speculative grounding
and interpretation of history, since it orients human reason to
the unforeseeable and unique. The function of reason in
theology then becomes "a higher kind of experience," to repeat
Kasper's phrase. Such an approach to theology can give full

value to the eschatological character of Christ as the unforeseeable and non-deducible event of divine freedom creating
history.

     This line of thought might be an important corrective to
any contemporary theology which would limit Christ's salvific
significance to what is intelligible in a theological frame of
reference constructed in abstraction from this central event of
history. Such a resolutely historical understanding of reality
could also provide an epistemological rationale for the present-
day interest in "narrative theology." If the decisive event
which casts light on all reality can only be discovered in
history (rather than being deduced or argued to), then knowledge of it can best be communicated in the form of a story.

     Despite these considerations, however, Christian theology
clearly cannot dispense with some general account of the human
condition which can be correlated with the Christ event.
Whether this takes the form of Drey's Reich-Gottes concept or
Rahner's transcendental anthropology, it must seek to show the
congruence and coherence between the unforeseeable gift of God
and the very nature of man. The category of "the New" must,
therefore, stand in dialectical tension with some kind of
rational account of the human condition.[65]

Religion and Theology

     This survey of Drey's contribution may appropriately be
concluded by recalling the importance of religion in his
theology. For Drey, religious life is primary, since it is
both the ground and the ultimate practical result of theological activity. The whole social fabric of the Church (including
beliefs, values, behavior, and liturgy) is an expression of
religion. The theology which grows out of this as its cogni-
tive expression must likewise be directed to the promotion and
development of the lived relationship to God.

     As we have seen, the mystical sense of the Infinite in
the finite is really basic to Drey's theology, beginning with
his account of creation and extending through his interpretation

---

     [65]Cf. Kasper's critical discussion of Rahner's transcen-
dental Christology in Jesus the Christ (New York: Paulist,
1976), pp. 48-54, 56-58.

of history as the "phases" of the <u>Reich Gottes</u>. The God-world
relationship, mentioned so often in these pages, is for him
most fundamentally a matter of immediate religious intuition,
out of which the whole rational account of Christianity is
generated. In particular, his careful analysis of the eternal
Creator-creature relationship is best understood as the
rational articulation of a mystery which is recognized only in
the immediate sense of the Holy.

        This feature of Drey's thought seems especially relevant
to our situation, where the very notion of "God" has become
problematic. Theology can hardly be attempted today without
showing how its propositions are related to authentic religious
experience. Moreover, the problem of how God is discovered to
be present and active within the world, addressed so carefully
by Drey, is still felt keenly. In this respect, his vision of
a world radically and intrinsically "open" to never-ceasing
divine influence is still challenging. Perhaps it can be
judged properly only by one who shares, to some extent, the
mystical intuition which is at the heart of Drey's theology.

SELECTED BIBLIOGRAPHY

The first part of the Bibliography ("Texts of Drey")
follows a chronological order. The first two items appeared
independently in print, but are so brief (8 pp. and 38 pp.,
respectively) that they are scarcely to be considered books.
The sections on Drey's articles and book reviews provide only a
partial list. For an exhaustive, annotated catalogue of all
Drey's contributions to the ThQ, see Ruf, J. S. von Dreys
System der Theologie, pp. 36-53. Also see Kustermann's critique and expansion of this catalogue in ThQ 156 (1976):232-34.
Finally, all MSS listed--unless otherwise indicated--are to be
found in the Library of the Wilhelmsstift in Tübingen.

Texts of Drey

Books

Observata quaedam ad illustrandam Justini martyris de regno
millenario sententiam. Gamundiae: Typis Joann. Georg.
Ritter, 1814.

Dissertatio historico-theologica originem ac vicissitudines
exomologeseos in ecclesia catholica ex documentis
ecclesiasticis illustrans. Elvaci (Ellwangen): Typis
Joann. Georg. Ritter, 1815.

Kurze Einleitung in das Studium der Theologie, mit Rücksicht
auf den wissenschaftlichen Standpunct und das katholische
System. Tübingen: Heinrich Laupp, 1819. Photographic
reprint ed., Frankfurt/Main: Minerva, 1966. Another
photographic reprint was published with a table of contents and introduction by Franz Schupp. Darmstadt:
Wissenschaftliche Buchgesellschaft, 1971.

Neue Untersuchungen über die Constitutionen und Kanones der
Apostel: Ein historisch-kritischer Beitrag zur Literatur
der Kirchengeschichte und des Kirchenrechts. Tübingen:
Heinrich Laupp, 1832. (Reprint of article in ThQ 11
[1829]:397-477; 609-723.)

Die Apologetik als wissenschaftliche Nachweisung der Göttlich-
keit des Christentums in seiner Erscheinung. Mainz: Fl.
Kupferberg, Vol. 1, 1838; Vol. 2, 1843; Vol. 3, 1847;
photographic reprint ed., Frankfurt/Main: Minerva, 1967.
A 2d edition of Vol. 1 was published in 1844, and of
Vol. 2 in 1847.

Articles

"Revision des gegenwärtigen Zustandes der Theologie," Archiv
für die Pastoralkonferenzen in den Landkapiteln des
Bistums Konstanz 1812, Erster Band, pp. 3-26. Reprinted
in GdChr, pp. 83-97, and in Schupp, Revision von Kirche
und Theologie, pp. 1-24.

"Vom Geist und Wesen des Katholizismus," ThQ 1 (1819):8-23;
193-210; 369-91; 559-74. Reprinted in GdChr, pp. 193-234.

"Grundsätze zu einer genaueren Bestimmung des Begriffs der
Inspiration," ThQ 2 (1820):387-411; ThQ 3 (1821):230-61;
615-55.

"Der katholische Lehrsatz von der Gemeinschaft der Heiligen,"
ThQ 4 (1822):587-634. Reprinted in GdChr, pp. 359-88.

"Über den Satz von der allein seligmachenden Kirche." In Der
Apologet des Katholizismus, Heft 5, pp. 39-85. Edited by
A. Gratz. Mainz: 1822. Reprinted in GdChr, pp. 333-57.

"Über das Verhältnis des Mystizismus zum Katholizismus, mit
Nutzanwendungen für unsere Zeit." ThQ 6 (1824):219-48.
Reprinted in Schupp, Revision von Kirche und Theologie,
pp. 25-54.

"Aphorismen über den Ursprung unserer Erkenntnisse von Gott--
ein Beitrag zur Entscheidung der neuesten Streitigkeiten
über den Begriff der Offenbarung." ThQ (1826):237-84.

Von der Landesreligion und der Weltreligion." ThQ 9 (1827):
234-74; 391-435.

Book Reviews

Review of Ignatz Thanner's "Wissenschaftliche Aphorismen der
katholischen Dogmatik." ThQ 1 (1819):26-33.

Review of Joseph Geishüttner's "Versuch einer wissenschaftlichen
und populären Dogmatik." ThQ 1 (1819):233-42.

Review of Marianus Dobmayer's "Theologia Dogmatica." ThQ 1
(1819):416-40; ThQ 2 (1820):38-55; 309-23.

Review of Georg Hermes' "Einleitung in die christkatholische
Theologie." ThQ 2 (1820):28-38.

Review of Marianus Dobmayer's "Institutiones theologicae in
compendium redactae ab Emmerano Salomon." ThQ 7 (1825):
116-33.

Review of F. W. Goldwitzer's "Compendium dogmatum christiano-
catholicorum systematicum." ThQ 8 (1826):527-42.

Review of F. Köster, M. Hagel, and J. B. Schreiner, under the general heading of "Offenbarung und Vernunft." ThQ 10 (1828):668-707.

Review of Fr. Brenner's "Katholische Dogmatik." ThQ 11 (1829): 298-308.

Review of Heinrich Klee's "System der katholischen Dogmatik." ThQ 13 (1831):660-81.

Review of A. Gengler's "Enzyklopädie der Theologie." ThQ 17 (1835): 192-210.

Review of Fr. Anton Staudenmaier's "Enzyklopädie der theologischen Wissenschaften." ThQ 17 (1835):384-403.

Review of Fr. Brenner's "System der katholischen speculativen Theologie." ThQ 20 (1838):83-103.

Review of Fr. Anton Staudenmaier's Dogmatics. ThQ 28 (1846): 295-320; ThQ 30 (1848):470-90.

Manuscripts

"Geschichte des katholischen Dogmensystems. I. Band. Geschichte der drei ersten Jahrhunderte oder erste Periode. Mit Benutzung von Münschers Handbuch dargestellt von Dr. J. S. Drey Pr. 1812-1813." No. Gf 1081. Printed in GdChr, pp. 235-331.

"Mein Tagebuch über philosophische, theologische und historische Gegenstände . . ." Vol. 2 (1812-15), Vol. 3 (1812-15), Vol. 4 (1815-16), Vol. 5 (1816-17). No. K 185. Excerpts printed in GdChr, pp. 99-192.

"Praelectiones Dogmaticae." Vol. 1 (1815-17), 246 pp. Vol. 2 (1817-18), 192 pp. Vol. 3 (1828-34), 590 pp. (Dates are written in pencil on the fly leaf of each volume.) No. Gf 582.

Students' notes on Drey's Dogmatics lectures:

1. "Dogmatik oder christliche Glaubenslehre, vorgetragen von Prof. Drey, Tübingen 1823. Heinrich Josef Wetzer, stud. theol." St. Peter (Schwarzwald), Library of the Archdiocesan Seminary of Freiburg, No. D 496. Quarto volume of 553 pp.

2. "Dogmatik von Prof. v. Drey," Kollegnachschrift von Kaspar Fuchs, 1828-29. 2 vols., 422 and 562 pp. No. Gf 1346b. A small portion of this is published in Geiselmann, Die Katholische Tübinger Schule, pp. 210-23.

3. "Skizzen aus Dr. Drey's Dogmatik, Tübingen 1829, Caspar Fuchs, theol. candid. Wilhelmsstift." 2 vols. No. Gf 2843. This is a summary of the preceding item.

4. "Vorlesungen aus der Dogmatik von J. S. Drey," Nachschrift
    von Josef Hefele. 2 vols., 264 and 479 pp. No. Gf 1346.

Published Collections of Texts

GEISELMANN, JOSEF RUPERT, ed. Geist des Christentums und des
    Katholizismus. Ausgewählte Schriften katholischer
    Theologie im Zeitalter des deutschen Idealismus u. der
    Romantik. Vol. 5 in the series "Deutsche Klassiker der
    katholischen Theologie aus neuerer Zeit," edited by H.
    Getzeny. Mainz: Matthias Grünewald, 1940. Abbreviation:
    GdChr.

SCHUPP, FRANZ, ed. Johann Sebastian Drey: Revision von Kirche
    und Theologie, Drei Aufsätze. Darmstadt: Wissenschaft-
    liche Buchgesellschaft, 1971.

Literature on Drey

Books

BROSCH, HERMANN JOSEPH. Das Übernatürliche in der katholischen
    Tübinger Schule. Essen: Ludgerus-Verlag, 1962.

GEISELMANN, JOSEF RUPERT. Lebendiger Glaube aus geheiligter
    Überlieferung: Der Grundgedanke der Theologie J. A.
    Möhlers und der katholischen Tübinger Schule. Freiburg:
    Herder, 1964; 2d ed. 1966.

_____. Die Katholische Tübinger Schule: Ihre theologische
    Eigenart. Freiburg: Herder, 1964.

KLINGER, ELMAR. Offenbarung im Horizont der Heilsgeschichte:
    Historisch-systematische Untersuchung der heilsgeschicht-
    lichen Stellung des Alten Bundes in der Offenbarungs-
    philosophie der katholischen Tübinger Schule. Zurich:
    Benziger, 1969.

RIEF, JOSEF. Reich Gottes und Gesellschaft nach Johann
    Sebastian Drey und Johann Baptist Hirscher. Paderborn:
    F. Schöningh, 1965.

RUF, WOLFGANG. J. S. von Dreys System der Theologie als
    Begründung der Moraltheologie. Göttingen: Vandenhoeck &
    Ruprecht, 1974.

SCHUPP, FRANZ. Die Evidenz der Geschichte: Theologie als
    Wissenschaft bei J. S. Drey. Innsbruck: Universität
    Innsbruck, 1970.

VERMEIL, EDMOND. Jean-Adam Möhler et l'école catholique de
    Tubingue (1815-1840): Étude sur la théologie romantique
    en Wurtemberg et les origines germaniques du modernisme.
    Paris: Librairie Armand Colin, 1913.

Articles

The Catholic Encyclopedia, 1909 ed. S.v. "Drey," by Joh. Bapt.
     Sägmüller.

CHAILLET, PIERRE. "L'esprit du christianisme et du catholicisme.
     I. Les antécédents de l'École de Tubingue. II. L'École
     de Tubingue: Drey, Baader, et Moehler." Revue des
     sciences philosophiques et théologiques 27 (1937):483-98;
     713-26.

FÜRST, WALTER. "Festansprache aus Anlaß der Feier des 200.
     Geburtstages von Johann Sebastian Drey (1777-1853)."
     Ellwanger Jahrbuch 27 (1977-78):116-30.

GEISELMANN, JOSEF RUPERT. "Die Glaubenswissenschaft der
     katholischen Tübinger Schule in ihrer Grundlegung durch
     Johann Sebastian v. Drey." ThQ 111 (1930):49-117.

_____. "Das Übernatürliche in der Katholischen Tübinger
     Schule." ThQ 143 (1963):422-53.

Dictionnaire de théologie catholique, Deuxieme Tirage. S.v.
     "Drey," by P. Godet.

GLOSSNER, MICHAEL. "Die Tübinger Katholisch-theologische Schule,
     vom spekulativen Standpunkt kritisch beleuchtet."
     Jahrbuch für Philosophie und spekulative Theologie 15
     (1901):166-94; 16 (1902):1-50; 17 (1903):2-42.

HEFELE, KARL JOSEPH VON. Obituary Notice for Drey. ThQ 35
     (1853):341-49.

HÜNERMANN, PETER. "Der Reflex des deutschen Idealismus in der
     Theologie der katholischen Tübinger Schule." Philo-
     sophisches Jahrbuch 73 (1965-66):48-74.

KASPER, WALTER. "Verständnis der Theologie damals und heute."
     In Theologie im Wandel: Festschrift zum 150 jährigen
     Bestehen der kath.-theol. Fakultät der Universität
     Tübingen 1817-1967, pp. 90-115. Ed. Joseph Ratzinger and
     Johannes Neumann. Munich: Wewel Verlag, 1967. Reprinted
     in Kasper's Glaube und Geschichte, pp. 9-32. Mainz:
     Matthias Grünewald, 1970.

Kirchenlexikon, 2d ed. (1884). S.v. "Drey," by Karl Joseph von
     Hefele.

KUSTERMANN, ABRAHAM PETER. "Zum 200. Geburtstag Johann Sebas-
     tian von Dreys: Biographische Hinweise und Quellen." In
     Tübinger Theologen und ihre Theologie, pp. 49-116. Ed.
     Rudolf Reinhardt. Tübingen: J.C.B. Mohr (Paul Siebeck),
     1977.

_____. "Vereine der Spätaufklärung und Johann Sebastian
     Drey: Ein Beitrag zum sozial- und ideengeschichtlichen
     Standort des Tübinger Theologen." Ellwanger Jahrbuch 28
     (1979-80):23-81.

292 Catholic Tübingen School: Drey

Lexikon für Theologie und Kirche, 2d revised ed. S.v. "Drey," by Josef Rupert Geiselmann.

MENKE, KARL-HEINZ. "Definition und spekulative Begründung des Begriffes 'Dogma' im Werke Johann Sebastian von Dreys (1777-1853)." *Theologie und Philosophie* 52 (1977):23-56; 182-214.

MILLER, MAX. "Professor Dr. Johann Sebastian Drey als württembergischer Bischofskandidat (1822-1827)." *ThQ* 114 (1933): 363-405.

New Catholic Encyclopedia. S.v. "Drey," by M. Csaky.

RIEF, JOSEF. "Johann Sebastian von Drey (1777-1853)." In *Katholische Theologen Deutschlands im 19. Jahrhundert*, 2:9-39. Ed. Heinrich Fries and Georg Schwaiger. Munich: Kösel Verlag, 1975.

SCHILSON, ARNO. "Lessing und die katholische Tübinger Schule." *ThQ* 160 (1980):256-77.

SCHUPP, FRANZ. "Die Geschichtsauffassung am Beginn der Tübinger Schule und in der gegenwärtigen Theologie." *Zeitschrift für katholische Theologie* 91 (1969):150-71.

_____. Review of Drey's *Kurze Einleitung*. *Zeitschrift für katholische Theologie* 90 (1968):222-28.

SECKLER, MAX. "Johann Sebastian Drey und die Theologie," *ThQ* 158 (1978):92-109.

_____. "Reich Gottes als Thema des Denkens: Ein philosophisches und theologisches Modell." In *Im Gespräch: der Mensch*, pp. 53-62. Ed. Heribert Gauly et al. Düsseldorf: Patmos Verlag, 1981.

WELTE, BERNHARD. "Beobachtungen zum Systemgedanken in der Tübinger Katholischen Schule." *ThQ* 147 (1967):40-59.

Dissertations

LAUPHEIMER, FRIDOLIN. "Die kultisch-liturgischen Anschauungen J. S. von Dreys." Doctoral dissertation, University of Tübingen, 1960.

LOHMANN, HERMANN. "Die Philosophie der Offenbarung bei J. S. von Drey." Doctoral dissertation, University of Freiburg, 1953.

Background

Books

ABRAMS, M. H. *Natural Supernaturalism: Tradition and Revolution in Romantic Literature*. New York: W. W. Norton, 1971.

ANER, KARL. Die Theologie der Lessingszeit. Tübingen: Verlag
    Max Niemeyer, 1929; photographic reprint ed., Hildesheim:
    Georg Olms, 1964.

BRUNNER, HEINZ. Der organologische Kirchenbegriff in seiner
    Bedeutung für das ekklesiologische Denken des 19. Jahr-
    hunderts. European University Papers, Series XXIII:
    Theology, Vol. 118. Frankfurt/Main: Peter Lang, 1979.

COPLESTON, FREDERICK. A History of Philosophy. Vol. 7, Part I:
    "Fichte to Hegel: Post-Kantian Idealist Systems." Garden
    City, N.Y.: Doubleday Image, 1965.

DULLES, AVERY. A History of Apologetics. Philadelphia:
    Westminster, 1971.

FUHRMANS, HORST. Schellings Philosophie der Weltalter.
    Düsseldorf: L. Schwann, 1954.

FÜRST, WALTER. Wahrheit im Interesse der Freiheit: Eine Unter-
    suchung zur Theologie J. B. Hirschers (1788-1865).
    Mainz: Matthias Grünewald, 1979.

GOYAU, GEORGES. L'Allemagne réligieuse. Paris: Perrin, 1905.

GRABMANN, MARTIN. Die Geschichte der katholischen Theologie
    seit dem Ausgang der Väterzeit. Freiburg: Herder, 1933;
    photographic reprint ed., Darmstadt: Wissenschaftliche
    Buchgesellschaft, 1961.

HÜNERMANN, PETER. Der Durchbruch geschichtlichen Denkens im
    19. Jahrhundert. Johann Gustav Droysen, Wilhelm Dilthey,
    Graf Paul Yorck von Wartenburg. Ihr Weg und ihre Weisung
    für die Theologie. Freiburg, 1967.

KRONER, RICHARD. Von Kant Bis Hegel. Tübingen: J.C.B. Mohr
    (Paul Siebeck), Vol. 1, 1921; Vol. 2, 1924. 2d ed., 1961.

LÖSCH, STEFAN. Die Anfänge der Tübinger Theologischen Quartal-
    schrift (1819-1831). Rottenburg: Bader 'sche Verlags-
    buchhandlung, 1938.

McCOOL, GERALD A. Catholic theology in the Nineteenth Century:
    The Quest for a Unitary Method. New York: Seabury, 1977.

RATZINGER, JOSEPH and NEUMANN, JOHANNES, ed. Theologie im
    Wandel: Festschrift zum 150 jährigen Bestehen der kath.-
    theol. Fakultät der Universität Tübingen 1817-1967.
    Munich: Wewel Verlag, 1967.

REINHARDT, RUDOLF, ed. Tübinger Theologen und ihre Theologie:
    Quellen und Forschungen zur Geschichte der Katholisch-
    Theologischen Fakultät Tübingen. Tübingen : J.C.B. Mohr
    (Paul Siebeck), 1977.

SCHELLING, F. W. J. Schellings Werke nach der Originalausgabe
    in Neuer Anordnung herausgegeben von Manfred Schröter.
    Munich: C. H. Beck & R. Oldenbourg, 1927; reissued in 1958.

SCHELLING, F. W. J. On University Studies. Translated by E. S.
    Morgan. Edited with an introduction by Norbert Guterman.
    Athens, Ohio: Ohio University Press, 1966.

SCHOOF, T. M. A Survey of Catholic Theology, 1800-1970.
    Translated by N. D. Smith. Paramus, N.J.: Paulist Newman,
    1970.

SCHWAIGER, GEORG, ed. Kirche und Theologie im 19. Jahrhundert.
    Göttingen: Vandenhoeck & Ruprecht, 1975.

SCHWAIGER, GEORG and FRIES, HEINRICH, ed. Katholische Theologen
    Deutschlands im 19. Jahrhundert. 3 vols. Munich: Kösel
    Verlag, 1975.

WELTE, BERNHARD. Auf der Spur des Ewigen: Philosophische
    Abhandlungen über verschiedene Gegenstände der Religion
    und der Theologie. Freiburg: Herder, 1965.

WERNER, KARL. Geschichte der katholischen Theologie seit dem
    Trienter Konzil bis zur Gegenwart. Munich: 1866; photo-
    graphic reprint ed., Hildesheim: Georg Olms, 1966.

WINDELBAND, W. Die Geschichte der neueren Philosophie in ihrem
    Zusammenhang mit der allgemeinen Cultur u. den besonderen
    Wissenschaften. Vol. 2: "Von Kant bis Hegel u. Herbart."
    Leipzig: von Breitkopf u. Härtel, 1880.

Articles

ADAM, KARL. "Die katholische Tübinger Schule, zur 450-jahrfeier
    der Univ. Tübingen." Hochland 24 (1926-27):581-601.

AUBERT, ROGER. "Das Schwierige Erwachen der katholischen Theo-
    logie im Zeitalter der restauration." Attempto (Univ. of
    Tübingen) 25/26 (1968):58-69.

CASPER, BERNHARD. "Der Systemgedanke in der späten Tübinger
    Schule und in der deutschen Neuscholastik." Philo-
    sophisches Jahrburch 72 (1964-65):161-79.

FUNK, F. X. "Die katholische Landesuniversität in Ellwangen u.
    ihre Verlegung nach Tübingen." In Festgabe zum 25jähr.
    Regierungsjubiläum S. M. des Königs Karl von Württemberg,
    dargebracht von der Univ. Tübingen, pp. 3-30. Tübingen:
    Heinrich Laupp, 1889.

GETZENY H. "Die Gemeinschaftsauffassung der Romantik in der
    frühen Tübinger Schule." Historisches Jahrbuch der
    Görresgesellschaft 74 (1955): 405-15.

GRANDMAISON, LÉONCE DE. "L'école catholique de Tubingue et les
    origines du modernisme." Recherches de science religieuse
    9 (1919):387-409.

MAURER, WILHELM. "Der Organismusgedanke bei Schelling und in
     der Theologie der Katholischen Tübinger Schule." Kerygma
     und Dogma 8 (1962):202-16.

REINHARDT, RUDOLF. "Die katholisch-theologische Fakultät
     Tübingen im 19. Jahrhundert: Faktoren und Phasen ihrer
     Entwicklung." In Tübinger Theologen und ihre Theologie,
     pp. 1-42. Ed. Reinhardt. Tübingen: J.C.B. Mohr (Paul
     Siebeck), 1977.

_____. "Im Zeichen der Tübinger Schule." Attempto (Univ. of
     Tübingen) 25/26 (1968):40-57.

SCHANZ, PAUL. "Die katholische Tübinger Schule." ThQ 80 (1898):
     1-50.

WEINDEL, PHILIPP. "Fr. H. Jacobi's Einwirkung auf die Glaubens-
     wissenschaft der katholischen Tübinger Schule." In Aus
     Theologie und Philosophie: Festschrift für Fr. Tillmann,
     pp. 573-96. Ed. Th. Steinbüchel and Th. Müncher.
     Düsseldorf, 1950.

ZELLER, JOSEPH. "Die Errichtung der kath.-theologischen
     Fakultät in Tübingen im Jahre 1817." ThQ 108 (1927):77-
     158.

INDEX OF PRINCIPAL SUBJECTS